D1229665

Keepers of the City

The Corregidores of Isabella I of Castile
(1474–1504)

MARVIN LUNENFELD

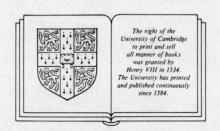

The right of the
University of Cambridge
to print and sell
all manner of books
was granted by
Henry VIII in 1534.
The University has printed
and published continuously
since 1584.

CAMBRIDGE UNIVERSITY PRESS

CAMBRIDGE
NEW YORK   NEW ROCHELLE
MELBOURNE   SYDNEY

Published by the Press Syndicate of the University of Cambridge
The Pitt Building, Trumpington Street, Cambridge CB2 1RP
32 East 57th Street, New York, NY 10022, USA
10 Stamford Road, Oakleigh, Melbourne 3166, Australia

© Cambridge University Press 1987

First published 1987

Printed in Great Britain at
the University Press, Cambridge

British Library cataloguing in publication data
Lunenfeld, Marvin
Keepers of the city: the corregidores of
Isabella I of Castile, 1474–1504.
(Cambridge Iberian and Latin American studies)
1. Corregidors–Castile (Kingdom)–
History
I. Title
354.46'3501 IN8140.C6/

Library of Congress cataloguing in publication data
Lunenfeld, Marvin.
Keepers of the city.
(Cambridge Iberian and Latin American studies)
Bibliography.
Includes index.
1. Corregidores–Spain–Castile–History.
2. Municipal government–Spain–Castile–History.
3. Isabella I, Queen of Spain, 1451–1504.   I. Title.
II. Series.

KKT246.L86   1987   349.46'3'09   87-14741
344.63009

ISBN 0 521 32930 2

TO PETER

Contents

Tables

Glossary

acemilero mayor   chief of the royal muleteers

acostamiento   stipend given to local political persons by aristocrats or kings to assure loyal service

adelantado   royal governor of a district

alcaide   military governor of a fortification or castle warden

alcalde   urban official combining functions of mayor and judge; justice of the peace

alcalde de casa y corte   royal official charged with prosecuting legal cases

alcalde mayor   urban official with formal legal training

alférez   standard-bearer; town military captain

alguacil   peace officer; constable

aposentador real   official who provides lodging for the court

asistente   royal municipal supervisor combining functions of mayor and judge

Audiencia   see under *Chancillería*

bachiller   holder of initial degree in liberal arts

caballero   knight or gentleman; noble of the higher grade, usually propertied

capitán   military officer

capitán general   senior military officer

Chancillería   supreme legal tribunal for Castile, divided into two major segments (Valladolid and, by 1505, Granada), plus two lesser tribunals, denominated *Audiencias*, at Santiago and Seville

comendador   knight commander of a religious military order

concejo   municipal council

consejero real   member of the royal council, or attached to the royal council

contador mayor   chief auditor and accountant

continuo real   royal guard or pensionary, often sent on mission *converso*   Jewish convert to Christianity and descendants; New Christian; *marrano*

convivencia   the coexistence, or "living together," of differing faiths

corregidor   supervisor for municipality combining functions of mayor and judge, appointed either by a lord or the crown

Cortes   assembly of delegates in the Spanish realms; parliament

deputado general   delegate, especially to the kingdom-wide assembly of the *Santa Hermandad*

doctor   holder of doctorate degree in law, medicine, or theology

entregador alcalde   with jurisdiction over cases involving pasturage and livestock

fiscal   public attorney and prosecutor

fueros   In Castile, royally-granted urban and provincial charters of rights and privileges; in Aragon and Catalonia, kingdom-wide privileges and exemptions negotiated with kings

gobernador   royally appointed governor of a district

hidalgo   holder of noble status (*hidalguía*) without indication of rank, although typically of the lowest grade

juez ejecutor   presiding magistrate

junta   deliberative or administrative council, specifically the various bodies that met in Castile from 1520 to 1521

jurado   urban councilor of second-tier body

justicia mayor   lord chief magistrate

kahal   the Jewish district within a Christian community; *judería*; *aljama*

letrado   university graduate in law

licenciado   holder of advanced degree in law (licenciate)

limosnero   distributor of alms

lugarteniente   deputy of a corregidor

maestresala   honorific title granted member of Castilian royal household

mariscal   marshal

maravedís   the main gold coin in Castile after 1497 was the ducat (*ducado*) and in silver, the *real*. Accounting was done not in these coins but in *maravedís* (abbreviation: *mrs*), which were once actual specie. A ducat was equivalent to 375 *mrs* and a real to 34 *mrs*.

mayorazgo   an entailed estate, or trust, used to pass on property intact to successive generations of heirs

mayordomo   chief steward or majordomo

merino mayor   chief magistrate

Meseta　table-land of the great Castilian plateau that dominates the center of the Iberian peninsula

mestas　local or kingdom-wide associations of stock owners; the *Real Mesta* gained exceptional privileges for its migratory flocks

mosén　"reverend" or "sir," which was a title given a cleric in Aragon and Valencia

Mudéjar　Muslim living within Christian territory

oidor　civil judge of a high court

pechero　member of the taxpaying portion of society

pesquisidor　judicial inquirer on mission

procurador　representative from a legally constituted body, such as a municipal council, to a Cortes or other deliberative body

regidor　senior urban councilor

regimiento　principal municipal governing council

repartidor　assessor of taxes

residencia　investigation into conduct while in office applied to corregidores and, to a lesser degree, other functionaries with judicial duties, typically undertaken at the end of a term by an appointed judge

Santa Hermandad　kingdom-wide "Holy Brotherhood" association of Castilian municipalities which policed rural districts and, during Isabella's reign, raised a militia

servicio　special "service" or grant of taxes awarded the monarchy by delegates through the Cortes

Siete Partidas　codification of law under Alfonso X, a thirteenth-century king

teniente　deputy of a corregidor

tesorero　treasurer and accountant

trinchante　honorary title granted member of royal household

vara　a slender wooden rod that is the symbol of governmental authority upon which oaths are administered, and which also signifies the jurisdiction of which it is the emblem

veedor　inspector on mission

veinticuatro　senior urban councilor in Andalusia

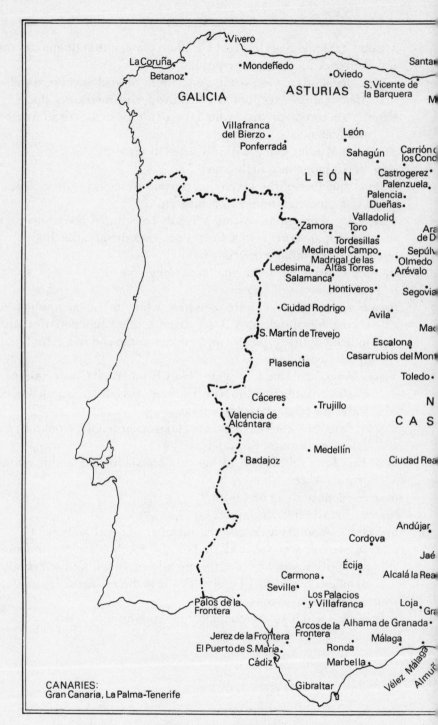

Distribution of royal jurisdictions (1474–1504)

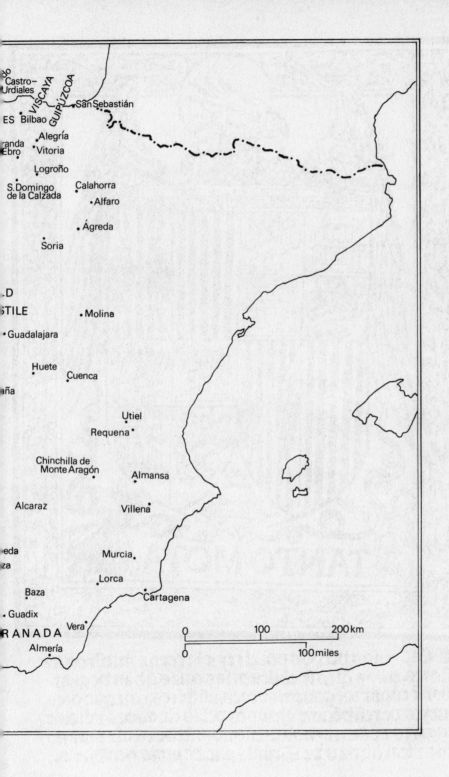

Castro-
Urdiales
VISCAYA
GUIPÚZCOA
San Sebastián
ES Bilbao
Alegría
randa Vitoria
Ebro
Logroño
S. Domingo Calahorra
de la Calzada
Alfaro

Ágreda

Soria

.D
STILE Molina

Guadalajara

Huete
Cuenca
aña

Utiel
Requena

Chinchilla de
Monte Aragón Almansa

Alcaraz Villena

eda
za Murcia

Lorca
Baza
Cartagena
Guadix
Vera
RANADA
Almería

0   100   200 km

0   100 miles

TANTO MŌTA

℃ Lap˙ ˙ulos hechos por el rey τ la reyna nueſtros ſe-
ñores.e₁˙₁˙₌s q̃les ſe cōtienen las coſas q̃ han de guar-
d₁.r τ cōplir los gouernadores.aſiſtétes.correcidores
juezes de reſidécia τ alcaldes delas ciudades villas τ
lugares de ſus reynos τ ſeñorios:fechos enla muy noble τ leal ciudad de Seuilla a.ix.de junio de.M.τ.d.

The cover page from the ordinances of 1500,
the *Capítulos de Corregidores de 1500*.

I

The omnicompetent servant

The facade of the city hall at Valladolid informs all who examine its portals that here is the House of the Corregidor. Isabella the Catholic was the first to make successful general use of this official to gain a new measure of authority over all areas in the royal domain previously under merely nominal jurisdiction. The august personage of the corregidor provided the enduring link between the municipality and the central government in whose name he ruled. Corregidores, and *asistentes* (assistants) or *gobernadores* (governors) – alternatively titled office-holders with equivalent powers and duties – were everywhere put in place to attempt to oversee many aspects of the day-to-day operations of provinces, cities with their outlying areas, towns, and hamlets. They made sure the ramparts were secure, the streets cleaned, and the market-place policed. By virtue of special judicial powers they presided over cases both civil and criminal, ranging from inheritance disputes to murder, adultery, and blasphemy. When necessary, they mustered urban militias and sometimes led them into battle. All in all, this was a full agenda for any bureaucrat.

Max Weber regarded functionaries of the monarchies of this era as key figures in the transition from decentralized feudal, or patrimonial, society to the "rationalist" centralized bureaucracy that characterizes both the modern state and contemporary business organizations.[1] Despite their importance to the Castilian crown, the group of individuals who held the post of corregidor under Isabella I have been examined inadequately. By assembling scattered records that cover a key period in the development of their office, it has been possible to construct a group profile for over 400 of these officials. This portrait delineates their jurisdictions (Chapter 2), military titles (4), career patterns, competence, salaries, and perquisites (5), and educational attainments and social levels (8).

A pioneering study of the officials, Fernando de Albi's *El corregidor en el municipio español bajo la monarquía absoluta,* typically presumed that they were a select group of university graduates, trained in law:

The Catholic Sovereigns entrusted government to a select social class, one with sufficient moral and professional preparation to fulfill their function adequately. This attempt at creating a governing *elite* is one of the most successful incentives of the monarchs and for that purpose, keeping in mind the absolute necessity of eliminating the restless and anarchic nobility, they resorted to legists [*letrados*], who were recruited among the lower nobility and the burghers.[2]

Current analysis of the Castilian bureaucracy as a whole demonstrates that Isabella was not an innovator in the employment of *letrados,* a trend which had been developing during the century, for, contrary to popular myth that she suddenly increased the rate of replacement of the titled by the academically trained, her reign actually saw the legal experts lose ground.[3] This book emphasizes the argument still further, in that, upon investigation, corregidores are indeed discovered, in Chapter 8, to have quite heterogeneous backgrounds that ranged from significant birth to modest origins. Most gained prominence through royal ennoblement rather than university achievement, for from 1474 to 1504 less than one-quarter of all appointments prove to be *letrados.*[4]

Benjamín González Alonso, principal student of permutations in the life-cycle of the corregidor over five centuries, provides a closely observed analysis of ordinances which governed the conduct of these officials. In *El corregidor castellano (1348–1808),* he found the ordinances of 1500 set high standards, in keeping with idealistic traditions of Iberian jurisprudence. This comprehensive decree he deemed to mark "the final crystalization of an institutional figure which due to its own nature demanded flexibility in order to adapt to the changing and different circumstances in which it developed."[5]

The weight of recent studies of the reign of Ferdinand and Isabella comes down on the side of constraints and limitations upon absolute power.[6] In the same manner that thinking has changed concerning the reign as a whole, the actual activities of the queen's urban officials must now receive the same close attention previously accorded only to their comprehensive ordinances. Jaime Vicens Vives counseled that merely examining codes never brings the observer very close to human reality: "These are the formulas that establish limits, but nothing more than limits. The expression of life is to be found in the application of the law, decree, or regulation."[7]

The study of Isabella's corregidores has remained too closely tied to a chronology bracketed on one side by the turn-of-the-century ordinances and on the other by parliamentary decrees issued at the 1480 Cortes of Toledo. That twenty-year frame presents a static picture, showing clear-cut continuity from sturdy beginnings. One inherent assumption of this approach as, for example, it is presented by Stephen Haliczer in *The Comuneros of Castile*, is that Isabella was a legitimate queen, whose reformist policies were well received by the municipalities:

The corregidores' earnest efforts to restore the integrity of municipal districts, improve urban government, and eliminate clan rivalries, and the care with which Ferdinand and Isabella and the Royal Council supervised their conduct, were important reasons for the undoubted popularity of these officials early in the reign.[8]

However, there is considerable evidence, not sufficiently taken into account, that Isabella was regarded by her foes as less immediately in line for the succession than her niece Doña Juana. This debate had to be fought out, from 1474 to 1479, during a bitter war of succession which involved an invasion of the country by Portuguese troops, in collaboration with Castilian aristocrats and urban elites supporting Isabella's rival. Thus there was a good deal of opposition, previously unexamined, to the installation of Isabella's corregidores. These officials often had to impose their rule by force against hostile aristocrats who dominated towns, or upon uncooperative urban dwellers.

Isabella's statutes, set down more clearly once she won uncontested power, certainly do present an all-competent official, leading Felipe Fernández-Armesto to generalize, in *Ferdinand and Isabella*, that her corregidores mastered urban government:

The characteristic royal official was the *corregidor*, whose powers lay in the supervision of justice and of the ordinances of the municipal councils: during their tenure, the local authorities actually handed over their powers and were confined to an advisory role.[9]

This perspective also pervades *Isabel la Católica* by Tarsicio de Azcona, which holds that, once in place, her corregidores quickly gained control of the municipalities:

Without being the creator of the institution, Isabella was able to modernize it and to wield it as a tremendously efficient medium in order to take to the municipalities the at times heavy, at times benevolent, hand of the royal power.[10]

A recent analysis by Henry Kamen, in *Spain 1469–1714*, takes an opposing stance which reduces the official to a virtual cipher:

The appointment of a corregidor gave the crown a voice in local affairs but in no way implied a policy of centralization. Although nominated by the king the corregidores were, in effect, local officials, since their salaries were paid by the city of residence. They might preside over meetings of a town council but were seldom in a position to control its deliberations, and the crown found it far easier to subvert towns by selling the office of *regidor*. Dual loyalty to crown and city must have restricted their initiative, and they were probably most effective in the newly conquered kingdom of Granada.[11]

It appears that the truth does not lie (as it often does) between the extremes, but that it must be determined on a case by case basis. Corregidores prove to be strong or weak in different cities, at varied times, depending upon the traditions and privileges of a municipality, the unity of the municipal elite, the fluctuating degree of support corregidores received from their superiors, and their own personal abilities.

A primary arena in which to test views concerning the imposition, and geographic spread, of the office is the Castilian municipality. There are three principally chronological chapters (3, 4, and 8) which focus most closely upon relations between the urban elite and the royal overseers. In these chapters, I recommend that, instead of presenting a "group portrait" of the corregidores as if it were akin to a single Renaissance canvas upon which historians have drawn one static picture, a more satisfyingly dynamic concept is required. I prefer to trace out the development of the office in the rather more complex metaphorical form of a late medieval triptych.

The first panel (1474–85) traces the outline of an unreceptive urban oligarchy forced to accept Isabella's men through a combination of coercive policies and favors, which included full recognition of the elite's total domination of their offices. Once the crown neutralized the landed aristocracy, the weak and disorderly municipalities had no alternative recourse in opposing the royal will. The second picture presents the high point of acceptance during the next decade of the reign (1485–94), when corregidores basked in well-deserved acclaim. A surface calm was at last brought to municipalities through ratifying the virtually hereditary hold on posts obtained by *regidores* (noblemen appointed by the crown), and by confirming the division of these positions among the competing aristocratic factions. The last panel illustrates a string of failures during Isabella's final decade (1495–1504), leading to renewed agitation on the part of city fathers, who began to lose sight of the rationale of their self-protective decision to support the crown, and to overt rejection of the corregidores by a broad segment of urban dwellers, tying the failings of their local masters ever more closely to the monarchy.

To move from the cities to a consideration of the great lords, it has long been posited by writers, J. H. Elliott's *Imperial Spain* offering a well-received example, that the officials reasserted royal authority against lordly dominance in all spheres of administration and justice:

Over the years, the insistence of the Crown on its own judicial primacy, together with the greater competence of royal justice in many fields of litigation, sapped the foundations of the Castilian aristocracy's independent judicial power. As a result, the influence of the *corregidor* extended by the end of the sixteenth century to every corner of Castile.[12]

Yet how much could have been achieved by any single corregidor without the constant intervention of his superiors? The actual strength of corregidores relative to aristocrats and significant prelates is examined in Chapter 6, where it is noted that the contest turns out to be less equal than assumed. Not only did by far the largest portion of the kingdom have no royal governors, but these seignorial estates were infrequently visited by outside officials. Only rarely did corregidores dare challenge the power of the aristocracy. Upon examination, it is also clear the unreformed clergy went its own way, virtually unresponsive to pressures from corregidores. Additionally, the powerful rural and highway police of the *Santa Hermandad* (Holy Brotherhood), the wealthy members of the Military Orders, and the officials and familiars of the Inquisition escaped either supervision or review by corregidores. Any significant issues concerning members of these corporate bodies or other important personages had to be settled in the end by the Royal Council, or by the monarchs themselves.

Just as the privileged were largely exempt from control by corregidores, so too the poor and lowly escaped attention if they (so far as could be seen in public view) kept to a life of virtue and piety. Those who felt the full brunt of the power of the queen's servants were taxpayers (*pecheros*), with special pressure reserved for propertied city dwellers who were forced to pay the most taxes, fined for infractions, and deprived of full control over affairs in their municipalities. It is this last group, the urban elite, which had the most dealings with the corregidores, and which thus held the royal officials to the highest standards – expecting that trade be properly regulated, guild status be respected, and government operate efficiently. Significant citizens jealously guarded their remaining privileges before the courts of the corregidores, looking for probity and respect for law in exchange for whatever cooperation they extended.

The Old Christian segment of this elite complained when corregidores protected competitors and rivals; but they could not have anticipated, at the start of the reign, that the regime would fulfill their fondest dreams by completely destroying the remnants of balance between Old and New Christians, Jews, and Muslims. The eventual application of police power by corregidores to resolve religious questions is addressed in Chapter 7. Although most corregidores did what they were told to do, some were laggard in carrying out their new role as persecutor. Further, some of the local royal officials at times even directly subverted the crown's intentions by protecting persons and property from the Inquisition.

The corregidores had so many and such varied tasks that any examination of their duties provides a panoramic view of life in Castile. Where sufficient biographical evidence exists, certain men – such as Diego Merlo at Seville, Gómez Manrique at Toledo, Dr Ramírez de Villaescusa at Valladolid, or Sánchez de Quesada, who served at six *corregimientos* – emerge from the group as fully-fledged individuals: a talented poet, a consummate public servant, or an irascible troublemaker. These men, and their counterparts, were set in place to ensure that funds were raised by municipal councils for public works, to see that amenities were kept in repair by city fathers, to protect boundaries, and to watch over pasture and farming lands. Morals fell under their scrutiny: games of chance were prohibited, and clerics were not to keep women. In rendering justice no local influence was to be permitted, and each city was to have a jail, with a scribe present to take testimony when corregidores made the required visits. Corregidores were to know the law of the land, especially statutes dealing with taxes, and were expected to learn a good deal about their jurisdiction, for they had to visit every part of their districts at least once a year. At all times the corregidores were to defend royal privileges against aristocratic or clerical encroachment. If the powerful molested the poor, the Royal Council expected to hear from its emissaries on the subject.[13]

Enumerating the proliferation of mandates or the continuing geographic spread of districts through the fifteenth century, as is so often done, places the stress upon continuity, yet there is one aspect of procedure in Isabella's reign which, if not totally new, is at least thought sufficiently developed by the late 1480s to have been treated by observers as a real departure. Municipalities were alert that cognizance be taken of a corregidor's activities in office so that he and his subordinates might be brought to book for malfeasance. A *residencia* – which was a formal judicial inquiry into activities during the term of office by a magistrate brought in for the task – was a longstanding demand.[14] Any corregidor who gave his community cause for concern should have been carefully investigated upon concluding his duty. But were they in fact interrogated with any degree of regularity?

Assessment of a representative survey of trial results shows that investigations were actually quite irregularly applied. Moreover, the analysis of the careers of the judges of *residencia* in Chapter 5 demonstrates that they were poorly prepared for their tasks. Only half are found to have the requisite law degrees, and few were ever called upon to conduct more than one investigation, despite the expertise they should have developed. The results of the exit examinations these judges produced, also included in Chapter 5, make it possible to evaluate the degree of corruption in their ranks, with the conclusion that there was far less malfeasance than one might expect, given the opportunities for graft and theft.

Beyond regularizing the *residencias*, Isabella's signal contribution to urban governance was to quieten the continuous strife between factions of the oligarchy. Wherever election still existed, it was replaced by appointments carefully measured out between the contending parties. The councilors could count on lifetime appointment to their posts, which were allowed to become virtually hereditary, so long as they acknowledged the legitimacy of the corregidores. The symbiotic relationship of the urban elites with the representatives of the crown managed to endure through Isabella's lifetime, despite the strains engendered by the Granada War's heavy taxation, the increasingly lax supervision of corregidores, and the weakening royal enforcement of laws protecting communal assets.

In the concluding Chapter 9, dealing with the period which runs from Isabella's death until 1525, hatred directed at corregidores by the urban elite played a part which has not been sufficiently recognized in igniting a conflagration against royal authority. Lacking an adequate comprehension of just how tightly their personal survival had become linked to the strength of the crown, the urban nobility defiantly parted company with inadequate corregidores over a variety of irritants during the varied governments that came after 1504. Pressure from all segments of the populace caused an explosion of resentment during the *Comuneros* rising, the most significant rebellion in sixteenth-century Europe and the biggest Iberian upheaval until 1640.[15] The union of oligarchic and royal interests made it inevitable that the populace would be obliged to turn against corregidores when they wished to strike at the tight-knit elite who dominated all lives.

When the great revolt arrived in 1520, corregidores and the urban oligarchy were swept away together, replaced in key areas by locally appointed officials responsive to urban needs, more representative of the community at large, and quite hostile to the ruler.

Too late, the old elite realized its best interests had been served by burying its differences with corregidores. The shattering confrontation between the poor and the comfortably affluent, which grew in intensity through the course of the *Comuneros* uprising, drove the displaced urban ruling group back to the crown. The Emperor Charles V thereupon reformed the office of corregidor, acting in concert with docile parliaments, and restored the fortunes of the post for the centuries to come.

Throughout these pages Fernando and Isabel appear in their well-established anglicized form, as do the Habsburg monarchs. Neither "corregidor," nor the naturalized "caballero," are italicized in the text. The older spelling of Spanish words and names has been modernized, with accent marks added where appropriate. *Maravedís*, abbreviated as *mrs*, were once actual coins, but by the fifteenth-century they no longer circulated. The sums they total in the text are merely an accounting device to equalize the diversity of coinage when rendering prices. The Glossary should be consulted for other frequently used technical terms – such as *regidor*, *jurado*, *alcalde* or *letrado* – which have no exact equivalent in English.

In space that is inadequate to the task I would like to thank a few of the many people who contributed to the shaping of this work. John H. Elliott, Robert Burns, Gabriel Jackson, and A. Collantes de Terán Sánchez offered support at varied points during the research. I am especially grateful to C. Julian Bishko, John Owens, William D. Phillips, Jr. and the reviewers for Cambridge University Press, whose names are not known to me, for the careful reading they gave the manuscript. Many useful suggestions came from them, and from various members of the Society for Spanish and Portuguese Historical

Studies. Valuable assistance always arrived when needed from doña Adela González of the Archive of Simancas and her efficient staff, as well as from the directors and staffs of the municipal archives and libraries consulted.

Research in Spain was financed by two major grants from the State University of New York Research Foundation, while the time to travel and write was provided by sabbatical and other leave extended by the trustees and administration of the State University College at Fredonia. An extremely generous subvention for the publication of the manuscript was awarded to the Press by the Spanish Government, under its Program for Cultural Cooperation.

My debt is extensive to Mary Notaro, who not only typed the tables and first draft of the manuscript but has always extended a helping hand. I am obligated to Katharine, who first suggested the book, and to Peter, who followed its slow progress with critical appreciation.

A part of the study appeared in preliminary form in "Governing the cities of Isabella the Catholic: the *corregidores*, governors and assistants of Castile," *Journal of Urban History* 9 (1982), pp.31–56. My thanks are due to the editor and publisher of the journal for permission to use this material.

2

Establishing authority

Illustrious gentlemen of high birth who govern Toledo city;
    As you ascend these stairs renounce ties, greed, love, and anxiety.
Eschew private benefit for the community's good and trust;
    For this God gave you power, making you pillars of the state, strong
    and just.[1]

This plea for civic responsibility, which graces the broad sweep of the
principal staircase in Toledo's *Casas Consistoriales*, has been attributed
to Gómez Manrique. He, and other corregidores, arrived at their
posts at a time when the urban oligarchies were certainly in need of
instruction and restraint. While preserving the traditional forms of
representative assemblies and elections a handful of dominant men
gutted the substance of self-government.[2] Making ostentatious claims
to constitutional rights, this powerful minority suppressed the
aspirations of all others to play a significant role in political life.

Closed corporations

Fundamental changes in the way municipalities were governed took
place in the late Middle Ages. Perhaps at one time town government
in Old and New Castile had actually been run by an open council
(*concejo abierto*) which incorporated all male citizens (*vecinos*) who met
qualifications of property holding and birth, beyond being mere
residents (*moradores*). The royal charters of privilege (*fueros*) allowed
the citizens to make all the decisions for their *comunidad y tierra*, or
municipality and its lands. No provision was made in the *fueros* for
councilors to be appointed by the crown, either to select magistrates or
to make decisions in the name of the community. In Andalusia,
however, owing to the pattern of royal settlement during the
Reconquest, citizens governed in conjunction with two magistrates
(*alcaldes mayores*) appointed by the crown. In lieu of an open council,
the southern municipalities were divided into parishes for administra-

tive, as well as ecclesiastical, functions. In each parish an elected citizen swore (thus becoming a *jurado*) to represent the community in council and to work with the magistrates. The slackening of the struggle with the Muslims by the late thirteenth-century allowed monarchs to turn their attention to the northern municipalities, coercing larger communities to delegate authority to magistrates, and to set up a separate body for *jurados* alongside any other council.

A major era of intervention in the governmental affairs of towns began with the centralizing efforts of Alfonso XI. His moves coincided with the stabilization of the frontier, which in its closing of opportunities seems everywhere to have been associated with a diminishment of freedom, and the reception of Roman law, the impact of which was to assist monarchy to override local statutes.[3] The dissemination of titles by the crown, and the increasing wealth within communities, introduced a range of disparities which overcame initial egalitarian impulses and led to self-appointed elites gaining control. The long view shows the gradual disenfranchisement of the citizenry, through the replacement of direct participation by representation, by *hombres buenos*, or *regidores* (municipal councilors). The quarrelling of these men among themselves over the division of spoils invited intervention by aristocrats. To retain a measure of urban autonomy in the face of challenges from lords, and to engender respect for the crown, kings began insisting upon their right directly to nominate magistrates, to suspend divisive elections, and to appoint *regidores*. A new council (the *regimiento*) for these appointees was, therefore, introduced on a broad scale during Alfonso XI's reign. In Andalusia, since the council at first had twenty-four *regidores* the post gained the name *veinticuatro*, although the number of *regidores* later became much larger.

Governance everywhere thus came to be completely dominated by a tightly knit group of nobles. By the fifteenth-century there was immense confusion about who could fit into the broad designation of nobility (*hidalguía*), which kept corregidores busy reviewing innumerable petitions for such recognition. In this book the term "nobility" is used to refer to the titled grades below the aristocracy, which ranks shade from caballero (knight) and *escudero* (squire) to the untitled *hidalgo* who claimed varied privileges and exemption from direct taxation. The minimum income within the range of a caballero at Seville was 50,000 *mrs* (133 ducats) from an estate, and it has been estimated that in 1480 only five out of 100 in the city approached that figure.[4]

The ruling nobles should not collectively be called a "patriciate," although this term is in vogue in current historical writing, because the description assumes a predominant role for burghers. While acceptable for Barcelona or Florence, the concept is not applicable to the municipalities of Castile. The oligarchies there owed their importance not to trade but to military service, real or presumed, and to royal appointment. The non-noble segment of the citizenry, who sullied their honor by engaging in commerce or dirtied their hands through labor, counted for less. Castile certainly did not lack a vigorous bourgeoisie,[5] but enhancing commercial prospects was not always the goal of those who dictated city policy. Finally, the denomination "aristocracy" will be limited in our text to the top rung of society – great dynasts who commanded the allegiance of many clients and the labor of a multitude of peasants.

By the late fifteenth-century, each city and town which swore fealty to the crown had a municipal corporation (*ayuntamiento*) populated by *regidores*, *jurados*, and *pecheros* sitting in separate groups. The weakest body, where it existed at all, was the assembly of taxpaying commoners (*pecheros*), which was permitted only a narrow consultative role in fiscal matters.[6] By far the more important body was the *regimiento*, whose members were generally drawn from the rank of caballero. While in theory the crown made free appointments, in practice kings confirmed designees presented after internal negotiations or the casting of lots. The oligarchies strove, usually successfully, to get kings to select *regidores* from a list of no more than three candidates they presented.[7] Positions were supposed to last for the lifetime of the holder, but became (as was typical of the age) virtually hereditary. Even during Isabella's reign, little effort was actually made to appoint royal favorites to a post when it happened to fall vacant, despite a strong statement that she intended to abolish hereditary office-holding by permitting resignation in favor of relatives only if the holder lived twenty days after making the assignment. While the timing might occasionally prove tricky for ailing *regidores*, they found they had no great trouble in keeping their positions within their families.[8] Indeed, so dominant did these nobles become that in this book the term "municipal council" is synonymous with *regimiento*.

The role of the assembly of *jurados* was considerably diminished from earlier times. They still kept order in their district and mounted guard on the city walls; but after the rise of the *regimiento*, all the *jurados* could do in governance was to watch what went on while the *regidores* argued and voted. *Jurados* were then expected to speak out on issues, for as the king's agents they were mandated to make reports.[9] Their membership, typically two per parish, was usually drawn from the rank of *escudero*, and their election was under the scrutiny of the corregidor. In 1480, for example, the *asistente* of Seville was petitioned by parishioners of S. Miguel that he be present at an election, thus impeding the pressure of certain powerful persons.[10] A corregidor might theoretically override elections if he wished, drawing his own appointee from the list of taxpayers. The elite were generally safeguarded from this eventuality, since approval of the other *jurados* was required and the choice had to be ratified by the *regidores*. In point of fact, elections were honored in the breach, since this office too had become virtually a hereditary possession. Thirty-four of forty-eight recorded cases of resignation, or announced intention to resign, in Cordova between 1474 and 1515 involve, according to Edwards, a transfer to the office-holder's son, and most of the others involved transfer to a close relative.[11] Thus *jurados* in that city were typically nominated by the crown from dynasties, rather than truly elected. What practical good did it do the crown to appoint *regidores*, and to have corregidores watch over the election of *jurados*, when in practice both posts were personal possessions that remained with families? These men need not abjectly favor the crown as a matter of course, when their grip on power was so unshakeable.

Regidores kept firm control over the lowest bureaucracy, which gave them considerable patronage when selecting the *mayordomo* who cared for public property and kept account of income, the *procurador mayor del concejo* who argued a city's case at court, the lawyers, and the public scribes. In addition, and depending upon a city's size, there could be a great many minor functionaries (*fieles*), such as accountants, clerks, collectors of funds, boundary superintendents, a public cryer, messengers, porters, and for war an *alférez*, or flag-bearer, who led troops into battle, along with trumpeters and drummers.

The municipalities dominated by the oligarchies can be graded into *ciudades* (cities) and *villas* (towns), with a step down to *aldeas* (villages) and *lugares* (lesser places, or hamlets). The first category was not distinguished by any significant size grading or high degree of urbanization, since it was the prerogative of the monarchy to raise a small country town to the legal status of city as a reward for loyalty and service. Valladolid, although of good size and a virtual capital during Isabella's reign, was denominated a *villa*. The second rank municipalities would, invariably, be entirely rural and have no magistrates of their own. According to Ladero Quesada they were also likely to consist of no more than 200 heads of household (which, at a multiple of five, yields 1,000 residents).[12] The population mass of Castile's quite modestly sized cities and towns drastically diminished from the Mediterranean to the Atlantic. During the late fifteenth century, the Guadalquivir area municipalities had from 15,000 to 40,000 inhabitants, and those in the Tajo to Duero region 10,000 to 25,000, while the far north possessed only 5,000 to 10,000 residents per site.[13]

Jane Jacobs offers a useful definition of a city as a settlement that consistently generates, or once generated, its growth from its own local economy; a town as a settlement that never generated its growth from its local economy; and a village as a smaller town.[14] In terms of this categorization, not all Castilian cities would qualify for their rank, since many a village and town set down during the Reconquest, which grew in size and developed an urban mentality, never developed further than a distribution point for agrarian or pastoral produce. Textile manufacturing did take place at Ciudad Real, Cordova, Cuenca, Palencia, Segovia, Toledo, Úbeda, and Zamora, while a network of commercial nodes incorporated Segovia–Medina del Campo–Burgos–Bilbao, and Seville and its satellites. Apart from these areas, and Valladolid, which served the bureaucratic needs of the royal court, the arena in which oligarchies and the corregidores alternatively struggled or cooperated was thus, whatever its title, primarily a small, economically dependent municipality incorporating a sizable rural district.

The corregidor arrives

Medieval kings employed a variety of expedients to assert short-term control over cities, beyond the long-term strategy of appointing magistrates and councilors. Administrators were sent out in various guises – inspector (*veedor* or *pesquisidor*), judge (*juez*), and royal *alcalde*.[15] A district head (*dominus villae*) appeared as early as the eleventh-century. This significantly titled official governed during periods of drawn-out conflict and was in turn superseded by the royal *merino*, who moved onto the stage at the end of the thirteenth-century, and off by the mid-fourteenth-century. What either of these two supervisors could achieve at a posting depended upon the leeway afforded them by a municipality's *fueros*.[16]

Alfonso XI – who in so many ways anticipated the *Reyes Católicos* – launched a concerted effort, upon reaching his majority in 1325, to reduce the independence of his cities, by declaring that henceforth the crown would nominate *regidores*, and that they should anticipate sharing power with an official whom he would send. The Ordinances of Alcalá de Henares (1348) followed up on these words by removing primacy from the long-cherished *fueros*, which thereafter were to have only supplementary status alongside royal decrees. The corregidor makes his first appearance in this document.[17]

There is some dispute about exactly what the new title signified. Albi holds that it derives from the intention to send a *co-regidor* ("co-administrator") to share power with local government.[18] Bermúdez Aznar, who undertook a rigorous study of the etymology, derives the title from the function of "corrector." He notes that from the late Roman Empire through the Middle Ages there existed a variety of such functionaries across Europe, whose titles were *corrector, reformador, reformateur, corregedor*, or *corregidor*.[19]

The dispute is not entirely insignificant. Albi was intensely proud of the achievements of corregidores. He wrote in the 1930s to defend them against accusations by liberals that they were tyrants who crushed urban liberties. Bermúdez Aznar published towards the end of the Franco dictatorship, when no apology was necessary for authoritarian rule. In an important sense, the two historians resurrect arguments between late medieval kings and their subjects over the proper role of the official. Was he to be a temporary visitor who would correct maladministration and judicial error, or would he stay to hold long-term supervisory rights in each jurisdiction?

It took centuries to settle the question. The process transcended the attention span of any particular monarch, although noticeable intensification of the process of keeping corregidores in place did occur during the reign of the usurper Enrique II (1369–79). The first of the Trastámara line, he responded to the demand of some cities for help in maintaining order in the face of a newly created and aggressive aristocracy.[20] Enrique III (1390–1406) resumed sending out corregidores, motivated by an expressed concern to combat municipal corruption and to adjudicate between factions.[21] He is the first monarch known to have stated an intent, in 1406, "to put corregidores in all the jurisdictions of his kingdom."[22]

The growing placement of representatives began to meet with a certain caution on the part of potential recipients. The 1419 Cortes of Madrid requested Juan II (1406–54) not to send any more corregidores, save at the petition of the jurisdiction in question.[23] When Toledo dared to close its gates to a corregidor in 1421, the king responded sharply by breaking the municipal corporation into segments, easier for him to manipulate.[24] Any presumed threat from a distant monarchy appeared far less of a danger to urban liberties in the early fifteenth-century than did the assaults of an uncomfortably close landed aristocracy. Grasping at aid from the crown to protect themselves from assault went hand-in-hand with the burgeoning of self-defense leagues within, and between, urban entities. Thus, for example, Juan II was encouraged by his cooperative subjects during 1444–5 to confirm a league for Segovia, to send a peace officer to Valladolid, to put a corregidor in Avila, and to assign a supervisor with a new title (asistente) to Burgos.[25] Opposition was sporadic, as when, in 1452, Murcia expelled its corregidor, in one of various isolated incidents.[26]

A troubled reign

Enrique IV (1454–74) continued along the interventionist path laid out by his forebears. Although much maligned for lassitude, Enrique's early years display activity, as from 1455 onwards he ambitiously dispatched envoys to cities and villages to "correct"[27] conditions. Enrique apparently wished to make the practice universal. According to Galíndez de Carvajal's chronicle, when the monarch was at Arévalo during 1459 he "determined to send corregidores to most villages and cities of the kingdom . . ."[28] That would not prove easy to do. Diego de Valera wrote to advise the king that his intention was against the laws of the kingdom.[29] His condemnation grew out of first-hand acquaintance with the low quality of appointees. He found corregidores encountered while he was dealing justice for the king in Palencia were "impudent and scandalous men, robbers and bribe-takers."[30] Alonso de Palencia enlarged upon this hostile evaluation with an intemperate outburst in his chronicle, where he asserts that corregidor passion for wealth had reached such extremes that these "well-protected scoundrels desirous of tyrannical domination" were no more than "army post slops provisioners, inn-keepers and black-pudding dealers . . ."[31]

The king was not deterred by insults, but his municipalities were becoming increasingly difficult to rule. In 1459 citizens of Burgos expelled corregidor Fernando de Fonseca amidst a sudden uprising over local issues, and the city fathers did not intervene.[32] Burgos struck again five years later, when urban notables objected to extending another corregidor's term. In recognition of his official's diminished ability to control the city, the king changed his title to *asistente* during 1464. Thereby the *regidores* won concessions which restricted interference in their activities and, for good measure, they unilaterally cut the *asistente*'s salary.[33]

Murcia offers another illustration of efforts to resolve increasing tension by means of titles. In 1460 Murcia suspended Diego López de Puertocarrero for staying on past two years.[34] As at Burgos, the king changed over to an *asistente* whose term was not subject to traditional restrictions. In a strongly worded justification for appointing Pedro de Castro, the king based his action squarely upon his "pleasure and will."[35] To skirt the limitations inherent in the *asistente* title, Pedro de Castro was endowed with special powers to supervise justice and to impose peace. He took over the castle and fortifications when the defense of the city was added to his duties. To Murcia's council, this *asistente* looked suspiciously like a corregidor in everything but name. When renewing his appointment in 1462, the king threatened *regidores* who voiced opposition with confiscation of goods and deprivation of office.[36] Because the *asistente* was still there in 1464, the council declared him "detestable and suspect for having many times surreptitiously broken the law and violated the privileges and good customs of the city," and for having attacked "the liberty that the administration of the city has for governance and for the common good."[37] Pedro de Castro then fled in fear of his life. Madrid refused, under similar circumstances, to accept an *asistente* by barring the gates to Diego de Valderrábano in 1465.[38] Popular hostility came into play elsewhere. A riot broke out during September 1463 at Seville, where an armed crowd attacked *asistente* Pedro Manrique. Manrique had earned their hatred when he proposed new taxes on meat and fish. *Regidores* stood aside while he was almost stoned to death.[39] By not suppressing disturbances the elite could always show its displeasure, of which more will be said in Chapter 8.

Assaults upon corregidores blossomed during the increasingly severe challenges made by aristocratic clans against the Trastámara dynasty. Through service, rapid advance had been made by several rapacious families: the Enríquez, Toledo, Mendoza, Guzmán, La Cerda, and others.[40] The clans, who had opposed Juan II and his hated favorite Álvaro de Luna, revived their agitation when the king's son acted against their interests. They were not happy when Enrique IV created and promoted new men, nor was it to their liking when he reduced his fiscal obligations to them by debasing the currency.[41]

The typical first stage of a revolt was to locate an alternative candidate from among royal children with a plausible claim to succession. Sultans of the contemporary Ottoman Empire were schooled to avoid such challenges by having all siblings executed on the day of accession to the throne.[42] This not being the case in Castile, Enrique's half-brother Don Alfonso was available for the cause. He was in direct line because Enrique's first wife failed to produce an heir and, therefore, a coalition looking to the future quite sensibly gathered around the boy's person. After Enrique divorced, his second bride unexpectedly presented the kingdom with a female heir on 28 January 1462.

Doña Juana was so inconvenient that the dissidents supporting Don Alfonso worked hard at inventing stories to prove why she did not deserve the succession.[43] It was alleged that her true father was a new star at court, Beltrán de la Cueva. Enrique was not only pronounced impotent, but it was insinuated that he was a voluptuary, a philanderer, and a homosexual as well, however inconsistent these allegations might be when taken together. The tack was also tried that Doña Juana's mother did not have a properly canonical marriage. Whatever the truth of any of these stories, the aristocrats were emboldened to persist by the defection to their cause of the king's mercurial follower Juan Pacheco, the marquis of Villena and master of Santiago, whose immense holdings sprawled over the boundaries of today's Albacete. Once Enrique's beloved companion, he had impulsively turned against him by the 1460s, forming the centerpoint for a powerful cabal that was augmented by Aragonese interests.[44]

Enrique IV was coerced by the coalition into recognizing his half-brother as legitimate successor, which meant setting aside the undoubted rights of his queen's daughter. The king followed this show of weakness by provoking uncertainty as to whether he intended to keep his word. Open rebellion then broke out in a curious ceremony held on a broad field near Avila on 5 June 1465, where Enrique IV was "deposed" by knocking his effigy off a mock throne. The thirteen-year-old prince then seated himself upon the vacant seat in an episode that smacks of magic.[45] Under pressure from the triumphant aristocratic party, Burgos, Cordova, Toledo, and Seville emphasized their hostility towards Enrique's corregidores by quickly joining the rebels, and in 1466 Murcia proclaimed its adherence. Although nominally under the rule of *adelantado mayor* Pedro Fajardo, Murcia received Alfonso López de la Cuadra as "King" Don Alfonso's *asistente*.[46]

Advent of a princess

The group around young "King" Don Alfonso encouraged his sister Isabella to join the rebel camp. When she hesitantly did so in 1467 her delighted brother gave her the village of Medina del Campo in celebration.[47] The joy was short-lived, for Alfonso unexpectedly died of the plague during July 1468. Hoping to present the seventeen-year-old woman as their new candidate, the leagued aristocrats found her unwilling to confront Enrique. Being female weighed heavily against any immediate chance of displacing a male ruler, no matter how disputed. Either acting alone, or on advice, she declined the proffered crown. She looked instead for negotiations to put her in line for the succession, knowing that a number of aristocrats were pressing the king to make peace at any price.[48] The agreement reached in the controversial pact of "Toros de Guisando" called, among other things, for the investiture in Princess Isabella of the principality of Asturias and seven towns: Alcaraz, Avila, Escalona, Huete, Medina del Campo, Molina, and Úbeda. Madrid was to be held in pawn for a year, pending her compliance with all terms.[49] Following through on his promise, Enrique allowed Isabella immediately to reclaim Medina del Campo. In December 1469, Alfonso Sánchez de Logroño, corregidor of the city and chancellor of the realm, met with the governing elite amidst a crowd of taxpayers. They all went to the church of S. Miguel to witness the brief ceremony giving the village to Alfonso de Quintanilla, in Isabella's name. Once again, she received "jurisdiction civil and criminal, high and low."[50]

Isabella's cause profited by her pledges from 1471 onward that, when queen, she would never alienate the royal patrimony. Several threatened municipalities thereupon shifted over to her side as an alternative to being severed by Enrique IV from the royal domains. Sepúlveda refused to accept its fate in 1472, as a new dependency of the marquis of Villena, who had by then returned to Enrique's service.

During the same time, both Agreda and Aranda de Duero escaped the clutches of local aristocrats by giving the princess their allegiance.[51] Bilbao came over in 1473, rather than accept meddling in its affairs by the count of Haro.[52] In 1474, the *regidores* of Tordesillas shifted to Isabella as a way of escape from Pedro de Avendaño, keeper of the fortress of Castronuño, who had been using terror to extend his territory.[53] Salamanca's united citizenry took up arms against Alba, to whom Enrique had donated their city. The king was absolutely sure that Isabella was the main cause of this last problem, completely disregarding opposition from within the city.[54] The degree of hatred directed against territorial lords is illustrated in the document whereby Moya gave itself over to Isabella. Burning, looting, extortion and cattle theft were crimes they charged to powerful men who, in the words of the villagers, acted as if they were Moors.[55]

Despite Isabella's hopes, there was no general movement of urban areas into her camp. Her strength stood at no more than some dozen important municipalities on the central table-land,[56] where she was regarded as legitimate successor, and in Vizcaya, where from 1471 she was recognized as ruler. Of far more importance to Ferdinand and Isabella's eventual success was the adherence to (or at least cautious neutrality towards) their cause demonstrated by the bulk of the aristocracy.[57] The final years of Enrique's life showed an understanding that to rebuild his standing with municipalities he had to reassure them they would not be separated from the crown.[58] He also continued to send out varied representatives, as had been done throughout the reign.

Assistants and governors

Over a twenty-year span, Enrique IV placed his men in at least thirty locations.[59] The fame of the corregidor should not be allowed to obscure the existence of other titles fulfilling analogous functions. The less well-known *asistentes* and *gobernadores* had duties and attributes so similar that this book generally subsumes both under the generic term "corregidor." What need was there for alternative titles? Bermúdez Aznar concludes that the *asistente* was invented to sooth tumultuous cities suspicious of the intervention of a corregidor.[60] During disturbances an *asistente* had a grant of special power to bring the troubles under control; but, other than the fact that no fixed term was established, he was somewhat circumscribed. At his inauguration the *asistente* was not permitted to give the *vara* (staff of office) to subordinates. That ceremonial privilege resided with a member of the municipal council in a graphic demonstration of independence. In judicial matters the *asistente* had only the same privileges as an *alcalde mayor*.

Enrique made use of this appointment sparingly, but kept a few *asistentes* in place for long periods. Six locations staffed with *asistentes* were Seville (11 years); Toledo (11 years); Murcia (5 years); Madrid (3 years); Burgos (1 year); and Guadalajara (1 year).[61] Representatives to the 1462 Cortes of Toledo complained vigorously about what they saw as a perversion of the use of the office. They wanted any such representative to be sent only for one year and then immediately be subject to a *residencia* investigation. Although the king indicated a willingness then, and again in 1465, to settle for the year term he neglected to keep his word.[62]

Isabella would make more limited use of the title; but the powers and voting rights she granted brought the office fully into line with the corregidores. Jurisdictions given an *asistente* up until 1477 were Burgos, Écija, Guipúzcoa, Toledo, and Requena–Utiel.[63] At Seville, the lack of a fixed term allowed smooth continuity, since only three men held the office during her reign.[64] Seville was the sole site where this title, and only this title, was used. For other areas, letters indifferently refer to *asistentes* by various titles. García de Cotes gained his *asistente* rank at Burgos in his letter of appointment, yet at other times was addressed as corregidor or judge.[65] A compound title of *asistente-corregidor* was granted by Isabella in 1477 to Juan de Sepúlveda at Guipúzcoa and to Gómez Manrique at Toledo.[66] After 1477 the title of *asistente* would be retained only at Burgos and Seville.

Governor is the last of the three titles to emerge, after a period of experimentation. Enrique IV had sent Murcia two investigators (*pesquisidores*) in 1455, one of whom was a captain and the other a student of law to serve as his lieutenant. Their rule was indistinguishable from that of corregidores.[67] Without any formal title, but with vast powers, Miguel Lucas de Iranzo loyally presided over the territory of Jaén from 1454 to 1473.[68] Enrique regularized these attempts to bypass conventional limitations by sending out men with a vague mandate to "govern" jurisdictions, without a term of office being set. Segovia (1468), Toledo (1468), and Écija (1469) received individuals who combined police powers with the right to guide municipal council meetings.[69]

Learning from this experience, Isabella's government coined the name *gobernador*. The governors were first placed in areas expected to be threatened by the Portuguese during the succession war – Galicia (1475), Ciudad Rodrigo (1476), and the Marquesado of Villena (1477). Fleeting references to a governor appear in documents for Murcia (1475), Los Palacios (1487), and Toledo (1492).[70] Uncertainty as to exactly what the powers of this position were led to conjoining the title with additional, short-lived titles such as president, or superior judge (*justicia mayor*). Diego López de Haro at Galicia (1484–92) was simultaneously governor, superior judge, and corregidor of La Coruña. He also received the unique title of *corregidor mayor* in an attempt to bolster his prestige at a difficult post.[71]

The governor title was then assigned to conquerors of new lands, such as the Canary Islands and Granada. A degree of uncertainty about what role Pedro de Vera would play in Gran Canaria from 1480 to 1491 can be seen in the titles given him when he organized the administration of the island after its conquest. He was named captain, *alcaide de la fortaleza*, and governor, ranks which carried a connotation of the domination of garrisons and frontiers. In addition, he was briefly entitled corregidor, which implies the supervision of a settled urban community.[72] It was in the islands, after this point, that the word "governor" began to take on the meaning of an administrator with sovereign powers representing the monarchy in an outlying province.[73] Such absolutism was certainly the case with Alonso de Lugo who combined the office of governor (1493–1525) of Tenerife and La Palma with suzerainty over Gomera and Hierro. Throughout his thirty-two years of iron rule he was charged with more, and worse, crimes against the natives than those alleged against any of his associates, but was rarely called to account.[74]

Along with the titles of Admiral of the Ocean Sea and Viceroy, Christopher Columbus received a governorship, one which was later granted to his son Diego.[75] In general, because Isabella's first governors ruled large, troubled jurisdictions – either near Portugal during the succession struggle, or in areas undergoing assimilation after conquest – they received extensive emergency powers, without time limit. As tensions diminished in these areas, a corregidor would virtually everywhere replace these more exalted officials.[76]

Only the corregidor is mentioned in the 1476 laws of the Cortes of Madrigal, but thereafter the three titles appear in varying combinations. Precedence was so vital a matter to aristocratic regimes that analysis of the order of titles will serve to illuminate social realities. At the 1480 Cortes of Toledo the sequence is, indifferently, "*asistente y corregidor*" or "*corregidor y asistente*" (clause 59), with mention of "*regidores y gobernadores y oficiales*" (clause 60).[77] In an expanded version of these ordinances, issued to Toledo in 1482, the title page reads: "*todos los asistentes o gobernadores o corregidores.*"[78] A set of ordinances dispatched to Cordova in 1493 leaves out the governors, limiting itself to "*asistentes y corregidores.*"[79] The long title of the code of 1500 lists "*gobernadores, asistentes, corregidores, juez de residencia y alcaldes,*" but in the text the order is shifted: "*asistentes o gobernadores o corregidores.*"[80] Clearly, the *asistente* is in the lead, appearing alternatively with governor, but both always preceding the corregidor. During Isabella's years, deference was thus always shown to the prominent men who typically held the two pre-eminent titles. Only much later would the less elevated corregidor at last forge ahead.[81]

During the late fifteenth-century, the prospect of unlimited expansion of control over municipalities in the royal domain was always in view, through the use of well-established corregidores, or through the introduction of officials with alternative titles. If the crown could then convince its subjects that these overseers were prepared to respect law and provide even-handed justice, the reception accorded to any new sovereign was likely to be enthusiastic. Immediately the news of Enrique IV's death, on 12 December 1474, reached her, Isabella initiated hurried preparations to declare her succession on the following day, with letters quickly dispatched to cities setting out her claim.[82] She was the type of strong female whom the Spaniards called a *mujer varonil*.[83] When the decisive moment comes, such a woman puts aside traditional feminine deference in order to take action. The ceremony in Segovia's main plaza was brief and austere: keepers of the fortress presented their keys, and those aristocrats who were in the city came forward to kiss her hand, paying homage in full public view. In turn, she promised to look after the good of the people, to keep the realms intact, and to respect the privileges of the high estates. A bright banner was displayed, and upon its unfurling a herald cried out: "*Castilla, Castilla, por la reyna la señora nuestra, la reyna Doña Isabel, e por el rey Don Fernando, como su legítimo marido!*"[84] In the weeks that followed, nothing was heard from Doña Juana's camp.

3

The naked sword (1474–85)

On the afternoon of 13 December 1474, Isabella rode in stately procession to Segovia's church of S. Martín, moments after she had heard herself proclaimed queen of Castile. Directly preceding her on horseback was a prominent Segovian, Gutierre de Cárdenas, who held aloft a naked sword, grasped by the point. The glittering foil was so much the archetypal symbol of justice and sovereignty that its use for a woman attracted unfavorable comment. Ferdinand's secretary, Luis González, asked if there was "in all antiquity a precedent for a queen to be preceded by this symbol . . . Everyone knows that these are conceded to kings; never was known a queen who usurped this masculine attribute."[1]

The chronicler who recorded this, and other complaints from onlookers about Isabella's insolence in "going against the laws of nature," agreed that it was indeed a novelty.[2] Later hagiographers throw so golden a glow on Isabella's life[3] that it requires imagination to recall that she was then a disputed contender for the succession, and not necessarily the one with the better claim. A sword certainly would be required to conquer the realms.

There were those who always believed that her niece Doña Juana had first right to the throne.[4] That young woman's claim was based solidly upon her birth in the Alcázar palace at Madrid as the only surviving issue of a legitimate marriage between Enrique IV and his second wife, Juana of Portugal. At the time of Enrique IV's death, León and Extremadura strongly favored Juana, with Andalusia wavering. Juana was in the keeping of Diego López Pacheco, the second marquis of Villena, and his cousins, whose party was then unexpectedly augmented by the volatile archbishop of Toledo, Alfonso Carrillo. As it fell out, the very families who saw profit in opposing Enrique IV during the 1460s had reassembled to back his intended heir in the 1470s, gambling once again to improve their

24

positions.[5] Doña Juana's supporters were slow to oppose Isabella's attempt at a *fait accompli* because their candidate was an as yet unespoused thirteen-year-old girl. Fortune widened its smile when Afonso V of Portugal agreed to conclude long-drawn-out marriage negotiations with his niece, upon assurance of obtaining the necessary papal dispensation. Afonso invaded Castile on Juana's behalf during 1476; but, after an inconclusive campaign, the coalition dissolved. There was a second invasion, much later on; but, because Afonso V never received anything near the degree of military support he was promised from the Castilian aristocracy, Juana's urban partisans were too demoralized to continue the struggle. Formal hostilities ended with a treaty in 1479.[6]

Submission of the realms

The internecine struggle to establish Isabella put her in direct conflict with municipalities under the control of hostile or neutral aristocrats. The vast properties held by the young heir to the Marquesado of Villena received her early attention. In January 1476, secret negotiations opened with two captains and some residents within the town of Villena. An attack launched by forces led by the duke of the Infantado brought success by early February, and generous pardons issued to the local family lines of Zapata, Vargas, and Luján secured their allegiance.[7] Because Ciudad Rodrigo held more staunchly to Juana's party, a battle appeared likely. To gain the aid of the keeper of the fortress, Isabella named him her governor during July 1476. Diego del Aguilar then used his guards to fine opponents and confiscate their goods to ensure that there would be no popular rising in favor of Juana.[8]

By September 1476 the marquis of Villena was ready to capitulate. He kept a vast tract of land in return for abandoning rights claimed to Alcaraz, Baeza, Madrid, Trujillo, Requena, and lesser sites.[9] Gonzalo de Ávila was named corregidor of Chinchilla, and Fernando de Covarrubias went to Baeza.[10] The new rule at Baeza brought unexampled order to municipal council meetings. When corregidor Fernando de Covarrubias ousted a *regidor* in 1476, the others were astonished that the miscreant was not just reinstated, and that they were forced to accept a substitute dictated by Isabella's court.[11] A series of short-term governors were sent to the territory, starting with Alfonso Navas in 1477.[12] The continuing state of war made their work difficult. The marquis of Villena equivocated, in anticipation of the fresh attack from Portugal; but when that incursion failed, he had left only the prospect of signing another settlement with Ferdinand and Isabella, which at one stroke reduced his lands by half.[13] Gaspar Fabra received a *corregimiento* at Villena and Almansa as a claim against the four million *mrs* he advanced Isabella for the northern campaigns.[14]

Turning to the south during the summer of 1476, the forces of Isabella undertook attacks against municipalities which were attempting neutrality. This brought her into direct conflict with the aristocracy of Andalusia, who held tight control over urban offices. The crown had tended to ratify all appointments recommended by the lords, and while a few new men infiltrated the ranks of the ruling nobility, they achieved this only if they already had some influence, much money, and the proper style. All of the well-rewarded *veinticuatros*, paid the sum of 7,000 *mrs* a year, were either themselves aristocrats or their closely watched clients.[15] The aristocrats maintained control by means of direct payments (*acostamientos*) to their clients until Isabella took a strong stand against payments for Seville during 1478.[16] The ban spread to other parts of the realm as her control widened.[17] She also strove, with success, to coax the aristocracy into ending direct participation on the municipal councils. After 1480, twenty leading families of the Andalusian region abandoned urban posts.[18]

Cordova was one city slow to accept the new order of the day, for it was under the tight control of Alfonso de Aguilar who held sway as *alcalde mayor*. Diego de Merlo was sent by Isabella as her first corregidor in 1476, charged with mediating the ancient quarrel between the lord of Aguilar and the *alguacil mayor*, Diego Fernández de Córdoba, third count of Cabra, who dominated the countryside. Merlo negotiated a four-month truce, but when attempting to enforce its provisions he fell under Don Alfonso's displeasure. The corregidor was forced to take humiliating refuge in a church, according to Palencia's account, where he waited on Isabella to gain his release.[19] When she came to Andalusia with Ferdinand in mid-year 1477, she first appointed a senior courtier to act in the corregidor's place, then reinstated Merlo for a few weeks, to save face. Merlo was soon shifted to Seville, in what may be regarded as a promotion for service under dangerous conditions.

Despite the brevity of his reappointment at Cordova, Merlo

managed to arrange another truce between the two bands. When Don Alfonso did not comply with its terms, he was condemned by Francisco de Valdés, a new corregidor, and ordered to pay a huge compensation to the count of Cabra. Both aristocrats were then forced out of the city, on Ferdinand and Isabella's insistence. Although keeping the titles of *alcalde mayor* and *alguacil mayor*, the aristocrats were induced to let the powers of their respective posts lapse. They thereafter took no part in municipal council business, although by retaining the titles they kept open a way for their immediate heirs to influence city government when the time was ripe. Aguilar also surrendered his jurisdiction over Andújar, which then saw the installation of a corregidor.[20] With their representatives firmly in place, Ferdinand and Isabella made their triumphant entrance into Cordova during the autumn of 1478.

In Seville, the aristocrat in virtual control of the city at the time was the duke of Medina Sidonia, Enrique de Guzmán, who with annual rents four times the municipality's ordinary tax revenues, was informally called the "duke of Seville."[21] Medina Sidonia had supported Doña Juana's cause, although in a lackluster fashion, causing Isabella to work assiduously to neutralize his allegiance by approaching his rival, the marquis of Cádiz. To weaken the duke's hold she had sent Pedro de Silva, her *maestresala*, to cajole the *veinticuatros* during December 1474. After nine months of hard work, he was pleased to inform her that, by confirming all the city's privileges in exchange for fealty, the way would be cleared for a state entrance on 25 July 1476.[22] The duke and the marquis then made their separate peace with her, although this did little to mitigate the ferocity of their personal rivalry.

Pacification of Seville began in earnest after 1478, with the appointment of Diego de Merlo.[23] There had been no *asistente* in the city for fourteen years.[24] It required all Merlo's conciliatory powers, backed by the crown's full attention, to bring the large population under control. The city had over 40,000 residents, not counting migrants or foreign merchants, and together with its lands accounted for 133,000 persons.[25] Half a millennium of Islamic occupation had created a totally Islamic town, bare of all traces of the regularity imposed upon it by the Romans' military camp. Seville's brown and white cityscape came instead to resemble a bazaar – disorderly, but so attractive that Christians happily settled in with little change. A sleepy torpor still suffused the warren of unruly streets at the core of the town on the right bank, away from the bustle of the riverside. One remnant of this maze lingers on: the Santa Cruz district surrounding the cathedral, where whitewashed houses crowd one upon the other, and where passageways shrink until scarcely wide enough for strangers to pass without touching.

Neutralization of the contending aristocracy proved to be the key to placing the municipal council and the populace in a subordinate position. Merlo's letter of appointment gave him far-reaching crisis powers. His vote, joined to the ballots of just one-third of the *veinticuatros*, could settle any issue. It was within his purview to work with any judge, and to sit with the *alcaldes* to pass sentence. Moreover, he had the power to raise troops when needed.[26] Protests erupted over the extent to which he might thus be tempted to attempt the domination of local affairs. Isabella backtracked for a time, announcing that he had been put in place temporarily to improve Seville's administration of justice.[27] Merlo, she wrote, was selected for the spot primarily because of his judicial experience.[28] During 1479, using unusually strong language – "as queen and sovereign, on my will and absolute royal power" – Isabella reappointed her *asistente*.[29] When renewing his term the following year, she acknowledged that, according to the laws of the kingdom, no one could hold the office of corregidor or *asistente* for more than two years, and yet asserted her will that the restriction be dispensed with in this instance.[30] The municipal council promptly dispatched two officials to the court with a letter denouncing this violation of law. Isabella had a brief but sharp rejoinder drawn up. At the end of the month she then demonstrated another side of her personality, with a consoling "we are very pleased" note, written when thanking the city for the good reception given Merlo upon the presentation of his credentials.[31] The councilors, not being ready to be cajoled into giving up on at least the forms of protest, launched a pointless lawsuit.[32]

For his strenuous work on Isabella's behalf, Diego de Merlo was set upon the high road to prosperity. His renowned father, Juan de Merlo "el Bravo," had been a *guardia mayor* under Enrique IV, and was a faithful servant of the marquis of Villena. Hernando del Pulgar thought Juan "inferior in merit to his father" and "in nothing resembling his father," but this assessment was not shared by all.[33] A strategic marriage to Constanza Carrillo de Toledo advanced Diego's prospects. His father's post of *alcalde* at Alcalá la Real was given over to him in 1454, and through the influence of the marquis of Cádiz he received a judgeship at Seville.[34] The judicial experience, combined with the positive impression he made during his brief spell as corregidor in Cordova, opened the way to the major opportunity of his life. At the time of his appointment as *asistente* he was already a caballero and a *guardia mayor*, indentified in documents as being "of the Royal Council."[35] Income-producing posts began to multiply in 1481 when he became a *veinticuatro* and chief auditor, afterwards adding posts as governor of the fortresses and of the castle across the river at Triana.[36] These stipends, plus his salary, yielded 550,000 *mrs* per year.

In recognition of his increasing status a respectable retinue of caballeros attached themselves to Diego de Merlo's house. His will lists slaves, servants, parcels of land in the city, a vineyard at Torno, and the ancestral home in Toro. In all, he was easily able to assign about half a million *mrs* in benefactions although his testament is, unfortunately, silent concerning the total for distribution to the heirs.[37] Two sons were cut out of any share because one, Martín, was a monk while the other, Juan Carrillo, was studying for the priesthood and so only required a modest gift for his church. That left Juan, an *alcalde* of the Holy Brotherhood (*Santa Hermandad*), whose reward from the crown for his father's services was a grant of all accumulated fortress posts.[38] A solicitor was appointed by the queen to protect the family from lawsuits, since Isabella took care of her own.[39]

Pacification of the municipalities

Diego de Merlo learned to contend with the perpetual conflict between leagues who fought over the selection of council members, for Seville was no different in this regard from other jurisdictions. Successive monarchs had attempted to reduce tensions by abolishing elections entirely in difficult towns, sometimes turning to selection by lot from a fixed pool of candidates. The typical procedure upon gaining such a post was to pass it on to a son or son-in-law, although private sales could, and did, take place.[40] Remnants of a once active political life were still to be found when Isabella appeared on the scene, but after some experimentation she became convinced that there was no alternative except to reduce competition still further. The abolitions of elections, selection by balanced factions, and the acceptance of virtually hereditable appointments came to be thought the only way to assure the active support of the urban elite.[41]

Whatever their show of opposition to infringements on their prerogatives, so long as the basic right to hold onto the posts was not contested,
the elite and their aristocratic supporters would attempt to learn to
live with Isabella's representatives.

Elections at Cáceres, for example, had been a persistent source of
conflict. In 1475, Isabella deposed *regidores* who supported Doña
Juana, replacing them with reliable new men, and at the same time set
her first corregidor in place.[42] Despite his efforts, yearly elections
remained tumultuous, requiring direct intervention from his royal
mistress. The poverty-ridden Extremaduran municipality had 2,000
Christian families and 160 Jewish and Moorish heads of household.
When Isabella visited in June 1477, everyone came out, standing in
distinct groups, lining the streets. Artisans carried the banners of their
trades and clerics brought their sacred vessels. The important
personages who greeted her at the center of town stood divided into
two groups – the "high line" and the "low line" – alluding to the
geographic setting of the strongholds of the two contending chiefs.
Isabella dismounted from her brightly caparisoned mule and was
escorted by Francisco Maldonado, her second corregidor for the
jurisdiction, to a house alongside the church of S. María, one room of
which had been transformed into an audience chamber. The 100
notables called to appear before her received a stern lecture. Why had
they disobeyed her earlier order to tear down the forest of defensive
towers? Why had they dared continue to meddle in elections?[43] To
reduce friction, her clerk prepared a new constitution which increased
the four municipal council posts to twelve, selected equally from the
two bands.[44]

There were still conflicts about who would fill these posts.
Ferdinand and Isabella visited the town in 1479, and this time made
the positions lifetime possessions of the holders. In case that privilege
should prove insufficient finally to quieten the obstreperous, militia
troops of the Holy Brotherhood would be unleashed against troublemakers.[45] To give substance to this threat, Maldonado was appointed
a delegate to the Holy Brotherhood, upon the lapse of his term in
1479.[46] Pulgar, usually one to look on the bright side of things for the
patroness whose deeds he chronicled, found a happy ending in the
perpetuation of upper estate dominance frozen into the new arrangement, which was "established as the regular law and custom of this
place, and all the inhabitants thereof rejoiced in it because it put a stop
to their quarrels and the evils that followed in their train, which
resulted from the elections of earlier days."[47]

Peace was concluded on similar terms in Ciudad Real during 1477, when the substance of the settlement again was to nominate for life *regidores* from opposing factions. Virtual bribes, of between 2,000 to 10,000 *mrs*, were handed out to convince the unwilling to go along with the pacification. Corregidor Pedro García de Cotes adjudicated contending claims which had been accumulating for years.[48] Ciudad Real also illustrates the high degree of New Christian penetration into urban ruling circles when, during 1477, New Christians were restored to five out of the twelve positions, from which they could be counted to hold the city to Isabella's allegiance in the succession fight.[49]

The turbulent city of Toledo required far more to bring it under control than juggling with elections or insisting upon the right to keep a royal representative in place. The city within its narrow confines was tiny, but self-possessed because of its height, and the deep river gorge that appears to make an island of the rock. From a distance tawny walls unify everything, embracing without distinction mosque, church, and synagogue, obliterating the demarcation of quarters. But quarters there were: the best area around Zocodóver Plaza was taken over by Christian conquerors, who handed the Jews a contained sector in the west, and left the Muslims to live where they could. Coexistence had run its course, giving way to ceaseless hostility and tension.

Unwavering royal attention was required to untangle the knot of conflicts that had kept the city of some 38,000 inhabitants in upheaval for decades. The Ayalas, the Silvas, and other aristocratic families were so deeply entrenched in civic administration that, at their will, they denied access through the gates of the capital city first to Enrique IV, and then to his half-sister.[50] Isabella's initial attempt to gain control had been to name Rodrigo Manrique, count of Paredes and master of Santiago, as her *asistente*. He was able to stage a triumphal entry for Isabella during May 1475, but by his death the following year he had made only a modest start to pacifying the jurisdiction.[51] Street fighting continued between the factions, while Old Christians still assaulted New Christians and Jews.

Ferdinand and Isabella brought with them on their return a well-regarded poet, Gómez Manrique, a brother of the deceased *asistente*. He took on his relative's post, at the age of sixty-five, with augmented powers. All leagues, confederations, and confraternities without overt religious content were banned.[52] *Regidores* and *jurados* were prohibited from accepting any payments from aristocrats, as was already the policy in Andalusia.[53] The fortress keeper, who held the municipal

gates and strongholds in the name of Pedro López de Ayala, count of
Fuensalida, was removed and executed, with dominion passing over
to the *asistente*.[54] These actions amounted to less than might at first
appear, because it was a serious handicap to Gómez Manrique that he
did not have the social prestige which had automatically been
accorded to his titled relative. When Toledo's families derided his lack
of significant rank, he wryly observed that change was the order of the
world, and that true nobility was that which virtue gives: "All are
made noble by God. Some take the clear road of virtue, while the
vicious take the road of error."[55]

Manrique's hold measurably strengthened during 1478, when he
dealt vigorously with a conjectured conspiracy. Doña Juana retained
partisans in the city, who were roused from quiescence by Archbishop
Carillo's sudden invitation to the king of Portugal to mount his second
invasion. Manrique asserted that he had been warned his assassina-
tion was planned as a means of restoring Juana's fortunes. This
became the occasion to plant Isabella's banner in Zocodóver Plaza,
and to raise 2,000 armed men to prepare for the resumption of the
succession struggle.[56] This strike force intimidated internal opposition, which was its intention, and the mark of its success is that the city
was sufficiently pacified to play host to the great Cortes of 1480. There
was less prospect of completely repressing the rivalry between the
Ayalas and the Silvas, which continued in a muted tone. Manrique
died in 1491 while still at his post, leaving peace negotiations to his
successor. The heirs of the original troublemakers signed a public
pledge of harmony in December 1506. Placards on the cathedral's
Puerta del Perdón and in the plazas, announcing the long desired
settlement, were a memorial to Gómez Manrique's achievements.[57]

It cannot, however, be said that this settlement or the other
pacifications brought about a fundamental change in who ruled.
Isabella played her part in a seemingly foreordained process of
stabilizing the hold that a few noble families had gained over cities, for
as it turned out her corregidores were everywhere to continue to be the
guarantors of oligarchical domination. The result was an enduring
boss rule, or *caciquismo*, to use a New World and metropolitan term
that closely fits the situation.

During his thirteen-year stay, Gómez Manrique strove as hard as
did his counterpart in Seville to enrich himself. His father was Pedro
Manrique, *adelantado mayor* of Castile under Juan II, and on his
mother's side he was descended from a sister of Enrique III, Leonor de
Castilla. Gómez, as the fourteenth child, carved out his own career,

using marriage to Juana de Mendoza as a way of securely joining his
fortunes to those of a prominent family. He fought alongside his
brother Rodrigo in several battles against Álvaro de Luna, the
favorite of Juan II. His faction of the family never did return to royal
favor with the legitimate ruling house, so he began his rise to fortune
by paying homage to "king" Don Alfonso of Castile, who appointed
Gómez corregidor of Avila in 1465,[58] and then immediately adhered
to Isabella. The rewards at his *asistente* post came quickly: by taking
control of Toledo's fortresses he gained the fees which went with
domination of the city, and his services prompted a gift of an interest-
bearing note (*juro*) of 100,000 *mrs*.[59] He purchased the office of chief
overseer (*veedor general*) for Toledo and Cuenca, which gave him the
right to obtain a fee from placing his seal on every bolt of cloth finished
in these towns.[60] The citizens of Cuenca deprived Manrique of at least
one office, given him as yet another royal gift, on the grounds that it
was not within the rights of monarchy to dispose of the position.[61]
After a decade in office he had accumulated a considerable fortune,
sufficient to request of the queen in 1487 that he be permitted to make
an entailed estate (*mayorazgo*) of his goods and land, thus assuring that
his branch of the family could try for greatness, passing its possessions
intact from generation to generation.[62]

Multiplying *corregimientos*

The traditional thesis that Isabella came to the throne as the favorite
of "the people" from the start continues to require correction. It is no
longer acceptable to hold that all urban areas in Castile favored her
advent because, as has been demonstrated, the cities were divided one
from the other, and riven with internal factions. Two other instances
of the old belief that municipalities especially favored Isabella should
be briefly refuted, to show why she had to move slowly when imposing
corregidores during her initial years. One ground for adducing
support for Isabella has always been the formation of the Holy
Brotherhood (*Santa Hermandad*), yet the founding meeting of the
league, under the supervision of her agents at Dueñas in 1475, saw
representatives arrive from only eight municipalities from northern
and central Castile.[63] The 1476 Cortes of Madrigal was also
something of a "rump" session, since it has never been clear how many
cities and villages sent observers. Even the seventeen municipalities
with voting rights who habitually sent delegates were probably not all
properly represented. Who would have represented hostile Toro, and

how would divided municipalities like Madrid, Cordova, Murcia, Cuenca, and Guadalajara have held elections?[64]

To gain maximum benefit from those few municipalities initially allied with her cause, Isabella dispatched corregidores. Their spread turned out to be slow, and not without incident, since even municipal councils which willingly joined Isabella's cause were not always willing to let her freely do as she wished. During February 1475, Salamanca insisted she swear on her "faith and royal word" that she would send no corregidor, save upon the city's request.[65] There were others to hold her to this word: when an attempt was made at Alcaraz to send Diego de Madrid in 1475, his nomination was met with a polite refusal. After the municipal council wrote that it "could not afford him and did not need him," Isabella quickly withdrew the nomination.[66] Along the same lines, at her first Cortes in 1476 she had to agree to a petition that affirmed that any town which did not wish to have a corregidor was free of obligation. The official was limited to a one-year term, with the prospect of a one-year extension only if the office was executed to the satisfaction of the jurisdiction.[67]

Isabella sent out as many corregidores as were permitted considering the opposition she faced, which meant that within a year of her self-proclamation she had placed merely twenty-five men.[68] During 1476 a further ten jurisdictions were added,[69] and during 1477 five more joined the list.[70] During the next two years she added four more officials, bringing the total to forty-four by the time of the formal conclusion of the War of Succession.[71] Finding herself at last in an unchallenged position, the work of bending municipalities under royal sovereignty to her will could begin in earnest. Pulgar records that the king and queen decided in 1480 "to send corregidores to all the cities and villages of all their kingdoms," in disregard of promises.[72] With the intention of easing the way, part of the package of reform bills promulgated at the 1480 Cortes of Toledo was a series of norms laid down to regulate the behavior of corregidores.[73] Soon enough, jurisdictions in the royal domain were all forced to accept corregidores, bringing to fruition the fondest hopes of Isabella's predecessors – a list drawn up a decade after the Cortes of Toledo shows that seventy-seven men were in place.[74]

The shape of jurisdictions

An effort was made to impose some equitable bureaucratic norms upon this rapidly expanding royal governance, but the constraints of tradition assured that these *corregimientos* remained a jumbled mix, which is just what one would expect to find at the dawn of modern times. The dim outline of rational shaping can be perceived, despite the willingness of the crown to accept pre-existing boundaries, no matter how irregular or inadequate. All districts which were already in being in 1475, save one, were retained during Isabella's reign.[75] *Corregimientos* were to be found wherever there had been major settlement: strung out all along the major pilgrim road to Santiago (9), following the course of the rivers Ebro (4), Guadalquivir (5), and tributaries of the Duero (8) or hugging the Cantabrian (11) and Mediterranean (19) coasts. Each municipality with Cortes representation[76] continued with its own administrative unit, such parliamentary jurisdictions forming a part of the full half of *corregimientos* which sat on the central table-land. A compass point placed on the map at Valladolid would see the arm swing across sixteen nearby jurisdictions, all concentrated within fifty kilometers of the old capital. By way of contrast, in a broad belt that stretches across the map from the 40° to the 38° there were only seven jurisdictions in poverty-stricken Extremadura, and but one on the vast wilderness of La Mancha.

The first districts which the royal administration had a fresh hand in shaping were the large northern kingdoms. Headquarters for the whole of the principality of Asturias was centered on Oviedo. This territory, along with other areas to be discussed, did not necessarily fall completely within the geographical limits of modern provinces which bear the same names. Thus, the isolated geographic unit of an irregular northern coastal strip of *merindades*, which ran fifty kilometers from S. Vincente de la Barquera to Santander and on to Castro-Urdiales, was allowed to remain separate from Asturias, as it had been since 1402. All of Vizcaya was run by a corregidor from Bilbao, and Guipúzcoa was directed from Vitoria. Galicia fell to the rule of a governor, whose seat was at La Coruña, although the capital also had its own corregidor.[77] The rationale for this dual rule is found in reasons of state. Aristocrats who had been granted posts giving control over vast domains typically attempted to create fiefs. Easily removable corregidores, beholden to the crown, provided counterweights to this tendency. In the Canary Islands, the quasi-seignorial rule of the life-term governor of La Palma and Tenerife was first brought under crown control by a lieutenant sent during 1511 to (in appearance) assist his superior. The governor did all he could to deny any power to his aggressive subordinate, but Ferdinand only reconfirmed the

powers of this first of a series of lieutenants who came to resemble
corregidores.[78]

A counterweight certainly was also necessary far to the southeast,
for the kingdom of Murcia, which had been virtually independent as
an *adelantamiento* – a district under an aristocratic governor, the
adelantado. "King" Don Alfonso had made a *corregimiento* out of the city
of Murcia to gain a measure of control over the area; and Isabella
followed suit by leaving the city out of the truncated remains of the
Marquesado of Villena that went to her governor. (Another zone was
chopped out from 1483 to 1493, when the city of Villena and
associated villages were formed into a short-lived *corregimiento* for an
aristocrat who contributed heavily to Isabella's side during the War of
Succession.) The whole of Granada was granted both a governor for
the kingdom and a corregidor for the capital city, following the policy
which placed officials not only to assist, but potentially to counter
great lords.

Apart from the unity of these six large regions, a certain further
administrative uniformity derived from the monarchs expanding an
inherited practice of sending out several men to a post, one typically a
caballero who took over the major *corregimiento*, plus one or more
lieutenants with legal training to administer subordinate jurisdictions. In this manner, Logroño was conjoined to Calahorra and
Alfaro, all three strung along the Ebro River, while, at Murcia, an
imaginary triangle reaching out from the key city touched Lorca and
Cartagena. The kingdom of Valencia saw Requena temporarily
combined with Utiel from 1476 to 1484, and in Andalusia, Baeza and
Úbeda were permanently paired from 1477 onward. Similar fixed
pairings appear from 1478 in the Kingdom of León for Carrión with
Sahagún, and in Old Castile from 1480 for Sepúlveda with Aranda.
When the monarchs organized newly conquered Granada they
replicated such joint districts, each with one corregidor who dominated another area through a subordinate. Five jurisdictions were
designed, of which four stretch out narrowly from the coast inland, all
separated by extensive aristocratic landholdings between the strips.

In virtually none of such teamings was the distance between linked
municipalities greater than fifty kilometers. This made it possible for
officials to keep in contact with no more than one day's journey,
avoiding both the dangers and inconveniences of travel after nightfall.
Eventually, forty-five jurisdictions (nearly 50 per cent af all *corregimientos*) were assembled into twenty administrative units. The

patchwork nature of these consolidated groupings can be explained by the fact that, by the start of the sixteenth-century, about one-half of all towns and villages in the realms were under aristocratic jurisdictions, with the concentration of private domination being most pronounced around the crown's large cities.[79]

Three broad groupings, in summary, developed during the reign. The central kingdoms and Andalusia accepted the least reshaping for their complex mix – individual Cortes municipalities with their territories, some lesser cities with their lands, and a handful of towns of roughly equal importance under joint jurisdictions – all remaining much as they were. In the northern kingdoms, the rule of a governor or corregidor was imposed upon large areas containing a few thinly populated municipalities, each capital typically also assigned its own official. The property conquered from Granada, as carved up by administrators, was granted several carefully designed parallel jurisdictions stretching inland from the sea. The map that emerged shows a land which continued fragmented into areas with vastly different backgrounds, interests, dialects, and grievances.

Hostility endures

The men who filled posts in the varied parts of the realms were on trial to prove their worth to the municipalities, for there is little evidence from the era when Isabella first struggled to consolidate her hold on the crown to suggest that her representatives expected to be popular. Even as Isabella drove her rival from the field and began to reign as if she were an unquestioned sovereign, the struggle commenced to bring Castile under the full rule of her representatives. She was not always fully successful during her first decade as, for example, in Asturias, which was unwilling to accept the continuing presence of corregidores without playing an important role in their selection. The junta formed by the municipalities of the principality intended that Isabella should keep the promise she made to the Cortes of Madrigal, and to that end ensured that its choices of corregidores to Oviedo were indeed nominated for limited terms, and their appointments renewed only with its active consent.[80]

In Galicia, it was soon clear that the military situation had stabilized, and what was needed after 1475 was not force but diplomacy. Officials sent there received the new titles of president and governor, the intention of which was to demonstrate that Isabella's

men had a higher than usual share of delegated power.[81] A period of
uncertainty, involving short terms for the counts of Alba de Liste and
of Ribadeo, was followed in 1480 by the long-term dispatch of a
military captain, Fernando de Acuña, to be governor and *justicia mayor*
(superior judge), along with a legist, López de Chinchilla, to act as his
corregidor.[82] The two men rode with 200 cavalry to Santiago de
Compostela, where they set about attempting to implement a strategy
of using the municipalities against the aristocracy.[83] Isabella requested that all the cities[84] and villages of Galicia should send representatives to a parliament. When these hastily chosen individuals arrived
for the meeting, the governor and his associate presented their
credentials and demanded obedience, taking the approach that they
were there to defend the populace against the lords. The representatives did not like the terms being offered and, despite their intense
hatred of local aristocrats, would not go along with Isabella's plans
until concessions were made to the municipalities which diminished
the control to be exercised by the governor.[85]

Group action in Galicia and Asturias was far more effective than the
isolated protests of individual municipal councils, such as those to be
examined at Murcia, Carrión, Aranda de Duero, Ciudad Rodrigo,
and Carmona. The kingdom of Murcia was under the domination of
adelantado mayor Pedro Fajardo.[86] A long-range plan to return his
holdings to royal control was eventually accomplished by Isabella
taking pains, with the bait of an enormous dowry, to marry a son of a
loyal royal servant to Fajardo's daughter and heir.[87] This was
preceded by a direct move to take the city of Murcia in hand, with the
appointment of García de Alcocer as corregidor in 1478. He stopped
at Molina del Segura to send ahead notice that a time be set to receive
him. Two *regidores* rode out to deny him access, professing offense by
both the tone and the language of his letter. García de Alcocer insisted
he would make good his arrival, whatever the reception; but the
municipal council insisted, in turn, that before it would let that
happen it would deal directly with Isabella, to explain why the official
was not wanted. On their way to her court, a *regidor* and his old servant
were set upon, strangled, and robbed, producing an enormous
indignation among the populace of some 13,500, one which would not
subside until the *aldelantado* smoothed matters over somewhat by
giving the vacant city post, for life, to the murdered man's son.
Considering the uproar, it was thought wise to withdraw the
nomination in November, and wait seven months until Lope Sánchez

del Castillo could be nominated, and received quietly by Murcia, as corregidor.[88]

This by no means indicated a willingness on the part of the municipal council loyally to go along with the idea of a permanent posting. In 1481 the *regidores* invited Isabella to retire their corregidor, alleging that he was unnecessary, since Murcia was "at peace and without scandal."[89] The officials assailed her with so many petitions that she curtly told them to cease writing and be content. Not that this stopped all agitation, for two years later the *regidores* tried to negate their agreement to receive Diego de Carvajal for another term. The corregidor had been using his "voice and vote" on behalf of the lesser social ranks too often to suit the oligarchs. The Royal Council enjoined them in October 1483 to desist, but they remained bitterly uncooperative.[90] Other towns had earlier discovered how ineffective protest could be. The commoners of Carrión alleged in September 1480 that custom did not require them to contribute anything towards a corregidor's salary, and the council of Aranda de Duero argued the following month that its privileges protected it from the charge.[91] Both petitions were denied.

Ciudad Rodrigo objected to renewing its corregidor and in 1483 surprisingly won its case (although when it refused a new term to another official in 1489 the crown pressed ahead).[92] Carmona's hostility emerged sporadically, but continued longer, because right from the start its corregidor was regarded as an extremely powerful force in municipal life. Following a precedent set in Seville, the municipal council had to comply with his orders so long as he garnered the support of one-third of the *veinticuatros*.[93] Sancho de Ávila, appointed in 1478, discovered that when his second year ran out the municipal council began petitioning Isabella not to consider him for renomination. The corregidor, and his allies, decided to go to court to make his case directly. The majority on the council strongly denounced the trip, although professing high personal regard for the corregidor. Isabella decided to approve his renomination to the municipality of 5,000 inhabitants for a third year. The council tried again, in 1484, when it argued that the city was so well governed and peaceful it did not require an outsider. Ferdinand and Isabella then made it very clear that it was their will "to have corregidores in all their cities and towns and they did not wish there to be any less in this town."[94]

Jerez de la Frontera was more daring, and thus more successful, than others in directly defying its overseer. When the city of nearly 15,000 inhabitants reverted to the crown in 1477, the marquis of Cádiz relinquished the title of corregidor, which he had held. Rodrigo Juan de Robles was sent to the municipality, where the *regidores* received him under protest. Residents made varied complaints at his *residencias* in 1478 and 1479, but each time he was exonerated of wrongdoing and, to the dismay of the city fathers, reappointed.[95] The opportunity to retaliate came when he was captured by the Moors in 1483 at the "disaster of La Ajarquía." To cover such eventualities, the ordinances mandated that a subordinate should take over, with powers equal to those of the corregidor. However, when *bachiller* Juan de Paz attempted to act in his superior's place at the first council meeting after the news arrived, the *veinticuatros* took away his staff of office and expelled him from the session. At the same time, they moved to deprive Robles' wife, María, of the control she was exercising in her husband's name over the fortress and the city gates. The municipal council then chose two of its members, by lot, to take over the corregidor's responsibilities, in a revival of Jerez's lost autonomy. María and the lieutenant fled to the royal court on 21 April to press their case.

However upsetting the upheaval may have been to the crown, it moved cautiously by opening intense negotiations with the municipal council. On 17 May 1483 Ferdinand authorized an investigator to be sent from Cordova with a letter empowering the official to restore the status quo.[96] After much haggling, the city fathers agreed to recognize Juan de Paz as heir to the powers of his imprisoned superior. First, though, full pardons were obtained from the court and sizable bribes accepted.[97] Isabella decided not to send Robles back immediately upon his ransom, to avoid stirring up the community again. What emerges from this summary presentation of opposition and objection at various locales is not a traditional portrait of city dwellers in complete loving harmony with a legitimate sovereign. Some municipal councils supported Doña Juana, while others struggled against Isabella because they, and their aristocratic patrons, anticipated that as she consolidated her hold their independence would diminish.

The lieutenancies

No matter how long it took to place corregidores in power, once in office the upper echelon of the bureaucracy fell to them to staff, as a welcome source of prestige. Generally, the *alcalde mayor* was replaced by ordinary *alcaldes* limited to judicial functions, or, if the title was held by an aristocrat, it was changed into an honorary title without powers. Minor jurisdictions too small to warrant a corregidor were sometimes allowed to retain an *alcalde mayor* so that he might deal on an equal footing with his counterparts.[98] A few jurisdictions managed to get an exception to the rule that *alcaldes* were mere tools of nearby corregidores, as in the case of Tudela (Valladolid), which kept the right to nominate *alcaldes*, who were then ratified by the official at the capital.[99]

Corregidores selected lieutenants (*tenientes* or *lugartenientes*), some to assist in judicial matters or to function as administrative officers (*ejecutores*), and others to keep the peace (*alcaldes de la justicia*, *alguaciles*). Although it has generally been presumed, based upon ordinances, that these subordinates were all academically qualified, a review of eleven lieutenants at Seville yields but three *letrados* and three holders of the bachelor's degree.[100] The *asistentes* of Seville typically designated one of these men as senior lieutenant, assigning him the significant role as chief administrative officer in charge of executive committee members (*fieles ejecutores*). This committee, which sat every working day, consisted of the senior lieutenant, two *veinticuatros*, and two citizens. Appeal from its decisions was made directly to the municipal council and, if that failed, to the court of the *Audiencia*. With such a tight group, public business was considerably expedited.[101] The senior lieutenant was also expected to oversee the operations of judges in criminal and civil cases, but not to direct the constables.

When Diego de Merlo was named Isabella's first *asistente* to Seville, he personally received the title of *alcalde de la justicia*,[102] but soon delegated this office to a junior lieutenant, sworn in to keep the peace. In most locales the *alcalde de la justicia* (or *alguacil*) typically had a deputy peace officer and a small group of constables in the parishes (*alguaciles de espada*). At Murcia – as turbulent a city as any, where virtually all men carried a sword or dagger – the *alguacil mayor* acted as chief during the day and the *alguacil menor* undertook night duty.[103] The chief peace officer had rather less initiative in dispensing justice than did the judges, being the enforcer of their decisions, but he could, of course, make arrests on his own cognizance. He also oversaw the direction of a *fiel* in charge of incarcerations, a chain of command which did not relieve any corregidor from his personal obligation to make regular inspections of the cells.[104]

If the corregidor in a small jurisdiction was fortunate enough to hold a law degree, he could dispense with the senior lieutenant – a large saving, since the aide was paid from his own salary. Cordova, Segovia, Salamanca, and Burgos had sufficient legal activity that they required two lieutenants within the walls, the one for directing civil law and the other for criminal cases.[105] The corregidor of Murcia had three: one for his principal jurisdiction, and the others for Lorca and Cartagena, where they directed government sessions in his stead.[106] To cover the far-flung northern coastal jurisdiction, four administrative lieutenants were sent out to the towns of the *merindades*.[107] The subordinates did earn their salaries, if only by providing useful continuity: García de Holguín was at Cáceres from 1468 to 1480, and Francisco Esquiván from 1480 to 1500.[108] Over this period the two *lugarteniente-alcaldes* served under more than fifteen changes of master, some of whom no doubt appreciated the guidance.

The varied titles for subordinates are not always a clear sign of levels of responsibility, since in certain cases corregidor, lieutentant, and *alcalde* turn out to be interchangeable titles. When Troilos Carrillo was nominated to Requena, he took on as his lieutenant Francisco de Molina, who was concurrently named corregidor of Utiel.[109] Instructions to the council at Seville, confirming Diego de Merlo in his post, state that rights and privileges of the *asistente* were equally granted to his lieutenant.[110] During a time when Juan de Silva was held hostage by Moors, the Royal Court gave his senior lieutenant the right to exercise all powers, and warned Seville not to innovate.[111]

This interchangeability of offices is typical of the mentality of all societies that gave low priority to bureaucratization. It was not at all necessary in the Europe that came into being after the decay of Roman authority that one hold a proper title before the privileges of an office could be exercised, since the important element was not the job description but the significance of the individual who gained the post. There was a constant delegation of powers in medieval offices, and all documents make provision for a lieutenant, whatever the title. Two reasons why this potential substitute had to be explicitly mentioned were either that the holder of the office might be a minor, or that a plurality of holdings made it impossible, or unlikely, that the holder would be available to exercise the duties of the position.[112]

The legal authorities were not very precise about just who a lieutenant was supposed to be – anyone delegated on the spot, or a specific, distinct, official. The cities of Castile wished to have a clear distinction made between leaving it to the corregidor to delegate

jurisdiction to whomever he chose or having a specific individual
named at the time the primary holder was sworn into office. Representatives to the Cortes of 1419 complained that corregidores were
abusing their right to nominate officials and judges in their stead.[113] At
Madrigal, in 1476, representatives to the Cortes tried to make sure
that a corregidor's lieutenant was specifically named by the sovereign,
and that he would bring his credentials to the municipal council when
those of his superior were being presented.[114] While it was fully
acceptable for a lieutenant then to delegate his powers, the councils
did not want him, in turn, to appoint a sub-lieutenant as his substitute.
The cities never got all they wanted, since corregidores were not
ordered to confirm their choices with the sovereign when naming
subordinates; but the documents do show that the *Reyes Católicos*
sometimes included the name of a specified senior lieutenant with the
credentials a new corregidor presented to his municipal council.

Shepherd among wolves

Having a staff beholden only to himself was a source of strength to the
corregidor, and one on which he was daily forced to draw in struggles
with municipalities. On all matters before city, town, and village
council sessions, the monarchy claimed for its corregidor a "voice and
vote." In the usual course of events each new official, after appointing
his staff, found himself facing seasoned parliamentarians. The *regidores*
could not always function as a monolithic bloc, but they did what they
could to keep their royal representative or his lieutenant from
influencing votes in a decisive way. Analysis by Gibert of voting
records in Madrid shows few unanimous ballots. *Regidores* typically
let personal interests predominate, with one or two breaking away
from the rest; wherever possible, however, issues were settled by a
majority, to forestall leaving anything up to the royal official.[115] Most
real business was accomplished in committees, which the councilors
attempted to limit to a few of their number; and while a commission
might include the corregidor, this was not obligatory.[116]

A look at the life of a corregidor in Madrid demonstrates some of the
problems a new man could face. Six persons held the post during the
first decade of Isabella's reign. Rodrigo de Mercado served from 1480
to 1483, and since little extraordinary happened during his tour of
duty in a town with only 4,000 inhabitants, these years offer a glimpse
of day-to-day operations. Upon being notified of his appointment,

Mercado presented himself in Medina del Campo for commissioning at a regular session of the Royal Council, on 24 November. It was not until the next month that he set out for his new jurisdiction. Until the most recent of times Madrid has been difficult to reach, somewhat isolated from foreigners behind doors doubly locked by mountains and arid tableland stretching for miles across one-third of the peninsula. Should a traveler come from the north, the Cantabrian mountains interfere; from the east, the Iberian. The south has the formidable Sierra Morena mountain chain. Even the rivers of the area, the Duero, Guadiana, and Tagus, conspire, with their turbulence, against easy contact with the coasts.

The day after arriving at his destination on mule-back, the most common way to travel, Mercado was escorted to the church of S. Salvador, where the Madrid council met throughout the year. After the presentation, and reading aloud of his letter of appointment with its enumeration of his duties and privileges, the *regidores* kissed it and placed it upon their heads, as was customary, both to show that they acknowledged it as coming from their sovereigns, and as a sign of compliance. Mercado, in turn, was asked to respect the rights and traditions of the commune. To conclude the brief and businesslike ceremony of 4 December he was granted his *vara*, an ashwood rod of office about the diameter of a finger and as tall as a person, capped by a silver cross. Mercado received the *vara*, symbol of the authority of office, from the hands of his predecessor, Alonso de Hereda, who stood to his left. In certain other towns his counterparts would receive their symbol of office from a senior *regidor*, which signified a stronger adherence to communal independence. As it was, the new corregidor at Madrid distributed, in his turn, the staff of office to his lieutenant. Soon afterwards Mercado went to visit each of his subordinate villages and hamlets to receive their accord, which was quickly accomplished, since the territory was not large. Also, he made a prompt visit to the jail and read over the charges against all who were incarcerated. Everything should have taken place the way described, if the rules were carefully followed.[117]

To narrow the focus, it is worth looking at one year to see what this official did when in the field. A summary look at municipal sessions for 1481 allows us to isolate Mercado by noting which issues council scribes indicate were specifically delegated to him, or on which he expressed a recorded opinion. Mercado attended most meetings throughout the year; however, enumerating what happened at these deliberations will not, of course, tell the full story, since controversial issues were often settled outside the chamber. With that caveat in mind, a look at procedure is in order. All through the year the Madrid council met in the portal of the church. The corregidor, with his lieutenant, would face his *mayordomo* and the public scribes, all ranged along the walls. The number of other participants varied: the front seats often held up to ten *regidores*, an equal number of *jurados*, and a minimum of nine commoners, with their spokesman. Since the sessions were public, and issues emotional, the noise level was high.

At the first session of 1481, the principal order of business for the corregidor, as recorded for Friday, 5 January, was that he carry out a council mandate to name an individual to check over the previous year's tax assessment distribution. The following Monday, Mercado was reminded that he and *regidor* Diego de Vargas had already received 2,000 *mrs*, for a twenty-day trip to court to plead a case for two residents. By royal mandate the council was supposed to meet three days a week, but sessions were skipped.[118] At the next meeting, on Friday, 21 January, Mercado reviewed a discussion about the division of imposts among taxpayers. At an unusual Saturday session, the last day of January, he mediated a problem between two taxpayers. The meeting of 7 February was a long one, with an agenda crowded with insignificant items. Mercado was called upon only once, being commissioned along with two *regidores* to look into conflicts over water rights and a mill. Protecting municipal land was the only business to come up for Mercado in the session of 14 February. A week later he had a busier day. Petitions had to be answered that he call an individual before him for justice; that he look into the distribution of tax assessments for the support of the Holy Brotherhood; and that he adjust the salary of the constable. On the last day of the month Mercado confirmed several sentences previously handed down, and designated two or three *regidores* to check into payment of a tax. At the request of one irate councilor, he ordered all the others to keep abreast of communal affairs.[119]

During March, Mercado appears in the record only twice, each time concerning taxes. On 2 March, along with the council, he petitioned Isabella to approve the distribution drawn up after an investigation by her treasury. On 28 March he ordered the rural areas of Valdemorillo and Nava to pay their assessments, about which they continued to stall. In April, Mercado saw to the execution of a fine of 20,000 *mrs* levied against an individual by the judges. That was on

Monday. On Wednesday 14 April, responding to a memorial from court, Mercado ordered that action be taken against anyone who damaged the El Pardo pasture grounds or cut down trees in the area without license from local officials. Much of the corregidor's work was routine. At the session of 22 June, Mercado reissued a standard prohibition against frivolities on Corpus Christi day. Moors were not to play music nor Jews to dance. Only one procession was authorized, and any confraternity which neglected to participate would be fined.

Meat markets were under discussion at the 27 June session, with much testimony concerning fraud and fixed prices. Mercado ordered an investigation. Another item which received his attention was the assessed charges due from tanners and makers of leather goods for using, and fouling, streams. Much of the corregidor's attention was given over to listening to similar complaints. At the 2 July session, the spokesman for the taxpayers was to the fore, demanding that Mercado put into effect a sentence pronounced against persons of high rank occupying various bits of land. After testimony, seconded by *regidores*, the corregidor agreed to carry out expulsions. A matter of personal interest came up towards the end of August when the council discussed the need to repair the house assigned to Mercado. A week later the *regidores* met at the house he rented to consider the problem at first hand.

Far more important business occupied the assembly in September. The crown had decided, after long deliberation, to restore major tracts of land to the town. The corregidor nominated a person of significance to conclude negotiation on the restorations with the duke of the Infantado, the *alcaide* of El Pardo, and the village of Alcobendas. This great matter out of the way, Mercado left on his twenty-day trip. During his absence he delegated powers to the *alcaldes*, on condition that the two men hand down joint decisions. In November, upon his return, the representative of the taxpayers was heard from again. At the tail-end of the 26 November session, he insisted Mercado detail at length all sentences handed down by judges regarding land quarrels, and clarify the status of all cases which had been subject to appeal. The last day of the year brought up minor items. Mercado saw to it that the council levied the final one-third of the costs for repairing his house, and concluded the session by ordering a resident to appear during the coming January with title to a mill.[120]

Rodrigo de Mercado's reported activities during 1481 appear to be those of a passive executive officer who responds to requests from interested parties, carries out other judges' verdicts, and complies with royal orders. He dealt most often with *regidores*, although there were times when commoners insisted on a say. The taxpayers' *junta de pecheros* could be brought in either by the corregidor or by the councilors, if consultation was thought necessary.[121] This gave Mercado a certain leeway to use one group against the other and thus, when it came to the costs of repair of a dangerous bridge, he was able to function as a mediator. The aristocrats took their position about the bridge to him on 15 January, the commoners on 23 November, and the *regidores* on 23 December.[122]

There is no hint in any of these deliberations of serious conflict with the oligarchy; but the third term was quite a different matter. Early in 1483, Mercado issued an ordinance breaking the monopoly maintained by officials on the sale of wine within municipal limits. During a moment when he was temporarily absent, the *regidores* struck by pushing through a reversal, over the objections of the lieutenant, which action Mercado chose not to fight upon his return.[123] The next run-in between the same forces was also won by the *regidores*. In March, Mercado removed two *alcaldes*, charging that they were not doing their jobs, and replaced them with Alonso Rodríguez de Medina. The councilors immediately complained to court that not consulting them was a serious breach of tradition. The crown let the decision stand, while the oligarchy bided its time. Mercado left office on 27 November 1483, with his replacement due to arrive 7 December; but on 1 December the town council met, pushed through nominations for the men it wanted, then hurried off the names to court. The crown acceded, since the two *alcaldes* appear in the record thereafter.[124]

The contest between the "omnicompetent" royal representative and the municipal elite was thus less unequal than it might appear from reading ordinances or reviewing thundering letters handed down by the Royal Council. When a corregidor went against the will of the *regidores* to attempt to mediate between groups the clamor from the privileged was loud. Clever *regidores* had a variety of ways to keep a corregidor off balance. In addition, there were broad areas where a lack of influence over judicial and police practices had the effect of reducing the official's prestige in the eyes of his audience.

The Holy Brotherhood escapes control

From the start of her reach for power, Isabella made sure that the entire apparatus of the Holy Brotherhood escaped a corregidor's control or review. Its national militia forces were so necessary in her fight to gain the crown, and its local police so important a force to terrify dissatisfied subjects, that she handcuffed her municipal agents. By 1476 the administrative organ of the soon-to-be-kingdomwide league was incorporated into her government as the Council of the Holy Brotherhood.[125] The league's growth thereafter was rapid, as cities were drawn into it on the tide of victory. With so high a degree of centralization, there was no interest in directly incorporating corregidores into the governing structure, as had been done in the past.[126] The corregidor of Vizcaya was exceptional during Isabella's reign in holding a mandated post with the brotherhood of the Basque ports: because that assembly had so independent a record, Isabella insisted it should never meet unless the royal official was in attendance.[127] The few other corregidores who took an office with Isabella's league did so only after they had left their municipal post, as in the case of a corregidor at Cáceres who quit upon election to the general assembly, and one at Jaén who left to be nominated as a chief judge.[128]

What small role remained for corregidores in the brotherhoods was played out strictly at the local level, as in the case of royal officials at Toledo who distributed decrees and took part in ceremonies.[129] Thus, when Toledo's treaty of concord with Talavera was renewed in 1477, its corregidor administered an oath to all assembled city officials obliging them to keep in force a pact dating back to 1300.[130] Although there was no guiding role for corregidores, a certain cooperation prevailed, since the royal officer supervised some elections and undertook *residencia* investigations, upon request, and judges for the brotherhood relied upon backup from municipal officials.[131] In a joint commission with the chief judge of the brotherhood of Trujillo, that municipality's corregidor investigated charges that the count of Medellín was intimidating the collector of taxes for the Holy Brotherhood in a seignorial village. A corregidor and a judge of the brotherhood in Vizcaya jointly petitioned the crown about disturbances caused by the master of the fortress of Valmaseda, and an *alcalde* of the brotherhood of Medina del Campo joined with his corregidor to review a sentence against a couple judged guilty of adultery; but apart from such cautiously limited instances, the force operated free from outside supervision.[132]

Holy Brotherhood police were allowed to reach deep into municipalities, for the first time, in their drive to punish Isabella's opponents, overriding urban ordinances to do so. Corrupt judges and brutal archers could not be kept from overstraying bounds, even by their own administrators, much less by outsiders. No interference whatever was allowed with trials, and the only appeal permitted had to be made directly to the Royal Council, in a troublesome and expensive process. During 1483 a corregidor at Asturias was, typically, prohibited from even looking into the circumstances surrounding an arrest.[133] That so little could be done locally about the outrages of the Holy Brotherhood reduced the prospects that Isabella's municipal representatives would find immediate favor in the eyes of all her subjects. There were thus communities which, for varied reasons, continued to reject corregidores, until forced to accept them at the point of a sword.

Breaking resistance

The opposition displayed towards a number of jurisdictions took its bitterest form at Alcaraz, where a delayed rebellion broke out as a consequence of a long history of conflict, analyzed by Pretel Marín, between deeply felt principles of urban freedom versus claims to pre-eminence by overlords. The tumultuous Andalusian city had risen six times since 1439, most successfully upon the death of Enrique IV, when it expelled his corregidor, known to be a pawn of the marquis of Villena.[134] The revolt came at a fortuitous moment, for Isabella was badly in need of support against the marquis, which help the city was happy to extend in exchange for her usual word that she would respect urban liberties and autonomy. With this promise in hand, a "revolutionary" government took over, featuring a reorganized council, placed under the joint rule of five *alcaldes* elected through widespread balloting. Reviving a thirteenth-century custom, the place of the dismissed corregidor was usurped by an *alguacil del concejo*.[135] In March 1475, overlooking her pledge to permit the city its own governance, Isabella prematurely attempted to send Diego de Madrid as her representative, with instructions that his salary be paid by the city, either through property rents or by raising new taxes. His nomination was met with polite but firm refusal from the new government, which wrote that it could not afford him and did not need him. Because the city's help was still required in the succession struggle, Isabella gave in, withdrawing her choice after fifteen days.[136]

The stakes in Alcaraz's struggle rose when the new city government seized holdings belonging to the marquis of Villena. As soon as he came to an agreement with Isabella pardoning him his transgressions, he naturally began agitating for the return of his property, which made it quite clear to the city that to accept an overseer meant to lose everything. A letter sent in 1476 to the community mentions a desire to send Gonzalo Chacón, who was highly placed at court; but quiet negotiations came to nothing, due to charges by urban officials that Chacón had so much land and so many benefices in the area that he was totally unacceptable.[137] Rumors began circulating in October 1477 that Isabella intended to resume the attack by sending García del Busto, a nobleman from Ocaña, who also held properties in Alcaraz. Her letter of nomination dated 9 September went beyond merely making the appointment, by completely suspending the new government.[138] The *regidores* dispatched a spokesman to present their case that all was tranquil, while also maintaining they could not pay the heavy costs everywhere associated with the official. After failing to dissuade the queen, the townsfolk began talking darkly of public disorders. It is not clear if García del Busto ever arrived to attempt to take his seat, or whether he prudently withdrew.[139]

As the *regidores* predicted, disturbances did break out, early in 1478, which proved all the pretext necessary to break the city.[140] Ferdinand sent a captain with troops, while at the same time threatening, if necessary, to call out the army of the count of Paredes. Juan Pérez de Barradas did not hesitate to use all necessary force during 1479 to impose his new authority. Most imprudently, this first of Isabella's corregidores to Alcaraz immediately set out to restore the property of the marquis of Villena, using threats and imprisonment.[141] Faced by the show of power, the city fathers changed their tactics, flooding the court with charges of corruption and mismanagement directed against the corregidor and his successors.

From the cascade of letters condemning Fernando de Talavera it appears he was particularly oppressive. When he was temporarily set aside by his judge, during a *residencia* investigation in 1485, the steaming resentments boiled over into revolt. Contributing to the strife was frustration over mounting assessments for the Granada War, which took no account of recurrent grain harvest failures. A royal messenger on his way to the corregidor was waylaid by a band of armed men who proclaimed the freedom of the city, once again.[142] Ferdinand and Isabella rushed in Día Sánchez de Quesada, with troops. He energetically repressed the revolt, and in collaboration with Talavera undertook a merciless program of banishment and confiscation.[143] The opposition was discovered to be quite widespread, with the accused ranging from a shoemaker to Juan Méndez de Sotomayor, scion of the most distinguished family.[144] Any remnant of Alcaraz's independence was eliminated when the size of the electorate was reduced, the corregidor authorized to intervene in elections, and municipal council membership limited to a few trustworthy families. The result, according to Pretel Marín, was a predictably supine acceptance of orders, and a craven servility towards the marquis of Villena. It was left to the undefended citizenry to forward their own petitions protesting abuses by corregidores, regidores, the Holy Brotherhood, or the Inquisition.[145] In Alcaraz, at least, it cannot be said that life improved for the ordinary person with the establishment of the corregidor system.

Looking back from the vantage point of the rubble of Alcaraz's failed rebellion, it is clear that the presumed alliance of cities and crown under Isabella is less solid in the early years than presented by historians following admiring chroniclers. Putting corregidores in place everywhere did not mean that they were always welcome. After Isabella's initial allies took up her cause, the rest either accepted their destiny or else fell before determined efforts. The municipalities were unable to present a united front against increased intrusion into their affairs because they remained sunk in isolation. Communities had failed to see advantages in lasting commercial alliances, and, except for infrequent general brotherhood leagues or the inter-municipal councils federated to administer common lands, remained aloof from one another. The Cortes, once a power in the realm, had few weapons left with which to force concessions. With its privileged membership jealously limited to a handful of cities presuming to speak for the rest, its representatives were drawn from too narrow a spectrum of the social order to persuade a monarch that they truly represented the entire political nation.

Long before 1474 the crown had been sending out temporary judges and officers to bring about order. Isabella invested her officials with increased stature through personal intervention and unceasing commitment. A sense of inevitability gradually developed around the office of corregidor during her first decade, when all municipalities discovered that it could be escaped neither through passive resistance nor through open rebellion. There is little to suggest that at the time this resigned acceptance meant that the officers were thought necessary by municipalities, for it remained to be seen if corregidores might ever be garlanded with popularity.

4

Faithful servants (1485–94)

"You are to be the head for this body, whose limbs are the city dwellers whom you govern. Study diligently that which the head must know," was the advice offered governors and judges by Pietro Martire d'Anghera, an Italian humanist resident at Ferdinand and Isabella's court. "You have been sent to these city dwellers not as their lord, but as their faithful servant."[1]

The promptings were well received during the second decade of Isabella's reign which, by contrast with the strife-ridden imposition of her rule, was virtually a golden age of corregidor accord with the urban oligarchy. The record is suddenly replete with complimentary remarks concerning the royal official. During the session of Madrid's council on 28 February 1485 a laudatory petition was drawn up requesting that García de la Quadra be granted another term. When, by April, there was no response from court, an even more fulsome letter was dispatched, pleading that it be "allowed to keep this good man who was always just and kept the peace."[2] Palencia was also well pleased, having originally requested the official as a way to escape onerous domination by the lord-bishop. The town continued to insist, during 1486 and 1488, upon its "right" to have a corregidor. The admiration it lavished upon its official is epitomized by a council session during January 1489, when the full body authorized sending two delegates to court to obtain an extension for Francisco de Vargas because of the many services he performed for the city.[3] Other municipalities just made the best of things when it became evident that corregidores were likely to become permanent fixtures. Intense lobbying for favored candidates became so customary that even the tenaciously rebellious town of Alcaraz, whose activities were considered in the previous chapter, changed its tactics. One of its *regidores* was granted expense money in 1492 to go in person to the Royal Council in hopes of influencing the choice.[4] The court became the

Table 1. *Geographic distribution of jurisdictions*

1. *By the Cantabrian coast*: Alegría, Asturias de Oviedo (principality), Bilbao–Las Encartaciones, Cuatro Villas de la Mar (*merindades*), Galicia (kingdom), Guipúzcoa (kingdom), La Coruña-Betanoz, Mondoñedo, San Sebastián, Vizcaya (county and seignory), Vitoria, Vivero.
2. *On the northern Meseta*: Aranda de Duero–Sepúlveda, Arévalo, Avila, Burgos, Carrión de los Condes–Sahagún, Castile (kingdom), Castrogeriz, Ciudad Rodrigo, Dueñas, Hontiveros (Fontiveros), Ledesma, León (city), León (kingdom), Logroño–Calahorra–Alfaro, Madrigal, Miranda de Ebro, Medina del Campo–Olmedo, Palencia, Palenzuela, Ponferrada, Salamanca, S. Domingo de la Calzada, Segovia, Soria–Agreda, Toro–Tordesillas, Valladolid, Villafranca del Bierzo, Zamora.
3. *On the southern Meseta*: Casarrubios del Monte, Ciudad Real, Cuenca–Huete, Escalona, Guadalajara, Madrid, Molina, Ocaña, Requena–Utiel, Toledo.
4. *In Extremadura*: Badajoz, Cáceres, Medellín, Plasencia, S. Martín de Trevejo, Trujillo, Valencia de Alcántara.
5. *In the Albacete–Murcia area*: Alcaraz, Almansa, Chinchilla de Monte Aragón, Murcia–Lorca–Cartagena, Marquesado de Villena.
6. *In Andalusia*: Alcalá la Real, Andújar–Jaén, Arcos de la Frontera, Baeza–Úbeda, Cádiz, Carmona, Cordova, Écija, Gibraltar, Jerez de la Frontera, Los Palacios y Villafranca, Palos de la Frontera, El Puerto de S. María, Seville.
7. *By the Mediterranean coast and in Granada*: Almuñécar, Baza–Vera, Granada (city), Granada (kingdom), Guadix–Almería, Loja–Alhama de Granada, Marbella–Ronda, Málaga, Vélez Málaga.
8. *In the Canaries*: Gran Canaria, La Palma–Tenerife.

scene of ever-increasing urban attention as the number of *corregimientos* to be staffed grew.

In terms of geographic distribution, Table 1 presents the maximum number of *corregimientos* reached by the second decade of the reign. In 1494 these jurisdictions were administered by 72 officials (63 corregidores, 5 governors, 2 *asistentes*, administrators for 2 *adelantamientos*).[5] The thickest cluster is centered on the table-lands of the Meseta, with lightly populated areas to the west and north showing far fewer districts. The kingdom of Granada was in flux, so soon after the war, with a few changes still to come. To all intents and purposes, however, the second decade of Isabella's reign set out the configurations followed during the Habsburg succession. (By the early sixteenth century, 87 localities were incorporated into 64 jurisdictions, which included 3 governorships, 3 *adelantamientos*, 2 districts for *alcaldes mayores*, and one city for an *asistente*.)[6]

Assault on the factions

The confidence that gradually developed in the swarm of corregidores as promoters of just rule emboldened the Vizcayans to support the use of the official. The bitter struggle of contending clans or bands (*bandos*) was a social malignancy, eating away at the northernmost province, for nowhere in Castile was the conflict more enduring and intense or the groups more diverse than in this isolated mountainous land.[7] During June 1487, the *Junta de Villas y Ciudad* held a seminal meeting at Bilbao where, with virtual unanimity, the representatives signed their names to the *Ordenamiento de Chinchilla*, thereby peacefully surrendering privileges once carefully protected. To end the internecine strife, Vizcaya's corregidor was granted far-ranging dominion, with administrative control of municipal councils virtually passing to the monarchs.[8] Corregidores in Extremadura performed a similar welcome service for their people, who suffered from the depredations of what were little more than gangs. The domination of society by a favored few was assumed by Ferdinand and Isabella, but that did not mean that their officials were to put up with violence from the privileged. Badajoz's corregidor was not only authorized to specify which caballeros were in secret league, but was to go beyond this, in 1488, to work with an emissary from the court to detain the guilty. There was also concern for dangerous conditions outside the city, as the next corregidor in line continued the struggle to control bands that roamed the hillsides.[9]

Strife between contending factions in Úbeda and Baeza pre-dated troubles already considered. As early as the 1420s the "Cueva" faction (descendants of the Traperas clan) was in the ascendancy over the "Molina" (offshoot of the Arandas clan). In return for support from the Molina, Enrique IV compensated the faction by giving it domination over Úbeda's government. The rise in their fortunes seemed unshakable, despite endless challenges – especially dangerous to bystanders on holidays, when Mass or Vespers brought out crowds in these two cities of some 12,000 to 15,000 inhabitants each. After attempts at negotiation, Isabella commissioned Pedro Gómez de Setúbal to quieten the strife in 1489.[10] Rebellious *regidores* were threatened with high fines and the loss of their positions. Above all, corregidor Alfonso Enríquez was instructed to show no partiality to either faction. A relative calm descended which lasted until 1505.

Isabella continued to work well past the mid-point of her reign at these efforts to pacify municipalities. In Trujillo, a locale with about 5,000 residents, it was long established that half the council positions went to the Altamiranos clan, and the other six posts were evenly divided between the Anascos and Bejaranos (two factions of a fragmented anti-Altamiranos clan). Despite this calibrated distribution, troubles continued until a royal reform took direct selection of municipal council members out of the hands of party chiefs. Electors for the *regidores* were chosen, after 1491, by lot under observation by the corregidor.[11]

At Seville, a new round of street fighting suddenly broke out during the spring of 1492. With no gainful military employment available after the conquest of Granada, disbanded forces of the duke of Medina Sidonia, the count of Cabra, and other aristocrats resumed their favorite sport. Ferdinand and Isabella could not come to the area during June, so they assigned fresh powers to their *asistente* to bring the disturbances under control.[12] Juan de Silva (1482–1500), who held the title of count of Cifuentes, suddenly found unexpected breathing space when, during August, both Enrique de Guzmán and Rodrigo Ponce de León died. The successors who took up the titles of Medina Sidonia and of Cádiz did not hate with the same intensity. This, more than anything Juan de Silva was able to do, brought long-term calm to the city.[13]

Salamanca was yet another city where confederations that disturbed the peace were brought under control at this time. Pedro García de Cotes, an experienced administrative specialist in urban problems, was alerted to inform himself about disruptive leagues of caballeros.[14] Despite exhausting struggles, he left office in 1487 without having resolved the basic issues. It was not until 1493 that corregidor Honorado Hurtado de Mendoza finally gained the negotiated settlement the crown had long desired between the San Martín and the San Benito lines. Thereafter, municipal offices in this city of 13,000 residents were split equally, bringing electoral strife to an end.[15] To assure calm in factious cities, both in the north and the south, broad administrative reforms were promulgated, for implementation through the 1480s and 1490s by royal officials.

Implementing the decrees of Toledo

The broad legislative program presented to the 1480 Cortes of Toledo had so many ramifications that its implementation was slow. It is difficult to envisage how Isabella would have been able to keep her promises of reform and lawful action without having the domains blanketed with agents on permanent duty, ready to press laggard municipalities to regularize governmental procedures, to keep their physical plant in repair, and to regulate the marketplace. Assiduous attention by corregidores to small details that improved everyday life eventually redounded to their credit with the populace. After the Cortes, although corregidores maintained pressure on jurisdictions to build a meeting hall within two years, or else improve on an existing building,[16] *regidores* proved in no immediate mood to spend money. Burgos proposed to provide a chamber in the tower of S. María, but for many years it continued to use the chapel of S. Juan in the cathedral, or rooms in inns and other unsuitable places.[17] The monarchs dispatched a letter in 1495 to the corregidor of Baeza asking him, in an irritated tone, just how far along the municipality was with its enterprise, and at about the same time ordered the corregidor of Asturias to forge ahead with fund-raising for a hall in Oviedo.[18] This renewed pressure to get government into permanent buildings came from the preference of legists on the Royal Council for regularized procedures. Corregidores, to give another example of this passion, had been mandated by the Toledo decrees to assure that all acts passed be recorded in a book, and that all letters and ordinances received be preserved.[19] A scribe at Segovia was admonished in 1495, by his corregidor, to write at length concerning sessions.[20] Although files were mandated, laggard Burgos would not allow itself to be rushed, and so did not get around to creating an archive until 1528.[21]

The pride with which communes were celebrated in panegyrics did not always mean that their inhabitants would save records or keep the physical plant in minimal repair, although late fifteenth-century Castile was fully recovered from the depressed economy of the preceding era, with the consequence that a confident middle-level social stratum emerged. The Cortes of Toledo charged maintenance of public works to the municipal purse, but newly prosperous inhabitants were loath to expend funds. Keeping fortifications in repair was the greatest single expense. Normally two walls, plus ancillary defenses, were required. Linking the two rows of stone was a platform where fighting men might mount their defense. The outer perimeter was often festooned with towers, and in front of the outer wall, at some distance, was a barricade. If the walls were to function effectively, a space had to be kept clear behind the inner perimeter, with up to thirty yards required so that troops could assemble, engines of war be set up, and the foe prevented from igniting houses. The scope of the maintenance problem on the principal structures is illustrated by the need for the inner wall to be at least thirty feet high and fifteen feet thick if it was to be effective.[22] The insatiable appetite of "defense" for land, funds, and manpower is a familiar enough concept in our own unhappy age.

Corregidores pressed for the repair of watch-walks atop the ramparts, or to have stones replaced after they were jarred loose by bad weather.[23] The walls surrounding Cáceres were in deplorable shape. An ordinance passed during 1479 had been expected to take care of all repairs through an assessment of 200,000 mrs. As it turned out, the money was diverted to salary purposes, with 125,000 going to the corregidor and other officials. In 1492 the royal representative was authorized to set a new tax to raise 150,000 mrs over a period of five years. To make sure the money would be used for the intended purpose, a committee was appointed whose membership consisted of the corregidor, two regidores, and one elected delegate from each parish.[24]

Bridges spanning rivers within cities were also costly items to repair,[25] or to build.[26] Grumbling over what was perceived to be enormous expense led to specific royal exhortations that corregidores do everything possible to reduce costs.[27] Bridges in Madrid, especially the narrow, but heavily traveled, Toledo span, were constantly in need of repair.[28] Periodically, attempts were made to get the privileged to pay a share of such costs.[29] In 1489 the municipal council insisted that only half the cost of the renovations be paid by commoners, in conjunction with the Jewish and Muslim communities. Madrid's corregidor then pressed to obtain the rest from clerics, hidalgos, and greater folk, but without success. Several years later, when 40,000 mrs were required to improve three bridges, a corregidor made a valiant attempt to get the duke of the Infantado to give a voluntary contribution, but the duke was not in a charitable mood.[30]

Sanitation was another unwelcome fiscal burden imposed by the corregidores upon laggard communities.[31] Isabella issued an order to Madrid's corregidor in 1491, insisting he press the community to clean its streets, thereby improving the health of its populace. The call to designate 40,000 mrs for the cleaning was repeated three years later.[32] Valladolid, a big town where some 32,000 inhabitants ran a greater risk of unsanitary conditions, asked Dr Alonso Ramírez de Villaescusa in 1494 to specify how it was expected to pay for clean streets. He told the regidores to lay a special tax on fresh fish to raise the needed 45,000 mrs.[33] To reduce the roadway damage inflicted by carts carrying heavy metal, he prohibited lorries from main thoroughfares. He was also alert to keep byways clear of overhanging balconies and other obstructions, for no one, he made it clear, had any right or privilege to build in, or control, any street.[34] This corregidor was a particularly enlightened administrator who typifies the best type of public official produced during this happy era.

Such vigilance about public property is one distinguishing characteristic of the change which took place when areas passed from Muslim to Christian rule. The Muslim city of the medieval period in Al-Andaluz or North Africa had little feeling for public space. One prosaic explanation for narrow, winding streets and a generally labyrinthine quality is that by the end of the Roman era camels and pack animals had completely displaced the wheeled vehicles which required wide, inflexible thoroughfares.[35] Conquerors of the Moors were not pleased with the resultant neighborhoods, encountered as they rode into their new possessions. "In most districts," noted Lucio Marineo Sículo concerning post-conquest Granada, "due to the great density of buildings the streets, of which there are many, are narrow, and likewise the plazas and markets . . . therefore, after Granada was taken these streets were made by the Christians much broader and distinguished."[36] It can be maintained in this larger sense that, even when not specifically enjoined to do so by ordinances, corregidores were concerned with every physical aspect of new jurisdictions.[37] Málaga needed such extensive attention at the close of the war that in February 1492 the crown dispatched corregidor García Fernández Manrique. His survey of Málaga included (but was not limited to) waterfront facilities, towers, fortifications, and walls, all of which he found in immediate need of repair.[38]

In the marketplace

Maintaining the market-place and regulating its activities thus quite naturally fell to the corregidor. In this role he was similar to an Islamic Master of the Market (*Sahib el-sūq*).[39] The exemplary Dr Alonso Ramírez de Villaescusa, noticeable in improving Valladolid's appearance, also took an active hand in improving its commercial life. He persuaded the municipal council to take over houses fronting on the "House of Spices" in the main plaza, giving them new vestibules with enlarged rooms so that they could function more effectively as shops for selling bread and other commodities.[40] He was also concerned about relocating the meat market to a healthier position.[41] At Ciudad Rodrigo, the government dithered over what to do about its busy meat market, unattractively located too near the municipal hall and the church of S. Juan. Three successive corregidores oversaw debates, before something was done in 1491.⁴² Turning to another issue, equally carnal, the corregidor of Ecija was faced in 1492 with having to move a brothel. It was not that this business was forbidden, just that the widow who lived across the way found the noise and traffic objectionable.⁴³

Residents at Burgos had more to be concerned about when complaining to their corregidor regarding a saddlemaker's shop, where the stench was too horrid to accept, year after year. In other cities, they noted, such enterprises were always outside the walls.⁴⁴ Fire was a greater threat than noxious odors to crowded commercial streets, since most buildings were made of wood. At Valladolid, merchants from the neighborhood of La Costanilla demanded that those in the trades of silver goods, baskets, linens, and clothes make a special contribution to fire watch squads. The record is not clear as to what action was taken, but since the corregidor they complained to was Dr Ramírez de Villaescusa, they probably received the protection they needed.⁴⁵

The improvement of commerce was thus a task given to corregidores, although they received no specific mandate in their principal ordinances. Ferdinand and Isabella seem to have had little clear understanding of what would be best for the economic health of their realms. Vicens Vives points out that the Catholic Sovereigns held unfortunate ideas concerning financial affairs, and sometimes did more harm than good.⁴⁶ Incessant war and the harassment of vital commercial families ran directly counter to economic well-being. Powerful old Christian families were allowed by the crown to make sure that many converts, and all Jews, were eliminated as a source of business competition, whatever the long-term fiscal consequences to the realms.⁴⁷ In keeping with economic postulates of the day, the crown satisfied guild-masters by assuring them that workmen would be stopped from banding together, employing the not unreasonable pretext that all confederations held potential for revolt. The corregidor of Salamanca broke up a league of shoemakers in 1493 who were "masquerading as a confraternity, without spiritual character."⁴⁸ The plebeian character of the group is indicated by the modest dues of 12 mrs a year. Since guilds organized by masters were encouraged, economic bias is very much in evidence.

Set against a background of skewed royal priorities, the economic role of the corregidor dwindles to police functions: the regulation of hours and conditions of sale, or the enforcement of laws concerning weights and measures.[49] He was to make sure sufficient meat, fish, and other staples were available at reasonable prices, set out for public display under hygienic conditions.[50] Tight regulatory policies also ruled the big seasonal markets and fairs, where every movement of traders was subject to suspicious control. Travelers who set up shop in Segovia during 1490 had to negotiate item by item with the corregidor concerning each privilege. Foreign merchants resident from 1488 onward at Guipúzcoa, Vizcaya, Logroño, and the smaller ports along the northern coast were constantly exhorted to report all changes in their stock to the appropriate corregidor.[51] The export of silk and fine goods was expressly forbidden and no gold, silver, or coins of any kind were to slip by the royal official without justification.[52]

Monopoly and protection were the goals of all producers, whether farm owners or urban jobbers. So long as corregidores watched over local interests, they increased their popularity with these groups. Vizcaya, for example, was permitted to restrict the metal industry to its own producers, despite high production costs. In 1489 Vizcaya's corregidor was petitioned, unsuccessfully, by the iron workers of Guipúzcoa, who asked to be allowed to sell their less expensive ironwork within his jurisdiction.[53] Only in the delicate area of foodstuffs did the corregidor's mandate demonstrate a greater concern for the interest of the community at large, since high prices and shortage inevitably led to unrest; and so, for the good of all, grain monopolies (outside seignorial estates) were prohibited.[54] Through the good harvests of the 1490s corregidores successfully maintained stable, locally regulated prices for grain, in keeping with Christian norms.[55]

Regaining the land

The greatest economic service corregidores could render their communities was to keep the common lands (*tierras baldías*) and municipal property (*tierras concegiles*) available for food production and grazing. Holdings in the surrounding countryside were sometimes quite extensive, as in the case of Toledo, whose rights and jurisdiction ran "seventeen leagues from east to west and eleven leagues from north to south."[56] It was always under threat, because the aristocracy's hunger for swallowing tempting morsels was insatiable. Elliott estimates that some 2 to 3 per cent of Castile's population owned most of the land by the end of the reign of the Catholic Sovereigns, and that over half this land was in the possession of a handful of great families.[57] Some of this property was boldly stolen from communities. The instrument to provide aid in resisting such thefts was at hand in the eighty-second decree of the 1480 Cortes of Toledo, which empowered judges to be stern in adjudicating charges of land theft brought to their attention.[58] Laborers in Vizcaya took complaints to their corregidor that small holdings had been chipped away at since the years of Enrique IV. Avila's council tried to enlist the aid of its corregidor during a struggle to get Las Navas del Marqués back from its lord, and Málaga demanded the royal supervisor do something to recover land from the count of Cabra.[59]

City fathers were undoubtedly right in their belief that corregidores would not get involved in such thankless, lengthy investigations unless forced to do so by their superiors.[60] Toledo bitterly protested, during 1483, against the judicial inaction of corregidor Gómez Manrique and his *alcalde*, after the local court handed down a decision to allow the alienated villages of Yeles, Azaña, Cobeja, and El Alameda to render obedience to territorial lords. It proved necessary, after insistent complaints from the city, for the sovereigns to write a strong letter to Manrique in October 1484, demanding that he use his authority under the Cortes of Toledo decrees to provide judicial remedies to determine the accuracy of charges of theft. Manrique maintained a lack of interest in the issue, and it was only after his death in 1490 that a new corregidor, Pedro de Castilla, made the first effort to satisfy the jurisdiction.[61] In other instances it might have been family connections that stayed a corregidor's hand. Don Juan de Silva, who usurped considerable land from Toledo, was the cousin of his namesake, the count of Cifuentes, who was the influential *asistente* of Seville from 1482: through the years, nothing was done to bother the former.[62] Madrid tried, with little help, to safeguard its pasture land of El Pardo from local troublemakers who constantly chipped away at the land or the vineyards, and also to police the closed season on hunting. The town designated two *regidores*, two nobles, and two commoners to adjudicate questions concerning the usurpations and abuses, but, typically, no corregidor joined the commission.[63]

The only way to get coordinated action throughout the realms would be royal pressure. In 1485 the crown at last directed all corregidores to begin resolving issues which had come before the courts. According to Pulgar, the crown ordered officials to review each decision rendered and to find out if it was being enforced. The men were to make personal visits to the territories in question, and anyone discovered occupying land contrary to a decree was to have their goods seized. If corregidores were apprehensive that strict application of decisions against the powerful would be too difficult or "the cause of scandal," then the Royal Council, or the monarchs themselves, would shoulder the burden.[64]

The response to pleas for restitution during the second decade of Isabella's rule proved gratifying to aggrieved parties. At Seville, the *asistente* set his lieutenant to work in 1488 examining case after case wherein more than seven leagues of city land, plus the salt-mines at Matrera, had been blatantly occupied by powerful families. Charges were filed against the marquis of Cádiz, *adelantado mayor* Pero Enríquez, and the countess of Los Molares.[65] Seville also defeated the count of Niebla, in a 1491 case involving the countryside of Andevevalo, and his heirs suffered a fresh loss three years later when the wasteland of Gamonal returned to the city's jurisdiction.[66] In June 1492, Cuenca's corregidor applied the law of Toledo to land usurped by the count of Tendilla at Huete, where an illegal castle sat on the property, boldly proclaiming lordly pretensions. During the same month the corregidor of Avila investigated heavy purchases made in the outlands of the city over the previous ten years by three members of the Dávila family. This noble plot against communal land was subtler than most, since their funds were rumored to have come from aristocrats, who intended to establish a disguised jurisdiction.[67]

It was well known that usurpations at Badajoz had been going on all through the fifteenth-century, although both Juan II and Enrique IV pressed the counts of Feria to make restitution. An emissary sent by Isabella's council to visit the city ascertained, yet again, that there had been an alarming amount of pilferage. The sovereigns backed their corregidor in his efforts to set things right, until Francisco Maldonado's vigorous enforcement of the Cortes of Toledo decrees caused too much of an uproar. His decisions were suspended while Dr Luis de la Villa did a minute, and surely superfluous, reinvestigation. The new finding, handed down in 1488, announced that Badajoz was to get back all the pastures and ancient sheep-walks awarded it in the days of Juan II. Ten more years would pass before all appeals were exhausted and the document of concession signed by the count of

Feria, Gómez Suárez de Figueroa. The then corregidor, Martín Vázquez de Rojas, appended his name, with further weight given by the signature of the president of the Royal Council.[68]

Guarding the collection of taxes

Tax flow dramatically increased during Isabella's reign. Ordinary revenue in 1479, already increased from Enrique IV's last years, stood at 94,401,000 mrs, and by 1494 collection had more than tripled, reaching 317,770,227 mrs.[69] The pressure for this increase is not entirely related to the Granada War, since non-military spending virtually doubled, going from 80,226,000 mrs in 1482 to 144,223,080 mrs eight years later.[70] The queen spent heavily on jewels and personal adornment, insisting as well that her court be more elaborate than previously thought necessary in Castile. This personal extravagance has been overlooked by those writers who still accept chronicles and official portraits that offer deliberately misleading public images of frugality and simplicity.[71]

Varied revenue sources were tapped to cover these expenses, which far outran income and revenues (rentas) from royal estates and direct taxes (moneda feorera, tercias reales) from towns under crown domination. Late medieval governments relied almost entirely upon indirect consumption taxes and user fees to increase ordinary income. The crown's two highest-yielding commercial levies in Castile were the alcabalas on general market sales, which grew in time to a 10 per cent charge, and the sisa or imposición excise tax deduction on foodstuff sales, which did not exceed 3 per cent. The next largest volume of income was generated from goods or persons in transit. Custom duty (almojarifazgo) was added to the other imposts set upon bridges, roads, and turnpikes, and herders in the mestas were instructed to pay a charge on the movement of sheep (servicio y montazgo). The monarchy increasingly competed with local jurisdiction for these fees and levies.

In emergencies, the Cortes might vote increased subsidies (servicios), especially agreeing in the heat of war to an extraordinary pedidos y monedas. During Isabella's time a great deal of such wartime funding was provided by servicios raised and collected by the Holy Brotherhood and, with the blessing of the papacy, by a crusade indulgence (cruzada) that was preached and gathered by special agents for the struggle against the infidel. There was also, as a last resort, the prospect of the crown issuing interest-paying certificates of indebtedness (*juros*) or selling government posts, two dangerous practices that blossomed in later reigns.[72]

Nothing was promulgated at the 1476 Cortes of Madrigal concerning a corregidor's responsibility in the gathering of this array of charges, or in the suppression of unauthorized taxation. Four years later, in the Cortes of Toledo there is only brief mention of investigating unwarranted sheep-pasturing charges, and notification that merchants traveling either by land or sea were to be protected against illegal poll or passage taxes.[73] Detailed instructions issued shortly thereafter fill in the substance of corregidor responsibility for the first time.[74] No one was to collect taxes unless approved by the royal recorder of taxes, who set out the proper authorized levels in the Book of Taxes and Revenues (*Cuaderno de las Alcabalas*), which was adapted with little change from the systematic lists of preceding reigns.[75] (A preliminary draft of the book, issued in 1484, was superseded by its definitive version in 1491.)[76] Corregidor ordinances at the turn of the century, therefore, presumed that the official would be completely familiar with the content of the book, wherein it was spelled out that no corregidor was permitted to impose an unlisted tax or use independent judgement that a tax was due.[77] Improper local revenue schemes were assailed by requiring the corregidor to investigate the warrant for all turnpike tolls (*portazgos*), tolls upon goods passing through a district with a castle (*castillerías*), custom duties, sheep passage charges (*borras*), or any other levy placed by a locality or a lord. Had charges increased? If so, why were they raised? Was there a right upon which the initial tax was based? If not, the impost must be removed.[78]

Collection of properly authorized charges was undertaken by tax farmers (*arrendadores*) – entrepreneurs who advanced funds in exchange for the privilege. During 1480–5, a comprehensive collection group was set up by prominent Jewish financiers, at the behest of the crown.[79] At the same time, less easily controlled individual farmers, notorious for corrupt accounting, were dismissed. Municipalities thereupon gained a satisfying new measure of control over resources, while harvesting a proportionally greater yield.[80] This also enhanced the significance of the royal official on the scene who, unaided, checked the accuracy of the count at small jurisdictions. In large cities like Seville, collectors continued to have to defend their renderings before the full council and its bookkeepers, with the *asistente* in attendance.[81]

The crown relied especially upon its official to assure the smooth collection of the extraordinary imposts. Successive general assemblies of Holy Brotherhood delegates were aggressively prodded to increase quotas, until yearly peaks of 64 million *mrs* were reached in the last stage of the Granada War.[82] Seville was always slow in paying its assessments, despite constant pressure from its *asistente*, and the same was true of other jurisdictions.[83] Villanueva de Alcaraz, citing the end of the war in 1493, refused to pay either its brotherhood contribution or its share of the corregidor's salary until charges against Pedro Ortiz were aired.[84]

Alfonso de Quintanilla administered the modest staff of accountants and lawyers on the Council of the Holy Brotherhood who checked on accounts and forced the pace of such collections. He allowed municipalities leeway on how quotas were to be met because so many groups were exempted. Aristocrats and *hidalgos* were freed of obligation after Isabella's one attempt at imposing a universal assessment was beaten back.[85] Individual Jews were not to be touched by municipalities, because their communities made separate lump sum contributions.[86] The church won total exemption at first, but then agreed that a contribution might properly be made in the fight against the enemies of God, which kept the administrators of the Holy Brotherhood busy trying to make good on this promise. The *asistente* of Seville received a typical letter from the Holy Brotherhood in January 1489, urging that he put pressure on the religious of S. Juan, who had not made a promised gift towards defraying general war costs.[87]

With so many groups placed out of bounds, the municipal elite protected their own purses by shifting burdens to those least able to resist. The rag-dealers of Cordova complained about heavy assessments to their corregidor, obtaining a promise that he would at least give their grievances a full airing. After Madrid's commoners attacked the burden of taxes their *regidores* set on fish and meat, Cristóbal de Toro saw to it that the contribution was raised somewhat more equitably.[88]

In the spring of 1488 a siege was undertaken of Baza which dragged on into winter, resulting in unanticipated war expenses, enormous by earlier standards.[89] The monarchy plunged into its worst period of fiscal distress. The near-bankruptcy years from 1488 to 1491 pushed the crown towards a variety of desperate expedients.[90] In February 1489, all corregidores were informed that large sums must be raised immediately. Local authorities who refused to cooperate would face trusted servants of the queen, sent to bypass them when setting assessments. Collectors squeezed at least 14,102,500 mrs out of thirty-one jurisdictions, primarily big cities. Forced loans, extorted from any individual with assets of more than 50,000 mrs, brought in over 145,000,000 mrs by 1491.[91]

The result of such frantic manipulation, as will be demonstrated later in this chapter, was to weaken the crown in its dealings with the aristocracy and to diminish corregidor power over the urban elite, although neither of these long-term threats counted for much in the heat of battle. Even if all the ordinary taxes and the special Holy Brotherhood charges due flowed promptly into the proper channels, income would not have been sufficient for the military campaigns. An additional major source of financing for the struggle was found in the bull of crusade, an indulgence settled at a fixed rate.[92] Ferdinand and Isabella desperately needed funds for the Granada War but resisted papal demands that quotas for the *cruzada*, or its timing, be left to parish churches. In exchange for a share of the spoils, the papacy gave up administrative control, with the result that the dissemination of apostolic bulls was first approved by prelates on the Royal Council, before they were promulgated. Corregidores were ordered to be alert to unauthorized indulgences, charities, or pardons in the districts.[93] Promulgators of the bull of crusade appeared with such alarming regularity to cajole funds by coercive activities that they lived under constant threat. A corregidor of Calahorra protected two collectors who arrived in February 1488, although that December nearby villagers successfully harassed the next round of visitors. During February 1490 a collector was despoiled at Loja, requiring that the corregidor recover the funds.[94] Preaching brothers were close to the populace and regularly articulated their hostility towards the *cruzada*. Friar Juan de Santo Domingo had to be restrained by corregidor Gutiérrez de Carvajal when public disturbances erupted in Zamora, after the cleric charged that the receiver of the bull was in usurious connection with Jews. Until he was silenced, the father was threatening to excommunicate all concerned.[95]

During the course of the Granada War, Castile was the scene of three extensive fund-raising drives (1484–5, 1487–8, and 1490–1), which yielded 361,997,230 mrs. Adding to this total the amount collected in Aragon and Navarre between 1485 and 1492, the chief treasurer of the bull showed the enormous balance on his books of 505,805,871 mrs.[96] Despite the vigilance with which corregidores watched over ordinary levels, special *servicios*, Holy Brotherhood assessments, and bull of crusade collections, the crown still suffered from deficient accounting and fraud. Father Azcona regretfully points out that the monarchy was surely denied access to vast sums by inadequate collectors and corrupt functionaries.[97]

Although the fighting ended the bull did not, since Ferdinand and Isabella found pretexts convincing enough for the papacy to allow the monarchs to go on receiving revenue. Between 1495 and 1503, the Castilian collectors brought in 169,045,136 *mrs*.[98] Thus corregidores continued to have to protect collectors of the bull, although the Reconquest once again began slipping back into memory. The anti-hero of *Guzmán de Alfarache* (1599) would still have good cause to raise his ironic prayer: "God free us from transgressions against the three Holies – Inquisition, Brotherhood, and Crusade Bull."[99]

Restraining the police

By relying upon the governing assembly of the Holy Brotherhood to finance troops during the Granada War, the sovereigns were saved the vexation of having to call a single parliament, where they might have had to answer for actions during the ten-year struggle.[100] To gain increased taxation cooperation from the municipalities in the collection of assessments for the national Holy Brotherhood militia during the Granada War years, the queen responded to insistent complaints from city fathers that the local brotherhood police be reined in. At the 1485 general assembly of Torrelaguna, police immunities were reduced, with the result that cases against archers and judges began appearing on the docket.[101]

A corregidor at Asturias undertook to carry a charge of rape in 1485 against *alcaldes* who were protecting constables. Police were investigated for hindering tax collection at Ciudad Real in September 1488, and at Salamanca in November of that year. Excesses led to a significant case for the corregidor of Santo Domingo de la Calzada. The charges, jointly brought by the *regidores* and the duke of Nájera, rated such careful attention that Fernando Gil Mogollón had his term extended for six months during 1494, specifically to complete the work.[102] Modest satisfactions granted to the urban populace never extended so far, however, as actually to let corregidores intervene in trials, or ever accept appeals on verdicts. When a persistent corregidor from Ciudad Rodrigo attempted to secure a prisoner's release in 1489, he was diverted and the case removed to the royal court to keep it entirely clear of local jurisdiction.[103]

Protecting communal lands

The integrity of cities and the welfare of their taxpaying members suffered when, in exchange for the extraordinary fiscal cooperation extended by the urban elite to the crown, royal ability to deal responsibly with communal resources became hampered. Theoretically, corregidores had no control over communal property, since the Catholic Sovereigns guaranteed the absolute right of possession, in the name of their jurisdictions, to municipal councils.[104] Yet there were sufficient *ad hoc* grounds established, via an ill-defined responsibility to look out for the "common benefit," to consider the corregidor a co-administrator of the communal patrimony.[105] The most secure foundation for his watchdog function was the necessity that his signature (along with that of two *regidores*) be on all orders connected with the disposition of the patrimony.[106] Evidence supporting the shared role can be found for all jurisdictions, as in the case of Carmona, where the largest category of letters dispatched from 1476 to 1504 by the royal court to its representative deals with common and communal lands.[107] There was thus hope in the municipalities that corregidores would make good the promise, made during Isabella's first years, that law would be respected.

Landholding was the foundation of the civic wealth that provided taxes, tithes, and wartime assessments. Prosperity, and an expanding population, brought formerly neglected wooded and scrub areas into use. Protecting title to these holdings was of profound importance to the urban elite who, despite their passionate self-interest, often altruistically protected public property benefiting the lower social orders. Conflict with other communities and with lords was inevitable as pressure mounted on this marginal land, since boundary lines were indistinctly marked. When the matter had been of little concern streams, boulders, ditches, or stands of trees were satisfactory markers to jog memory; but these no longer served when competition for resources increased. It is the role the corregidor played in the clashes between contending entities over these indistinct demarcations which is of concern here. Cáceres was fortunate to have in Diego Ruiz de Montalvo at least one official who constantly repaired boundary stones, checked on borders, protected streams, and implemented the court order which ruled in favor of possession of common lands in an area of Valhondo.[108] In the cold of January 1492 he was out chasing interlopers who were damming the river with nets, to the dismay of herdsmen, and worse, poisoning streams for fast catches.[109]

The hardworking corregidor was, at times, a bit too impartial for the urban elite. Ruiz de Montalvo caught the wrath of *regidores* that September, when he attempted to allow villagers of nearby Casar freely to gather firewood and catch fish and game, which he knew to be customary.[110] Similarly, the reality behind a barrage of criticism directed by Carmona's *regidores* against their corregidor, Juan de Ulloa, during February and March 1493, was that he opposed their greed. The chief lieutenant from Seville was sent to investigate charges that the corregidor was making unjust decisions when allocating water to orchards and vineyards. That April, a contrasting petition was received from the commoners of Carmona, who supported Juan through his difficulties. They pointed out that previous corregidores had always sided with the oligarchy in giving the lion's share of water to the possessing group, but that this official "alone had given them benefits." At his public *residencia* sessions, Juan came under such strong attack from the *regidores* that he was forced to hire his own attorney, at a cost of 13,000 *mrs*. The crown neglected to back up its man, who was fortunate to escape with a token fine of 4,000 *mrs*.[111]

Few other corregidores pressed as hard to enforce their protective role over communal holdings, despite a flood of complaints from the queen's lesser subjects.[112] The cooperation the urban elite extended during the final stages of the war effort was rewarded by royal passivity in the face of theft and malfeasance. Corregidores soon lost what reputation they had built up as protectors of the common good. They had the right to audit municipal accounts; yet during these years the corregidor at Cuenca stopped supervising disbursements from the treasury.[113] Bilbao's long show of hostility towards its string of officials began to bring modest results, as royal unwillingness to antagonize the nobility intensified. Lope Rodríguez de Logroño's tenure was secure as corregidor of Vizcaya (1483–8), but as soon as he departed the council struck by holding onto an entire year's salary of 150,000 *mrs*, and was not forced to disgorge the money.[114] Jerez resumed its opposition to the imposition of royal domination when the crown decided, in 1488, to return Juan de Robles. Relations had been so stormy that two *regidores* locked themselves into the jail to dramatize their hostility to the reappointment. This time, the councilors were able to apply the lever of the war-related fiscal emergency to extract advantages previously denied to them. The Jerez council unilaterally reduced the corregidor's salary and perquisites, and two years later made sure that no portion of fines levied for violation of city ordinances would go to him.[115]

Even the resolve to punish more openly rebellious activities against the corregidores started to dissipate. A local court found Fernando de Galacha guilty of fomenting an uprising at Trujillo against corregidor Diego López de Ayala; but after the crown insisted charges be dropped in May 1490, he was fully pardoned by the Royal Council.[116] Madrid's authorities felt free to act irresponsibly in the more permissive atmosphere, especially after being greatly provoked by Tristán de Silva. In 1490 he pressed for free housing and gifts of clothing, and two years later was found guilty of imposing unjustified charges on residents, with the result that his goods were seized in 1492 as a way of satisfying claims.[117] The antagonism to wrongdoing surfaced aggressively after the next corregidor suddenly died within the year. Upon notice of Juan de Valderrama's death, during December 1492, tumults and robberies broke out; yet, because the regidores refused to act promptly to repress the disturbances, the crown was forced to dispatch its own investigator.[118]

It is likely, though unprovable at this distance in time, that two corregidores were murdered at the behest of regidores during permissive years when conspiracy went unpunished, due to the crown's need to obtain cooperation. Bartolomé Santa Cruz was attacked in Alcalá la Real during June 1492 and left for dead. Was he assassinated on the orders of the elders? Two court attorneys, Gonzalo Sánchez de Castro and Gonzalo Fernández Gallego, were promptly assigned to this important case. They investigated assiduously, calling a number of regidores and jurados to court for further questioning. The Royal Council then suddenly acted upon the behest of the suspects, ordering that the investigation be ended. Two sons of María Sánchez were eventually seized and convicted, with no wider conspiracy alleged.[119] The following year, a corregidor at Badajoz was murdered under equally suspicious circumstances. Gonzalo Fernández del Castillo was on his way to Sunday mass when he was stabbed by a son of the commander of Calatrava, García Sánchez, who fled with his accomplice, Fernando de la Rocha, to the church of the Trinity, where they claimed sanctuary. The crown dispatched Pedro de Cuba to handle the case, along with Esteban de Palacios, an expert on police matters sent to examine the wounds. Because the assassins remained lodged in the church, another emissary from the queen was sent out the following month to have a quiet personal talk with the vicar general. During the lag, while the vicar general dragged his heels, *regidor* Fernando de Sotomayor was suddenly implicated, and then equally as quickly released. It was determined by the Royal Council, from a distance, that he was not part of a city-wide conspiracy, and the books were immediately closed, with the decision that the first two suspects had acted entirely on their own.[120] There are thus instances of renewed hostility directed against officials, activities which were not fully suppressed by the monarchy. Yet it was hardly apparent upon the conclusion of the Granada War that Isabella's corregidores might not be able to regain the stature they had acquired by the mid-1480s, or that the queen's middle decade would appear, in retrospect, as a golden age of acceptance.

During April 1493 a festive caravan traversed the coastal road through Tarragona, on its way to Barcelona, where the city and court came out to greet it. Columbus and his crew were graciously received in the Alcázar by the king and queen, where for an hour or more the sovereigns, and their courtiers, examined the plunder of "the Indies" and exclaimed over exotic natives.[121] It seemed from his evidence that the Admiral of the Ocean Sea was placing before Isabella an all-water route to the spice islands which would open the way for Castilian enterprise. The queen stood high in the eyes of her subjects at this moment, when few would care to recall in public that she once had to fight for her throne, for there was little prospect that a factious aristocracy would dare to resume the horrors of civil war. Peace had also descended upon formerly tumultuous municipalities, whose councilors were guaranteed their tenure as a part of their acceptance of a settlement which made corregidores an apparently permanent part of municipal life.

Promises of just rule, made long before at the Cortes of Toledo, seemed well on the way to being kept. Chapter 5 addresses this issue by demonstrating where the courts of the corregidores fit into the legal system as a whole, and how well the servants of the queen fulfilled their legal and administrative functions over the years. This last question is also tightly tied to an analysis of the qualifications of corregidores in terms of their education levels, the adequacy of their remuneration, and the extent of their honesty. Chapter 6 isolates the dealings of the corregidores with the aristocrats and the prelates of the kingdoms, weighing just how effective the queen's officials could actually be in the context of social privilege. Chapter 7 addresses the most contentious and emotional issue which disturbed the reign, that of how to deal with the separated religious communities. After completing the examination of the role of corregidores in handling religious strife, we then return, with Chapter 8, to our chronological survey, which will cover the troubled final decade of the reign.

5

Careers open to talent: judicature, remuneration, *residencia*

The legal hierarchy

Whereupon the corregidor must be attentive to hear and to see with diligence the civil and criminal cases that will come under his judgement, without perverting the *vara* of Royal Justice; and also no one should be made corregidor who has not vanquished the passions and the cupidity for augmenting his patrimony.   Bartolomé de Góngora[1]

The queen made few significant innovations in the Castilian judicial system of local courts, appellate tribunals, and Royal Council, all of which were in place by the fifteenth century.[2] At the bottom of the ladder were the trial courts of the corregidores and other judges. These tribunals also accepted appeals from the decisions of *alcaldes* of villages or estates. The *Real Audiencia y Chancillería*, at the next tier up, became so overburdened with work once it was settled at Valladolid, during the start of the reign, that a second *Chancillería* was created for Ciudad Real in 1494. In 1505 this new high tribunal was moved to Granada, with geographic jurisdiction between the two courts split at the Tagus River. Two lesser tribunals, denominated *Audiencias*, sat in Santiago and Seville to help with the growing workload.

Appeals were heard at the highest level by the Royal Council, which had judicial as well as administrative functions. There was, finally, always the last resort of a plea to the crown. Since the bulk of preserved documents concerning the corregidores deals with their close relation with the Royal Council, it is to the latter that we must turn. Various monarchs attempted to make the unwieldy body into a usable tool for decision-making.[3] A bilateral commission of royal and aristocratic representatives, meeting in 1465, set out to reform the body, but, for fear of offending important lords, Enrique IV did not fully implement the plan.[4] The group Isabella assembled – indifferently called the *consejo real, consejo de justicia* and, in time, the *consejo superior de Castilla* – therefore continued to reflect the judgements of a military elite.[5] One-third of the ordinances at the 1476 Cortes of Madrigal dealt with Castile's judicial structure, and the first order of business at the 1480 Cortes of Toledo was to reshape the Royal Council. Aristocrats were phased out, for although they could continue to attend sessions they no longer had a vote.

The revised Council was presided over during its first ten years by a trusted prelate who eventually took the title of president. He pulled together the work of the group of eight or nine *letrados* (legists), three nobles, and various secretaries.[6] Judicial review was retained, and so the body continued to divide its time in an unproductive manner.[7] Everything was mandated to be put into writing and secured, although there was no central archive. Since the monarchs were continuously on the move, leather-covered chests of documents were left trailing along the way. During 1486 the Royal Council had to ask the corregidor of Carmona about the jurisdiction's salary precedent, having lost the papers during one of its moves.[8]

There was one other, short-lived, body besides the Royal Council which had an equally close relation with corregidores. In 1496 the monarchs transferred to Don Juan's personal council of state a number of municipal jurisdictions – Alcázar, Alhama, Baeza, Cáceres, Écija, Jaén, Loja, Ronda, Toro, and Trujillo.[9] Appeal against a corregidor's decision in these jurisdictions ended up before the prince's advisors. This move was made simply to increase their young son's prestige, without consideration for the supposed virtues of bureaucratic centralization. The prince's death in 1497 saw appeals revert once more to the Royal Council.[10]

The presumption that the Cortes of Toledo change was a "reform" is based, according to Nader, upon a historical tradition first formulated by legists themselves.[11] A government of legal experts, directed by a cleric, is not inherently more efficient, or less open to corruption, than one dominated by military professionals. What is clear is that a bias becomes evident in favor of a more theoretic approach to untidy aspects of life. *Letrados* posited a uniform world drawn from Roman law and medieval scholastic political theory. The king stood at the apex of a divinely ordained and immutable hierarchy of institutions administered by anonymous servants, uniformly trained in law. Transferring the desire for a rational juridical order from speculation into practice demanded that ministers evaluate all aspects of life, then devise suitable rewards for proper behavior and punishment for offenders.[12] There was less place in this lofty view than before for the untidy patchwork of local rights preserved from early times.

The principal agents immediately at hand to introduce at least some of the desired uniformity into municipal life proved flawed, since few corregidores were sympathetic to such abstract ideas. The majority of officials, as will be noted, came from a service nobility and thus were presumably most comfortable with pragmatic approaches to the business at hand. The chancery turned out a vast quantity of letters aimed at its municipal official, in a continuing attempt to enforce uniform policies. One year's correspondence with the corregidor of Segovia yields a fairly typical quota of documents. Out of forty-two directives preserved, there are nine *incitativas* and seven *comisiones* from January to December 1495. In administrative matters the most common document issued to a corregidor was this *comisión*, or commission, to take action, and in judicial matters this *incitativa*, or writ, from a superior court to a lower court urging that justice be done. The remaining letters cover a wide range, including three *ordenanzas*, or statutes, to be promulgated, a *pragmática*, or rescript that answers a written question, an *inhibir*, which prohibits an inferior court from proceeding further on a case, an *ampara*, calling for the seizure of chattel, a *notificación*, announcing a law, and a *sobrecarta*, or warrant, repeating a previous order.[13]

What was it, moving from the form of documents to their content, that the monarchs acting through their Royal Council wanted their *asistentes* in the crowded metropolis of Seville to do when administering the affairs of the community? City scribes meticulously recorded each letter from the crown in the large bound volumes of the *Tumbo de los Reyes Católicos*. Although an *asistente* presumably dealt with most matters of substance, out of hundreds of letters in the volumes dated 1479–92, less than seventy are specifically directed only to him. Of this number, fifteen deal with raising troops and war supplies and sixteen with the appointment and conditions of service of urban officials. Nine letters treat the role of the *asistente* in the assessment of taxes, seven his intervention in minor aspects of the city's economic life, five his role as judge, and two are concerned with boundary issues. The Inquisition was called to his attention in four letters, nobles and their privileges in five letters, and clerics in two. The remainder of the correspondence ranges over matters as disparate as the price of falcons, or protecting the rights of an inventor of a way to raise water without the need for animal or human power.[14]

Juan de Silva, count of Cifuentes, held the governing post at Seville for eighteen years. Appeals from his decisions, found in the *Archivo General de Simancas*, create another body of royal instructions to be considered. A sampling from 1487–8 is of special interest because it allows a view of the office separate and apart from the holder: Cifuentes was as yet unransomed from a Moorish prison, and so his lieutenant, Fernán Yáñez de Lobón, undertook his functions without thereby gaining the title. The municipal council was ordered not to innovate while Cifuentes remained out of the city.[15] In twenty-seven letters dealing with appeals, the Royal Council instructed the lieutenant in five cases dealing with land disputes, four cases involving slaves, two cases where merchants ran into trouble, two about title to ships, and two challenging tax assessments. There were two appeals regarding civil suits between natives, and a petition from a person who wished to become a resident. There was also, to conclude, a squabble over who would have the monopoly of soap manufacture, and a complaint that funds left on deposit with a moneylender were stolen by the duke of Medina Sidonia.[16] From the sources considered, apart from matters connected with the Granada War, having the *asistente* or his lieutenant take action in economic issues and government appointments received the highest concern in the missives which flowed from the Royal Council to its officials at Seville.

Before the bench

The Royal Council's agenda shows far less attention being paid to directing municipal matters than to judicial review since, despite its restructuring, the Council continued to function as a supreme court for Castile. The king and queen reinforced this function by attending sessions themselves to administer justice. An old man nostalgically recalled the scene: "I remember well to have seen the Queen, together with the Catholic King, her husband, sitting in judgement in the Alcázar of Madrid every Friday dispensing justice to all such, great and small, as came to demand it."[17] The monarchs were really there as much to watch that the Royal Council did not get out of bounds, since in its own name it could issue orders, proclamations, and pardons that had the force of the law.[18] When Ferdinand and Isabella came to trust council members they entirely abandoned the Friday sessions, allowing the imperatives of law to unfold without constant intervention. Common formulas found at the conclusion of documents without royal signature are "by your petition, before our council" or "seen by our council."[19]

To make sure its commands were carried out, the Royal Council had an unlimited right to send special investigators to look into any matter.[20] It is under this authorization that the corregidores fell to its direct supervision.[21] On correspondence to the municipal officials there is typically always a signature of a chancellor, such as Dr Diego Vázquez, Dr Lope del Castillo, Rodrigo Díaz, Francisco Díaz, Pedro de Maluenda, Antonio del Rincón, or Alonso Álvarez. In addition, there are from three to five signatures by staff, plus the occasional autograph of the constable of Castile, the admiral of Castile, or other aristocrats. Judging from the frequency with which the names of certain staff appear, the three Royal Council members charged with some degree of attending to corregidores from the 1470s to the 1490s are Dr Gonzalo Fernández, Dr Juan Rodríguez, and Fernán Álvarez de Toledo Zapata. Through the end of the century, their successors are Diego Sánchez, Dr Johanes, and Dr Filipus. Almost all signatories identified by academic title are *doctores* until the early 1490s, when for the first time *licenciados* begin to appear. At first there is typically only one, but by 1500 the signatures of three or four of these legally trained officials might appear in any document.

The relationship between these members of the Royal Council and corregidores was necessarily an intimate one in judicial matters. Courts of the corregidores were where many cases had their first hearing, although certainly not the last. Because, as will be established later in this chapter, three-quarters of the corregidores of Isabella's era lacked professional legal training, they were allowed two experts, one for civil and the other for criminal matters. In criminal cases, the corregidor and his judges had unrestrained jurisdiction to pronounce sentence. The first line of defense for those judged guilty was to attempt to have the findings negated on the grounds that the judge was biased or had a special interest. This (almost automatic) delaying tactic meant the case was then retried by the original judge in the company of two assessors, chosen by the *regidores* from among their own ranks. The sentence was confirmed if at least one assessor agreed with the verdict.[22]

The range of criminal infractions that passed before the trial courts is vast, but difficult to document statistically, because prior to the eighteenth-century Castile's lower courts made little effort to develop or keep archives.[23] The full records of successful resolution of certain disparate cases do survive. The royal chaplain had his mule stolen at Alcalá de Henares in January 1488. It was located alive and well in Avila and returned by that city's corregidor during April. At the port of Cádiz in 1493, a ship under the flag of the Portuguese pirate Castil Blanco was seized by the lieutenant of the corregidor, after a struggle. Its crew had picked off boats carrying Jews into exile. Since the ship was discovered to belong to Juan López de Narruondo, it was returned to its previous master, much the worse for wear.[24] Of typical murder charges which started out before corregidores, there was a woman from Jerez de la Frontera who had the satisfaction of seeing the son-in-law who maltreated and then murdered her daughter brought to justice in 1485, while at Alcalá la Real in 1499, the husband of a woman discovered poisoned was adjudged not guilty and had his property restored.[25] These cases have in common one aspect typical of the full range of criminal verdicts encountered: decisions reached by the lower court were upheld upon appeal to the Royal Council.

Most pleas heard before the corregidor did not involve anything so dramatic as murder or piracy. Court actions concerning civil judgement were an outgrowth of petty bickering, in the main concerned with the enforcement of contracts, quarrels over inheritances and dowries, struggles over the rights of widows, arguments concerning bits of land, and "honor" disputes involving presumed insult. Judgement could be pronounced in the originating court for sums of up to 10,000 mrs. Appeal in a civil suit first led to a local ad hoc tribunal consisting, once again, of the corregidor or judge, and two members selected by the municipal council from its own ranks.[26] All arguments, including appeal, were brought by mature men over the age of twenty-nine, the legal majority. Since women, save for widows in certain instances, were not permitted to argue on their own behalf, their complaints were brought forward by male relatives and guardians.[27]

Two inheritance cases which worked themselves out in 1495 demonstrate that, despite this masculine bias, the courts at times protected the defenseless. Pedro Arias de Ávila, regidor of Segovia, had married Isabel de Herrera and, in order to gain her inheritance, had imprisoned her daughter, and heir, in the fortress of Turégano. A cousin, Antonio de la Cueva, called in August upon the corregidor of Segovia to free her. Before any action could be taken, the stepfather transferred the young woman to a convent, where she was forced to take holy orders. The corregidor of Arévalo was the one who, in the end, went into the religious house for the rescue, in September.[28] In keeping with the traditional nasty fable about the new stepmother, the second wife of Pedro Suárez coaxed him into placing his daughter, Beatriz Guiera, in the convent of the Incarnation. Through a male relative, Beatriz requested first the corregidor of Avila, and then the corregidor of Salamanca, to take her to a safe place from which she might sue to regain her mother's inheritance.[29] In these two instances, once again, lower court decisions, intended to protect these young women, were sustained.

The form suits took was a *pleito ordinario* or *pleito entre personas*. This "pleading" was quite a mass of documents: notarized proofs, testaments, and lawyers' briefs. As years passed the required files grew voluminous, with judges basing their decisions ever less on verbal testimony and ever more upon proper form. The importance of the *pleito* was ratified by the sovereigns in 1499 and its structure codified.[30] From the sheer bulk of *pleitos* piled upon tables at any time, it would appear that early modern Castile was highly litigious. Kagan observes that the land surely was a quarrelsome "hair-trigger" society, just learning to sublimate its taste for direct action by channeling conflict into judicial form, so that the reliance upon lawsuits does not necessarily reflect a willingness to resolve differences peacefully. Court was seen as another arena for revenge, where litigation was recklessly, passionately, and ruthlessly conducted with a minimum of restraint, more an extension of brawling than a way to obtain reasoned justice.[31] So argumentative was this society that the *asistente* of Seville was asked to intervene in 1484 in a bitter fight between neighbors over who possessed a tiny, newly created island in the Guadalquivir River.[32] It was this sort of case that kept corregidores busy, not fascinating criminal matters, struggle with powerful lords, or the glamor of leading troops into battle.

Perusal of verdicts from appeals preserved in the *Registrado General del Sello del Corte* at the *Archivo General de Simancas* yields the conclusion that in both civil and criminal cases the largest category – one-sixth of all reviewed documents – deal with land, which is what would be expected in a highly agrarian society. Details on the size or specific locations of the holdings in dispute are too inconsistent to allow analysis of a statistical nature; but the bulk of disputes between private parties concern lands newly brought under cultivation in wooded or scrub areas. Most areas had a remarkably complex and hybrid property structure, ranging from crown lands, seignorial property, municipal lands, inter-municipal property, and common lands to ordinary "private" property hedged round by all kinds of restrictions.

Vassberg estimates that at least one-fifth of all arable land in Castile was owned by independent peasants, while they and others also had access to varied long-term leases, rental of municipal holdings, and free use of the commons.[33] Conflicting local and royal laws regarding these parcels was the cause of much of the problem. There was a constant need for those who lived or died by the product of the soil to go to court to defend any new bit of earth they put under cultivation.

Owing to this propensity to go to law, the courts offer other glimpses of life, far away from distant woods and fringe scrubland, which demonstrate marginal judicial involvement of corregidores in cultural and intellectual matters. The Church was, of course, the great patron of the arts, and so its officials were always in the midst of disputes, such as one in 1488 when the prior of the monastery of Parraces went to the corregidor of Segovia to force his episcopal superior to pay, as he had promised, for improvements to a chapel, which enhancement consisted of decorative details for the main altar and the acquisition of a new organ. Craftsmen always brought their grievances to court, as in the instance of Francisco Sánchez, a painter from Seville who went to Baeza in 1490 intending to take up a church commission but found himself blocked. He soon complained to the corregidor that he was being annoyed by a jealous local rival, Martín Rodríguez, who found many ways to delay the project.[34]

In the realm of education, the corregidor of Cordova had to act in 1495 on a number of complaints received from teachers of arithmetic and geometry, who maintained that the city was hiring unqualified masters of these subjects. They needed to protect their profession, since teachers were grossly underpaid. The annual stipend for a grammar teacher in Madrid was 1,000 *mrs*, which had to be supplemented by fees from the families of students. Since the *regidores* received 2,000 *mrs* for part-time work, this confirms, once again, that government service proves more lucrative than education.[35] University life came under increasing corregidor scrutiny when the crown began displacing the papacy as the arbiter of advanced education, leading the former to deep entanglements in academic disputes, the appointment of officials, and the policing of internal university statutes. Corregidores at the university towns of Valladolid and Salamanca were naturally the most concerned with academic issues, overseeing voting on professional positions to assure impartiality.[36] When a rector at Valladolid insistently protested against what he regarded as an arbitrary decree on scholastic matters by a member of the Royal Council, it was the academic who was told by a corregidor to hold his peace.[37]

Affairs of the heart

Judges covered a far wider spectrum of malfeasance than the theft of pigs or the clash of professors. Corregidores were mandated to pay special attention to "public sins" (*pecados públicos*)[38] for, as far as possible, secular courts were obliged to aid in reshaping the imperfect City of Man into the sublime image of the City of God. In that better world there would be no gaming tables or other forms of wager.[39] The corregidor of Valladolid, reminded in 1494 that gambling was still rampant in his jurisdiction, was ordered to close the tables down immediately, and oblige past winners to reveal how large were their gains.[40]

Love might also be regarded as a form of wager. Most aspects of romance, from courtship to adultery, find their way into court, with emotions as recognizable today as then. A young Jewish woman from Trujillo complains that she is being pestered by unwanted protestations of love from a Christian.[41] At Nájera, a young man espoused too long wants his corregidor to find out if he will marry or not.[42] A lonely Genoese merchant, Marco "de Rota," resident at Cuenca, wants help to soothe his wounded heart and damaged pride, for Juan de Chinchilla has defrauded him by falsely insinuating that he, Juan, has an attractive unmarried woman in his house, whom he will give in marriage to Marco, for a price.[43]

Marriage hardly guarantees happiness. Isabel flees her home in Alfaro for the nearby convent of Los Lirios and Pedro wants her back. Each time a new corregidor takes office the thwarted husband repeats his story.[44] Tales of adultery are common: unlucky Beatriz Fernández, native of Granada, asks her corregidor to get her convert husband, Juan Loarta, to return to her bed. He has resumed living with a Moorish woman, with whom he had taken up when the kingdom was still under Islam.[45] Francisco Delgado wants the corregidor to return his wife, María de Palencia, to him from Logroño, where she is another's mistress. Antón Ortiz de Salcedo has worse to complain about to the corregidor of Puerto de Santa María. Not only is his wife, Ana de Vargas, having an illicit relationship with Diego Espadero, but the two rifled the household before they absconded.[46] Vows of celibacy were no clear answer for those who attempted to avoid the manifest failings of marriage, since the clergy displayed their own share of weakness. The husband of Martina goes before the canon of the abbey of S. Martín de Elmes to complain that a monk, Luis Manrique (brother to the marquis of Aguilar), is cohabiting with her. The canon then calls upon the corregidor of Aguilar de Campóo to punish the partners in sin.[47] So, too, the corregidor of Madrid investigates purported adultery between the sacristan of the church of S. Cruz de Valladolid and Isabel Díaz, wife of a servant of Prince Don Juan.[48]

Being as human as clerics or peasants, corregidores are sometimes caught in these snares. Fernando Sevillano charges in 1480 that both Juan Rodríguez de Baeza, corregidor of Medina del Campo, and archpriest Alfonso Rodríguez Manjón have been intimate with his wife. Investigators agree, after taking depositions, that both men are "criminal in their correspondence."[49] A major scandal breaks in Trujillo during 1484, when corregidor Sancho del Aguilar is caught in brazen adultery with a vivacious Jewish widow, doña Vellida. She also made free with the keeper of the fortress, Gonzalo de Herrera, yet only Sancho del Aguilar is forced to resign his post.[50] The fact that his disgrace goes this far is probably due to the machinations of a local enemy, angered by an unpaid debt, who writes a brother-in-law on the Royal Council to interest that august body in the peccadillos of its man at Trujillo.[51] The person placing the charge of adultery during January 1487, at León, is Alfonso de Valderrábano, corregidor at Asturias. While he was off at his posting his wife, Mencia de Corral, stayed behind. Alfonso notified the corregidor of León that he should proceed against both Mencia and her presumed lover, Pedro Díaz de Tablares. Mencia vigorously denies the charge but in December she is adjudged guilty, along with her paramour, who has his goods confiscated.[52] Morality and the sanctity of marriage are preserved in all such cases, following the demands of the guardians of standards and the presumed wishes of the public at large.

The Royal Council bombarded corregidores with instructions on a vast range of such social issues, and with responses to appeals concerning a multitude of private disputes. In a society becoming ever more disputatious, corregidores dealt with a complex bramble of legislation. Radical pruning was needed to shape an orderly code of jurisprudence, but that was never done.[53] Because each change undertaken by the Catholic Sovereigns often simply made law even more of an enigma, a conscientious judge certainly earned his salary.

Remuneration

The corregidor's span of office was usually brief yet, like the life cycle of
the mayfly, it had a pleasant side. The salary typically ran to 73,000
mrs a year, or 200 *mrs* at the daily rate. In terms of buying power, a
corregidor earned more salary for his day's effort than did a
specialized worker in a craft during a five-day week. The rate of
compensation, shown in Table 2, was not uniform because it
depended both on local traditions and the social standing of the office-
holder. Rodrigo Valderrábano, who took over at Burgos in 1475, was
considered sufficiently important to have the rate quadrupled.[54]
Toledo was normally worth 187,000 *mrs* a year, and Segovia 200,000.
Where all elements were maximized, as at Seville for the count of
Cifuentes, the yearly stipend rose to 400,000 *mrs*, with 187,000 for
expenses.[55]

The salaries of corregidores were covered by the localities to which
they were sent, not the crown. Heads of household in the *merindades*
of the northern coast were assessed at five *mrs* a day.[56] Wherever there
was a sizable Jewish community it paid far out of proportion to its
numbers, providing anything from one-fourth to one-third of the cost
of the corregidor. After the Expulsion, the loss went so hard on
Badajoz that its corregidor lost 100 of his 300 *mrs* a day; but the crown
insisted that Ágreda increase taxes in March 1493 to make up for the
50 *mrs* a day the Jewish community had paid towards the 200 *mrs*
salary.[57] Corregidores occasionally took salary cuts when communities were in financial straits, which was an especial phenomenon of the
lean years of struggle against Granada. Diego López de Haro agreed
to a 50 per cent reduction midway through his stay at La Coruña,
because his area had been hard hit by contributions to the Holy
Brotherhood's militia and other war-related obligations. Aranda and
Sepúlveda successfully argued that, because of war costs, they could
only afford one-half the usual salary.[58]

Various privileged groups assumed they would avoid payment:
there was a storm at Sahagún when Juan de Luzón decreed that
hidalgos would be called upon, an order against which they successfully
appealed to the *Audiencia* in 1492. In Avila, soldiers dunned for
contributions protested, until the community was ordered to desist in
1494.[59] Creative financing had to be employed, due to the determined
refusal of the exempt to contribute any amount whatsoever. Baeza
and Toro used land rents, La Coruña apportioned 20,000 *mrs* from

Table 2. Corregimiento *salary contributions*

Location	Mrs per year	Location	Mrs per year
Ágreda[1]	73,000	Cuatro Villas de la Mar[14]	150,000
Andújar–Jaén[2]	109,500	Cuenca–Huete[15]	109,500
Asturias de Oviedo[3]	150,000	Escalona[16]	29,200
Badajoz[4]	109,500	Jerez de la Frontera[17]	100,000
Baeza–Úbeda[5]	40,000	León[18]	70,000
Burgos[6]	146,000	Logroño[19]	18,500
Cáceres[7]	97,000	Madrid[20]	73,000
Carrión de los Condes–Sahagún[8]	73,000	Medina del Campo[21]	50,000
Carmona[9]	97,000	Murcia–Lorca–Cartagena[22]	73,000
Ciudad Real[10]	40,000	Seville[23]	420,000
Ciudad Rodrigo[11]	20,000	Toledo[24]	187,000
Cordova[12]	183,000	Vizcaya[25]	150,000
La Coruña[13]	73,500	Zamora[26]	71,000

Notes:
[1] *AGS, Sello,* 14 Mar. 1493, fol. 169. 200 *mrs* a day.
[2] *Ibid.,* 8 June 1478, fol. 83. 300 *mrs* a day.
[3] *Ibid.,* 11 Oct. 1494, fol. 423.
[4] *Ibid.,* 19 June 1493, fol. 101. Salary reduced from 300 *mrs* a day to 200 *mrs* a day in 1493 (73,000 *mrs* a year).
[5] *Ibid.,* 16 Mar. 1480, fol. 169.
[6] *Ibid.,* 20 Apr. 1475, fol. 418. 400 *mrs* a day salary was doubled for Rodrigo Valderrábano (1475–6), to 292,000 *mrs.*
[7] *Ibid.,* 19 Dec. 1477, fol. 511. An additional 20,000 *mrs* was allocated for expenses.
[8] *Ibid.,* 2 Apr. 1486, fol. 8. 200 *mrs* a day. Carrión contributed 30,000 *mrs* per year to the total. *Ibid.,* 8 June 1492, fol. 177.
[9] *Archivo Municipal de Carmona, Provisiones Reales,* 1500–16. 6 Dec. 1503.
[10] Municipal budget of 1715 (which includes unchanged corregidor salary) *AGS, Sello, lib.* 468, transcr. Carla R. Phillips, *Ciudad Real, 1500–1750.* (Cambridge, Mass., 1979), appendix.
[11] *AGS, Sello,* 26 July 1487, fol. 70; 5 Mar. 1492, fol. 199.
[12] *Ibid.,* 3 July 1478, fol. 77. 600 *mrs* a day (includes 100 *mrs* salary as governor of fortress of the Calahorra).
[13] *Ibid.,* 14 Jan. 1489, fol. 203. 200 *mrs* a day.
[14] *Ibid.,* 20 Feb. 1475, fol. 190.
[15] *Ibid.,* 13 Dec. 1485, fol. 28. 300 *mrs* a day.
[16] *Ibid.,* 12 July 1479, fol. 52. 80 *mrs* a day.
[17] *Ibid.,* 9 Apr. 1488, fols. 26, 86.
[18] *AGS, Diversos de Castilla, leg.* 1, fol. 3.
[19] *AGS, Sello,* 9 Apr. 1491, fol. 25. Logroño only – 50 *mrs* a day.
[20] *AM Madrid, Acuerdos,* vol. I, fol. 3v, 10 Jan. 1481. 200 *mrs* a day.
[21] *AGS, Sello,* 30 Sept. 1494, fol. 34. Medina del Campo only.
[22] Francisco Chacón Jiménez, "Una contribución al estudio de las economías municipales en Castilla: La coyuntura económica concejil murciana en el período 1496–1514," *Miscelánea Medieval Murciana* vol. III (1977), p. 257.
[23] *AMS, Tumbo* vol. II, p. 169, 10 Sept. 1482. In addition, the *asistente* received 187,000 *mrs* for expenses.
[24] *AGS, Diversos, leg.* 1, fol. 3.
[25] *AGS, Sello,* 29 Nov. 1488, fol. 162. Salary paid by the Bilbao city council.
[26] *Archivo Municipal de Zamora, Documentos varios. S. XV, Documentos Reales–Reyes Católicos, Documentos Reales, leg.* 20, fol. 1, 7 Jan. 1502.

fines, and Ciudad Real allocated one-half of its sales taxes towards its corregidor's salary.[60] Without question, corregidores were luxuries as far as these hard-pressed communities were concerned. At Murcia, *regidores* and the *mayordomo* earned 2,000 *mrs* each, per year. The peace officer took home 3,000, the chief scribe earned 3,700, the prosecutor received 6,000, and at the top of the scale was the *alcalde*, who earned 13,000 *mrs*. In terms of these salaries the corregidor's 73,000 *mrs* was grand indeed, for it represented almost 57 per cent of all salaries, and virtually 28 per cent of the community's total expenditures. Madrid's budget was more badly thrown out of balance by its corregidor's 73,000 *mrs*, which far outdistanced the 47,000 *mrs* allocated for all twenty-six other members of the government.[61]

Communities with grievances struck at their corregidores through the purse. In November 1480 Ágreda tenaciously refused to pay its corregidor any salary, as did Sepúlveda in December of the same year, and Alcaraz in November 1494, although all were eventually coerced by the crown into paying.[62] There were a few safeguards built into law that proved more helpful to communities in protecting their residents than did such outright opposition. Corregidores had to supply financial guarantees, put up by bondsmen outside the municipal council who would indemnify anyone proven to have just charges against the royal official.[63] An equally successful device was for the municipal council simply not to hand over back salary, since the last one-third of the year's stipend was held as a bond to satisfy judgements uncovered during the course of a *residencia* investigation. There were struggles over this last issue at Cáceres (1478), León (1479), Cáceres, again (1480), León, again (1485), Ciudad Real (1488), Carrión (1493), Guadix (1494), Málaga (1495), and Cáceres, yet again in 1495.[64] Pedro de Castro had more than his share of such troubles due to this loophole in the ordinances. Jerez de la Frontera refused to return his goods, including two horses and two mules, which were kept under embargo long beyond the time he left his post in 1486; and as for his salary, the last one-third remained unpaid despite two years of litigation.[65] Juan de Luzón vacated his post at Carrión–Sahagún during 1492, while lawsuits on the part of the councils and some Jews were still pending. His investigation went well enough, so that in November the judge ordered the 21,000 *mrs* back salary paid in full. The *regidores* appealed to the *Audiencia*, which obliged by sending an investigator, who backed the original judgement. After vain attempts to collect in January and July 1493, Juan insisted that the original judge return to issue an order attaching the goods of the councils and dunning leading citizens. In time, the cities released the money; but, so far as debts to the Jews were concerned, since they were exiled it was a case of out of sight, out of mind.[66]

The amount involved in all these struggles was minimal. When Diego de Merlo died in office in 1482, the stake for the family of this *asistente* of Seville was considerably higher, for his heirs were besieged with claims against the estate. The queen sent a competent lawyer to assist the family in negotiating its way through charges laid by the municipal council, former aides, and servants. He was there to block any judge from taking preemptive action.[67] Protection from creditors was also required upon the death in 1488 of Fernán Yáñez de Lobón, a lieutenant at Seville. Letters from the Royal Council to the city insisted that his widow, Nicolasa Fernández, and their four children should not be held responsible for anything he did while in service or for any costs he incurred. The pressure faced is illustrated by a demand upon the widow by a Genoese, who alleged he was owed 80,000 *mrs* for firearms, sold for use in the Moorish strife. In addition to shielding the lieutenant's family against such suits, the attorney also ordered Seville to give the family all salary and rights due the deceased.[68]

Even when the full salary was paid and creditors were fended off, the statutory compensation for the ordinary run of corregidor was less princely than at first appearance. Salaries during the fifteenth-century fluctuate, but show no persistent rise, so inflation has to be taken into account when evaluating the erosion of the "traditional" daily stipend of 200 *mrs*. From 1400 to 1435 prices were stable, but then there was a rise, which intensified in the decades of the 1460s and 1470s, accompanied by serious debasement of the coinage.[69] Despite diminishing real salary income, there was the continued need to cover expenses of relocation and housing rental, and personally to absorb the costs of a staff. The corregidor of Murcia was expected to pay the salaries of an *alcalde mayor* and a lieutenant-corregidor, necessary because his extensive jurisdiction included both Lorca and Cartagena. Medina del Campo's corregidor received 50,000 *mrs* to direct that town, plus Olmedo. The *alcalde* at Medina was paid 12,000 *mrs*, and the one at Olmedo received 6,000 *mrs*, both from the corregidor's purse. Some posts took the extra costs into account, one example being Cáceres in 1477, when Ruy González de Puebla received a one-time 20,000 *mrs* allocation for especially heavy expenses.[70] In the case of Seville, the *asistentes* were given an ongoing expense allocation to defray costs in the great city, and their principal lieutenant received a separate 15,000 *mrs* annual salary.[71]

Perquisites of office

All early modern European monarchies failed to provide adequately for public servants, anticipating that posts would be exploited and supplementary income found. A corregidor at Badajoz earned a commission of 20,000 *mrs* in 1480 for working on the peace treaty with Portugal, paid him by his community. Pedro Fernández de Aranda received a modest fee in his jurisdiction of León by arbitrating a quarrel between the bishop, the marquis of Astorga, and the count of Luna. Confiscations constitute a significant accepted windfall, with one consignment of goods, taken from a merchant at Seville in 1478, yielding Gómez Manrique 150,000 *mrs*. When arms illegally on their way to Portugal were seized in 1495, the royal official at Medina del Campo was there to claim, and to obtain, one-third of the value of the shipment.[72]

Most satisfying of all was to make successful claims of service to the crown in order to receive *mercedes* – the gifts which came in all amounts. At Vizcaya, 124 benefices were granted during 1479, totaling 625,693 *mrs*, one of which, worth 48,000 *mrs*, went to corregidor Diego Martínez de Astudillo.[73] In return for assuring a sizable tax yield from the bishoprics of Málaga in 1503, Alonso Enríquez, corregidor of Granada, benefited from the largesse the following year when he shared, equally with the archbishop and the captain-general, 1,200 gold ducats (45,000 *mrs*).[74] Smaller gifts were not beneath notice: a corregidor of Plasencia was granted a mill and a bakery; and the corregidor of Málaga had only to ask in 1504 that the post of prison guard be given to his barber – who was crippled – to have his wish honored.[75]

The queen of Castile had clearer ideas than most rulers of the age about what she expected from her officials, for, unlike sovereigns who winked at corruption while giving lip-service to demands for honesty, Isabella insisted upon high standards of rectitude, anticipating that corregidores would live on traditional salaries and legitimate fees. Punishment followed admonishment, at least until the third decade of her reign. So long as the royal court remained consistent in holding its officials within the boundaries of agreed-upon remuneration, this eased their acceptance as a feature of urban life. Honest officials who lingered at jurisdictions, such as Gómez Manrique at Toledo or Diego de Merlo at Seville, managed to gain riches through the slow accumulation of favors; but, with most men at their posts for a short term, there was great temptation to seek wealth quickly, by whatever means. That not all tried an illegal road to fortune is undoubtedly due to the elaborate safeguard of a formal judicial inquiry into activity during the term of office.

The *residencia* exit investigation

The vices or virtues of the corregidor ruin or save the republic.
                                        Lorenzo Guardiola y Sáez[76]

There were so many opportunities for illegitimate enrichment that judicial inspection of the activities of royal representatives during their tenure was vital to assure upright behavior. The inquiry at the end of a term so far predates Isabella's reign that it is necessary to go back at least to the *Siete Partidas* law code of Alfonso X the Learned to locate a point at which the Roman concept of judicial review enters Castilian law.[77] Versions of the *residencia* were tried out around 1300, although the *Ordenamiento de Alcalá de Henares* (1348) was the first to lay down a comprehensive list of procedures, including the proviso that there be fifty days available during which an aggrieved party could speak out.[78] When this period was cut to thirty days, deputies to the 1419 Cortes petitioned that *residencia*[79] investigations were not being completed.

The inquests were not willingly authorized by the crown without intense communal pressure, since monarchs were little interested in tying the hands of their officials, who might be intimidated by the prospect of lengthy investigations upon the expiry of their office. Juan II faced demand for a resumption of the practice at the successive parliamentary sessions of 1435 and 1436, along with complaints that judges had not asked questions, had left early or, worst of all, had appointed agents to do the actual work. The king finally took notice of this agitation by declaring in 1438 that he would send "good persons" who would be sure to stay the full fifty days. He appears to have put into operation a reformed system of end-of-term examinations; at least the Cortes record is void of complaints until 1462, when the demand resumes, in the face of Enrique IV's activism in placing corregidores, that there be an automatic investigation after each year's stay.[80]

There matters stood until Isabella's arrival. How well did she deal with longstanding grievances? Legislation instigated at the 1480 Cortes of Toledo called for the nomination of inspectors, whose mission it would be to inform the Royal Council of the situation of each corregidor, *alcalde*, judge, *merino*, and keeper of a fortress. Exactly how long a stay at a post was required before the investigation would be initiated was not specified, but at least the principle of regular *residencias* was laid down. The amount of time allocated reverted, once again, to thirty days, "and no more."[81] To safeguard communities against retaliation, an innovative petition called for no corregidor or *asistente* to be reappointed at the same locale for at least one year after the investigation.[82]

Did this legislation mean that a functioning *residencia* system, with safeguards and proper procedures, was active and operating relatively smoothly in, or shortly after, 1480? Although historians of urban government have generalized that, once established, such a program at once proceeded,[83] so elaborate a scheme was only sporadically applied. Pulgar's chronicle account is emphatic that a thorough invigoration of the program was necessary in 1487. With so much else to occupy them, the monarchs then once more neglected to assure that procedures were being scrupulously followed. During a lull in 1490, they wintered in Seville, where they once more reviewed the judicial structure, with the result that squads of investigators were sent out to examine corregidores and their subordinates.[84] Pulgar's dates fit closely what is revealed by the archives: the flood of exit investigations commences in 1488, peaks by the mid-1490s, and then subsides.

Whatever the fluctuating level of governmental concern regarding corregidor and *asistente* misdeeds, the crown was slow to take an interest in the conduct of its highly-placed governors. There were few end-of-term examinations undertaken during the fifteenth-century: two in the 1480s and four in the 1490s. Governors who dealt with native populations outside the peninsula were even more rarely called to task. Pero de Vera's indignities against the small Canary island of Gomera, from 1480 to 1490, were never given judicial review.[85] Following that governor's forced return to Castile, Francisco Maldonado Álvarez was sent to assess Pero de Vera's records, which inspection turned into a belated effort to correct the worst aspects of ten years of misrule.[86] The only Canary Island *residencia* of the century was launched against Alonso de Lugo, late in 1497 or early in 1498, for unjustly imprisoning the Guanche natives of Tenerife, and although many were set free Alonso was not removed from office.[87] He did, at least, receive three *residencias* during his last twenty-five years at Tenerife.[88] The system gradually regularized, as each governor on Gran Canaria after 1500 unfailingly underwent an investigation at the end of his term.

On the mainland the system operated sufficiently well through the second decade of the queen's rule, despite the gaps and delays enumerated, to stifle doubts. The paucity of sustained complaints from the urban elite during that period indicates satisfaction with delivery of the promise of evenhanded justice, although at no time did the *residencia* become the widespread and automatic procedure it is often pictured to be. The costly investigations of corregidores, *asistentes*, and governors were ordinarily carried out only at the urgent request of injured parties. This stubborn unwillingness of the crown to regularize the *residencia* appears to be a remnant of early medieval decentralization of judicial rights and privileges. Crimes committed by corregidores were not placed within an impersonal bureaucratic context, but were instead treated as injuries committed by private persons, who happened to hold public office. Infractions on the part of such persons against individuals or corporate bodies were matters best left to be punished on the initiative of the aggrieved party. It was up to the plaintiff to begin the process; to present evidence; to press the case; or to withdraw at any time.[89]

Investigative norms

Prior to 1500 there was modest experimentation with norms for *residencias*, which were tested at Murcia on Pedro Gómez de Setúbal in 1495, and on Fernando de Barrientos during 1498 and 1499. Apparently no other municipal council received this specific set of 1494 instructions, which has not been located elsewhere.[90] With slight modification this procedure was then made applicable to the realms.[91] The model judge was to set to work without delay, his arrival announced by notices posted in the market and other prominent places. Collection of evidence in the principal seat of the jurisdiction was followed, where feasible, by an investigative tour of subject villages. If grave accusations were made against the corregidor, contact was to be made with all interested parties, including those who had left the district. A standard set of questions were drawn up for the guidance of the judge, who was instructed to learn the good as well as the bad, the general as well as the particular.[92] Open hearings were followed by a secret proceeding which assured confidentiality. The accused was permitted to give his questioner a list of all who hated him, to provide protection from false secret accusation. This was balanced by a proviso that the judge was not to accept favorable petitions or letters from influential personages at the royal court.[93]

Where no substantial charge of wrongdoing was forthcoming, the case could be brought to a rapid close without a need for written justification on the part of the judge, who might then allow the corregidor and his subordinates to stay on or else ask them to leave within thirty days. At the judge's discretion, officials could be suspended from office, or a fine could be levied for up to 3,000 *mrs* – a fine which had to be paid before appeal was permitted. Where damages were greater, judgement could be appealed against before payment, which permitted proceedings to be dragged out. The amount of the initial sentence could be decided upon the spot, or those adjudged guilty could be sent to a higher court for hearings on their penalty. What the Royal Council did not want, above all, was for the judge on the scene to send uncompleted cases on for decision.[94] Judges presumably discarded court registers and other documents upon completion of their work, which is why there are so few local judicial records of complete late medieval *residencias*. During the mid-sixteenth century, procedure was given more of a permanent direction, in keeping with a general movement towards paper-ridden government; and the full report, labored over by the judge on the scene, was forwarded to the Royal Council.[95]

During Isabella's reign, the thirty days provided gave too little time to polish such reports, let alone to complete all work. Judges typically sat from morning to midday, although if there was a great deal to do they might stay on till Vespers. Even with the best will, hours depended upon the amount of light available, for, although sessions might be somewhat prolonged from Easter to mid-October, inevitably they shrank as the year declined into winter.[96] For this reason, and for ease of travel, *residencia* investigations encountered in the course of research were found invariably to take place in the spring.

Numerous loose ends noted in many of these cases indicate that it was often difficult to reach judgement. An examination into the doings of a lieutenant to the *asistente* of Seville took seventy days "because the city is so populous."[97] One investigation in Salamanca took exactly three months, while another, in Cáceres, took more than four months.[98] Suspicions were sometimes aroused that these procedures were dragged out simply to enlarge the bill to the community, thus causing Murcia to object strongly to the Royal Council about a lengthy proceeding in 1488.[99] At times there were in fact good reasons for delay, as when, in 1494, judge Juan de Raja asked that his assignment, begun in March, be extended into May. His investigation of Pedro García de Cotes at Burgos in the end produced a mass of evidence that the principal scribe and most of the corregidor's subordinates were trading in rentals of public land.[100]

One striking example of inadequate work is offered in a case begun by judge Francisco Muñoz at Marbella–Ronda in 1495. The regime of the *licenciado* Remón quickly proved exceedingly corrupt: he had not resided continually in his jurisdiction as required, yet claimed full salary; he illegally diverted water and public grazing lands to cattlemen for fees; and he extorted clothes and bed furnishings. The corregidor had taken every opportunity to extract funds from Moors, including fees on bread, overcharges at their market for bringing animals in for slaughter, and the outright theft of their silk, fish, and cattle. Another major swindle was uncovered when it was found that weapons seized from Moors were being concealed from city and royal treasuries, through diversion to a peace officer who collaborated in private sales. To complicate the *residencia* further, the judge found himself called upon to reassess over fifty civil and criminal cases whose participants claimed that justice had miscarried. Judge Muñoz then submitted a bill for 58,000 *mrs* to Ronda. The Royal Council reviewed his report, and the packet of papers, with distaste:

Many complaints and accusations were made before our judge investigator in the public sessions of the *residencia*, and before his assistant, against the *licenciado* Remón. There were so many complaints, quarrels, and accusations concerning law cases that neither our judge investigator nor his assistant could decide upon definitive sentences. Some of these cases could be given definitive sentence upon receipt of evidence, others were ready for definitive sentence, and others were remitted to our Council for determination. It appears that they should all be remitted to the lower court. For the present, the cases are being returned in the state that they are in to our [new] corregidor, who is now in the city.[101]

Complex judicial investigations obviously outran any willingness of royal councilors patiently to review incomplete work sent them from the field.[102]

The judges assessed

The minimal qualifications for such judges were that they be at least twenty-six years old.[103] It was taken for granted that women were

Table 3. *Degree-holders at* residencia *postings*[1]

	1474–84	1485–94	1495–1504
Total postings	14	150	29
Number of *licenciados*	3	50	8
Percentage of *licenciados*	21.4%	33.3%	27.6%
Number of *bachilleres*	3	20	5
Percentage of *bachilleres*	21.4%	13.3%	17.2%
Number of *doctores*	5	8	1
Percentage of *doctores*	35.8%	5.3%	3.4%
Number without degree	3	72	15
Percentage without degree	21.4%	48.1%	51.8%

[1] Data drawn from Table 4.

incapable of holding public office, since an elaborate theoretic structure was reared from the legal base of the *Siete Partidas* to show why females were incapacitated on moral, physical, and juridical grounds. The higher claims of gentle birth alone could overcome this deeply held sentiment, for it was grudgingly agreed a lady might herself wield the sword of justice on seignorial land, so long as she sought the advice of a council of wise men.[104] No educational standards were set for *residencia* judges, and out of 124 men evaluated, only slightly under a quarter (thirty) held the licenciate in law most appropriate to the judicial function they fulfilled. The best showing came in the period 1485–94, when one-third of the postings in Table 3 were filled by licenciates. In all, however, only a half of all appointees held any degree whatsoever.[105]

A certain confusion sets in when analyzing the judges, since they did not form a clearly defined group. Few undertook more than one investigation, which was surprising, considering the expertise that needed to be developed. In all, less than one-third of the judges carried out more than a single tour of duty. This total includes twenty who undertook two investigations, twelve who saw duty three times, and only nine who were employed more often.[106] A few of the judges sent out to conduct investigations stayed on to become the new corregidor, engendering many irregularities. Since the search for wrongdoing was a time-consuming obligation, it delayed anyone getting into the administrative side of a corregidor's job. Further, such appointments seriously hampered the integrity of investigations, because judges were not likely to be too hard on the occupant of a post they themselves were set to occupy. Recognizing these difficulties, the "typical" judge was given a task and then told to depart, although the system began to slip after 1500, when ever more investigators stayed on to govern.[107] By the mid-sixteenth-century the initial pattern was completely reversed, for each legist sent out to do the investigation took over as the next corregidor in line.[108]

Every judge who functioned as corregidor, however briefly, might in turn be examined. For the part of a month that Álvaro de Porras governed Guipúzcoa in 1490, his investigation revealed no taint of corruption.[109] Others got into varied difficulties while undertaking a lengthy examination, such as Pedro de la Cuba in 1493, during his investigation of Gutiérrez de Carvajal at Zamora. When, in turn, the examiner faced a judge, he was forced to disgorge 57,000 mrs in fines to the city and the royal treasury. His peculation did not stop the crown from planning to send him on the sensitive assignment of investigating the murder of corregidor Gonzalo Fernández del Castillo. Pedro de Cuba's dallying at Zamora meant that he never did make the trip to Badajoz, although he kept his advance salary from the Badajoz council.[110] To prevent similar duplications, that year Cuenca was instructed by the Royal Council not to pay anything to Lope Sánchez del Castillo because he was passing directly on to Carrión, where he would undertake a second residencia with ample compensation. Cities regularly complained, as already noted, that costs were high. After Carmona spent 45,000 mrs to have López Ruiz de Antillo undertake a brief residencia, the crown, upon petition, requested that the record be sent and that the judge appear before the Royal Council to justify his charge.[111] Málaga was informed that it need not pay Diego Martínez de Astudillo, who had taken far too long in his 1504 assignment; besides, his appointment to an audiencia meant that the judge was no longer eligible for a city salary.[112] Whatever the cost, however, the work of these judges was invaluable to cities for keeping corregidores in line, temptations being so great and opportunities for corruption so abundant.

Prohibited practices

With a short stay presumed, corregidores entering new jurisdictions were usually quick to make the most of their chance by importuning housing, bed linens, and clothing – corruption which persisted from earlier reigns.[113] The first ordinances drawn in Isabella's reign to guide corregidores specifically prohibited such gifts, for any reason.[114] It was necessary to enlarge on the prohibition a few years later, when a

Table 4. *Judges of* residencia

Name	Academic degrees	Place and date
Alonso de Aguilar[1]	*licenciado*; *doctor*	Madrid 1485; Palencia 1487; Madrid 1494
García de Alcocer[2]	—	Marbella–Ronda 1495
Juan Álvarez Guerrero[3]	—	Toledo 1491
Diego Arias de Anaya[4]	*bachiller*	Alcalá, Loja, Alhama 1495
Pedro de Avellán[5]	—	Carmona 1502; 1503
Gil de Ávila[6]	*bachiller*	Baeza–Úbeda 1490; Jerez 1490; Baeza–Úbeda–Jaén 1493
Gonzalo de Bañuelos[7]	—	Carrión–Sahagún 1495
Sebastián de Bilbao[8]	*licenciado*	Cáceres 1485; Baeza–Úbeda 1486; Alcaraz 1487
Álvaro de Bugia[9]	—	León 1493
Diego de Burgos[10]	*licenciado*	Aranda 1483
Juan de Burgos[11]	—	León 1488; Alcaraz 1490; 1496; Carrión 1492; Alcalá 1492; Jaén 1492
Juan del Campo[12]	*licenciado*	Murcia 1487; Carrión–Sahagún 1488; Jaén 1488
Antonio Carnejo[13]	—	Cuenca–Huete 1486; Medina del Campo 1487
Bachiller de Carrión[14]	*bachiller*	Olmedo 1494
Martínez de Cascales[15]	*doctor*	Alcaraz 1484
Doctor de Castilla[16]	*doctor*	Seville 1489
Rodrigo de Céspedes[17]	*bachiller*	Carmona 1484; La Coruña 1495
Pedro de la Cuba[18]	—	Carmona 1491; Zamora 1492–3; Toro 1495
Diego Díaz[19]	—	Seville 1491
Fernándo Díaz del Castillo[20]	*doctor*	Villena 1484; Plasencia 1492
Pedro Díaz de Madrid[21]	—	Carmona 1498
Pedro Díaz de Zumaya[22]	—	Asturias 1493
Alonso Escudero[23]	*bachiller*; *doctor*	Medina del Campo, Olmedo 1495; Málaga 1498
Licenciado Espinar[24]	*licenciado*	Avila 1475
Francisco Francés[25]	—	Palencia 1490; Écija 1492; Molina 1494; Ágreda 1494; Écija 1494
Sancho de Frías[26]	*licenciado*	Ciudad Rodrigo 1493; 1494; Huete 1495
Alvar García[27]	—	Salamanca 1487
Gonzalo Gómez de Córdoba[28]	—	Madrid 1487; Ciudad Real 1487; 1488
Pedro Gómez de Escobar[29]	—	Jerez 1487; Palencia 1491
Pedro Gómez de Segovia[30]	*bachiller*	Cuatro Villas 1484
Pedro Gómez de Setúbal[31]	*licenciado*	Lorca–Murcia–Cartagena 1493
Gonzalo Gómez de Villasandino[32]	*doctor*	Salamanca 1494
Francisco González del Fresno[33]	—	Avila 1494
Ruy González de la Puebla[34]	*doctor*	Aranda 1484; Cuenca 1494
Lope de Gordejuela[35]	—	Vizcaya 1495
Íñigo de Guevara[36]	—	Carmona 1499
Juan de la Hoz[37]	—	Carrión–Sahagún 1485
Honorado Hurtado de Mendoza[38]	—	Salamanca 1492
Bernaldino de Illescas[39]	*bachiller*	Antequera 1492

Table 4 (*cont.*)

Name	Academic degrees	Place and date
Pedro de Loaisa[40]	*licenciado*	Villena 1488; Salamanca 1491
Juan de Loarto[41]	—	Jerez 1492; Vizcaya 1494
Sebastián de Lobatón[42]	—	Ciudad Real 1488; Medina–
		Olmedo 1490; Ciudad Real 1492
Andrés López de Burgos[43]	—	Avila 1479
Juan López Navarro[44]	—	Olmedo 1485; Madrid 1485;
		Vélez Málaga 1495
Diego López de Trujillo[45]	—	Úbeda 1485; Madrid 1492
Juan de Luján[46]	—	Logroño 1485; Carrión–Sahagún
		1493
Francisco de Luzón[47]	—	Medina–Olmedo 1491
Francisco de Madrigal[48]	*bachiller*	Loja-Alhama 1494
Francisco Maldonado[49]	—	Canarias 1492
Diego Maldonado de Aguilera[50]	—	Lorca–Murcia 1493
Licenciado de Maluenda[51]	*licenciado*	Tenerife 1497–98
Diego Manuel de Huete[52]	*licenciado*	Requena 1490; Madrid 1490
Antón Martínez de Aguilera[53]	—	Murcia 1492; Palencia 1493;
		Madrid 1498
Juan Martínez de Albelda[54]	*bachiller*	Madrid 1483
Alfonso Martínez de Angulo[55]	—	Madrid 1498
Diego Martínez de Astudillo[56]	*licenciado*	Asturias 1488; Málaga 1502; 1504
Antón Martínez de Cascales[57]	*doctor*	Alcaraz 1483
Diego de Mendoza[58]	—	Salamanca 1493
Fernando de Mogollón[59]	—	Plasencia 1491
Carlos de Molina[60]	*licenciado*	Trujillo 1493; Palencia 1493;
		Toro, Zamora 1495
Juan de Molina[61]	*bachiller*	Jerez 1492
Francisco de Molina[62]	*licenciado*	Badajoz 1489; León 1490;
		Ponferrada 1491
Fernando de Montealegre[63]	—	Logroño 1490
Licenciado Mora[64]	*licenciado*	Miranda de Ebro 1494
Bachiller Morguía[65]	*bachiller*	Medina–Olmeda 1494
Bachiller Mudarra[66]	*bachiller*	Ágreda 1494
Francisco Muñoz[67]	*licenciado*	Alcaraz 1493; Marbella–Ronda
		1495
Bachiller de Nájera[68]	*bachiller*	Cuatro Villas 1495
Francisco Núñez[69]	—	Alcaraz 1494
Pedro Núñez de Peñalver[70]	—	Andújar 1490; Requena 1494
Juan de Olarte[71]	—	Jerez 1492
Alfonso Ortiz[72]	—	Carmona 1487
Francisco Ortiz[73]	—	Carrión–Sahagún 1494
Pedro Ortiz[74]	—	Alcaraz 1492
Juan de Pedrosa[75]	—	Toledo 1494
Alonso de la Peña[76]	—	Cáceres 1484
Gómez Pérez[77]		Molina 1493
Juan Pérez de Barradas[78]	*licenciado*	Madrid 1490
Juan Pérez de Segura[79]	—	Plasencia 1492
Doctor de la Plazuela[80]	*doctor*	Cuatro Villas 1490
Álvaro de Porras[81]	*licenciado*	Guipúzcoa 1490; Jerez 1490
Lope de Porras[82]	—	Guipúzcoa 1491
Juan de Portillo[83]	—	Santo Domingo de la Calzada
		1496
Juan de Raja[84]	*licenciado*	Valladolid 1493; Burgos 1494

Table 4 *(cont.)*

Name	Academic degrees	Place and date
Francisco Ramírez[85]	*bachiller*	Carmona 1492
Licenciado Remón[86]	*licenciado*	Ronda 1492; Jerez 1492
Juan de Ribera[87]	—	Arcos 1493
Bachiller de Riomayor[88]	*bachiller*	Olmedo 1480
Juan Rodríguez de Jaén[89]	—	Alcaraz 1486
Antonio Rodríguez de Lillo[90]	*doctor*	Trujillo 1480
Gonzalo de las Risas[91]	—	La Coruña 1493
Antón Rodríguez de la Rúa[92]	*licenciado*	Molina 1490; Villena 1493
Licenciado Romany[93]	*licenciado*	Alcázar de Consuegra 1492
Rodrigo Romero[94]	*bachiller*	Segovia 1490
Licenciado Romo[95]	*licenciado*	Murcia 1490
López Ruiz de Antillo[96]	—	Carmona 1493; 1494; 1495
Juan Ruiz de la Fuente[97]	*licenciado*	Jerez 1484; Molino 1490; Medina–Olmedo 1492; Carrión–Sahagún 1492
Licenciado de Sahagún[98]	*licenciado*	Valladolid 1490
Francisco de Salinas[99]	*licenciado*	León 1493
Pedro de Salinas[100]	—	León 1493
Pedro Sánchez de Briviesca[101]	—	Villena 1478
Gonzalo Sánchez de Castro[102]	*bachiller*	Cordova 1490
Pedro Sánchez de Frías[103]	*doctor*	Madrid 1487
Lope Sánchez del Castillo[104]	*licenciado*	Cuenca, Huete 1492
Alfonso Sánchez del Hermosilla[105]	*licenciado*	La Coruña 1485
Sancho Sánchez de Montiel[106]	*licenciado*	Badajoz 1491
Día Sánchez de Quesada[107]	—	Alcarez 1490
Licenciado de San Esteban[108]	*licenciado*	Villena 1496
Bachiller San Millán[109]	*bachiller*	Cuatro Villas 1493
Álvaro de Santisteban[110]	—	Écija 1492
Juan de Santo Domingo[111]	—	Carmona 1491
Juan de Segovia[112]	*licenciado*	Medina–Olmedo 1485
Pedro de Soto[113]	—	León 1485
Fernando de Talavera[114]	—	Alcaraz 1484
Francisco de Tapia[115]	*licenciado*	Aranda 1494
Alonso Téllez[116]	*bachiller*	Toro, Zamora 1491; 1492; Sepúlveda 1492; Toro 1493; Molina 1494
Cristóbal de Toro[117]	—	Avila 1488; Vizcaya 1491
Juan de Torquemada[118]	—	Jaén 1490
Alonso de Torres[119]	*bachiller*	Ciudad Rodrigo 1487
Bachiller Tórtoles[120]	*bachiller*	Almería 1494
Pedro de Valencia[121]	*bachiller*	Murcia 1484
Francisco de Vargas[122]	*licenciado*	Alcaraz 1485; Cáceres, Trujillo 1490; Avila 1493; Guipúzcoa 1493; Asturias 1493
Fernando de Vega[123]	—	Asturias 1493
Francisco de Yepes[124]	*licenciado*	Segovia 1494; Ciudad Real 1495
Díaz de Zumaya[125]	*licenciado*	Asturias 1493; Málaga 1496

Notes:
[1] *AGS, Sello,* 30 Mar. 1485, fol. 166; 27 Jan. 1487, fol. 30; *AM Madrid, Horadado,* M-338, fols. 381r–382r, 26 Sept. 1494.
[2] *AGS, Sello,* 23 June 1495, fol. 21.

Notes to Table 4 (*cont.*)

[3] *Ibid.*, 6 Nov. 1491, fol. 179.

[4] *Ibid.*, 16 Mar. 1495, fol. 64.

[5] *AM Carmona, Actas Capitulares*, 1510, fols. 123–4, 5 Nov. 1502.

[6] *AGS, Sello*, 4 Jan. 1490, fol. 199; 27 Feb. 1490, fol. 302; 16 Mar. 1490, fol. 243; 19 Feb. 1493, fol. 85.

[7] *Ibid.*, 15 May 1495, fol. 276.

[8] *Ibid.*, 13 June 1485, fol. 223; 22 Apr. 1486, fol. 94; 30 Sept. 1487, fol. 54.

[9] *Ibid.*, 4 Feb. 1493, fol. 84.

[10] *Ibid.*, 5 Dec. 1483, fol. 82.

[11] *Ibid.*, 13 June 1488, fol. 173; 8 Mar. 1492, fol. 289; 16 Apr. 1492, fol. 209; 14 July 1492, fol. 64; Aurelio Pretel Marín, *La integración de un municipio medieval en el autoritario de los Reyes Católicos* (Albacete, 1979), p. 34.

[12] *AGS, Sello*, nd, Sept. 1487, fol. 102; nd Mar. 1488, fol. 130; 2 June 1488, fol. 167.

[13] *Ibid.*, 12 Nov. 1486, fol. 19; 26 Apr. 1487, fol. 155.

[14] *Ibid.*, 25 Apr. 1494, fol. 119.

[15] *Ibid.*, 10 Mar. 1484, fol. 36.

[16] *Residencia* conducted in 1489, *ibid.*, 11 Apr. 1491, fol. 150.

[17] *AGS, Sello*, 26 Aug. 1495, fol. 239; *AM Carmona, AC*, 1484, fol. 65, 16 Aug. 1484.

[18] *AGS, Sello*, 19 Jan. 1491, fols. 186, 222; 16 July 1492, fol. 66; 20 Sept. 1493, fol. 55; 18 July 1495, fol. 175.

[19] *Ibid.*, 4 Mar. 1491, fol. 158.

[20] *Ibid.*, 28 Oct. 1484, fol. 205; 4 May 1492, fol. 261.

[21] *Ibid.*, 15 Apr. 1493, fol. 205.

[22] *AM Carmona, AC*, 1488, fol. 43. 19 June 1488.

[23] *AGS, Sello*, 5 May 1495, fol. 329; *AM Málaga, Provisiones*, vol. I, fols. 82v–87, 12 Aug. 1498.

[24] *AGS, Sello*, 18 Jan. 1475, fol. 65.

[25] *Ibid.*, 26 Mar. 1490, fol. 235; 26 Sept. 1492, fol. 45; 13 Mar. 1494, nf; 19 July 1494, fol. 92; 18 Oct. 1494, fol. 379.

[26] *Ibid.*, 25 Sept. 1493, fol. 38; 19 Mar. 1494, fol. 334; 8 Oct. 1495, fol. 189.

[27] *Ibid.*, 28 Jan. 1487, fol. 18.

[28] *Ibid.*, 11 Apr. 1487, fol. 147; 12 Apr. 1487, fol. 85; 22 Jan. 1488, fol. 161.

[29] *Ibid.*, nd Mar. 1487, fol. 58; 10 Oct. 1491, fols. 142, 148.

[30] *Ibid.*, 14 June 1484, nf.

[31] *Ibid.*, 17 Jan. 93, f. 66.

[32] *Ibid.*, 15 Oct. 1494, fol. 459.

[33] *Ibid.*, 31 Oct. 1494, fol. 333.

[34] *Ibid.*, 6 Feb. 1484, 233; nd Oct. 1494, fol. 51.

[35] *Ibid.*, nd Mar. 1494, fol. 77.

[36] *AM Carmona, AC*, 1499, nf 5 Sept. 1499.

[37] *AGS, Sello*, 21 Jan. 1485, fol. 132.

[38] *Ibid.*, 13 Jan. 1492, fol. 36.

[39] *Ibid.*, 4 June 1492, fol. 116.

[40] *Ibid.*, 24 Mar. 1488, fol. 116; 29 Jan. 1491, fol. 162.

[41] *Ibid.*, 5 Sept. 1492, fol. 173; 28 July 1494, fol. 94.

[42] *Ibid.*, 15 June 1488, fol. 286; 12 Feb. 1490, fols. 84, 85; 13 Mar. 1492, fol. 145.

[43] *Ibid.*, 22 Sept. 1479, fols. 66, 74, 115.

[44] *Ibid.*, 29 Mar. 1485, fol. 165; 25 Mar. 1495, fol. 125; *AM Madrid, Cédulas*, M-339, fols. 47r–49r, 18 Dec. 1485.

[45] *AGS, Sello*, 24 Feb. 1485, fols. 249, 262; 25 Mar. 1492, fol. 370.

[46] *Ibid.*, 9 Feb. 1485, fol. 255; 12 Sept. 1493, fol. 273.

[47] *Ibid.*, 28 Mar. 1491, fol. 195.

[48] *Ibid.*, 20 May 1494, fol. 341.

[49] *Ibid.*, nd Sept. 1492, fol. 97.

[50] *Ibid.*, 17 Jan. 1493, fol. 66.

[51] L. de la Rosa y Serra Rafols, *El adelantado D. Alonso de Lugo y su residencia por Lope de Sosa* (La Laguna, 1949), pp. xiff.

Notes to Table 4 (*cont.*)

[52] *AGS, Sello*, 18 July 1490, fol. 383; 26 Aug. 1490, fol. 31.
[53] *Ibid.*, nd Sept. 1492, fol. 46; 24 Aug. 1493, fol. 93; *AM Madrid, Actas Capitulares*, v-1498, fol. 172r, 8 Oct 1498.
[54] *AM Madrid, AC*, 1-1484, 133r-v, 17 Feb. 84.
[55] *AM Madrid, Cédulas*, M-339, fols. 61r–64v, 21 Sept. 1498.
[56] *AGS, Sello*, 27 July 1488, fol. 231; AM Málaga, *Provisiones*, vol. III, fols. 24v–26v, 26 Feb. 1502; vol. III, fols. 74v–75, 2 Nov. 1504.
[57] Pretel Marín, *Integración municipio*, p. 34.
[58] *AGS, Sello*, 28 Feb. 1493, fol. 51.
[59] *Ibid.*, 30 June 1491, fol. 52.
[60] *Ibid.*, 30 Jan. 1493, fol. 70; 24 Aug. 1493, fol. 93; 9 May 1495, fol. 389.
[61] *Ibid.*, 16 July 1492, fol. 104.
[62] *Ibid.*, 30 Mar. 1489, fol. 356; 27 Feb. 1490, fol. 297; 16 Dec. 1491, fol. 160.
[63] *AGS, Sello*, 12 Feb. 1490, fol. 99.
[64] *Ibid.*, 7 Apr. 1494, fol. 389.
[65] *Ibid.*, nd Apr. 1494, fol. 580.
[66] *Ibid.*, 30 Nov. 1494, fol. 430.
[67] *Ibid.*, 17 May 1493, fol. 169; 23 June 1495, fol. 21.
[68] *Ibid.*, 9 Mar. 1495, fol. 376.
[69] *Ibid.*, 24 Mar. 1494, fol. 409.
[70] *Ibid.*, 9 May 1490, fol. 384; 9 Mar. 1494, fol. 363.
[71] *Ibid.*, 15 May 1492, fol. 283.
[72] *AM Carmona, AC*, 1487, fol. 39; 2 Apr. 1487.
[73] *AGS, Sello*, 30 Oct. 1494, fols. 191, 256.
[74] Pretel Marín, *Integración municipio*, p. 35.
[75] *AGS, Sello*, 17 Oct. 1494, fol. 324.
[76] *Ibid.*, 23 Mar. 1494, fol. 212.
[77] *Ibid.*, 14 Oct. 1493, fol. 45.
[78] *Ibid.*, 23 Jan. 1490, fol. 32.
[79] *Ibid.*, 4 May 1492, fol. 261.
[80] *Ibid.*, 26 Mar. 1490, fol. 170.
[81] *Ibid.*, 9 Feb. 1490, fol. 108; 18 Feb. 1490, fol. 321.
[82] *Ibid.*, 20 May 1491, fol. 342.
[83] *Ibid.*, 12 Nov. 1497, fol. 42.
[84] *Ibid.*, nd Aug. 1493, fol. 28.
[85] *AM Carmona, AC*, 1492, fols. 1–2. 24 Feb. 1492.
[86] *AGS, Sello*, nd Feb. 1491, fol. 284; 5 Sept. 1492, fol. 173; 17 Sept. 1492, fol. 236.
[87] *Ibid.*, 21 Mar. 1493, fol. 356.
[88] *Ibid.*, 13 Sept. 1480, fol. 127.
[89] *Ibid.*, 2 Apr. 1486, fol. 88.
[90] *Ibid.*, 24 May 1480, fol. 206.
[91] *Ibid.*, 5 July 1493, fols. 58, 59.
[92] *Ibid.*, 25 Oct. 1490, fols. 225; 5 June 1493, fol. 110.
[93] *Ibid.*, 22 Dec. 1492, fol. 69.
[94] *Ibid.*, 25 Mar. 1490, fol. 231.
[95] *Ibid.*, 22 June 1490, fol. 16.
[96] *Ibid.*, 3 June 1493, fol. 90; 15 May 1494, fol. 399; 29 Aug. 1495, fol. 250.
[97] *Ibid.*, 15 Feb. 1484, fol. 203; 3 Feb. 1490, fols. 86, 87; 30 Mar. 1490, fol. 173; 26 Nov. 1492, fol. 190.
[98] *Ibid.*, nd Mar. 1490, fol. 392.
[99] *Ibid.*, 17 June 1493, fol. 93.
[100] *Ibid.*, 10 Dec. 1493, fol. 94.
[101] *Ibid.*, 12 June 1478, fol. 56.
[102] *Ibid.*, 12 Dec. 1490, fol. 5.
[103] *AM Madrid, AC*, II-1487, fols. 58v–59r, 10 Feb. 1487.
[104] *AGS, Sello*, 26 Aug. 1492, fol. 161.

Notes to Table 4 (*cont.*)

[105] *Ibid.*, 23 July 1485, fol. 103.
[106] *Ibid.*, 18 Jan. 1491, fols. 138, 144.
[107] *AM Alcaraz*, docs. 311, 324, 16, 17 Sept. 1490.
[108] *AGS, Sello*, 12 Mar. 1496, fol. 124.
[109] *Ibid.*, 24 Nov. 1493, fol. 98.
[110] *Ibid.*, 26 Sept. 1492, fol. 45.
[111] *Ibid.*, 14 June 1491, fol. 98.
[112] *Ibid.*, 23 Dec. 1485, fol. 58.
[113] *Ibid.*, 7 Feb. 1485, fol. 247.
[114] *Ibid.*, 5 Mar. 1484, fol. 184.
[115] *Ibid.*, 7 Feb. 1494, fol. 200.
[116] *Ibid.*, 10 Oct. 1491, fol. 166; 8 Mar. 1492, fol. 290; 14 July 1492, fol. 78; 20 Apr. 1493, fol. 83; 6 Mar. 1494, fol. 458.
[117] *Ibid.*, 11 June 1488, fol. 221; 5 Aug. 1491, fol. 335.
[118] *Ibid.*, 12 Feb. 1490, fol. 290.
[119] *Ibid.*, 28 Jan. 1487, fol. 17.
[120] *Ibid.*, 19 July 1494, fol. 90.
[121] *Ibid.*, 9 Feb. 1484, fol. 236.
[122] *Ibid.*, 26 May 1485, fol. 61; 9 Mar. 1490, fol. 190; 26 Oct. 1493, fol. 47; 17 Jan. 1493 *residencia* (in doc. 11 Mar. 1493, fol. 317); 24 Aug. 1493, fol. 25.
[123] *Ibid.*, 24 Aug. 1493, fol. 27.
[124] *Ibid.*, 7 Apr. 1494, fol. 401; 4 Jan. 1495, fol. 245.
[125] *Ibid.*, 24 Aug. 1493, fol. 25; *AM Málaga, Provisiones*, vol. I, fol. 73, 10 June 1496.

rambling letter was sent in 1488 to every city and town reiterating in the strongest terms that no one was to give gifts or housekeeping money.[115] The heavy penalties enumerated in this edict finally stayed the hand of most corregidores, for I encountered only a few incidents thereafter where individual warnings were sent out by the crown regarding requests for clothing and cloth,[116] pressure for free rental on houses,[117] and one case where a domestic animal had been accepted.[118]

Jewish communities were always likely to come under pressure from officials wishing to set up temporary households.[119] Following the Expulsion the absence of Jews became a matter of immediate concern to Gonzalo Bernaldo Gallego. When he reported for duty at Cáceres, he was informed that his predecessors had depended entirely upon Jewish merchants to rent bed furnishings and hangings. He naturally wanted to obtain these necessities for his family, and was irritated to find that not one Christian in the poor region had anything to rent. The new corregidor demanded they be of aid, but all refused, backed up by the Royal Council, which reminded him that gifts were forbidden.[120] The documents do not tell us whether Gonzalo ever did find anyone to help him get a restful sleep in his new home.

Not only was the Royal Council insistent that each corregidor pay for housing, it also had firm ideas where those lodgings should be. The center of the city was the place – not an outlying district – and as close as possible to the jail.[121] To meet these requirements, some municipal councils bought houses to rent out, and to use as a lockup, as when Ciudad Real agreed to provide lodgings and expense money in 1478 because the salary was low.[122] Cáceres paid rent for house number 14, Calle del Atrio del Corregidor, until it bought the building from a widow in 1503, for 29,500 *mrs*.[123] Málaga finally got around, in 1514, to setting up a permanent *casa del corregimiento* and prison, after taxes in the amount of 400,000 *mrs* were raised to purchase the building from a merchant, plus providing a fund for maintenance.[124] The crown had no policy of asking communities to buy a house, but when Burgos wanted to divest itself of its buildings in 1493 the Royal Council ordered the properties be kept.[125]

There were any number of possibilities for supplementing income from judicial practices that were more lucrative than demanding lodgings or garb. Albi estimated that legitimate court fees alone worked out to yield judges the equivalent of one-tenth of the property or money in question.[126] Abuse of fines had been condemned at the 1480 Cortes of Toledo.[127] Corregidores and judges were ordered to turn over to local authorities or the crown whatever excess was left after persons who had sued for justice received payment.[128] In 1491 and 1493, administrators were reminded that they could not double fees for litigants, on pain of a fine four times the amount extorted.[129] The need to reiterate such injunctions indicates that banned practices continued in the teeth of the *residencia* system, which reached its most active point during these years. The hostility of the populace towards allowing corregidores and other judges to take any part of their income from fines, legitimate or otherwise, was strong, for the reasonable presumption was that this led to unnecessary and excessive condemnations.[130]

Instances of corruption

One name appears far more frequently than others in the roster of trial verdicts. Día Sánchez de Quesada held a greater number of corregidorial posts than any of his fellows, which makes him especially visible. His career in public life began modestly enough at Baeza, where he served as *regidor* when his father ceded him the position.[131] Not until ten years later, in 1486, did he gain appointment as corregidor, at Segovia, which was next followed by a stay at the

Cuatro Villas, from 1488 to 1490. The same year in which he left that post, he put in a few months at Madrid, before receiving an assignment to Alcaraz, where he stayed from 1490 to 1492. He returned to Segovia during the year, for a period that stretched out until 1494, with the last stage of his career bringing him to Salamanca from 1494 to 1496.[132] There was a pugnacity about Sánchez de Quesada which made him a useful crown servant, fit to take on ugly tasks, but which always landed him in the midst of controversy. The line between aggressiveness and corruption is easy to transgress, and he crossed it often. Not without reason did a fellow corregidor characterize him as "detestable."[133]

During Sánchez de Quesada's first appointment, in Segovia, the *regidores* and commoners rose up to complain about a tax he levied which they regarded as illegal. Going on to the Cuatro Villas, he and his officials used the excuse of the Granada War to harass and overtax residents, at least according to the depositions. Juana Gutiérrez Calleja accused him of criminally causing the death of her husband, and María Sánchez de Herrera alleged she was assaulted when she came to visit her brother in jail. In Alcaraz, he attempted to get the government to give him a clothing allowance, for which he was condemned at his exit investigation in 1492. Despite earlier troubles, Sánchez de Quesada was sent back to Segovia, where he caused a new sensation. The queen was much interested in the subject of priestly *barraganas* and in him she found a corregidor willing to follow the letter of the law. In May 1494 his men raided homes of clerics and took any women found to jail, where they stayed until heavy fines were paid. At two *residencia* hearings in Segovia, aggrieved parties assailed him anew for improprieties and "immoralities," which each time resulted in the impounding of his movable goods.[134]

Certain other jurisdictions had more than their share of problems with equally troublesome officials. Of the ten most nettled *corregimientos* – Alcaraz, Avila, Carrión–Sahagún, Madrid, Baeza–Úbeda, Ciudad Rodrigo, Jerez de la Frontera, Medina, Salamanca, and Zamora – only the first three will receive detailed attention. Avila saw its problems develop over a short time span. Juan Flores was temporarily suspended in 1479 under suspicion of involvement with counterfeit money, and after Jews complained that he had improperly meddled in their business. The following year, Pedro Sánchez de Frías was condemned for allowing a suspicious death to take place in his cells. During 1493, Álvaro de Santisteban's peace officer was condemned, along with his superior, for unjustly shaming Antón Sánchez Cubero in public, and for whipping Juan de Conde without cause. The corregidor had also refused to pay any rent on the house he occupied in Avila.[135] Similar problems turned up in a five-year period of trials at Carrión and Sahagún. Francisco de Luzón was adjudged guilty in 1489 of accepting clothes, and at an exit investigation in 1490 was once again found guilty of petty extortions. During April of the following year Juan Ruiz de la Fuente was condemned for infractions, along with his brother, whom he had appointed his subordinate. When no action was taken by September to carry out the sentences, citizens petitioned the royal court to punish the two offenders. The next corregidor in line, Lope Sánchez del Castillo, also found guilty of corruption, was fined.[136]

The city where the exit investigations present the most luxuriant crop of deficient corregidores is Alcaraz. As a consequence of the bitterness of the crown's long fight to reduce Alcaraz to subservience, officials perceived that they could cite the exigencies of having to deal with a refractory populace to justify misdeeds. Virtually every corregidor was charged with corruption, and investigation most often bore out such complaints. To present an example, all through March 1484 judge Antón Martínez de Cascales took evidence concerning the same Lope Sánchez del Castillo we just encountered, at a later date, in Avila. The case went against the corregidor, who had by then gone on to a new post at Trujillo, from which he slandered his accusers and the judge. Sánchez del Castillo lost an appeal to another judge in Toledo, with the penalty that, for not promptly paying his initial fine he was to pay an additional 10,000 *mrs*.[137] Not unexpectedly, when Martínez de Cascales moved from being judge to becoming corregidor of Alcaraz, he too dipped into public funds by diverting money supposed to go towards the repair of walls. The city's case was taken to the Royal Council, which ordered a *residencia* investigation for the magistrate in 1485 that confirmed the charge.[138]

To offer a later instance, Pedro Ortiz survived the public part of his trial in 1493, but after the secret hearing was condemned for a variety of offenses, receiving a heavy fine. Ortiz was given time to defend himself, unlike his *alcalde*, whose goods were immediately impounded. The record was called for by the Royal Council in September, and until the final appeal was turned down the following March, Ortiz was allowed to live securely with his family in the house he rented.[139] He, along with other corregidores in Alcaraz, undoubtedly pocketed fines levied on gamblers. In July 1496 a royal investigator finally confirmed this longstanding charge, leading to an edict that the bad custom of treating such fines as personal remuneration should cease.[140] Sweeping prohibitions had little effect, as indicated by the case of Ortuño de Aguirre, who incited a wide variety of complaints in 1500 about his abuse of office and favoritism.[141]

Subordinate officials

Regulations governing appointments of subordinates stated that, in addition to being from outside the community, they were not to be related, up to the fourth degree, a rule that was in the main observed.[142] In instances which suggest a slackening of Royal Council attention, Juan Ruiz de la Fuente, at Carrión–Sahagún from 1490–2, appointed his brother, Pedro, *alcalde*, and during 1503 another corregidor placed a relative as his lieutenant at Cuenca. In neither case was the offender rebuked.[143] Because higher officials had an otherwise unfettered right to appoint subordinates, the potential for corruption was significant.[144] Corregidores were under strict orders not to take any portion of salary designated for functionaries or subordinate judges,[145] but the way was always open for hard-to-trace "kickbacks." Juan de Luján, charged with extortion by his *mayordomo* at Alfaro, offered the weak excuse that he had only taken back a part of his own salary. The former subordinate dared speak without fear of retribution only after he had left the jurisdiction.[146] Avila also managed to disgorge funds earmarked for salaries from a corregidor when his underlings complained.[147]

In such *residencia* proceedings a corregidor's aides were under examination as well. Twenty-five subordinates, out of all noted in the records reviewed,[148] committed offenses sufficiently serious to warrant a separate investigation that led to suspension or fine. The list of the guilty included a high proportion of cell-keepers and peace officers.[149] Lieutenants generally escaped unscathed: one such subordinate at Jerez de la Frontera had his back salary released, upon review, in 1493 and his counterpart at Asturias was cleared that same year of charges of causing the death of an ironworker.[150] Only four lieutenants located in our study were actually convicted of charges raised at their trials – an example being the functionary at Jaén, who paid a fine of 25,000 *mrs*, after appeals stretching over two years.[151] Since many more corregidores than subordinates were caught in the net, the *residencia* system during Isabella's reign proves not to be directed merely against small fish.

Scribes, whose profession gained prestige in Castile's increasingly paper-ridden society, were deeply involved in petty larceny. The tedious verbosity of documents has one origin in the scribal propensity to charge by the sheet, thereby also making it common to find only a few lines on concluding pages. Another way of increasing income was to charge each of several persons involved in any trial separately for the same work.[152] *Residencia* investigations offered excellent opportunities for such gouging, due to the uncertain scope of the work.[153] Charges assessed to León for a small bit of work by scribe Juan de Portugal illustrate at what rate costs could run: Judge Francisco de Salinas insisted, upon reflection, that the scribe return fifty *reales* (1,700 *mrs*).[154] To keep their lucrative practice free of such meddling, scribes constantly agitated that corregidores respect all qualifications the trade set for itself.[155] They could count, in this regard, on highly placed friends to hold the local royal overseer at bay. When Cáceres complained, in 1497, that although the established salary for the chief scribe was 500 *mrs* he was actually collecting 3,500, the Royal Council, with its sympathetic secretaries and notaries, would authorize the corregidor only to reduce the charge to 1,500.[156]

The verdict

The number of charges alleged against corregidores which actually reached the stage of prosecution is low in relation to the hundreds of officeholders over three decades. It can further be said in defense of the administration of justice during the reign of Isabella I that, wherever substantial evidence of malfeasance was revealed by *residencias*, the Royal Council consistently confirmed lower court verdicts. In only seven out of eighty-three exit investigations whose complete final verdict is known to me was a condemnatory decision reversed. Two other cases saw pardons granted, relieving offending corregidores of the necessity to pay assessed fines.

Yet even when the penalties for wrongdoing were imposed, the result was generally a light rebuke, for punishment meted out conformed to the social level of appointees. The basic form of judicial punishment for privileged groups in European society of the day was a fine.[157] Token payments of 3,000–10,000 *mrs*, with the temporary seizure of personal property as bond for payment and court costs, show up in fifteen decisions (18.4 per cent), and in a further eighteen decisions (21.6 per cent) corregidores were ordered to restore funds, goods, or property to aggrieved individuals or communities. The offenders were not jailed or permanently barred from any office, despite the most adverse judgements, at worst suffering the rare failure to be reappointed.

On balance, the corregidores were fairly honest servants, their probity guaranteed by their dependency upon the crown. By way of contrast, bribes for favorable action to officials in France, such as the *sénéchels* and *prévots* sent to govern, or negotiate with, towns during our period, were so common as to be almost normal.[158] Governors assigned by the Venetian patriciate to the mainland towns of the *terraferma* were, despite myths of perfection that cling to Venice, notoriously corrupt yet seldom called to task.[159] In Castile, examples of serious malfeasance on the part of corregidores prove so scanty, considering the many officeholders, that Isabella's officials would probably prove less culpable than their counterparts elsewhere were firm evidence available for all of Europe. The constant reissuing of proclamations forbidding illegal practices in the queen's realms indicates both that abuse of position did take place and that, when this happened, attention was generally paid at the highest level.

6

Lords and prelates: a matter of privilege

"Through her was destroyed the haughtiness of the wicked aristocrats, who were disobedient, and traitors to the royal crown," wrote
Andrés Bernáldez, upon recording the death of his queen.[1] Isabella
and her advisors did check abuses, although on a selective basis that
escaped the notice of the humble curate of Los Palacios. Troublesome individuals were chastised, yet the high estates as a whole were
little diminished, for the most significant finding in the modern
literature is that Isabella relied so heavily upon the great families to
govern that she felt compelled to advance their fortunes with
augmented prestige, titles, enormous grants of land, and rich gifts.[2]
She needed support and she bought it.

From the stature accorded genealogical studies at this time it might
be supposed that this aristocracy was ancient; but, on the contrary,
the houses which dominated Castile saw their rapid growth in the
fifteenth-century, when some two dozen seignorial estates mush-
roomed in size until they overshadowed all others.[3] In lower
Andalusia the council of Seville administered fifty hamlets, compared
to the lords' eighty in the same jurisdiction. For Cordova, the city
ruled twenty while the lords had over thirty. These areas also saw an
additional fifteen hamlets in the hands of military orders and the
cathedral of Seville.[4] The reign shows a continuing increase in the
assembling and legal confirmation of entailed estates (*mayorazgos*).
Confirmation of the secure right to hold and pass on this land in the
name of the family was a key reason why the aristocrats finally
accepted a stable monarchy, abandoning serious challenge to the
throne during Isabella's lifetime.[5] When a village close by his area of
jurisdiction claimed free status in 1480, the corregidor of Écija was
ordered to make sure it continued in fealty to Doña Beatriz de
Guzmán.[6] The maintenance of control in *villas de señorío* is demonstrated by the seignorial right to name corregidores.[7] If, at times,

aristocrats allowed minor communal functionaries to be freely designated, without question they always nominated this officer, or an
alcalde mayor.[8] The count of Castañeda, Juan Manrique, himself served
as corregidor for Aguilar de Campóo until he took on the title of
marquis of Aguilar, whereupon he nominated a servant to the post.[9]
In the case of the Ponce de León line, Don Rodrigo received a
corregimiento along with his title of marquis of Cádiz. It proved quite
expensive for the crown to obtain the return of Cádiz, and the office,
after his death.[10]

Time added justifying theory to reality. Following a law set out in
the *Siete Partidas*, the concept developed that seignorial regimes were
true mechanisms for governing the community. In the *Ordenanzas
Reales de Castilla* – a judicial code drafted by Dr Montalvo under the
inspiration of the Catholic Sovereigns – the naming of all *alcaldes* and
judges was held to belong to the crown by right but practices
consecrated by usage were approved, giving *de facto* approval to what
the lords were doing all along in their properties.[11] The logical
conclusion, reached by jurists in the sixteenth century, was that
aristocrats were privileged to rule on their estates, so long as they
observed royal law.[12] Castillo de Bovadilla went so far as to observe
that "dukes, counts, marquises and other lords of vassals are in their
estates and lands vicars of the kings and perpetual corregidores."[13]

On the estates

Facing aristocratic powers as strong in theory as in fact, what role
could the queen's corregidores play in overturning injustice? Cities
forming a part of the royal domain were a few fires shining in the dark
expanse of lordly holdings. It cannot be said that the queen's
corregidores threw much additional light on what happened in the
hidden recesses of privilege. So far as the lives of their subjects were
concerned the lords had, according to the common formula, "jurisdiction civil and criminal, high and low."[14] Justice in a *mayorazgo* was
administered by the *alcalde*, who typically adhered to customary
rather than codified law, after which a plea could be attempted by a
defendant to the lord. This judicial apparatus was not much interfered
with by the Catholic Sovereigns, beyond an insistence that their own
courts should accept appeal under specified conditions, after lordly
justice had done its best, or worst.[15]

This did not mean that the estates were totally insulated. In response to a petition (actually prepared at court) from the *Junta General* of the principality of Asturias, Isabella did mandate in 1475 that her corregidores be allowed to enter estates in the area to search for criminals, and that they be empowered to look into all crimes committed since 1470.[16] The impulse for this exceptional decree derived from the exigencies of the War of Succession, for the pertinent ordinance under which all royal corregidores came to operate after 1480 was more limited. Officials could reach into estates only to check on a fortress or stronghold being built or expanded without royal permission, and to gather information about malefactors in hiding.[17] All aristocrats and clerics at Zamora and Toro had to be reminded that they must grant admittance to the royal official. In the same manner, Segovians were admonished that, since the reign of Enrique II, it had always been a part of a corregidor's work to seize troublemakers hiding in towers and keeps. There are scattered instances which prove that corregidores did exercise their presumed right of search. The count of Osorno got into such hot debate with an official in Trujillo over which one of them had the power to appoint a *mayordomo* that he ended by imprisoning the official, obliging a corregidor to get the prisoner out. So too, when Alonso de Fonseca, lord of Coca and Alaejos, arrested citizens from Arévalo, Avila's corregidor visited their cell.[18]

Vigilance against fortifications was exercised to a fuller extent when numerous fortresses in the hands of partisans of Doña Juana fell to Isabella's forces during the War of Succession. The year 1478, for example, opened with the destruction, at the hands of Galicia's corregidor, of the marquis of Villena's enormous new La Roda castle. This was followed by demolitions ordered by corregidores at Úbeda, Huete, and Andújar.[19] Fortresses were sequestered at Jaén in 1479 and Alegría the following year.[20] Regarding new fortress construction, Isabella's insistence that her approval be obtained was followed up by her aides, rather consistently, during the first two decades of the reign. The governor of Galicia was upheld when he stood fast against allowing the count of Monterrey to rebuild at Caldelas in 1484.[21] Corregidores were ordered to investigate reports in 1485 that Pedro Suarez de Alcalde was building at Cuenca, and that Diego Pérez de Martiarto was rebuilding in Vizcaya during 1488.[22] In 1487 the corregidor of Ciudad Rodrigo was ordered to visit Fuenteguinaldo, which belonged to a son of the count of Castañeda: if he found any building in progress he was to destroy the structure. Unauthorized castles were demolished at Trujillo (1487) and León (1489).[23] During 1492 a corregidor from Ciudad Rodrigo was sent to Coveña, on the outskirts of Madrid, to demolish a recently built fortification owned by the count of Coruña. The count of Miranda, caught in the midst of construction the following year, ceased work in the village of Iscar when pressure was brought to bear by the joint action of the corregidores of Burgos and Toledo.[24] Most dramatically, the corregidor of Castrogeriz was commanded in 1493 to enter Socastro (Zamora), where he smashed a stronghold built illegally twenty-three years previously.[25] Overall, despite this anecdotal evidence, the record of demolitions during Isabella's years is less impressive than that of the much-maligned Enrique IV, who eliminated more than twice the number of fortresses, in one-third less time than it took his successor. From 1475 to 1505, some eighty-four fortresses were demolished, which works out on the average to less than three for every year of Isabella's reign. By way of contrast, between 1454 and 1474, 180 fortresses were destroyed, an average of nine per year.[26]

The most notable document in a long string of prohibitions is the *pragmática* of 1500 which, in a sweeping command, again ordered *asistentes*, governors, and corregidores throughout the realms not to allow castle-building without royal license.[27] The severity of this decree is belied by the numbers, which show that a slightly higher proportion of fortifications per year were actually initiated or built during Isabella's three decades than during Enrique's two: a total of 265, contrasted with 148.[28] After the initial impulse to enforce prohibitions slackened, Isabella's agents in the field became increasingly loath to act. When Badajoz complained that Fernando de Sotomayor was constructing a stronghold six leagues from the city, the crown told its corregidor to investigate. Diego López de Trujillo failed to respond to the July 1490 order, and, although prodded again in September, managed to finish out his term safely without taking action.[29] Corregidor lassitude worsened significantly as aristocrats gained increasing exemption. Fortresses sprouted throughout Cuenca by the end of the century, with newly-appointed military governors, under direct aristocratic control, who were not harassed by royal officials.[30]

Problems of rule

The elimination by the crown of all threatening strongholds was certainly never considered, much less attempted, but domestic conflict was somewhat reduced. Unwavering royal support for a corregidor role in negotiations between factions brought the positive results described in Chapter 3: comprehensive settlements at Ciudad Real, Cáceres, Seville, and Toledo. Where aristocrats were united, or temporarily willing to set aside their rivalries, the record of corregidor achievement is less brilliant. Valladolid's ten families dominated their region throughout the years; as consolidated into two bands – the Reoyo and Tovar – they brawled and raged, with notable flare-ups in 1332 and 1428.[31] In time, they learned to keep the peace by making sure that all appointments to government were evenly split, and as a consequence the intervention of Isabella's corregidor in the life of Valladolid was kept to a minimum.[32] Factions were in permanent control of Vizcaya as well, strengthened by the War of Succession, which placed in suspension the enduring rivalry of the count of Treviño and the count of Haro, both of whom supported Isabella; and, in return for that aid, any thought by the monarchy of repressing the factions was abandoned.[33]

The Marquesado of Villena was another area in which corregidores were kept from doing as they wished. Because of its huge extent of land, strategically placed between Portugal and Aragon, the holding was long a decisive factor in destabilizing plans for the pacification of Castile. Its leagued aristocracy was difficult to master, owing to the solidarity it maintained behind the second marquis, Diego López Pacheco. In 1475 Isabella attempted a partial dismemberment of the estate, by sending corregidores to all municipalities which either refused to recognize Pacheco's dominion or else seized the opportunity offered by the war to revolt. With the withdrawal of Portuguese forces from his land, Pacheco was forced to negotiate a fragile accord in September 1476, recognizing his losses.[34] After uncertainty in 1477, which involved the sending of three successive legists, Fernando de Frías settled down to work as governor and *justicia mayor*.[35]

Shortly after Fernando's arrival in November, Pacheco began complaining that Fernando de Frías was persecuting vassals, usurping jurisdiction, and in general acting in a greedy and criminal manner.[36] Pulgar, in his chronicle, interprets the charges as a sign that the Portuguese were preparing a new invasion, which would give the marquis an opportunity to reject the pact.[37] Isabella took his complaints seriously enough to rush a special judge to the area in June 1478, while suspending Fernando from his post throughout a seventy-day investigation.[38] The charges were not substantiated, so he was

restored without admonishment and permitted to remain until
November 1479.[39] No effort was made to send a new man until shortly
before a fresh settlement was signed with the marquis in March 1480.
Pedro Vaca was designated governor with reduced authority, judging
from titles and jurisdiction, for he was not designated *justicia mayor*,
and lost control over the town of Villena and three villages to a
nobleman who gave funds to Isabella in her long succession struggle.[40]

In Galicia, despite initial prospects of success with the cooperation
of the cities, the aristocracy proved far more difficult to subdue than
that in the *Marquesado*. The count of Lemos, Rodrigo Enrique Osorio,
and his followers hardly ever muted their opposition to Isabella. The
attempted assault on aristocratic privilege by governor Fernando de
Acuña and his lieutenant had damaging counter-effects. In 1482 the
king came in person with troops to compel a truce which had proved
beyond the capacity of representatives on the scene to obtain.[41] When
the governor dared to execute a persistent opponent, *Mariscal* Pedro
Pardo de Cela, in December 1483, the amazement this caused
throughout Galicia brought the territorial lords together behind the
count of Lemos as nothing else could. At a meeting in Santiago at the
start of 1484, they agreed among themselves not to consent to let the
governors do all they wished to do.[42]

To calm the storm, Isabella replaced Fernando de Acuña in March
with a new man, Diego López de Haro, the first official sent to Galicia
with the title of *justicia mayor*, indicating that his role was to be viewed as
predominantly judicial. He followed a cautious policy which involved
few prosecutions of aristocrats – a show of weakness which encouraged
the count of Lemos to resume his rebellion. Corregidores had to be
called upon at Sahagún, Toro, Zamora, and Salamanca to aid the
governor in raising troops.[43] Ferdinand broke off his persecution of the
Moorish war to free Ponferrada, halt the strife, and regain submission
from the count.[44] To patch over the conflict as quietly as possible,
López de Haro and his *alcalde mayor* were delegated power to give as
many pardons as they saw fit.[45] In a later effort to demonstrate
strength, López de Haro jailed two of the count's partisans. A
companion, who eluded capture, fled to Salamanca where he pleaded
before the Royal Council for the release of his two friends on grounds
of "advanced age." The Council outflanked the governor by granting
a pardon to all three.[46] Since the best the crown could get for its
officials was a stabilized situation, it allowed the governor to slip
gradually into becoming a decided advocate for the privileged. In

June 1490 López de Haro protected Juan Pimentel's vassals in Allariz, and in December of the following year he stepped in to stop a corregidor from meddling in the lord's estates.[47] The governor agreed not to interfere during 1492 in areas of jurisdiction claimed by the count of Ribadeo.[48] Galicia's aristocrats were thus never brought under the crown's control to the degree hoped for when governors were first dispatched.

Powerful troublemakers

The aristocracy could not easily be weaned from its anarchistic ways, for certain individuals, such as the count of Aguilar, were a constant source of trouble to a string of corregidores. Alonso de Aguilar imprisoned a tax collector at Alfaro in 1483, and would not let him out until the corregidor entered the estate. Six years of stalling passed before the count finally restored the 70,000 mrs he had expropriated from the collector.[49] In March 1488, the count entered the house of Pedro de Tejada and took away wedding gifts stored there for his vassal's niece, which the corregidor of Alfaro ordered to be restored in July. Another corregidor ruling went against the count in 1489, when he was ordered to force his chaplain to surrender an illegally held prebend.[50] Corregidores at León had continual troubles with the count of Luna, Diego Fernández de Quiñones. He made life difficult in a variety of petty ways for Pedro Sánchez de Frías,[51] and a good deal worse for Pedro Ortiz, the next supervisor in line.

During the latter's regime, the count of Luna's armed men invaded the convent of S. María de Orto de las Dueñas in 1487. They broke in the door, bloodied the guards, and roughly evicted María Robles as abbess, replacing her with Mencia de Quiñones, a member of the count's family. The corregidor's orders that the position be restored to its rightful owner were ignored. That August, the peace officer and the Royal Council ordered the count of Luna to obey Ortiz. When he did not, captain Bernal de Avendaño was assigned, later in the month, to resolve the matter, and also to look into other troubles the count had caused. Charges continued to pile up. During November, abbess Doña Mencia was accused of using her new position to despoil residents of their homes.[52] The monks of S. Isidoro de León and the populace of Riosequillo joined together in a complaint, during January of that year, that under threat of beatings they were forced to accept illegal pasturing on their lands. During February, after

Cristóbal de Ávila complained that he had been robbed by horsemen acting on the count's orders, it took the combined efforts of the royal investigator and the corregidor to bring Diego to account. With firm backing from the queen, Ortiz dared to ban the count and make the order stick, while restoring Doña María to a rightful place with her nuns.[53] There is no happy ending to the story, however, for long after Pedro Ortiz left his post at Alfaro the count's men molested residents and disturbed travelers.[54]

The aristocracy and its wide-ranging network of dependents and servants thus posed constant challenges to alternative authority. A humiliated chief constable in Madrid had to turn to his corregidor for help after servants of Juan de Mendoza took away his weapons.[55] Unruly friends of the marquis of Denia created a worse uproar in Carrión, after Pedro Gómez de Villamohol administered poison herbs to Padre Pedro de Escobar and other brothers, in a refectory plot to replace the abbot. The culprit was jailed, but broke away from the corregidor with the aid of Denia's *mayordomo*.[56] Despite these instances of attempts at firm action by corregidores, the record of enforcement against recalcitrant lords sharply diminishes with the passage of time. The increasing dependence of the crown upon the financial resources of its aristocracy, so marked during the last years of the queen's rule, manifested itself in slackened effort. The heads of the great military orders were even more insulated from punishment, although as arrogant as the secular lords. Corregidores found themselves at a loss to do anything about these powerful men without the constant intervention of the crown.

Military orders

The military orders provided their members with a satisfying blend of aristocratic privilege and ecclesiastical immunity. These remarkable institutions of fighting monks had long since moved past original vows of holy war and personal chastity, to evolve into landholding trusts, especially significant in the case of Santiago, Calatrava, and Alcántara, the three principal orders. Their territorial spread, primarily in New Castile, is indicated by figures from the smaller orders: Calatrava's two principal seats were augmented by an additional forty-four estates, and Alcántara accumulated thirty-eight far-flung estates, in addition to its original seat.[57]

Free municipalities, founded by kings in the flux of the Reconquest, were set down right in the midst of holdings of the orders, to serve as chess pieces in a long game. Ciudad Real, positioned in the dead center of Calatrava power, was foreordained to fight out such a bitter match.[58] Cáceres, squeezed by both Alcántara and Santiago, had an equally unhappy destiny. Hatred and vindictiveness on all sides – which no one corregidor could hope to mitigate – resulted in endless litigation. In 1482, María de la Cerda bought land near Cáceres, which she sold six years later to the grand master of Santiago, Alonso de Cárdenas y Osorio. He then immediately denied villagers their traditional rights to cut wood, to gather acorns, or to take advantage of other benefits they believed they were guaranteed. Combatants were regularly jailed by the corregidor, after fights broke out and bitter language was hurled.

With his new acquisition in hand, the grand master decided to rebuild its decayed fortress. Well aware of the queen's distaste for unauthorized strongholds, the residents protested through their prosecutor, bypassing the corregidor. A *regidor* from Palencia was dispatched by the Royal Council in March 1490 to investigate the fortification, with the result that work ceased. The separate matter of rights was settled with the aid of the corregidor of Badajoz, Diego López de Trujillo. A lengthy hearing was held in July on the forests and pastures, conducted jointly by the two outside officials, without the presence of the corregidor from Cáceres. The municipality had so high a pile of documents that it was granted a clear "act of possession"; yet the grand master fought on through appeal courts, until October, when the queen personally asked him to desist, so slight were his prospects.[59]

Next it was the turn of the grand master of Alcántara, Juan de Zúñiga, to set his subject town of Alcántara to spar with Cáceres. The lines between jurisdictions had been redrawn by a royal emissary in March 1491, with the happy result for Cáceres that it was put into possession, once again, of its pastureland of Cantillana. The corregidor of Cáceres was charged with the responsibility of seeing that this settlement was respected, but the grand master, not one to accept any judgement as final, sent armed men into pastures to destroy markers. The queen responded by firmly ordering corregidor Diego Ruiz de Montalvo to restore all to what it was. A bitter subterranean fight raged on between the communities, subject versus free, due to the unwillingness of the order to give up its attempts to tax, by means of sheer pressure of wealth and arms, all livestock passing through its pastures. Cáceres tried to avoid local arbitration, going over the head of its corregidor to get the crown to obtain a justice less susceptible to local interests. Lope Sánchez de Villarreal, who arrived with the hope of bringing the parties together, gained Cáceres' agreement that the discussion he planned for February 1496 would be presided over by the corrigedor, Fernando de Ribera, but that the ultimate decision would remain in his own hands. Immediately upon the convocation of that meeting, the municipal council brought out testaments showing free passage through the pasture in dispute dated back to 1217, with the happy result for Cáceres that the verdict by the visiting royal official went solidly in its favor.

The grand master then shifted ground, sending his officials to appear before a judge at another site that June, with the claim that markers had been moved by unknown parties from Cáceres. The ruling this time went in favor of the order, convent, and town of Alcántara. Cáceres immediately appealed, forcing a meeting in August of all parties, chaired again by Fernando de Ribera. Argument against the adverse ruling was left entirely to the prosecutor from Cáceres, who made the successful case that all markers were exactly where they had been in 1436 and in 1491.[60] During these involved adjudications, the corregidor of Cáceres never took an advocate's role, for the municipality's argument was always put forward by its prosecutor, and appeals made by councilors. The corregidor presided impartially over these meetings, arranged by visiting royal representatives, and then merely carried out decisions reached by others.

Cáceres and Ciudad Real struggled tenaciously against the greed of the grand masters. What emotions communities more directly subject to the orders felt are graphically conveyed by Lope de Vega's *Fuenteovejuna*. Lope read about the bloody result of the 1476 rising in Rades de Andrada's *Crónica de las tres órdenes* (1572).[61] The town of 4,500 inhabitants, once in the orbit of Cordova, had become a possession of Calatrava administered by a knight commander, Fernán Gómez de Guzmán. Ground down by exactions and Don Fernán's "fierce tyranny and cruelty," the people rose as one to kill him. When asked, in the play, who had done the deed, all made the famous reply: "Fuenteovejuna did it!" The judge sent to discover the truth and punish the guilty abdicated his responsibility to the monarchs: "Since it is so hopeless to reach any conclusion, either pardon them or kill the entire population."[62] Magnanimous Ferdinand chose the first course, giving the 1619 play its optimistic ending. Lope blamed the incident entirely on the knight commander's pride and lust, neglecting economic and political motives which might not have played as well on the boards.

The reality, as research has begun to demonstrate, is that the rebellion may not have been as spontaneous as has been assumed. Twenty-three years earlier, Fuenteovejuna had been encouraged by Cordova to rise against the Order of Alcántara, only then to be given by Enrique IV to Calatrava. Its knight commander may have been personally favorable to Isabella during the civil war, but the leadership of Calatrava stood with Doña Juana. With this leverage, Cordova managed to get Isabella to concede, in a decree dated 20 April 1476, that Fuenteovejuna was under its jurisdiction. To make this concession into a reality, a rising was planned for dawn, two days later, when three *veinticuatros* from Cordova would be on hand.[63] It is also probable that Alfonso de Aguilar, *alcalde mayor* of the city, was a driving force behind the presumed conspiracy, owing to his fierce competition over properties with the order.[64] Over the next few days, Cordova's council started making good its claim through a hail of lengthy resolutions and letters.[65] It is not clear exactly when in 1476 Diego de Merlo arrived to take up his post as corregidor; but, since he is not mentioned in documents concerning the rising, he must not have been in the city at the time, nor does he play any part in the immediate investigations or the litigation which followed.

Ferdinand and Isabella dispatched an investigator in May (which would indicate that Merlo was still not in place), but took no action on his report, probably because Cordova had sufficient military force to hold onto its restored property, whereas the young couple then had little to spare. They waited to reaffirm the order's possession of the town the following year, after the new grand master of Calatrava joined Isabella's faction.[66] The assault is tidied up in the play by leaving out the riot with its attendant looting, since a single murder, properly justified, makes for a satisfying script; but the end result in Castile, typically, was a series of mundane lawsuits. As late as 1495 a corregidor was still being petitioned to recover property for the knight commander's children, Juan, Carlos, and the nun, María San Bernardo.[67] Fuenteovejuna was placed in the hands of a lieutenant of the *asistente* of Seville until the courts could adjudicate to whom it belonged. The Order of Calatrava eventually won the suit, so to retain its town Cordova had, in the end, to pay a handsome price.[68]

Inspecting the clergy

From the vantage-point of corregidores the life of the clergy was not edifying, for what ends up being heard in a courtroom tends towards the seamy. Judging solely from legal actions, ecclesiastical life might appear no more than stolen benefices, unpaid bills, and rampant immorality. Only a bit of the spiritual regeneration slowly taking place shows up in records involving corregidores. A church council, meeting at Seville in 1478, restated such desirable norms as celibacy, proper dress, residence at an assigned post, and regular visitations by bishops.[69] The total failure of this modest effort at internal reform led to a significant role for the *asistente*. When he met with the canons during June and July of 1503, bad customs still flourished. That August he dispatched his lieutenant to inspect all of Seville's churches and monasteries, giving the lieutenant a mandate that the secular arm be used "with all rigor" to assure churchmen were tonsured and wore decent habits.[70]

Elsewhere, the corregidor of Olmedo was instructed by the crown to accompany an official who was being sent to reform the customs at the monastery of S. Vicente. The corregidor of Burgos also provided protection in March 1495 to a delegation come to inspect an abbey; and later the same year commander Juan Alonso de la Mota was in Santiago to reform the church and hospice of the Order of Santiago. He ran into serious opposition, which necessitated his obtaining active help from the corregidor of Talavera de la Reina.[71] At times the line between the clerical and the secular was more blurred. The corregidor of Málaga, himself armed with papal bulls from Innocent VIII and Alexander VI setting out qualifications for office, went on his own inspection tour in 1494 to make sure that non-ecclesiastics were excluded from posts in churches and monasteries.[72]

Weaknesses of the flesh

Inspection always involved the search for sexual improprieties, for corregidores had standing instructions to enforce clerical celibacy, under ordinances which specified that they had church approval, sanctioned by ecclesiastical congregations, to act on these matters. Priests who kept *barraganas* ("concubines," as female companions were called) could expect reprimands. Isabella systematically followed through the assault on this offense, the only clerical social misdeed singled out in ordinances for corregidores.[73] A royal official at Calahorra, for example, was reinstructed by the crown in 1488 to punish concubines wherever found; and, in 1500, Isabella went out of her way to chide the bishop of Calahorra that in his diocese, "the greater part of the clergy are said to be and are in concubinage publicly and if our justice intervenes to punish them they revolt..."[74] The queen's preoccupation with the subject was fully in line with the wish of her subjects, but the failing was difficult to correct. At Avila, a corregidor heard charges that fourteen sacristans and chaplains were married, yet took no action. A corregidor at Toledo alleged he feared his life would be in danger if he dared act against the chaplain of the church of La Sisla, who openly flaunted breaking his vow.[75]

Caution seemed indicated, but corregidores were given a strong personal motivation to persist, since prosecuting moral failings offered excellent opportunities to collect fines. A storm was raised in Segovia when one official went ahead and attempted to carry out the standing orders to the letter. The corregidor was Día Sánchez de Quesada who, as has been noted, stirred controversy wherever he settled. During April 1484 this pugnacious functionary made a series of night raids. His men kicked in the doors of rectories and homes, seizing all females found within. The dean and chapter protested, as did lesser clerics, who bombarded the royal court with complaints that "honest women" did not deserve such vile treatment. In the face of bitter opposition not much was accomplished, other than enriching Sánchez de Quesada, who extorted what he could before dropping all charges.[76] Obviously, then, no corregidor by himself could hope to accomplish significant change in the moral climate.

In January 1495, the crown launched an all-out attempt, analyzed by García Oro, to reform the independent church of Toledo. This struggle, which was to last almost a decade, brought into play all the talents of Jiménez de Cisneros, the new archbishop, who let the cathedral chapter know that he intended to reform its lax ways.[77] Corregidor Pedro de Castilla was urged to begin to apply the law on concubinage, backed up by a commission which reported in September that serious deficiencies were found in both personal and ceremonial life.[78] The Royal Council gradually became aware that a revolt was simmering. It was said some clerics maintained they would die before they kissed the hand of the archbishop. Alarmed, the Council wrote to its corregidor on 29 March 1496, ordering that he undertake an investigation in the utmost secrecy. Who was in the conspiracy? Were they planning to call for aid from the pope? Juan de Valladares gave the investigator a full account: Toledo's clerics were planning a wide appeal to all the clergy of Castile, for they did not like having a friar as their archbishop, nor did they want him meddling in communal life. Secret meetings had been held in various spots, notably Seville and Guadalajara, with one especially dangerous result that Alfonso de Albornoz was being dispatched to Rome. The appeal to the pope threatened a recently approved subsidy, so the crown had its agents seize Alfonso de Albornoz upon his disembarking in Italy. Cisneros decided not to press on blindly, but to act instead in a conciliatory manner. His canonical visitors, sent out in 1496, cautiously made allusion only to possible transgressions.[79]

A visitation team which studied the situation in Toledo at a calmer point was allowed to be more forthright. During 1499 it was given access, for the first time, to files collected by Gómez Manrique covering 1478 to 1490, which were in the safekeeping of the corregidor's old secretary. Here was irrefutable evidence, according to García Oro, of sodomy and other irregularities, inculpating twenty-five members of the chapter in crudely vivid testimony.[80] Cisneros suppressed the report. In 1503 yet another visitation team was sent out with a letter of commission that the guilty be punished, causing a great tumult to be raised anew as city dignitaries, under clerical prompting, took a stand against the commission. The upshot was that Cisneros again proved conciliatory, which is contrary to the bulldog image that clings to his public personality. He was prepared to accept reality to the extent of drawing up a letter of concord with the chapter in 1504 that effectively annulled whatever small degree of reform had been accomplished.[81]

Degrees of immunity

As the troubles in Toledo indicate, clerics had to be handled gingerly because they had unlimited potential for agitating an easily aroused populace. Ecclesiastical courts did not hesitate to fight to keep under their jurisdiction all business remotely concerning their own. Pulgar tells an illuminating story about a disturbance at Trujillo in 1486 where a culprit, who had committed an unspecified misdeed, claimed that he was tonsured and so might be judged only by a church court. The lines of who was, and who was not, a cleric were so loosely drawn that the proper haircut and a smattering of Latin prayers might

suffice. Corregidor Lope Sánchez del Castillo's decision to disregard
the claim of privilege caused agitated clerics to take up a large cross,
which they carried round Trujillo while calling upon the populace to
defend the faith. Aroused by the tumult, a crowd charged the house of
the corregidor, broke into the cells, and released the prisoner. "Seeing
how royal justice was offended," the corregidor denounced the fathers
to the court, which sent a local captain with men under arms to arrest
principal rioters, whom he ordered to be executed, and to expel the
meddling clerics from the realms.[82]

Sanctuary was an equally sensitive issue, and one that had to be
faced in Badajoz in 1487, when corregidor Francisco Maldonado
went into the monastery of S. Trinidad to capture suspects. The vicar-
general was incensed, but limited himself to a vigorous complaint.[83] A
struggle which broke out at Salamanca during January 1485 was
fought more tenaciously, after Pedro García de Cotes and his *alcalde*
entered a church to drag out a criminal. Canon Fernando de
Maluenda excommunicated the corregidor and, to make his point
more strongly, laid an interdict on the city. If García de Cotes had
hoped for support from the council he would have been mistaken, for
the *regidores* just wanted the ban removed. Early in February, the
Royal Council dispatched a Dominican father to reason with the
canon and then, when his mission failed, relied upon the cleric's
superiors to bring an end to the drama.[84] The frequent, and
inevitable, struggles over sanctuary went on elsewhere, as corregidores continued to enter shrines and seize troublemakers, whatever
the protest.[85]

Struggle for preferment

It is not necessary to set out in much detail the clergy's vast wealth to
comprehend why the struggle for preferment was fierce: the archbishop of Toledo enjoyed 80,000 ducats income per year in the
sixteenth-century, making him second in wealth only to the emperor;
and, as a whole, the Spanish church in that period produced an
annual income estimated by Elliott to be over 6 million ducats.[86]
Conflict over who would reap this harvest thrust the corregidor into
the heart of the institution's economic life. Why did the new abbot of
S. María de Valdedios not pay a pension due to an old monk?[87] Would
a cleric in Murcia be able to regain a revenue – his first fruits –
improperly taken by the cardinal vice-chancellor?[88] When would the

corregidor of León carry out the order to return the Observant Brothers of S. Francisco to their house?[89] How long would it take at León to restore a curate to the church of S. Miguel, after he was ejected by force of arms by the canon of Palencia, acting in the name of a cleric resident in Rome?[90] If it were true that Padre Rodrigo de Valderrábano had been ejected, under threat, from his parochial church, would the corregidor of Ciudad Real be able to put it right?[91] And when would a bishop in Avila, a cleric in Salamanca, an abbot in Toro, or monks in Valladolid and Burgos be restored to their rightful holdings?[92]

Clerics were thus quite willing, when it suited them, to invite the royal official into the midst of quarrels. An *asistente* of Burgos was called upon in 1479 to adjudicate a struggle over fishing rights between two monasteries, and a corregidor at Madrid was brought into an argument concerning grain mills on the Jarama river, claimed in 1489 by opposing houses.[93] Lacking a personal stake in the communities to which they were sent, corregidores might often as not support clerics against municipalities. Commoners of Zamora were forced to pay taxes to the monastery of S. Clara de Tordesillas, despite protest; and when a monastery in Málaga thought municipal bakeries were prejudicing its exclusive rights, it relied upon the corregidor to protect its monopoly.[94]

Although turning to the secular power in time of need, the body of clerics jealously defended church immunities. The question was squarely presented by Pope Sixtus IV in 1476 concerning Tórtoles de Esgueva (Zaragoza), which Pedro Férriz, the cardinal-bishop of Tarazona, held under his sole power and jurisdiction. His only obligations to the crown, the obstinate prelate claimed, were to give fidelity and to pay traditional contributions. He, therefore, objected strongly to the intrusion of any royal officials into his jurisdiction. Responding to the cardinal-bishop's plea for support, the pope declared forthrightly that church officers had absolute temporal domination over their vassals.[95] The monarchs found it difficult to present resistance at that moment, since they needed the pope's help on other matters; but, beginning in 1480, corregidores were mandated to defend royal law and jurisdiction wherever challenged by ecclesiastical pretensions. The church's judges and estate managers were not allowed usurpations, and should a corregidor run into their opposition he was to go directly to the royal court for a remedy.[96]

Repair of the rift was accomplished in 1485 by Cardinal Mendoza, a loyal servant of the queen. To oppose claims made by the archbishop of Toledo, Mendoza advised Isabella to state that, even though the great prelate maintained jurisdiction on his land *by act*, she had a higher theoretic claim *by right*.[97] Having established a basis for future royal action to her satisfaction, the queen could tactfully neglect pressing on, for the moment.[98] Clearly then, there were sharp limits recognized by the crown on the amount of interference permitted it in church affairs. A prior of the Order of S. Juan de Jerusalén, who received his village of Consuegra in 1499, was allowed to deny outside corregidores first instance jurisdiction.[99] At Ciudad Real, both the corregidor and a Royal Council member who set out to investigate a problem in Almagro during 1492 were totally beaten back by clerical privilege, which made sure that neither official dared claim to render justice or even to hold a hearing.[100]

Corregidores were useful for maintaining the crown's interests and for mediating quarrels between contending factions; but it is wise to avoid projecting back in time a prestige that would only come with the centuries. The Catholic Sovereigns checked abuses, yet did not expect to pry over-much power out of well-groomed hands, power which could then be independently used by mere bureaucratic functionaries. Without doubt, there was certainly little fear on estates of thoroughgoing outside meddling. The mighty took full advantage of their privileged access to the crown to bypass any corregidor regarding disputes outside seignorial lands by appealing directly over his head. Major issues involving prelates or aristocrats always found their way to the Royal Council or wound up at the foot of the throne, for justice and good government remained a prince's responsibility, despite delegation.

7

The end of *convivencia*: Jews, Christians, and Muslims

"I have caused great calamities and depopulated towns, lands, provinces and kingdoms," Isabella wrote her ambassador in Rome, who was to defend the Castilian Inquisition by telling the pope that she had done all "for the sake of Christ and His Holy Mother."[1] Any such mono-causal explanation for the policies of the *Reyes Católicos* was instinctively distrusted by Francisco Guicciardini, a canny Florentine, who saw enough of Ferdinand when serving as ambassador to the Castilian court to observe with cynical admiration: "This is what made the enterprises of his Catholic Majesty so glorious – they were always undertaken for his own security or power, but often they would appear to be done either to strengthen the Christian faith or to defend the church."[2]

Whatever the mixture of motives, few foresaw before they came to power that Ferdinand, together with Isabella, would completely destroy the last of an ancient Iberian tradition of *convivencia*, which had permitted creeds to coexist. Much of the survival of the remnants of this toleration depended upon prompt action by corregidores. They were often all that protected the separated communities from the hostility of the clergy, the brutality of the populace, and the envy of the urban oligarchy. We trace during the new reign the gradual, often imperceptible, shift of the royal official from protector of Jews to their persecutor, and from adjudicator of Muslim rights to their foe.

At first, many individuals who suffered from prejudice and riot actually hoped for better times from Isabella's advent. With good reason Jews, New Christians (*conversos* or *marranos*, as they were variously called), and *Mudéjares* (Muslims within Christian territory) preferred any slight promise of firm government to the anarchy of faction. It was necessary for corregidores to assure the minimal survival of the non-Christian communities by, for example, safeguarding access to food supplies in the face of vindictive acts. Olmedo closed down the only street which opened directly upon the market-place from the Jewish quarter. One corrigedor reversed this ruling in 1480, then another had to do so six years later.[3] The *asistente* of Seville would not allow Jews to be hindered in 1480 from freely bringing animals into the city to have them slaughtered there, according to ritual.[4] Likewise, the official at Segovia heeded complaints from Jews in 1488 that they were being prohibited from buying foodstuffs at accustomed hours. They had been told by *regidores* that they could no longer buy fowl or meat at hours when Christians shopped or purchase fish on Friday.[5] That same year, Avila's corregidor also had to warn his city that it must not impede Jews and Mudejars from selling provisions, although his stance was then weakened by his acceding to local demands that meat be kept on the prohibited list.[6] At Medina del Campo, Jews had to look to the royal official in 1489 to protect them against new ordinances forbidding them to sell bread, firewood, and carbon.[7]

In 1490 Jewish merchants were being prevented from trading at fairs. Bilbao would not let them freely land goods for the great fair at Medina del Campo, inventively imposing a fine of 2,000 *mrs* on any Jew caught sleeping in town overnight. Lodgings were few, and dangerous, outside the limits, which was the point of the harassment. Acting under orders from the constable of Castile, the corregidor of Vizcaya forced the *regidores* of Bilbao to revoke the legislation.[8]

Those few Jews who clung to urban centers required constant protection because they were so visible. After bloody pogroms in the cities during 1391, most Jews had scattered to the safety and obscurity of some 400 small communities.[9] Urban areas, such as Trujillo or Segovia, thereafter averaged only fifty Jewish families.[10] By choice, most Jews lived within defensible enclaves, as did the Muslims. Each settlement (*kahal*, in Hebrew; *judería*, in Castilian; or *aljama*, in Arabic) had its own legislative council, executive officer, and magistrates, who judged internal matters according to the laws of respective faiths. In April 1487 Abrahán Seneor complained, in the name of the Segovian *kahal*, that the friar Alonso de la Peña was inventing tales to whip up the hostility of the Christian populace. Ruy González de Puebla was instructed by the royal court that, if this were true, "it was a scandal to the city and a disservice to God." The corregidor was to attend sermons at the monastery of S. Cruz and to send a full clean copy of what he heard to the Royal Council.[11]

Agitation engenders assault – an *alcalde* of the Holy Brotherhood,

Sancho de San Martín, broke into a synagogue in Zamora that same month, injuring worshippers. Rabbi Abráhan Caba petitioned the royal court that the corregidor punish the assailant.[12] The situation at Zamora worsened after friar Juan de Santo Domingo's thunderings against usury in 1491 led to the passage of an ordinance that no Christians be permitted to enter the *kahal*, nor any Jew to leave. Acknowledging that residents would starve if this edict were allowed to stand, the crown ordered Gutiérrez de Carvajal to see the law struck down, and to check if this preacher of the Bull of Crusade had strayed from his assigned topic.[13] Given this constant flow of directives that communities should be shielded, it is not certain why protection was gradually withdrawn.

The turn to repression

It is likely that Isabella did not start out with a clear vision of her policy towards the religious question.[14] In 1478 the crown was still granting permission for Jews to take their judicial oaths on the Torah, and Muslims on the Koran.[15] Enactments concerning judicial procedures for Avila, a city with 7,000 persons, of whom perhaps half were Jewish (the largest concentration in Castile), bore all the marks of traditional policy. So many malicious lawsuits were being brought there by Christians that the corregidor and his judges were rebuked late in the year for not first checking facts before letting suits go to court. He was ordered to impose a fine of 10,000 *mrs* upon anyone found to have instituted a baseless action.[16]

There were faint signs elsewhere that policy might, however, take a turn towards repression. In a letter from Seville, dated August 1478, Jerónimo de Valdivieso, corregidor of Cáceres, was admonished, unexpectedly, that it was such a scandal to allow the faiths to live together that he was to encourage Jews to move to one single area by selling lots and houses at bargain prices.[17] With the War of Succession completely behind her by 1480, Isabella convoked a Cortes at Toledo where, only half a century before, mobs roaming narrow streets had slaughtered the innocent. The hostile provisions of a succession of late medieval parliaments calling for the segregation of Jews (and Muslims) were revived.[18]

Royal emissaries were central to implementing and policing the regulations, should the crown actually choose to follow through with a thoroughgoing repression. Rodriguez Álvarez Maldonado was dispatched to Avila with a specific commission to draw up fresh boundaries. During 1480 he consolidated two districts into one intolerably narrow Jewish quarter, with few points of egress.[19] Rodriguez Álvarez Maldonado decreed that all tanneries and leather treatment sites were to be removed from the area. So far as the Jews were concerned, his allegation that smells were a hazard to health and the skins a source of filth were secondary to his desire to deprive them of income.[20] To stabilize their diminished fortune Jews petitioned the crown, with some success, that corregidores protect the quarter from further, unlicensed, encroachment. When someone blocked Moisés Tamanno's houses with two rows of barriers, making it impossible for him to use the street to sell his goods, corregidor Alfonso Portocarrero responded to royal approval of Tamanno's plea by removing the barriers.[21] The question of the narrowness of Avila's ghetto eventually came under general review by its corregidor, who was asked by the Jews to reopen gates that once gave access to the river, but by shirking his responsibility, Portocarero managed to avoid having to render a decision before his term ran out.[22] The cause of delay in this, and other, instances may be undisclosed bribery, or a deepseated unease.

The confusing nature of royal instructions did not then, and does not now, fit neatly into a single category of conviction or opportunism. Through coercive legislation, the monarchs conveyed the message that persecution was to be the new order of the day; yet corregidores continued to be ordered to protect minorities from the hostility of municipal government, the taunts of preachers, and the brutalities of the mob. The conflicting psychological pressures corregidores faced might be understood by adopting a theory popularized by R. D. Laing.[23] What he calls the "double bind" works as follows: one person conveys to another, by means of verbal or written instructions, that he should do something, and, at the same time, on another level (often by means of inference), that he should or should not do something completely different. The situation is then "sealed off" by a further injunction forbidding him to get out of the situation or even to dissipate the tension by commenting on the conflict. The servant, relative, or lover, is thus placed in an untenable position. The result will be a confused or "neurotic" response. Projecting this slender theory, if it can bear the weight, from an individual to a group, corregidores were put into the "double bind" of officially defending by command those who, by deeper indications, were to be persecuted.

The queen of Castile insisted that "her" Jews be protected at the same time as she undermined their status. The corregidor of Trujillo was ordered to investigate allegations that one Jew had a house outside the *kahal*[24]. That was in 1489, the same year the corregidor of Soria was urged by his superiors to respond to complaints against a single blacksmith who still had a shop beyond the ghetto. The presence of horses being shod by a Jew had been condemned by a priest at the nearby church of S. Gil as a dishonor to divine service.[25] Yet an orderly application, in this manner, of the harsh Toledo decrees was difficult, because at any moment the crown might shift ground under its representatives.

Madrid's commerce had received a hard blow as a consequence of the first wave of repression. Ferdinand, wanting to do something in 1482 about depopulation and declining sales, authorized the corregidor to allow small shops in the Plaza Mayor, so long as proprietors returned to the ghetto at night. The Madrid council, outraged, asked that no action be taken locally until the king had heard from them.[26] In Seville, upon the exposure of an alleged conspiracy by New Christians to have inquisitors assassinated, the Holy Office took advantage of the tension to order, with the approbation of the municipal council, that all Jews in the area sell their houses and leave within thirty days after 1 January 1483. When this news reached the heads of the Jewish community at Jerez de la Frontera two days later, they rushed to the municipal council to beg protection. The city dispatched a *veinticuatro* to Seville to ascertain if Jerez was included in the zone of expulsion. Jews not only remained under the protection of the council, after his report was delivered on 21 January, but the *regidores* wrote to the monarchs in their favor.[27] The key figure in protecting the Jewish community through that tense month was the corregidor, Rodrigo Juan de Robles. According to a local chronicler, Benito de Cárdenas, the corregidor had become disturbed over the extent of economic disaster caused in Seville by the upheaval. To eliminate similar panic selling in his own community, he expressly forbade anyone to enter the *kahal* to buy out the Jews, at the penalty of a public whipping and incarceration. Juan de Robles managed to stabilize the situation until the following January, when the queen sent a representative formally to suspend the expulsion order.[28]

At Medina del Campo, Francisco de Luzón dutifully confined the Jews to their quarter. When Abrahán Segrano asked in the name of his community, during 1490, that shops be permitted in the main plaza, the corregidor was suddenly authorized by the crown to give approval. This shift did not please the monastery of S. Francisco, whose monks agitated so strongly that an inspector had to be sent in 1491 by the Royal Council. He decided that the decision had to be reversed to end turmoil.[29] It became increasingly necessary, in light of countervailing policies, to bring in more such outsiders to do the work for corregidores caught in crosscurrents. The ghetto at Palencia, a city with 7,500 inhabitants, was designed with malice by a tough local judge, *licenciado* Segura. At the petition of the Jews that the narrow area they were given was too small, Pedro Gómez de Setúbal was authorized in May 1491 to improve the design. Segura ignored the corregidor, and when the Jews resumed their protest the judge imprisoned the messenger they sent to the royal court. So frightened, or confused, was the ineffectual corregidor by then that the crown had to dispatch an emissary to Palencia, the following month, to take on the task.[30]

The golden goose

It never proved simple for the crown to decide what to tell its local officials to do about Jews, because of the valuable services they rendered, and the wealth commanded by a few. A first sign of the financial pressure to come was the load put on Avila after *asistente* Juan del Campo was notified in 1475 that four investigators would arrive to take a fresh count. The accountants struck fear in the community by alleging that Jewish officials held their posts illegally, and that they had rendered inaccurate accountings.[31] Disregarding protests, a later corregidor forced the community to pay supplements for the period 1473–7.[32] Municipalities, outraged that the crown took what it wanted, but blocked them from direct access to assets for their own mounting tax needs, seized property on any pretext. When several Jews in Segovia complained that *regidor* Juan de Talavera was breaking into their homes to impound goods, the corregidor on the scene in 1485 assigned an *alcalde* to investigate and then send the results off in a sealed packet to the Royal Council.[33] At Aranda de Duero it was left to the corregidor in 1487 to ascertain if dowry goods of Bien Venida had been improperly taken when property of her husband, Yucef de Soto, was seized.[34]

Faced with royal vacillation, corregidores began cooperating with jurisdictions to fleece Jews. The Jewish community at Murcia petitioned Juan Pérez de Barradas in 1491 that they had contributed fully to the Holy Brotherhood assessment, but he turned down their plea that they should not be charged a second time. By then there were few Jews left in Cáceres, which did not stop its corregidor from ruling that, so long as they had assets there, even if their residence was elsewhere, they were obliged to provide one of the forty lancers due from the town.[35] The screw was turned even more tightly at Jerez de la Frontera in 1490. Juan de Robles, who seven years earlier had taken initiatives to protect Jews, now obliged merchants who long before had left the area to pay a second set of taxes on merchandise they had sold when resident in the town.[36] The monarchs attempted to restrain such unofficial connivance of their officials with municipalities, even in the last, expensive, stage of the war when urban cooperation was most necessary. Yuçe Cohen, his wife, and their nephew Davi were systematically overtaxed by Cárceres. When Davi dared to protest in 1491 two *regidores* had him thrown in jail, where he languished a month until released by the sovereigns, who admonished the corregidor that all the proper taxes and assessments had been paid.[37]

The expulsion

The Granada War intensified public pressure to take action against non-Christians, while at the same time reducing exploitable Jewish resources to the point where the community became less valuable to the kingdom. Areas not in immediate proximity to the arena of the war which attempted to expel Jews were, at first, rebuked by the crown.[38] Burgos tried to limit the number of Jews resident in the city, proposing in 1486 to expel any couple who had married within the previous three years. When Andrés de Ribera made no response to the *kahal*'s pleas, the Royal Council called urban representatives to appear before it to answer for the legislation, bypassing their *asistente*.[39] During 1488 Valmaseda (Vizcaya) expelled its handful of families. After their desperate petitioning, the crown ordered their return but the corregidor of Vizcaya, Lope Rodríguez de Logroño, did nothing to help. He could easily have intervened in local affairs, had he chosen to do so, because during the previous year municipalities under assault from aristocrats had all given him the right to override the charters of privilege (*fueros*). The royal court seems not to have pressed him to do so, eventually contenting itself with an order that he get Valmaseda to compensate the expellees for the loss of their property.[40] It is understandable that corregidores stopped protecting Jews when all signs pointed towards increased repression.

Groundwork for a final act of general exclusion was laid during the sensational trial of Jews and Christians accused of ritually murdering the so-called "Holy Child of La Guardia." Charges that a youth had been crucified, and a consecrated wafer abused, turned out to be difficult to prove, in part because no Toledo family ever came forward to claim they were missing a child. The trial was moved out of Toledo to the more sympathetic and reliable environment of Avila, where the absence of proof that a crime had actually been committed would be less troubling. For maximum publicity value a *consulata de fe* was assembled, bringing together lay and clerical experts, with Álvaro de Santisteban, the town's long-term corregidor, placed at the committee's head.[41] Allowing him so prominent a role in the show trial indicates royal connivance. When the brief of condemnation, more a tragic story than a judicial verdict, was presented and distributed the emotional impact was profound.[42] Public opinion was prepared to look for retribution.

The blow fell on 31 March 1492.[43] Jews unwilling to accept baptism were granted four months, by order of the monarchs and the inquisitor general, to put their affairs in order before departing. The bitterly anti-Semitic curate of Los Palacios professed himself moved by the sight of the People of Israel leaving "as if from the captivity of Egypt," tired, hungry, and beset by robbers.[44] Improvised armadas were hastily assembled to ferry out the exiled. At Cartagena, for example, Juan de Negrón had the lucrative contract to put together the principal fleet under the direction of the corregidor, Juan Pérez de Barradas, who was charged with coordinating the fevered labors.[45] The last ships sailed from varied ports at dawn on Friday, 3 August 1492. Christopher Columbus noted in his log that his voyage was delayed till then by the crowding at the harborside. Leaving Palos, his ships swung into the Saltés and passed La Rábida, where his three vessels turned west and a single accompanying craft, carrying the last of the Jews, turned east.[46] On shore, corregidores would be kept busy for years sorting out property and hearing lawsuits regarding debts.

The ejection of the Jews was a heaven-sent opportunity for debtors to get out of paying obligations by crying usury. High interest rates during pre-modern times are typically found wherever currency was unstable and life insecure for the lender. It was easy to avoid anti-usury legislation at the start by concealing the interest, with the connivance of the borrower, but dangerous at the end, when the debtor had good reason to confess his sin.[47] Corregidores were alerted to refer all usury charges to the royal court for settlement.[48] Isaac Abenzemerro petitioned the Royal Council in May 1492 that many who owed money were refusing to pay, so the corregidor of Badajoz was ordered to hear his complaint promptly and to report results. In August, Francisco de Luzón, corregidor of Medina del Campo, was reminded that lawful obligations should be respected.[49] There was profit to be made out of the chaos. Two natives of Segovia petitioned the Royal Council in November that they had been friendly with Jews and that, desiring to do a good deed at the time of leave-taking, had bought the right to collect obligations. What they wanted was the corregidor's aid in getting debts paid, since "none was let at usurious terms."[50] A year later, a debtor at Villena was still maintaining to his governor that he would never pay a debt he considered usurious.[51]

The expulsion edict specified that Jews could freely dispose of their property. Isabella was furious with the corregidor of León, Juan de Portugal, who extorted 30,000 ducats (11,250,000 mrs) "protection money" and seized property without pretext. Día Sánchez de Quesada, the tough corregidor to whom the crown frequently turned for quick results, was dispatched from his post in Segovia to deal severely with Juan and his subordinates.[52] They were made examples, although to little effect. The Jewish community ejected from Cádiz made it clear, through pleas transmitted to their former royal official, that they had been thoroughly robbed.[53] Even with fear of punishment, or good intentions, to spur them on, how effective could corregidores have been? The expulsion edict under which they had to operate was poorly drawn, indicating the haste in which it must have been written. It also betrays optimism about the numbers who would accept baptism, and while it may never be known exactly how many Jews decided to abandon their homes, estimates by historians and demographers range from 75,000 to over double that number.[54] Atypically for the sovereigns, little advance thought had been given to the problems of a wholesale evacuation.

Goods held in safekeeping by corregidores were hostage to debts, real or invented.[55] All obligations had to be satisfied before the parties were permitted to go.[56] There were debts in 1493 to worry the corregidor of Badajoz, while at Madrid Jewish property was held to satisfy the claims of a former corregidor.[57] Zag Cohen was still in prison at the end of May 1493, where he would be kept by the corregidor of Huete, on the express orders of the Royal Council until he paid 400,000 *mrs* to the count of Lemos.[58] The following year the corregidor of Valladolid, Alonso Ramírez de Villaescusa, was petitioned by the widow of an *audiencia* judge who complained that her 3,000 *mrs* annual income from former Jewish property was not being paid.[59] In January, that corregidor sold off all remaining communal assets in the hope of putting the problems to rest. Conscientious as always, Dr Ramírez de Villaescusa brought the judge charged with control of these goods back in September 1495, once it became clear that much was still left undone, and ordered him not to delegate any work.[60] Corregidores continued to have to deal with such problems all that year.[61]

The insistence in the edict of expulsion that strict legality be observed in the sale of property, and that all debts be paid to the Jews, was something of a deception, in view of the queen's simultaneous prohibition against removing gold and silver from the kingdom. Only bills of exchange, payable abroad by Genoese bankers, were authorized. It was understandable that, given the protectionist economic theory dominant at the time, the state did not wish to allow the depletion of its bullion reserves. Individuals forced rapidly to exchange real property for unreliable paper naturally attempted to use influence and subterfuge to get around the prohibition. The corregidor at Ciudad Real during 1492 fell under suspicion that he had allowed Jews to transport coins across the western border, although upon subsequent investigation he was cleared of charges.[62] Peasants in Plasencia found a buried leather bag full of precious metal, presumably left behind by Jews who fled to Portugal, intending to dig it up at a later time. The corregidor put the bag in the possession of a "trustworthy person" until disposition should be made.[63] What incidents of concealment or smuggling were uncovered became the occasion for the crown cynically to disavow all letters of exchange carried away by the unlucky exiles, visiting the sins of the few on the many.[64]

Apparently sincere prayers were offered up at court that all Jews might convert for, dismayed at the unexpectedly large number who chose to leave, the monarchs made strenuous efforts to retain useful families. Rowdy elements in the populace, not about to make the same fine distinctions between fresh converts and once-hated Jews, freely took revenge. The duke of Alburquerque, acting for the Royal Council in June 1493, told the corregidor of Segovia to insist villagers of

Cuéllar promptly return all they had seized from the newly baptized.[65] The carnival mood abroad in the country did not make it easy
to have obligations honored. The word went down in December to the
corregidor of Atienza that he make sure that debts owed to a new
convert, Francisco de Aguilar, be respected. Alfonso Pérez Coronel
struggled with the corregidor of Avila throughout 1493 about who
was responsible for bills left by his expelled mother and brothers.[66]

The Inquisition

Exiles might return, until 1499, if they could prove that they were
baptized abroad, or had accepted baptism at the borders. Some fairly
large sums were restored to give those who came home reasons not to
doubt the soundness of their decision.[67] Regaining property and
clearing debris away from households were only the first hurdles faced
by converts. Soon enough the calibre of their adopted faith might be
carefully tested, and it would go hard for anyone under suspicion of
having relapsed. The corregidor of Avila was instructed, in a typical
edict, that anyone who reverted to Judaism be executed.[68] The
greater threat, however, came from the "Holy Office." The Castilian
Royal Inquisition had its own spy network; an enforcement apparatus
for secretly arresting any under suspicion; cells to hold suspects; places
to store movable property; and courts to try as many cases as need be.
There was thus little apparent place for corregidores to insert
themselves into the mighty struggle to control the populace, for
ordinances say only that cooperation is to be extended to constables of
the inquisitorial tribunal.[69] The limited nature of this instruction
obscures the reality that the investigation into religious practices was
instituted, in part, to resolve an urban clash over inequities of power
and wealth, crucial to the success of the mandate of corregidores to
pacify jurisdictions.

Continuing turmoil over the status of New Christians (*conversos* or
marranos) had greatly complicated Isabella's quest to bring as many
municipalities as possible to her side when the succession still hung in
the balance. Her initial answer had been to rely upon pre-existent
urban leadership, assuring the adherence of New Christians to her
cause through reconfirmation of their rights, in complete disregard of
the clamor from the street.[70] The old order was fully restored by 1477,
when most dispossessed New Christians were reinstated on municipal
councils. Questionable cases were put to the decision of Pedro García

de Cotes, a trustworthy individual with much experience as a corregidor.[71] At the same time as the displaced regained their posts, a more comprehensive solution to ending continuing disturbances was initiated by the Catholic Sovereigns through reviving an investigation, previously started by Enrique IV and then dropped, into the quality of the faith of suspect New Christians. The crown anticipated thereby that Old Christians would feel reassured that their complaints were being accorded serious consideration.

The inquest was born at Seville in 1478, after Isabella and Ferdinand were presented with accusations that descendants of converts were covertly practising their ancestral faith. The monarchs apparently became convinced that an "emergency" existed which required immediate action. As the investigation spread, it sought out cooperative witnesses, some of whom were corregidores who gave testimony in their private role as prominent personages in the communities to which they were sent. Alonso de Cáceres was helpful to inquisitors struggling to establish themselves in Ciudad Real. The corregidor, his wife Mencia, and their daughter Isabel de Santa Cruz, testified for the prosecution a number of times. He proved especially useful in the key case of Juan de Fez, tax farmer for both the crown and the archbishop of Toledo. During the trial, which opened in 1483, Alonso de Cáceres testified that he had known the accused twenty-five years, and that, during that time, Juan had bought kosher meat from a Jew who sold to many New Christians. So minor a charge, by itself, would bring no one to the flames, but added significantly to this flimsy case. Juan fled, was captured, and brought back with the expectation that he would confess what he was expected to confess, and was burnt along with his wife. By the end of the first round of questioning, at least one member of each of the fifty or more New Christian households in the town was tainted, and many families were on their way to being destroyed.[72]

Inquisitors were now ready to move on to Toledo, where help could be expected from Gómez Manrique, who had frequently expressed anti-convert sentiments. The Christian poet Juan de Valladolid had been, typically, slandered by him as "the best of the Hebrews."[73] To do justice to Manrique, he had shown exquisite tact maneuvering between hostile factions facing one another within the swollen *regimiento*. (When Enrique IV settled with the city in 1462, he allowed New Christians to be displaced, then, reversing himself nine years later, the king reinstated all the old officials, but without eliminating their replacements.)[74] The clerics arrived to issue their announcement of a forty-day "grace period," when all were obliged to come forward to confess, or to turn in others. There was, however, no way of knowing exactly what constituted an offense against orthodox Christian practice, until the first clear bill of particulars was published in 1500.[75] Many in the city of 38,000 inhabitants decided to resist imposition of the Holy Office. Two weeks passed without response to the edict.[76]

Then Manrique struck, announcing the discovery of a sensational plot set for Corpus Christi day. An anonymous informant revealed that when processions were out on all four great streets the inquisitors would be assassinated, along with the notables and "all the Christian people."[77] That September, an inquisitor actually was murdered in Zaragoza's cathedral.[78] Whatever the truth of the broadly drawn allegations concerning the conspiracy in Toledo, Manrique rounded up suspects, including his own lieutenant, the *bachiller* de la Torre – one of six principals charged in the plot – and seized arms.[79] Inquisitors invaded synagogues and coerced rabbis to pronounce anathemas upon any of their flock who would not denounce Judaizers. The grace period was extended, as a thoroughly frightened populace rushed to come forward to save themselves, or to do what they now saw as their duty.[80] As Toledo's tribunal prospered, a modest continuing role was found for the corregidor. His *alcalde mayor* took part in the *consulta de fe* sessions that set sentence after trial. Since the church was theoretically prohibited from spilling blood, the condemned was then "relaxed," as the euphemism put it, to the secular power for the grisly business of execution.[81]

In distinct contrast to Manrique, Iñigo López de Mendoza, first governor of Granada, of whom more will be said later in this chapter, was a man of wide toleration who did his best to protect New Christians and freshly converted Muslims from the Inquisition. Among the first investigated in the city of Granada were two constables, whom the corregidor refused to hand over, surely with Mendoza's connivance, claiming that he alone had jurisdiction in his *corregimiento*. The sovereigns summarily rejected this argument, with the tart observation that the Inquisition's terrain was everywhere, because all jurisdictions belong to the crown.[82] The Holy Office attempted to strike back at such meddling by insisting that municipal officials meet *its* qualifications to hold office. A royal ordinance was obtained in 1501 which decreed that no heretic, or child of a "reconciled" family into the first generation feminine, or second generation masculine, be appointed corregidor or placed on a municipal council.[83]

The expansion of the Inquisition's duties immensely increased jurisdictional overlap, which created some potential for the obstruction of the Holy Office's work by other magistrates. Courts were always in competition, since so much of the income of judges depended directly upon fines and fees. In 1485, a servant of the duke of Medina Sidonia relied upon the court of the *asistente* of Seville to get his property released from the Inquisition. The daughter of heretical parents in Valladolid appealed to Dr Alonso Ramírez de Villaescusa in 1492 to return some property, which he was willing to do. When Francisco de León made a claim on money owed him by a condemned heretic in 1495, he, too, looked to the court of the conscientious corregidor of Valladolid to pry funds out of the hands of the Inquisition's receiver of property.[84]

Despite confiscations, torture, burnings, imprisonments, and exquisite humiliations, the Inquisition never fulfilled all the fond hopes held for it by those old Christians who wished to see every last descendant of converts rooted out. The New Christians had too many friends in high places for that to happen. Dr Alonso Díaz de Montalvo, for example, was a New Christian who had served Enrique IV as corregidor at Murcia and Baeza, with a stay as *asistente* at Toledo. He specialized in assisting Ferdinand and Isabella with problems of urban administration, and gained enduring fame as compiler of their one comprehensive codification of law.[85] A more socially prominent career at court was carved out by Andrés de Cabrera, marquis of Moya, corregidor at Segovia for Enrique IV, who was an assiduous collector of urban posts at Seville. An opportune marriage to Beatriz de Bobadilla, friend and confidant of the queen, greatly enhanced his prospects. Isabella restored posts he had lost in Seville during riots against New Christians and installed him at her court. In recompense for his support to her at a critical moment, Isabella alienated Segovian land to Andrés de Cabrera, with 1,200 vassals.[86] Pedro Vaca, from an Aragonese convert family, was the powerful governor of the Marquesado of Villena from 1480 to 1487, and along the way picked up a lucrative position at Seville.[87]

Diego de Valera, also of convert descent, offers an example of the well-educated caballero who gives the lie to any notion that all were thick-headed warriors.[88] Throughout his life he composed excellent poetry and observant chronicles, for which he was well remunerated by patrons; and a long diplomatic career, in the service of three monarchs, took him to many foreign courts. He was the son of a doctor, Alonso (Chirino) García de Guadalajara, who sent him to be educated at the court of Juan II. Diego received his knighthood after battle, at the hands of his patron, the marquis of Santillana, and then used his early support for Ferdinand of Aragon during the Castilian succession struggle to achieve the dignity of joining the Royal Council. Diego de Valera was one of the carefully chosen men employed by Ferdinand and Isabella to bring cities under control. When serious rioting against New Christians broke out in Segovia, he was dispatched there to serve eleven months as corregidor, from 1479 to 1480. Fortifications blocking the gates were destroyed, and high fines set to cover the expense of the repression. It was undeniably galling to the aggrieved public to find themselves still governed by men drawn from the ranks of the enemy. Diego de Valera had a son, by María de Valencia, to whom he gave the English name Charles. After the family settled in Cuenca, at Puerto de Santa María, Charles became a *regidor*, ruler of the fortress, and then occupied the post of corregidor until 1505.[89] Later, long after Ferdinand and Isabella passed into memory, various New Christian families survived because friends obstructed efforts to eject them from office or seize all their assets.[90] Converts from the Islamic faith, and Muslims, were not nearly as fortunate in this respect.

The Mudejars

Somewhat less than 20,000 practising Muslims lived in Christian areas outside the kingdom of Granada.[91] It was a commonly held prejudice that these Mudejars (*Mudéjares*), as they were called, were prolific breeders, yet the only sizable community, at Murcia, was not growing.[92] Avila alone may have seen an increase, as evident from a long-running argument concerning assessments. Jews complained that the agreement with the Muslims about how much each community would contribute was no longer just, since their quarter of Avila was depleted, with only the poorest remaining, whereas, they alleged, the Muslims flourished and had "become rich." The queen intervened in 1479, through her corregidor Juan Flores, who froze collections until taxes might be restructured.[93]

So long as self-rule was permitted, each Muslim *alcalde mayor* had charge of civil and criminal matters within his assigned community.

Isabella regarded the posts as patronage plums, and in January 1475 nominated Abrahán Xarifi to Toledo, at the petition of the arch-bishop. When, eight months later, that powerful cleric switched sides in the War of Succession, the post went to Farax de Belvis, whose patron was Diego Hurtado de Mendoza.[94] The judicial prerogative granted to the official was to head a tribunal which reviewed decisions, following norms of Islamic law. Appeal against its decisions was permitted only to the Royal Council or the monarchs. An *alcalde mayor* also had the privilege, in theory, of nominating judges and aides; but Isabella never respected this right, freely intervening to fill offices herself.[95] The powers of the tribunal were diminished by legislation from 1476 onward, first in criminal and then in civil cases, with the result that the workload for corregidores grew heavier.[96] This new era is evident in instructions given to a corregidor at Avila during 1489, that he acquaint himself fully with Muslim rules of inheri-tance.[97] Notice under the revised procedures went out to several corregidores on 10 January 1493 concerning the murder of Ahudalle "the Rich" by a fellow Muslim. It suggests efficiency that two days later Ali Moharrache was arrested in Arévalo and jailed on the charge.[98]

Along with such a presumed benefit of royal (as opposed to mere communal) justice went unpleasant restrictions on ordinary life.[99] In Cordova, Francisco de Valdés anticipated the decrees of the Cortes of Toledo by forcing residents out of their homes near the central square during 1479. By moving everyone to a single street in the old castle area, the corregidor delivered a virtual death sentence, since the loss of contact with their customers put an effective end to their livelihoods. In laments to the crown during early 1480, the community elders note that many had already died and many more suffered greatly from hunger. Although the crown sent an investigator, who concluded that a larger quarter should be found, no action was taken, then or later.[100]

Muslims were viewed by outsiders much the same as were Jews – performers of necessary services, but regarded with suspicion and envy. When Mudejars were persecuted simply for following their customs they could only look for aid to aristocratic protectors or to the crown. In Valladolid, the brotherhood of Christian shoe and buskin makers were agitated, during 1489, that their competitors were willing to work excessive hours. They tried to stop them from sewing by candlelight on Saturday evenings, and on Sunday, but the corregidor resisted the demand.[101] Under the impulse of prejudice, a variety of other local harassments were devised. Muslim residents of the village of Palomar, in the jurisdiction of Murcia, for example, were forced to petition their corregidor in 1489, before they were allowed freely to bury their dead outside their small quarter.[102] During the height of the Granada War, tax-collectors scoured the *aljamas* for gold coin, but the heavy assessments levied on domestic Muslims for the conquest of their co-religionists to the south did not thereby make their enforced patriotism any less suspect.[103]

Realms of the Moors

There was no overriding historical imperative which drove Ferdinand and Isabella to distort domestic priorities by expanding their mature years upon the conquest of Granada, since the queen was provided with useful tribute income from this client state and the king's interest, immediately upon ruling Aragon in his own right, lay in fighting in Italy, and elsewhere, against the French. Aristocrats who ruled southern frontier areas, where they were forever probing Muslim lines for weakness, were allowed by default to set the agenda for the monarchs.[104] Shortly after the crown itself became involved in the frontier quarrels, it was apparent a major blunder had been made in presuming that royal campaigns could be mounted as inexpensive forays. By 1484 the war was at an impasse: either far more funds and men must be provided or else the struggle would have to be abandoned.[105]

The bulk of troops for the initial phases of the struggle against the Moors came, as in the past, from aristocratic contingents. Augmentation of these forces was requested by the monarchs from the cities, both indirectly through increased Holy Brotherhood contributions and directly from urban militias. The mustering of militias in plazas was not an elaborate exercise, for the main distinction made at the assembly point was between those who arrived from their districts mounted, and men who arrived on foot. Responsible home-owners (*vecinos*) were thought more likely to have the requisite skills and equipment than residents without property (*aldeanos*). The soldiers, grouped in larger towns by neighborhoods, moved out for the campaigns shoulder to shoulder, all behind the city flag.[106]

Cities lost control of the disposition of these troops once militias were placed under the nominal direction of either a military governor (*adelantado mayor*) or a captain-general. When the principal commander was not available, the heads of the varied municipalities might still exercise implicit reserve power, as in Navarre, where the corregidor of Logroño acted as captain-general in the absence of the viceroy, or in Gibraltar, where the corregidor had charge of defense when the captain was not present.[107] Murcia's corregidor was authorized to muster its militia and take it to the point of concentration, although he never superseded the *adelantado mayor*, which title was hereditary in the house of the marquis of Vélez.[108]

Some corregidores held military posts in their own right and thus had a fighting role, especially important during the first stages of the Moorish struggle. A count of officials shows twenty-two individuals with a military title (twelve were military captains and four captains-general).[109] Some held such titles while simultaneously retaining urban posts.[110] A sitting corregidor of Carmona, Alfonso Porto-carrero, led that village's troops in several early Granada campaigns, including the taking of Alhama in 1483.[111] The formation drawn up for an assault on Málaga in 1484 includes four corregidores from Andalusia, with their respective city militias. The battalion put together under the command of the duke of Medina Sidonia included Cordovan troops, led by García Fernández Manrique, and the Jerez contingent headed by Juan de la Fuente. A battalion directed by the grand master of Santiago incorporated Úbeda's corregidor, Diego López de Ayala, together with Andújar's Francisco de Bobadilla.[112]

A fresh war

Isabella's second decade on the throne opened with a full-scale propaganda effort to stoke the engines of religious enthusiasm, needed because Castilians were not the eternal crusaders as which they are so often portrayed. The time elapsed since the previous great anti-Muslim push was longer than the years which would later stretch from the launching of the Spanish Armada to the end of World War I. Under Ferdinand's inspired leadership, campaigning was divided into successive theaters of operation: Málaga, to the west; Almería, to the east; and finally the capital, at the center.[113] During 1487, militias from Jaén, Andújar, Úbeda, and Baeza, with commanders including corregidores Francisco de Bobadilla and Diego López de Ayala, joined the massive troop assemblies held in Cordova for the push on Vélez–Málaga and its capital.[114] The stubborn resistance at Málaga ended in mid-August, bringing the first phase of the "new war" to a successful conclusion.

Chivalry gives way in long struggles, as was the case with the vital port which, instead of submitting as twice requested, had to be stormed in 1487, with the result that its entire Muslim population was enslaved and uprooted, freeing Málaga for new settlers.[115] García Fernández Manrique, who, in order to take part in battles, had neglected his Cordovan jurisdiction (1483–6), captured the fortress. [116] The complex task of reorganizing the territory was entrusted to him, and to another experienced official, Juan de la Fuente. The second in command, as former corregidor at Jerez de la Frontera, brought to the task a background of a legal career as attorney for the crown, experience which was helpful as the two men strove to bring order to the captured city.[117] Fernández Manrique, as a corregidor who had already settled Ronda and Marbella, thought it best to work closely with a native magistrate, Ali Dordux.[118] Not unexpectedly, the status of a corregidor in relation to his city was initially quite high in areas conquered and reorganized in this fashion. Nominees to Málaga's governing body were expressly told during the first meeting that their office came directly from the monarchs. During the ceremony on 26 June 1489, each *regidor* placed his right hand in Fernández Manrique's, when pledging on the gospels to use the office well and loyally, a clear enough symbolic investment. The corregidor then took his seat in the central position, ready to make use of ordinances which gave him full power to eject any disobedient member.[119]

During the spring of 1488 it was the east's turn to be attacked. The siege at Baza dragged on into winter, resulting in unanticipated expenses, enormous by earlier standards.[120] A massive program of taxation and forced loans allowed the struggle to continue, with the yield invested in a number of intelligent ways: factions of Granada's ruling house were bribed, the coastline blockaded to prevent supplies from Africa reaching the Nasrid dynasty, and the latest technology in cannonry employed to batter down walls. Juan de Silva, *asistente* of Seville from 1482 to 1500, played the most important role of any urban leader in raising, and spending, these funds during the years of trial. Again and again, letters preserved in the books of the *Tumbo* exhort him to locate troops and lead them into battle. In 1487 Seville raised 500 lances and 5,000 peons, as either foot soldiers or laborers, along with pay for twenty days. During 1489 the *asistente* collected 600 lances and 6,000 peons. In the last stage of the war, the *asistente* scraped together 1,500 horsemen and 7,000 foot soldiers by calling out every male in good health, however old, to fight.[121]

Despite the burden placed upon Andalusia, the war was not

exclusively a southern responsibility. A corregidor from Asturias made a troop muster, and a governor of Galicia fought at the head of his municipal forces.[122] The corregidor of Vizcaya watched over the welfare of foreigners imported to cast artillery pieces.[123] The crown, striving to develop a monopoly over cannon and gunpowder, sent orders out to all its corregidores in 1487 to ensure that none of this advanced technology fell into the hands of aristocrats.[124] The prohibition of high explosives, although not initially effective, did more in the long term to tip the balance against the aristocracy than did exalted claims of royal preeminence.

Baza's capitulation on 4 December 1489 was followed by the surrender of all nearby strongholds without a fight, before the year was out.[125] The campaigning then could turn to the heart of the kingdom. Ferdinand and Isabella opened fresh negotiations, hoping to gain a settlement in two months, but instead the fighting dragged on for two years.[126] The major contribution to success during this stage of the war was made by Iñigo López de Mendoza, count of Tendilla and marquis of Mondéjar, who placed his fortune and retainers at the complete disposal of the crown. He was richly rewarded for his loyalty. On Tuesday, 6 January 1492, the celebrated day the royal couple made their first glittering entrance into the Alhambra, he was granted control of the Moorish palace.[127] Writers of romances found it pleasant to concentrate upon the brilliance of that day, which offers the opportunity to relate well-polished anecdotes concerning Christian chivalry and mournful Islamic regret; but, since others have done the task so well, my immediate focus here will be upon administration of the new territory.

When Mendoza was named governor, he felt so sure the position would be made hereditary in his family that he moved his household from their estate in Guadalajara into the Alhambra, and then bought heavily in land to build up the holding.[128] He retained the full confidence of the *Reyes Católicos* all through a long career which had begun in earnest when he assisted the monarchs at the Cortes of Toledo. That same year of 1480, he made a strategic marriage to a daughter of Juan Pacheco, master of Santiago and marquis of Villena, and was sent by the queen on a delicate mission to Rome. His prestige mounted during the Granada War, when he was named governor general and *alcaide* of Alhama in 1483, and then *adelantado mayor de la frontera* and governor of Alcalá la Real in 1490. Through these years he multiplied his property several times over, gaining control of four fortresses along with numerous villages and farms, all of which generated an income calculated at some 300,700,000 *mrs*.[129]

So long as he retained the full confidence of the crown, Mendoza was all-powerful in the kingdom of Granada, since as captain-general he was granted control of all royal military forces, and when the monarchs were absent from Castile he was invested with the regal powers of a viceroy for Andalusia. The royal decree which granted his jurisdiction over Granada on 4 June 1492 was reconfirmed, and amplified, by Queen Juana in 1505 and again in 1508.[130] He alone administered justice until 1505, when a high court of *Chancillería* was shifted from Ciudad Real to his district to reduce his power. Even then Mendoza insisted so tenaciously upon his right to be the initiating judge in all civil and criminal cases that in 1513 the crown ordered the *Chancillería* to respect all his rights.[131]

The "team" that Mendoza first established in 1492 to administer the prostrate kingdom of some 300,000 inhabitants consisted of Fernando de Zafra, a secretary of humble origins who handled negotiations with the Moors, *Fr.* Fernando de Talavera, then bishop of Avila and confessor to the queen, who oversaw the teaching of the triumphant faith, and a corregidor. From 1492 to 1500 this last office was held by Andrés Calderós, a loyal functionary in the lord's personal service.[132] The corregidor oversaw the workings of a municipal council for the 50,000 inhabitants of the city and its surrounding *vega*, one that was an unusual mix of Christians and Moors. The council included the *alguacil mayor*, Mahoma el Pequení (who converted in 1500, by which date the government contained nine former Muslims).[133] Mendoza was personally granted a post as *regidor* by the crown, which office he renounced in favor of his son Luis, and ultimately assigned to his heir, Bernardino.[134]

Mendoza had a quasi-paternal interest in his charges, and defended their rights as best he could over the years. In 1492 he had entered the Alhambra quietly, through the north portal, so as not to upset the city dwellers, and he soon reduced his militia to a modest guard.[135] To create an ambience of abundance, the governor and his corregidor imported large quantities of wheat and fish, while crops favored by Christians were planted in model farms as a way to teach cultivators new ways. Unfortunately, the governor's hopes for peaceful development were dashed by failure, despite his prestige, to hold the crown to a moderate religious policy. This issue typifies the conflict noted by Nader between the realism and compromises of a military elite versus the abstract dogmatism of the clerics and the *letrados* who increasingly surrounded the royal couple. Mendoza's contempt for theorizing bureaucrats shows up in a pithy comment: "Advice should come from where the action is."[136]

There was a strong guarantee in the treaty against forced conversion, but with the Jews out of the way, the last remaining separated community received ever-closer scrutiny.[137] At first, clerics followed the patient lead of *Fr.* Fernando de Talavera, who learned to preach in Arabic. Conversions took place, but too slowly to suit the court or tough-minded Archbishop Cisneros. The clash between the governor and the archbishop was intense, but cautious. Years later, Mendoza recalled a time when his corregidor came to him agitated about a letter he received concerning a plan Cisneros had contrived to exile all *alfaquís* (religious leaders) from the land in a summary procedure. The governor decided the sovereigns would never agree to such a scheme. Much better, he wrote in 1513, to have kept that conflict a secret than to have talked openly at the time.[138] It is difficult to believe, however, that Isabella did not suspect that, when Cisneros replaced Talavera, he would order the corregidor of Granada to burn Muslim books and, on his own, inaugurate a policy of forced mass baptism.

An uncoordinated rising in favor of the faith broke out, with rebellion flickering like brushfire through the Alpujarras mountains and threatening to engulf towns.[139] Granada's governor lost favor as a result of the troubles. Fedinand wrote to Mendoza on 22 December 1499, concerning forced conversions as the cause of fighting: "ever since I heard the method in use I did not expect any other result . . ." His conclusion was harsh, if somewhat unfair:

as to the archbishop of Toledo, who never saw Moors, or knew them, I do not marvel but [I do] that you and the corregidor, who have known them so long, did not protest . . . see that you, principally, and the corregidor of justice, take responsibility for this city.[140]

The battles in the mountains were cruel, but short-lived. Ferdinand came with 15,500 mounted troops and 80,000 peons, while Mendoza personally headed a force of 4,000 lancers.[141] Juan Gaitán, Málaga's corregidor, raised 500 lancers plus 300 peons and, accompanied by most of his municipal officials, successfully led the city's forces in clashes through the terrain around Ronda and Villaluenga.[142] After the fires were extinguished the 1492 treaty was rewritten, under pretext of its abrogation by rebellion, presenting Moors with the necessity to accept baptism or leave by 1502.[143] All was not quiet thereafter on the southern front, since guarding the long coastline remained a constant preoccupation for corregidores. At Málaga, in collaboration with the captain-general, checks were always being made on fishermen, to ensure that no one was being transported to or from Africa.[144]

On the heels of the turmoil the legists at the royal court seized their opportunity, according to Nader, to encroach upon Mendoza's powers. In 1500 the long-term corregidor was dismissed by the crown, to be replaced by a series of one-year appointees with whom the governor found it more difficult to arrive at agreements. A Muslim consultative body which had looked to him for direction was abolished, at the same time that the municipal council was expanded from twelve to twenty-four regidores, which made it harder to intimidate.[145] From this year on, the governor's name begins to appear after the corregidor's in municipal council minutes. He continued to do his best, for another decade and a half, to care for the practical welfare of his charges in the face of economic decline, as the region started on a long demographic slide.[146]

From the evidence, royal policy was never very consistent when dealing with religious differences. This could prove confusing to corregidores, for those who moved faster in repression than the crown wished were rebuked. All along the officials were expected to shoulder the burden of protecting food supplies, preventing unauthorized taxation, resisting the impact of inflammatory sermons, and assisting financiers, merchants, and craftsmen. That they had so to guard separated communities, even while enforcing humiliating restrictions and strict segregation, sometimes led to unexplained delays in carrying out orders. When clear and unambiguous messages for full repression emerged, corregidores promptly enforced the stringent regulations, and then struggled with knotty leftover problems. Of all groups, the New Christians (if indeed they may be considered a separate community) alone managed to survive, for, although badly clawed by the Inquisition, not all bled to death, as had been once assumed. With the connivance of highly placed patrons and friendly officials, including the occasional corregidor who was himself from a convert family, they bound up their wounds and endured through subterfuge or disguise. By the opening of the sixteenth-century, then, the pattern of Castilian society was greatly simplified. Corregidores did not have to learn anything about the complexities of Hebrew or

Islamic custom. What heresy or apostasy existed would be handled by the Holy Office. The corregidor was no longer the fulcrum around which revolved the fortunes and lives of separate, but interacting communities.

8

Difficult governance (1495–1504)

It is no less dignity for the good corregidor to govern the republic than to administer justice, inasmuch as both functions look to the common good and the necessities of human life. But always, it is more difficult to govern than to judge, because to govern requires perfect prudence, since all the virtues depend upon it.

Jerónimo Castillo de Bovadilla goes on in his voluminous handbook to maintain that such skill in ruling comes only with long experience.[1] During the last years of Isabella's reign, a number of corregidores were repeatedly reappointed;[2] but length of stay, upon examination, turns out not to be the key element in assuring that her officials would be allowed to govern with wisdom and prudence.

In an era of fresh crisis for the monarchy, the insistent claims of privilege pushed aside the common good. Laws were increasingly disregarded, under royal instruction, to favor those who claimed exemption or held high title. In other cases decrees were rewritten and traditions overturned to facilitate the assault of the privileged upon the rest of society. Corregidores were highly visible as enforcers of this new order of the day, and suffered an according loss of the prestige granted them in the previous era of acceptance.

On the roads

As the Granada War receded into the past protests increased from the municipalities both against continued taxation for the militia of the Holy Brotherhood and against the total freedom from outside review claimed by its police. In 1494, for example, the executive body of the Brotherhood in the province of Seville found that the city was successfully preventing it from collecting funds and fulfilling its duties.[3] Faced with widespread communal opposition, based upon an unwillingness to cooperate once the war was over, the monarchs

148

decided to replace the Holy Brotherhood militia with a new force more directly under their control. Corregidores throughout the realms were instructed by Alfonso de Quintanilla, chief administrator of the Council of the Holy Brotherhood, to maintain a census of fighting men, arms, and horses.[4] The old militia was dissolved, and fresh recruiting began in 1495 for a permanent troop of 83,333 foot soldiers and 2,000 light cavalry; but, as it quickly turned out, the ill-conceived new force proved so prohibitively expensive, and came under such strong criticism from aristocrats, that it was stillborn.[5] This blunder left the crown without its own troops, back to relying upon *ad hoc* forces.

Without a militia to maintain, there seemed no need for the Holy Brotherhood's executive body, which was eliminated in 1498.[6] Along with the suppression of the governing council, the system of assemblies was also dismantled, with the result that an important direct link, more universally representative than the Cortes, was thereby severed between the crown and the urban elites. Abolition of the governing structures left local brotherhoods free, again, to do as they chose on the highways, in rural areas, and in the cities. Corregidores were given no right to interfere to protect their constituents from a privileged group dealing out vigilante justice. The inadequate remedy for those who ran foul of the brotherhood remained an expensive and difficult direct appeal to the Royal Council.[7] Inability to place any restraint upon the police, even after the elimination of the conciliar structure, was one way in which Isabella's urban overseers continued to fail their jurisdictions.

Corregidor attempts to perform other constructive functions ran into varied obstructions. A healthy commercial life required that roads be kept open and passable in all seasons. The expense of maintaining thoroughfares and bridges was defrayed by a modest tax (*repartimiento*) on each community and a comprehensive transit charge (*imposición*) on through passage. The luxuriant growth of the latter charge provided communities sufficient surplus to allow the highway network to keep up with the needs of an expanding economy, although users naturally grumbled. In particular, the carters and sheepherders made their complaints known at court. The carters' newfound ability to pressure the sovereigns to quash tolls grew out of their wartime services against the Moors, when in order that a constant supply of skilled drovers from 1488 onward could be maintained, carters operating out of Segovia to Granada were allowed to move without arbitrary delay or fees. These privileges were soon extended to other locales, and although no "national" organization came into being at this time, according to Ringrose, blanket rights were granted in 1497 to a protective legal corporation, the *Cabaña Real de Carreteros*.[8] To ensure achievement of the strategic goal of having teams available in case of renewed fighting, the crown issued a series of laws, from 1497 to 1499, that placed municipalities under pressure to charge only fees authorized by the monarchy, and to allow beasts to graze freely on their uncultivated communal pastureland, while declaring invalid all local ordinances contradicting these mandates. The sheepherders also managed to get sweeping edicts directed against unwarranted local tolls, and against illegal fees on the pasturing of flocks.[9]

At the same time that municipalities faced diminished income, they were given the entire responsibility of maintaining roads used by all.[10] To compensate to some extent for projected losses, the monarchs set aside limited funds to repair roads and to have new ones built, primarily in Granada.[11] The crown did not think to do much for Valladolid or Burgos, its principal commercial centers on the northern Meseta, for, realistically, the sums that would have been required merely to keep the various bridges around Burgos in repair were far beyond the capacity of the treasury. An estimate by two master-builders at Burgos in 1508 totaled up costs, simply for labor, on the spans at 11,500 ducats, or 4,312,500 *mrs*.[12] Corregidores struggled to raise funds, but found themselves blocked time and again by the Royal Council, which had few practical ideas about how to meet commercial and municipal needs. The case of the Buniel bridge outside Burgos, as presented by Molénat, illustrates why little could be done. It was in the hands of Sancho de Rojas, an aristocrat who rendered great service to Isabella during the War of Succession by his attack on the castle of Burgos. Secure in her favor, he would not allow his villagers to make payment for repair. A confidential mission by the corregidor of Palencia, during 1488, developed so strong a case that the crown was again obliged to press for a contribution. This modest initiative collapsed in 1496, when the Royal Council decided to allow the aristocrat to stand fast against any imposition. In July 1500, after an urgent request from Burgos, a corregidor tried, but failed, to raise the necessary money from regional assessments, leaving the Buniel bridge to decay.[13]

The result of placing all burdens on those least likely to have assets is seen in the failure of efforts to improve the primary artery connecting Burgos with Valladolid, which passed through the territory of Torquemada, where eroded passes obliged traffic to make detours far out of its way. In 1492, settlements along the route authorized the brotherhood official in charge of roads to collaborate on reconstruction with the corregidor of Palencia, Pedro Gómez de Setúbal. Because sufficient money could never be raised from poverty-stricken hamlets, the highway continued to decline.[14] In one last instance analyzed by Molénat, at the turn of the century the corregidor of the Cuatro Villas worked in cooperation with the *alcalde mayor* of Old Castile to repair the only direct route north from Burgos to Laredo on the coast. They hoped to raise 1,113,000 *mrs* by means of a carefully drawn agreement between the drovers of Valladolid, the municipality of Laredo, and villages along the way. When the villages pled poverty, officials compromised by placing a user fee on beasts of burden, which was to bring in 260,000 *mrs*. On the complaint of the drovers, a royal investigator was sent who, although accurate records were not presented by the carters, nevertheless insisted that whatever refund was requested be paid in full. Because sufficient funds could never be collected from residents alone, a report by the lieutenant of a later corregidor notes that twelve bridges destroyed by flooding were abandoned, and that roads were in wretched condition.[15]

The *mestas*

The newfound ability of the carters, with corregidor help, to bypass unauthorized local taxation was a modest loss to municipal resources when compared to the successful campaign by the *Real Mesta*. This powerful kingdom-wide association of sheepherders supervised the complex journeys of vast flocks across the peninsula. Although strictly a trade association which did not itself own any sheep, the *Real Mesta* carefully watched over the interests of members. Analysis of the organization continues to be dominated by *The Mesta: A Study in Spanish Economic History*, which Julius Klein published in 1920. In the section of his work devoted to the era of the *Reyes Católicos*, Klein underlined three points: (1) the crown favored the organization to the extent of incorporating it into government because the taxes it contributed resolved fiscal problems; (2) in the effort to obtain this subsidy as directly as possible, Isabella favored wealthy owners against smallholders, and both against farmers or burghers; (3) the consequence of royal favor to pastoral interests was to blight agriculture. The thrust of recent scholarship has been to maintain that Klein gave birth to something of a "Black Legend." Modifications of his study show that the executive body was not yet entirely dominated by rich owners, since anyone with a few sheep could join the organization, and small herders did need redress for their problems.[16] Sheepwalks (cañadas) actually required constant protection from aggressively expansionist agricultural interests, as wilderness land came under increasing cultivation.[17]

There were four sheep "highways": the Leonese, the Segovian, the Sorian, and the Manchegan. The Leonese cañada, some 850 kilometers long, was a model of skillful organization. In autumn, seemingly endless numbers of beasts flowed like whitewater rapids from the mountains in the north, through Zamora and Salamanca to Béjar. There they were joined by another stream of walking wool from Logroño, which had passed through Burgos, Valladolid, and Segovia across the northern slopes of the Guadarramas. The flood poured on through Palencia, Cáceres, and Mérida–Badajoz, where it branched off finally into Portugal or terminated at Seville. By April the flocks were started north again, this time sheared along the way.[18]

It was the mandated function of traveling judges (alcaldes entregadores) of the Real Mesta to make sure these established sheepwalks suffered no reduction in their traditional 250-foot span. Municipalities relied upon six "good men" to accompany, and to observe, these judges on their rounds. So long as differences were locally adjudicated, the long-distance sheepherders were at a disadvantage in maintaining their routes, as Bishko has pointed out, more from hostile local cattlemen and sheepherders than from agriculturalists.[19] Traveling flocks faced the most objections when they were driven south to go where grass grew the whole year round: in La Mancha at the Murcian plains around Chinchilla and Albacete, the countryside of Montiel and Calatrava, and the Sierra Morena valleys near Alcaraz and the valle of Alcudia; and in Extremadura at the pastures of La Serena, the tierra of Barros, and the countryside of Badajoz, Cáceres, Alcántara, Coria, and Plasencia.[20] As the northern flocks passed through Cáceres, to provide a typical example of conflict over pasturing, residents engaged in vigorous struggles with the travelers which degenerated into abusive denunciations that could only be restrained by outside officials. In April 1490, the crown sent in a special investigator to adjudicate conflicts that had been building up for years. Ruy González de Sepúlveda, instructed to work upon arrival with an official of his choice, selected Ferrand Sánchez de Tovar, a corregidor who graced Cáceres for a single year. Together the two heard complaints from Pedro de Haro, solicitor for the *Real Mesta*, and countering allegations from García de Holguín for the municipal council. The verdict shows an evenhandedness betraying no partiality: a peasant was found guilty of plowing pasture land in the walkway before it had been used by sheep, and a shepherd was judged to have taken flocks illegally through certain public lands.[21]

Ferdinand and Isabella were aware, despite such Solomonic judgements, that having corregidores in place strengthened their hand in readjusting the balance between drovers of migratory sheep, stock-breeders, and agrarian interests. To this end, corregidores in 1486 were reminded they must safeguard privileges claimed by the *Real Mesta* so that it would not continue to suffer diminution of its routes.[22] The crown's growing need for funds in the late 1480s was a further incentive to listen closely to the association's brilliant attorney general, Jorge Mexía.[23] He convinced the sovereigns that their yield from taxation on the *Real Mesta* would be much greater if corregidores freed shepherds from unauthorized assessments, and eventually the organization was relieved even from paying the *alcabala* charge. Corregidores throughout the kingdoms were reminded in 1495 to enforce these fiscal incentives for increased sheep-breeding.[24]

Shifting attention from the glamorous kingdom-wide organization's trouncing of its opposition to the neglected topic of local *mestas*, which has been called to our attention by Bishko, it is notable that cities of the Guadalquivir valley and its periphery developed municipal bodies which contributed significantly to the expansion of sheep ranching.[25] Terrain in the orbit of Seville, Jaén, and Granada had sophisticated *mestas*, which were as hostile to the *Real Mesta* as were farmers or stock-breeders. Since these *mestas* had no way of enforcing their ordinances either upon outsiders or upon powerful local agrarian interests, they looked to their municipal officials and their corregidores to protect their interests. A series of royal orders, set out in Cordova during 1492, ordered that one-half of all grasslands be treated as common pasture open to local herders. Francisco de Bobadilla made use of the mandates in 1494 to strike against lords around Cordova who refused to comply with the regulations against enclosures.[26] Yet, despite the enthusiastic efforts of municipalities to ensure enforcement, Edwards observes that the long-term result favored the wealthy, since court tests generally confirmed private title to land against over-enthusiastic challenge.[27]

As a rough kind of counterweight to policies which had the effect of favoring pastoral interests, corregidores were given the task of instructing peasants about improving farming techniques. The queen asked her officials to get cultivators to switch from a two-field to a three-field system, thereby leaving two-thirds of their land untilled each year.[28] The system offered the advantage of increased fertility for exhausted soil, especially were sheep to pass over the two fallow portions, since so highly prized were sheep droppings that the beast was said to have a "golden hoof." Mitigating the prospect that large numbers of peasants might switch to the superior system, with which they had long been familiar, was the sure prospect that leaving additional land untended might set a precedent for permanent right of passage. This indeed was the intent of the law of 1501, which reserved in perpetuity for pasturage all land on which flocks had ever moved. The issue of property rights was promptly put to the test by Cáceres, whose solicitors argued before the high court at Valladolid that such things could not be called just or honest, since they were not for the public good but for the private advantage of a few favored men.[29] The judges gave more weight to the case made by Jorge Mexía. A happy result was not long in coming for pastoral interests, as the sheep population rose from 2,700,000 in 1477 to almost 3,500,000 by 1526.[30] Trade boomed with Flanders and England. There is no good reason for such expanded wool production to be viewed negatively, while agricultural expansion, for example, in the viticultural sector, should receive higher praise.

Time of famine

The role of corregidores in enlarging the domain of sheep at the expense of human cultivators is, however, vigorously assailed by Klein. Was starvation actually a direct consequence of favoritism to sheepherding interests? This was long the traditional view.[31] It has been argued alternatively that, when easing oppressive local jurisdiction over migratory flocks, the Catholic Sovereigns were mostly restoring the medieval balance between pastoral and agrarian interests. Due to the spurt in cultivation, often in forbidden locations, central Castile may have become self-sufficient in wheat.[32] There was just no way that *mestas*, large or small, could stop the advance of the plow despite help from corregidores. Andalusia, on the other hand, certainly suffered a series of agricultural collapses. Yet its bad harvests antedate the augmented privileges of the *Real Mesta*, since, from 1468 to 1490, the south was hit by five periods of crisis (1466–8; 1472–4; 1481–2; 1485–6; 1489). Production then dramatically increased during the abundant harvests of the "happy nineties," which saw falling prices for consumers.[33] It is thus injudicious to maintain that the famines which arrived in full force during the sixteenth-century can be attributed entirely, or primarily, to pastoral assaults on farmland, aided and abetted by corregidores. Hunger stalked the land because of natural disasters, poor internal transportation, and the mismanagement of the market for economic and political reasons.

The role of the corregidor, at least in terms of regulating the food supply, was actually quite positive. Officials attempted to restrain the price of grain under local regulations, while maintaining stocks for emergency use. Low prices were vital to human survival, since considerably more than 60 per cent of each day's calorific intake for an ordinary European came from cereals.[34] Shortages threatened social order whenever expensive or scarce grain led to bread riots, the most common form of urban disturbance in pre-modern times. Alcaraz did not allow wheat sold during 1487 to be priced at over 140 *mrs* per Spanish bushel (*fanega*). The corregidor of Baeza reprimanded Martín de Guzmán for attempting to sell at a slightly higher price in 1495.[35] Such admonishments were, of course, ineffective in times of shortage, such as when famine struck Andalusia in 1502–3, then returned with full force in 1506–7. "Many places were depopulated," wrote the curate of Los Palacios, "and fathers and mothers wandered down the roads carrying their children, dead of hunger, on their shoulders, searching for bread."[36]

The queen's first response, set out in an edict of 23 December 1502, was to maintain that the shortage was due to hoarding, since she had been told, correctly, that the harvest had been abundant. Corregidores were ordered to investigate, and to force the holders of grain stocks to sell at the usual prices, on pain of very heavy fines.[37] When this mandate proved insufficient, all stocks of grain were ordered to be registered. To make sure that the edict was not evaded through technicalities, the *asistente* of Seville also took a listing of flour and bread, although such a policy, which relied primarily upon coercion for its impact, kept supplies off the market. The *asistente* and the council wrote to the queen on 6 April 1503 begging her to get bread anywhere, at any price, until the crisis sent by God ceased.[38] The *asistente* was also in direct contact with cities of the interior about obtaining any of their excess grain.[39] Since little was to be had, there was nothing left for the queen to do but authorize importations. Agents under the direction of the president of the Royal Council made purchases in Perpignan and wherever else possible. The corregidor of Málaga, Juan Gaitán, was alerted to permit the ships to dock at Valencia, and elsewhere along the coast, without delay or customs duty.[40] Massive imports sharply depressed grain prices for regional producers and, combined with an unexpectedly large harvest in 1504, brought further ruin to cultivators.

The aristocracy resurgent

Whatever enthusiasm had been slowly engendered in the urban elite to support corregidores, when wheat prices were kept low, the communal patrimony protected, and government perceived as just, dissipated rapidly during the last decade of the reign. Haliczer posits an "aristocratic offensive"[41] to expand estates, which began growing in strength during the late 1490s. The aristocracy made use of private armies, returned to their exclusive service upon the conclusion of the Granada War, to intimidate neighbors. A sign of new times was the abrupt resumption by the lords of overt meddling in municipal council business when the royal prohibition against *acostamientos* was abandoned. As soon as Isabella permitted direct payments from the duchess of Cádiz and the duke of Alba to reach supporters in Seville, during 1493, the game was lost and the practice gradually resumed throughout the realms.[42]

The similar ease with which aristocrats made good a renewed drive to usurp land is illustrated by the loss by Cáceres of the hamlet of Arroyo. Even though its affairs had been administered by the town's corregidor, the duchess of Frías, wife of the constable of Castile, seized it on various pretexts in 1494. For the next three years Cáceres did everything it could to recover its property. With the aid of the local royal official, appeals were forwarded to the Council of Prince Don Juan, then later to the Royal Council, but both bodies refused to bring the duchess to task.[43] At Santo Domingo de la Calzada, corregidor Juan de Portillo set out, in 1497, to reoccupy land stolen by the duke of Nájera's villages. Although the crown sent an envoy to stop him from so doing, this new arrival unexpectedly cooperated in continuing the legal struggle. Their defiant course was halted when the duke alleged the two officials were also trying to gain jurisdiction over his village of Haro, at which point the Royal Council took matters out of the hands of its representatives.[44]

Demoralization set in with such clear evidence that the crown was no longer interested in enforcing the laws on restitution of communal property. Avila's corregidor in 1500 simply refused to visit any outlying area. Francisco de Bazán, by stubbornly avoiding a trip through Cuenca's district, despite complaints in 1501 from the municipal council, was probably wiser than his successor, Fernando de Rebolledo, who in his naiveté tried to enforce land decrees dating back twenty-five years. To refresh the faded promise of Isabella's youthful days, the corregidor ordered peasants from seignorial villages owned by Juan Hurtado de Mendoza off Cuenca's land. Mendoza appealed to the *Audiencia*, with the result that the corregidor was ordered to cease enforcement in 1502, although it was conceded that Cuenca had an undeniably valid decree.[45] So marked a failure of corregidores to defend communities from assault profoundly increased dissatisfaction with them, and with their mistress, by the reign's end. The contempt with which corregidores came to be regarded by the city fathers was compounded by a reduction in individuals sufficiently well qualified to fill posts.

A decline in status

Either military prowess or a university degree was vital in the contest to gain status. Humane letters competed with law for the leading role in Castile's educational system, and it was by no means sure which course of study would win out as the more desired for public service. The basic university degree, a bachelor's in *estudios generales*, showed the deep impact of the Renaissance through a curriculum which emphasized the classics and developed rhetorical skills.[46] A holder of the baccalaureate might then seek admittance to the *colegios mayores*, to study law or theology.[47]

For corregidores in the years prior to 1474, Bermúdez Aznar's tables list fifty-one degree recipients (21 per cent of 238), of whom fully half held the doctorate.[48] Isabella's reign produced more degree-holders in corregidor ranks, but the rapid expansion and routinization of the post called for less heroic intellectual qualification than was previously thought necessary. Our listing presents 488 postings out of an estimated total of between 600 and 700.[49] Data for 408 individuals appointed to the royal postings shows that 36 per cent (148) held academic degrees. Of this total of 148 university men, 14 per cent (20) had doctorates, while 30 per cent (45) made their careers with a bachelor's certificate. The dominant 56 per cent (83) were *licenciados*, with the status of *letrado*.

The term *letrado* is difficult to translate into a modern equivalent that does not distort the meaning. It was applied broadly to any lettered individual with an advanced degree, but specifically to a civil or canon jurist. The legally trained had a certain advantage in government, since many significant posts, from seats in the Royal Council downwards, combined judicial with administrative duties. A full separation of functions had not yet taken place, because the medieval concept still held that the king was the fountainhead of justice, as well as ruler. The licenciate degree obtained at Salamanca and Valladolid, or in Italy and France, qualified the holder to be an *abogado*, with the right to plead before the bar. The legal profession did certify its practitioners as minor nobility, which was of inestimable value in a pedigree-ridden society, but lawyers were often treated as mere clerks. Their slow but steady rise in status gained momentum during the late fifteenth-century.

Kings were rarely under pressure to appoint *letrados* to the urban post. Universities did not offer courses in Castilian law, so anyone who had to administer it learned about the subject outside the classroom. Petitions from parliaments merely ask that a "good person" be sent. The 1462 Cortes of Toledo requested, for example, that the corregidor "be a powerful person, of good reputation."[50] This was in keeping with a presumption that the all-encompassing office might require an astute compromiser trained in the humanistic arts of persuasion or a military man with leadership experience. Vizcaya was unique in demanding legal qualifications. The officers of the *Contado* complained to Isabella in 1477 that she was violating their charter of privileges by naming Juan de Torres, who was not a *letrado*, for it was their right to be sent one.[51] Isabella's entire government, in general, shows surprisingly little overall advance in staffing with officials trained in law. William Phillips calculates that Isabella actually did less well than her two predecessors when it came to appointing law school graduates, for both Juan II and Enrique IV placed a higher ratio of *letrados* to aristocrats than did she.[52] A principal cause for this shortfall is that not enough law graduates were being produced by the domestic universities to staff the rapidly expanding administration. Of 201

Table 5. *Degree-holders at* corregidor *postings*[1]

	1474–84	1485–94	1495–1504
Total postings each period[2]	172	200	138
Number of *licenciados*	14	50	31
Percentage of *licenciados*	8%	25%	22%
Number of *bachilleres*	12	29	12
Percentage of *bachilleres*	7%	14.5%	9%
Number of *doctores*	10	6	8
Percentage of *doctores*	6%	3%	6%
Number without degrees	136	115	87
Percentage without degrees	79%	57.5%	63%

[1] Data drawn from Table 7.
[2] The listings in Tables 5–6 take into account individuals whose terms overlapped one or more of the three periods.

graduates from Salamanca and Valladolid during the reign, only a quarter chose posts with the crown.[53]

It is an important feature of our review that far fewer corregidor positions overall were held by individuals with legal training than has sometimes been presumed. Out of the entire company of royal office-holders throughout the reign, less than one-quarter were *letrados*. Distributing this proportion into periods, in the first decade of Isabella's rule only 8 per cent (14 of 172 postings) had legal training. The following decade shows a significant effort to recruit graduates, which increased degree-holders to 25 per cent (50 of 200 postings). This dramatic improvement, presented in Table 5, very probably eased the acceptance of corregidorial regimes in the years 1485–94.

The desire of Ferdinand and Isabella to surround themselves with a corps of properly trained servants led to legislation in 1493 that decreed that any *letrado* hoping to gain a government post would have to produce notarized documents attesting to ten or more years of study.[54] Recognizing the difficulty this might cause when staffing the less attractive short-term urban offices, corregidores were specifically exempted from the ten-year requirement.[55] Despite this encouragement, the rate of recruitment of *letrados*, even ill-qualified ones, was not maintained. The figure dropped slightly during the last decade of the reign, to 22 per cent (31 of 138 postings).[56]

Rather than being filled with legal drudges, then, the ranks of corregidores present a bright panorama of social levels. The Cortes of Toledo decrees specifically prohibited commanders of military orders (and all clerics) from holding the post, but were silent about other titles.[57] Aristocrats were thus by no means legally excluded at any point. Seven counts were appointed: Castañeda (1475), Alba de Liste (1475–6), Ribadeo (1477–80), Cifuentes (1482–1500), Fuensalida (1487–9), Tendilla (1492–1516), and Penamacor (1494–5).[58] Some three dozen officials in all are referred to as "Don" in the correspondence reviewed.[59]

One locale which stands out beyond the rest for having a series of especially well-connected corregidores is Baeza–Úbeda. In 1477 Isabella nominated Rodrigo Manrique, the third son of the count of Paredes, to Úbeda. His marriage to Mencia de Benavides confirmed a family alliance with the count of Santisteban del Puerto. During April of the year of Rodrigo's appointment, his brother conquered Baeza for Isabella.[60] The two towns were given a united *corregimiento* in August 1477, under Pedro de Rivadeneyra, whose father was a loyal servant of the constable of Castile, Álvaro de Luna. Pedro was also *alcalde mayor* of Toledo and a caballero of Santiago.[61] The Order of Santiago appears frequently in this locale. Alfonso Enríquez (1488–93) was a caballero of the order, and a military captain. This corregidor was related by marriage or blood to Isabel Enríquez, *señora* of Villalba. The next appointee was Lope de Alburquerque, count of Penamacor.[62] One other official whose social status is worth mentioning is Alfonso Martínez de Angulo, assigned his post at Baeza–Úbeda in 1500. Another caballero of the order and *veinticuatro* at Cordova, he was the son of *Mosén* Juan Martínez de Angulo, also of the Order of Santiago.[63]

The significant presence of caballeros at Baeza–Úbeda is illustrative of the direction taken by appointments elsewhere, which led to predominance for these nobles. Denominated *capa y espada* (cloak and sword), their military honors carried freedom from direct personal taxation, along with other privileges. Ferdinand and Isabella distributed knighthoods widely during the reign, especially during the War of Succession and the Granada War,[64] which accounts for caballeros holding almost 35 per cent (175 of 510 postings) of all the royal corregidor positions from 1474 to 1504, listed in Table 6. An additional 31 per cent (160) of the appointments during this same span of time form a mixed company of untitled nobility – *hidalgos*, to be sure, but without diploma, court position, or military dignity.

So long as there was a sufficient number of well-qualified and high-status nobles in the corps of corregidores, the urban elite could be satisfied that their municipalities were being accorded proper respect.

Table 6. Corregidor *titles held in postings*[1]

	1474–84	1485–94	1495–1504
Total postings each period	172	200	138
Number of caballeros	67	74	34
Percentage of caballeros	39%	37%	25%
Number of *hidalgos*	68	41	51
Percentage of *hidalgos*	39.5%	20.5%	37%
Number with academic title	37	85	53
Percentage with academic title	21.5%	42.5%	38%

[1] Data drawn from Table 7.

Because posts on the *regimiento* were held in absolute domination by caballeros, served by faithful lesser nobles tied to them by marriage and political alliance, social solidarity might serve to bind these cliques to acceptable corregidores. González Jiménez maintains, specifically for Carmona late in the reign, that such an arrangement had reached "the climax of its evolution," consisting of the following elements: (1) the consolidation of the regimen of the corregidor; (2) a disproportionate increase in the number and permanence of municipal offices; (3) the total failure of the meager representation for the commons.[65]

The turn of the century shows the start of an oligarchic crisis of confidence in such ripe compacts, engendered at least in part by the declining calibre of executive appointees. The proportion of *letrados* in Table 5 for 1495–1504 falls from the previous 25 per cent to 22 per cent (31 of 138 postings).[66] More significantly, officeholders in Table 6 without a university degree or caballero status rose sharply during the final period, almost doubling to 37 per cent (51 of 138 appointments).[67] This drying up of the pool of candidates to whom *regidores* would be likely to give automatic deference due to social standing alone contributed to the resumption of an agitation which will be discussed shortly.

What was hardly considered by the crown, despite the developing shortfall in qualified men, was dispatching the most acceptable to multiple postings. Indeed, over the entire period 1474–1504, only 9 per cent (35) received a second assignment, while a mere nine corregidores went to three or more cities.[68] Instead, the Royal Council chose to extend the length of stays. A source of strength during Isabella's early years had been her insistence that decrees of the Cortes be respected; and although a few *asistentes* and governors stayed on through open-ended terms, this was defensible by her on the legal grounds that they were exceptional appointees. The extensive control she quickly acquired over cities might have allowed her to place men in corregidor positions for extended periods, had she so chosen; but at first she avoided doing this lest she appear a tyrant. The "typical" twelve-month stay during the first decade did give way to a virtually automatic one-year extension, but this still fell within traditional boundaries. Multiple extensions, which only began to develop towards the end of the 1480s,[69] were followed by stays of four to five years, or longer, at *corregimientos* during the 1490s.[70]

Escaping control

This option, taken late in the reign, to stretch out the length of service instead of moving candidates about, risked trouble when such stays coincided with reduced assurance that systematic end-of-term investigations would take place. Complaints from cities during the post-Granada War period demonstrate that *residencias* were thought as necessary as ever. Pedro García de Cotes (1492–1502), his head scribe, and other officials at Burgos were found guilty of illegally renting out public lands, despite his defense that the practice had been going on "from time immemorial," a typical plea.[71] The count of Penamacor, corregidor at Baeza–Úbeda, was similarly charged in 1495 with accepting personal benefices of land. Baeza had to go to battle again in 1499, complaining that its latest corregidor put pasture lands up to auction, with prejudice to the farmers and cattlemen to whom it belonged, until the crown agreed that municipal and common land was specifically protected by royal decree.[72] At Carmona in 1501, with the corregidor's salary close to 100,000 *mrs*, the *jurados* began complaints to the Royal Council. By the time Bernal Flores del Carpio had put in another two terms, the municipal council was strongly insisting that he should not be reappointed. Only after the crown agreed to have him replaced was the Council willing to look into the salary issue.[73]

As the sixteenth-century opened, some individuals seized newfound opportunities to escape investigation. The corregidor of Cuenca came under attack by *regidores* and the major families; but when he was nevertheless reappointed in 1501, without a *residencia*, he arrested opponents to silence them.[74] A variety of charges against Ortuño de Aguirre (1496–1502), protesting abuses and favoritism in Alcaraz, proved well-founded, yet he was allowed to leave office in 1502 without an inquest. Not until 1505, following successive complaints, did the former official submit to a *residencia*, an indication that the routinized justice promised long before was a lost hope.[75] One reason for such failures was that supervision and review of personnel never kept up with the expansion of the network. At first the queen handpicked officials to place in the more sensitive or dangerous spots, but as postings became routine the task increasingly fell to the Royal Council. Candidates themselves, and delegates from municipalities, lobbied the Royal Council vigorously.[76] After the initial scrutiny led to appointment, corregidores were then left wide leeway, since distances were relatively great and communications slow. When the time came to evaluate performance, if it proved inadequate, the crown did little more than arbitrate between an officeholder and his irate constituents.

The Royal Council even neglected to consider *residencia* reports in its letters of reappointment, which routinely assigned culpable individuals in the midst of ongoing investigations. The budget for judges and secretaries on the Royal Council never rose (taking inflation into account) in line with increased responsibilities for supervision. The sum of 1,618,666 *mrs*, allocated in 1480, only rose to 2,368,000 *mrs* by 1492 – although the total cost of the monarchical household had tripled.[77] The Royal Council never appointed a specified director, or watchdog subcommittee – as in the case with the group which oversaw the Holy Brotherhood – to coordinate the activities of corregidores.

Unrest increases

Cortes gatherings from the post-Granada War era do not provide a measure for gauging urban dissatisfaction with criminal, inadequate, or lazy corregidores. Representatives (*procuradores*) from northern cities should have felt free, at least in theory, to voice dissatisfaction because, although elected in the presence of the corregidores, they represented the authentic voice of the oligarchs. The situation was quite different in Andalusia, for at Cordova and Jaén the corregidor directly controlled the process, and although Granada elected its two representatives from the ranks of the *regidores*, these were political clients entirely under the thumb of the governor.[78] The selection process was more complex in Seville, where three representatives were chosen – an *alcalde mayor*, and one each from the ranks of *regidor* and *jurado*. In 1498 a conflict erupted when the *jurados* would not quietly accept the candidate chosen for their rank by the *asistente*. A group met secretly to elect their own man, then bypassed the *asistente* by writing directly to the queen to make their argument. Not surprisingly, she assailed them for their "disorders," and let the *asistente* see that troublemakers were sent into exile five leagues out of the city.[79]

The Cortes had not met for eighteen years when it was called in 1498, after Prince Don Juan's tragic death. Inexperienced representatives were tightly limited to paying homage to the new line of succession and to voting funds.[80] There were brief sittings of the Cortes at Ocaña and Seville (1499), again at Seville (1501), and at Toledo (1502–3), at which the crown made very sure that delegates did what they were told. When the Toledo meeting was announced, all cities were ordered to send representatives with full powers to settle "whatever things that are needed to be complied with for the service of our Lord God and for the common good of these our realms . . .," the point being not to allow representatives the prospect of returning to their cities for consultation on any matters the crown chose to raise.[81] Another effective way in which discussion was muted was by isolating the royal persons from intimate contact. Sovereigns had always addressed the Cortes when possible; but in 1499 Juan de Fonseca presided, speaking in Ferdinand and Isabella's stead, and two years later the archbishop of Seville took over this role.[82]

With so ineffectual a sounding-board, the only way for cities to have attention called to grievances was to resume direct action. A ruler in violation of law, who paid no attention to subjects, was considered a tyrant against whom it was permissible to rebel.[83] The urban elite could thus, with good conscience, abstain from suppressing disturbances as an effective way to call their sovereigns to task. Sensitive rulers responded to revolt by bargaining, taking few reprisals, and spreading pardons around.[84] Ágreda attempted petitioning the queen to replace its "odious" long-term official, Ruy Gutiérrez de Escalante (1487–96), but when no response was forthcoming, unopposed street brawls broke out in 1494. A *residencia* was provided the following year, at which the corregidor was condemned on several counts, although reappointed nonetheless.[85] As soon as Diego Fernández de San Millán left his post at Toro in May 1495, serious rioting took place in protest against his arbitrary decisions.[86] During that November, at León, there were uprisings and revolts against corregidor Pedro Fernández de Aranda, who bitterly complained that the municipal council was laggard in coming to his aid.[87] *Regidores* at Murcia, who had failed to overawe their corregidores in the 1480s, resumed meeting secretly. In 1497 the crown ineffectually protested that the *regidores* were deciding important matters without the presence either of the corregidor or of the *jurados*.[88]

Distrust of royal willingness to protect communal interest even spread to Palencia, which was once so anxious to shelter under the umbrella of royal justice. Here the oligarchy pushed beyond its fellows by taking the drastic step of demanding, in 1503, that the crown absolutely remove its corregidor.[89] Elliott notes that privileged and propertied groups in pre-modern Europe were always in a quandary over how to find a balance between their persistent fear of social upheaval and their hostility towards unresponsive monarchies.[90] The oligarchs of urban Castile were generally cautious in the ways in which they expressed opposition to policies followed by the crown, despite provocations. Corregidores profited from this prudence much more before 1504 than they would thereafter, for *regidores* were still sensitive, during Isabella's lifetime, that they owed their status to a tacit agreement that they accept the royal representative as a fixed part of city government.

9

The queen in heaven: troubled aftermath

The topic of conversation at the refined court of Urbino, one evening, was rule by females. A courtier, as reported by Castiglione, maintained that much attributed to the late Queen Isabella was actually the work of her husband. Giuliano de' Medici sprang to the defense, eloquent on the subject of her justice:

Wherefore among the people there arose a very veneration for her, composed of love and fear, and a veneration still so fixed in the minds of all that it almost seems that they expect her to be watching them from heaven and that she might praise or blame them from up there.[1]

Not every observer was as sanguine. García Sarmiento, a corregidor at Medina del Campo in 1506, complained: "these kingdoms have been very badly governed and Queen Isabella, for her evil rule, was in Hell," and as for Ferdinand, "with her he never did anything save rob and dissipate these kingdoms."[2]

Just as the *Reyes Católicos* have had their partisans and detractors, so too the corregidores attract a mixture of praise and blame. The queen did reach her goal of placing these officials throughout her domain, yet they were not thereby made self-sustaining, because the alert administrative presence of a stable monarchy was required to permit them to function adequately. Isabella left the kingdom so troubled a succession that the fate of this legacy was put in doubt. She had the misfortune to see her son die, leaving Castile to an obviously distressed daughter, with a foreign consort. Unable to decide what should be done in case Juana became totally incapacitated, Isabella left contradictory instructions in her will and its codicils about who would serve as regent: Philip of Austria, Ferdinand, or Cardinal Cisneros.[3] The confusion, which uncomfortably resembles the muddle left behind by Enrique IV, deepened with the sudden death of Philip I in 1506 and the subsequent rapid mental deterioration of Queen Juana. Their son Charles (eventually styled Carlos I in Spain and, in German speaking lands, Karl V of the Holy Roman Empire) was but four at the time, so the next few years resounded with the struggles of supporters of Cisneros to prevent Ferdinand from claiming the regency. The old fox maneuvered a return from Aragon to Castile in 1510 with the approval of the Cortes, adroitly managing affairs of the two kingdoms until death took him away from his burdensome chores during 1516.

Under assault

A "post-Isabelline" period that runs from 1504 until the Cortes settlements of 1523–5 can be discerned in the relations between corregidores and the urban elite. During these decades corregidores presented four successive aspects to their communities. The esteem in which they had once been held continued its downward spiral, from 1504 to 1516, due to their dereliction of duty, their high salaries, and the aristocratic domination of their selection – all of which deepened the marks of corruption upon their features. With the advent of Charles, corregidores were asked to don the mask of hard taskmasters for cities, as from 1517 to 1520 they prevented unauthorized protest meetings, repressed dissent from *regidores* and clerics, and attempted to assure docile representatives be sent to the Cortes. During the height of the *Comuneros* uprising of 1520–1, corregidores showed a grimace of fear, as they were driven from rebel cities and saw their places usurped by men drawn from the communities. Returning with the vanguard of conquering armies, corregidores displayed a cruel visage in their central role of gathering information for a purge of urban offices, punishing conspirators, and repressing lingering disturbances. As soon as the general pardon of 1523 brought an end to the crisis, the crown relieved corregidores of such extraordinary duties and began to undertake reform of their office.

Disarray in the ranks of corregidores appreciably worsened immediately after 1504, as a result of unstable dynastic fortunes which permitted the aristocracy to dig itself deeper into urban life by tearing away at the prestige of the crown's representative. The issue of who would control the appointment of the official reopened fighting at Úbeda. In 1505 Philip I nominated Antonio Manrique, the Molina candidate, to the post in the city of 15,000; but the Cueva band seized their opportunity, upon the king's death, to persuade Ferdinand to nominate Hernán Gil Mogollón. The Molina, in turn, reached

Charles's Habsburg advisors with the recommendation that Manrique be renominated. A bitter armed struggle ensued, until Ferdinand and Charles came to an agreement that Manrique would withdraw from Baeza and Úbeda, thereby ending forty years of Molina ascendancy.[4] At Jerez de la Frontera, the muted rivalry of the Ayala with the Ribera line resurfaced over the same issue. Philip I gave the position to Hernando de Ávalos, who was from a family allied to the Ayalas, and Ferdinand took the post away to hand it to a nominee from the rival clan. When Ferdinand was no longer on the scene Hernando de Ávalos started petitioning Charles to regain the post, but his restoration was blocked by the new King's minister, Guillaume de Croy, sieur de Chièvre. Sour discontent flared into hatred of all Flemings, with the result that Hernando de Ávalos would become a principal leader of the *Comuneros* rising at Toledo.[5]

As soon as Murcia heard that Philip I had died, wrangling began about how to get rid of its crown representative, most council members being pleased to maintain that the office lapsed upon the death of a monarch. On 27 October 1506 a majority of *regidores*, joined by the *jurados*, voted to offer the executive post to their lordly *adelantado mayor* and so informed the corregidor, adding the ironic rationale that he had not brought peace to the city.[6] Toledo was an equally significant target of aristocratic pressure from November 1506, when the count of Fuensalida recovered his daughter's right to nominate the keeper of the fortress. His campaign to overawe the city culminated in an armed attack on corregidor Pedro de Castilla's house, but residents came to their official's aid, in this instance at least, to repel the hated count.[7]

The succession squabbles, coming as they did in a difficult economic climate, encouraged some corregidores in dereliction of duty. Throughout the south, harvests were lean from 1504 to 1507, with the nadir being reached in 1506. The impact of bad weather was worsened by excessive taxes, market speculation, and heavy requisitioning for royal troops.[8] Tensions were so high in 1506 at Cordova that a number of *veinticuatros* left to protect their estates and, in June, the long-term corregidor, Diego López Dávalos, fled. Pedro Fernández, the first marquis of Priego, who had been granted his father's title of *alcalde mayor*, came to an agreement with the third count of Cabra – the *alguacil mayor* – to take over the supervision of the city from the corregidor's officials. The municipal council decided that, unless there was a royal document forbidding this action, it would go along with it. This state of affairs lasted only until August, when a new corregidor, Diego Osorio, arrived.[9] Plague added its toll the following year, and, despite the direct order of the municipal council that he stay in place, Osorio left in April. When he did not return by August for a renewal of his term, the marquis expelled his officials, and managed affairs in collaboration with a deputy from the count. Finally, Diego López Dávalos returned that December to the post he had fecklessly abandoned a while before. The aristocrats gracefully surrendered their powers to him but, as Edwards notes, their intervention broke the spell of automatic *veinticuatro* acceptance of royal supervision.[10]

Corregidores at Murcia also scandalously neglected their post. Through a particularly long absence of a corregidor in 1510, his constables were so heedless that Murcia suffered a series of ugly crimes.[11] One consequence of similar neglect was the decay of the urban fabric. At Alcaraz, corrupt *regidores* and a series of uninterested corregidores allowed water conduits to disintegrate. During 1511 a petition was filed with the crown requesting that an investigation be made into just how, and when, the decorative fountain which once graced the main square had disappeared.[12] At Cuenca, corregidor Fernando de Rebolledo was so frequently absent during 1516 that the municipal council withheld part of his salary, as it had every right to do under the ordinances.[13] During the following year both corregidor Martín Vázquez de Acuña and his lieutenant were out of the city at the same time, leading the disgruntled municipal council of Cuenca to elect its own officers to keep the peace.[14]

Yet, in justice to other corregidores who continued to do their work in a professional manner, one example is provided for balance. Meneses de Bobadilla, who was at Logroño, Calahorra, and Alfaro in 1517, confessed himself overwhelmed by problems. In a lengthy letter to Cardinal Cisneros (briefly regent after Ferdinand's death), he humbly requested any help he could get. Somehow he had to learn how to deal with bitter conflicts within an aristocrat's family over a dowry; to intervene in a fight between two churches over the manner in which they held processions; to get the clergy to conform to the proper mode of making payments to the bishop; to sequester the goods of the canon of the cathedral; to mediate a debate between Calahorra and an aristocrat over boundaries; to diminish the perpetual small-scale armed struggle between Alfaro and neighboring hamlets; and to deal with large-scale fighting involving 1,000 men on the frontier.[15]

Defective procedures

Residencia investigations, which might have kept corregidores less conscientious than Meneses de Bobadilla in line, had been neglected for some time. The demand for a *residencia* each year was once again put forward in early discussion at the Cortes of 1506, the most open held in almost half a century. Delegates were not bound by stipulations that they arrive with full powers, an oversight that would be corrected in later assemblies.[16] Philip I and Juana flatly rejected the demand for an automatic *residencia* in favor of continuing to leave the initiative for an investigation to the community. Ferdinand expressed a willingness in 1512 to regularize investigations, but his apparent agreement proved to be mere pacification.[17]

Representatives asked for far more than exit investigations in petitions put forward from 1512 through 1518. Corregidores and other judges, they claimed, were neglecting to render justice except when they profited from fines and salaries that were far too high. Also, judges were so poorly trained in the law that they were sending everything to the Royal Council for decision, with resultant errors deriving from the long-drawn-out appeals. So inadequate were local royal officials that the crown was itself constantly bypassing them in favor of rapacious special envoys. Corregidores were beginning to allow *regidores* to display open favoritism to friends, and to dissipate the communal patrimony. Above all, the petitions lamented, when the time came for reappointment no consideration was given to community sentiments. Corregidores must not return to office until at least two years had passed, to prevent retaliation against hostile witnesses who had testified in exit investigations. What representatives to these meetings of the Cortes really hoped for at best, despite the aggrieved tone of the protests, was still minimal Royal Council consultation with the concerned jurisdictions.[18]

Documentation for at least one allegation made at the parliaments is found in a transition paper prepared by a Royal Council official for the new Habsburg king.[19] Complaints dating from late in Isabella's reign about excessive salaries are fully borne out by figures showing that the "typical" remuneration, which once ran to 200 *mrs* a day, or 73,000 a year, was by then found in only eight locales, and these the tiniest jurisdictions. Out of 57 listed salaries, 45 per cent (25) earned under 100,000 *mrs*. Through a combination of salary inflation and expense padding,.35 per cent (20) now earned between 100,000 and 199,999 *mrs*, while 21 per cent (12) show incomes in excess of 200,000 *mrs*. Corregidores collected fines worth 70,000 *mrs* in Segovia, and were paid in kind at Molina, where the official received 180 bushels of wheat a year. The rate of improvement was uneven: Madrid went up by merely 50 *mrs* a day, but Murcia almost doubled its salary, to 380 *mrs*. Burgos shot up from 154,000 *mrs* to 270,500, and the fortunate aristocratic holder of the post at Toledo received 330,000 *mrs*, up from 187,000.

The sixty-four officeholders in the listing continue to be drawn primarily from the ranks of the military nobility, plus a sprinkling of aristocrats. Commander Pedro Barrientos was at Logroño, and the powerful duke of the Infantado dominated his family holdings in Guadalajara. The level of those with formal education had dropped slightly, again, from Isabella's last decade: three bachelors join only thirteen men who held the licenciate in law.[20] The jurisdictions to which these officials were sent had little to be pleased about concerning their quality.

The *Comuneros* rising

Grievances accumulating from late in Isabella's rule and through the changes following her death were greatly exacerbated in 1517 by the arrival in Castile of the inexperienced and physically unattractive young heir, Charles of Austria. His "alien" court of Flemings was thought to be robbing the kingdom so thoroughly that when the king left for German territory to collect his expensive title of Holy Roman Emperor, leaving behind a regent, there were many who thought the monarch would never return, all the while draining them of taxes. The *Comuneros* rising began in earnest during the last week of May 1520, and continued in strength until the popular forces succumbed to defeat at the battle of Villalar on 23 April 1521.[21]

The principal rebels resided in towns grouped about a triangle formed by Segovia, Valladolid, and Salamanca, which incorporated municipalities little involved in international commerce and thus unlikely to profit from royal monopolies or foreign dynastic connections.[22] Pressure for the expulsion of the corregidor of Ciudad Real, for example, came from the lesser guilds of weavers, carders, and fullers, who were fearful that the new king would give competitors in Flemish cloth centers too big a price advantage, and that they would have to absorb the loss with no relief from crown or city.[23] Municipalities with workers involved in significant international trade, however, such as

Seville to the south or Burgos to the north, actively resisted the rebels, after an initial flirtation. Although the main historical platform is crowded with city folk, there was also a large-scale agrarian adherence offstage during early phases, both by rural nobles and by anti-seignorial peasants. The aristocrats stayed in the audience, until they decided that their best interests lay with Charles.

The millenarian ideal of a self-directed association of communities delegating powers to representatives was the only suitable alternative to God-granted royalty that could be accepted by the age. This communitarian image offered the most widespread and powerful of symbols to early modern Europeans, in Castile or Aragon, France or the Germanies. Wherever revolt took deep root, the *comunidad* ideal meant the establishment of a degree of popular power and active participation.[24] The core of rebel municipalities had been used to working together at sporadic Cortes meetings since 1498, and before that very closely through twenty years of the Holy Brotherhood's assemblies. It should not be forgotten that corregidores played virtually no role once those various bodies had been convened, and could thus be decisively rejected as outsiders when new assemblies were constructed.

During the stormy time that preceded this rising, the crown relied upon its supervisors to hold back demands for unauthorized meetings, and to make sure that *procuradores* selected for official parliamentary sessions were both submissive to the royal will and ready to vote subsidies. Out of the cascade of events of those tumultuous years, we will select only the few which most deeply involved corregidores. Burgos, with a major stake in preserving its position in international trade under a new regime, began agitating in February 1517 for a meeting with other cities, to set policy before the young king and his lands had their first encounter. Cisneros was concerned about the revolutionary aspect of such a call, and relied upon his corregidores to oppose the action, being successful at least to the extent that Burgos found only León, Valladolid, and Zamora willing to meet with it that June.[25] Thus, when Charles arrived in Castile for the Cortes of Valladolid, during February 1518, the event passed without conflict.

As the extent of outside appointments to Castilian positions became clearer, and when, at the request of the crown, the papacy approved an exceptional ecclesiastical contribution (the *décima*) in 1517, xenophobic clerics looking to their own fiscal interests became a central focus of agitation. The Royal Council urgently requested that the count of Palma, its corregidor in Toledo, undertake a secret inquest into who was preaching subversive themes. A gradual inflation of rhetoric on the part of these preachers provided a millenarian ideology for the masses, by going so far as to identify Charles with the Antichrist.[26] Toledo tried to convoke an unauthorized meeting of the third estate during 1519. Although its letters received a positive response from Cordova, Cuenca, Granada, Guadalajara, Jaén, Madrid, Murcia, Seville, Segovia and Soria, corregidores in the respective locales successfully aborted the meeting.[27]

Because the king desperately needed a special grant from Castile, his advisors scheduled the second official Cortes of his reign for March 1520 at Santiago. The crown demanded that corregidores ensure that the eleven cities and two towns privileged to send *procuradores* reject any individual pledged to opposition, and that the communities be prevented from coordinating strategy. Toledo was the primary fomentor of the opposition to these pressure tactics. Charles's advisors made a serious mistake in this city by removing the count of Palma because he was too closely identified with dissenters on the municipal council. Antonio de Córdoba, the new corregidor, was told bluntly by the king to manipulate the elections to the Cortes because time was too short for subtler means. The aggressive replacement also attempted to enforce the king's order of 27 February, which insisted that no messengers be sent from Toledo to other cities, on pain of a heavy fine of 2,000 ducats. When all the votes went consistently against the corregidor, by large margins, he ordered the chief scribe not to cooperate and his lieutenant not to allow messengers to leave. When the time came to select *procuradores*, the councilors wanted to exclude the corregidor and his officials from witnessing the vote. Antonio de Córdoba wrote to the king that his efforts to reduce propaganda within the city were proving ineffectual, and that he could also not stop it from stirring up Valladolid.[28]

Other royal officials proceeded with a similar lack of finesse, as was shown in Toledo, encouraged by the king to admit strangers to the municipal councils, on any pretext, to rig elections for *procuradores*. Valladolid was divided over the nominations, and its council meetings had several times to be reconvoked by its corregidor. The *regimiento* objected bitterly to having the king's official authorize outsiders to vote in its convocation.[29] In Salamanca, monks who cooperated with the municipal council in drawing up a declaration preached that the city should not be intimidated by its corregidor. These clerics also wrote to other cities that they should not be servile, but should resist. At Segovia, the troubled voting eventually went according to the corregidor's wishes after he arranged an ambiguous compromise, through bribes and promise of office, that a special fiscal grant – a *servicio* – would be voted at the Cortes in exchange for allowing *procuradores* to have their demands heard. With less effort, the corregidor of Burgos was happy to report to the Royal Council that he had completely impeded all efforts to have the city's *procuradores* speak against royal policy at the Cortes.[30] Despite such successes, Toledo and Salamanca did not get their delegates seated at the Cortes, which began at distant Santiago as scheduled, during March 1520, and then was shifted to the even less accessible La Coruña, so that the king could hurriedly set sail from the port to his imperial coronation.

Distinguished family heads at Toledo immediately moved to create the *Santa Comunidad*, a new regime led by the popular heroes Juan de Padilla and Hernando de Ávalos. When Antonio de Córdoba appeared before this body on 8 May 1520, a clamor arose to take away his staff of office, forcing him to flee, along with his officials.[31] Wherever there was a significant rising thereafter, corregidores and Cortes representatives, not the aristocracy, took the first brunt of popular hostility. Segovia expressed its outrage during a meeting held on 29 May at the church of Corpus Christi, where residents of that parish complained about the corregidor, Juan de Acuña, that "he never came to Segovia and that his officials had more of an eye to rob them than to govern them...."[32] Leaving the gathering, the agitated crowd hanged two police informers. The next day a *procurador*, who had voted for additional taxes in Santiago as his price for negotiating a corregidorship for himself, was murdered. All of Juan de Acuña's officials were driven out of the city when the nobility took charge, under the leadership of Juan Bravo. The *regidores* claimed, when questioned by the regent, that no natives were responsible for these outrages, which they asserted were fomented by foreign workers.[33]

At Burgos, corregidor Meneses de Bobadilla called a meeting of parish representatives during June to end rumors, but because he was unable to allay anger over new taxes to be placed upon wine the strategy backfired, leading to the occupation of the fortress and the pillaging of the house belonging to a *procurador*. The scrupulous corregidor was jostled by the crowd, who seized his staff of office and forced him to take shelter in a monastery. The populace then happened to encounter the corregidor of Cordova, Diego Osorio, who was in town on a visit. Responding to the popular clamor, he reluctantly accepted the abruptly vacated office, but he was unable to end attacks on *procuradores*, protect their houses, or stop an assault upon his prison. To retrieve the situation, the constable of Castile took over from Osorio, which led to agitators firing the aristocrat's townhouse.[34] In Madrid, Antonio de Astudillo entered office as its corregidor on 19 May. When he attempted to prevent the municipal council from receiving letters and briefs from Toledo, a crowd invaded the church where the session was being held on 17 June and drove him out of the town. The council was presided over thereafter by an *alcalde mayor*.[35]

Meanwhile, the south looked equally precarious during these early months, causing the regent, Cardinal Adrian of Utrecht, to write to Charles on 20 July 1520 that the corregidor of Cordova had abandoned his jurisdiction, that Sancho Martínez de Leyenda was afraid to enter his at Seville, and that such serious crimes were alleged against Antonio de la Cueva, the corregidor of Granada, that it was perilous to avoid an immediate *residencia*.[36] With the passage of time the Andalusian situation stabilized, as the higher social orders, who dominated its towns, took fright and closed ranks behind their sovereign in the League of La Rambla. Diego Osorio, corregidor of Cordova, was one of the eight directors who coordinated the collection of troops and took part in the fighting, while the *asistente* of Seville took responsibility for keeping the league's books and disbursing payments.[37]

In the central highlands, radicalization had proceeded apace. Luis Mega, corregidor at Jaén, was suspended from his post and replaced, in August 1520, with ordinary *alcaldes*. When much of Medina del Campo was burned to the ground by forces acting on the regent's orders, the populace condemned the corregidor, Gutierre Quijida, and his lieutenant, Joanes de Ávila, as authors of the destruction. Quijida fled with the departing troops.[38] The ejection of such corregidores was merely one aspect of a generalized protest against entrenched oligarchies, working in collaboration with royally appointed officials who shared their values and backed up their grip.

A city's rallying to the *comunidad* is always presented in contemporary texts as a transfer of power from both the corregidor and the narrow *regimiento* to citizens represented by elected delegates.[39] Composition of the new governments demonstrates an overt desire completely to replace the old order of royal selection with widely drawn, elected administrations of lawyers, merchants, artisans, municipal functionaries, and some members of the mendicant orders.[40] Those caballeros who still retained popular respect, such as Juan Bravo, former *regidor* at Segovia, sat with newly prominent delegates from parish and cathedral chapters. Executive power was invested in locally chosen individuals, typically *alcaldes*, but often civil servants given designations other than the despised title "corregidor" – for example, *justicia mayor* in Madrid, *caudillo* in Zamora, and *capitán general* in Valladolid.[41]

The first quarter of the sixteenth-century was a time of varied troubles in Iberia. Despite the expansion of the royal corregidor system throughout Castile during the fifteenth-century, the officials had failed to create a sense of urban community in which they would be seen as an invaluable part. In fact, it came to be thought in various parts of the peninsula that corregidores blocked good government and should be removed. At the moment that Castilian municipalities were in full revolt, unrelated social revolutionary upheavals were taking place in Valencia and Mallorca, directed against the upper stratum of Aragon's society and the protected Muslims on their estates.[42] Fighting also flared in Guipúzcoa, where the conflicts since 1516 were directly associated with the desire of the regent to force a corregidor, selected without consultation, upon the community.[43] Rebels revived a brotherhood during February 1520 that soon evolved into a dissident junta for Tolosa, Irún, Hernani, and other towns which refused to accept the crown's choice. The junta claimed that the privilege once extended to the towns by Enrique IV not to send a corregidor "without our supplication and petition" was perpetual.[44] An opposing, royalist, junta centered in San Sebastián fully sided with the appointment, and, in conjunction with the aristocracy, suppressed the dissidents.[45] The insular rebels at Guipúzcoa never sought to link up their struggle with those in the other kingdoms, and so suffered ignominious failure.

In Castile, with the backdrop of new city governments coming into being during 1520, the commune at Toledo urged that an assembly be held at Avila, where sympathetic urban regimes might establish a confederation cautiously rival to the government of the regent, Adrian of Utrecht. This *Junta General* or *Santa Junta*, which at first consisted of only four cities, made a series of modest demands upon the sovereign entirely in line with previous Cortes petitions, until the apparently retaliatory burning of Medina del Campo, that August, greatly accelerated radicalization. When Tordesillas, site of Queen Juana's confinement, joined the revolt, the junta transferred its sessions there, assembling thirteen cities in September. The junta decided to administer all royal revenues to fund its activities, and decreed that it would nominate all corregidores and judges, save for those in the *chancillerías*.[46]

Making use of the occasionally lucid queen against her son, a thoroughgoing sharing of power was given a cover of legitimacy. After three months of work, a broad platform of reforms was agreed upon and sent off to Charles, with an insolent letter. Suggestions initially put forward by advanced or "democratic" elements, which attract increasing attention today, were swept out of sight by the newly dominant group, as were most radical dreams in various pre-modern risings, be they Jacqueries or urban worker agitation. The demands of the Tordesillas junta for reinvigorating the Cortes were thus kept modest enough, and would not have considerably diminished royal prerogatives if carried out in their entirety, although they were naturally seen by the king and his regent as an intolerable interference with governance.

The principal request from the junta was to hold regular Cortes meetings, at which tighter urban control would be exercised over requests for fiscal aid. Given the past record of various monarchs, who agreed to take somewhat similar action and then blithely disregarded their word, it is difficult to believe that acceptance of this point would have crippled the monarchy. A hope was also expressed at Tordesillas that the number of deputies be expanded from two to three per municipality, providing broader representation in the person of one delegate each from the commons (*comunidad*), the clergy, and the nobility. A principal difficulty for Charles was a xenophobic tinge in the reform program that insisted he return to Castile and pledge to exclude non-Castilians from all aspects of government and religion. These initial requests were couched in terms implying that nothing more was called for but a return to time-honored norms, which appeared to be the case with the recommendations concerning the corregidor. The assembly revived demands, last aired in the Cortes of 1478, that no corregidor be forced upon a village or city unless called for by the community, the stay to be no longer than two years, followed by an obligatory *residencia*.

Such familiar requests were eventually overshadowed by innovation: free to express their deepest feelings without any need for circumspection, townsmen soon decisively rejected the corregidor, whom they neither required nor wanted. The deputies asserted that in most cases an ordinary *alcalde* would be sufficient. Rejection of the royal superintendent was incorporated into a broad attack on the corruption of the old urban oligarchy, so long winked at by the corregidores. *Regidores*, for example, were not to profit from being lawyers to the jurisdiction they served, and no license was to be given to permit regular payments to flow from aristocrats to their clients on the municipal councils.[47] (A last list of demands that the junta of Tordesillas made on the emperor, submitted in February 1521, presents little new concerning corregidores, save that the offices should never be sold, and that absenteeism ought to prohibited.)[48] What was at issue in the petitions and demands was the lifting of some weight from the shoulders of hard-pressed subjects. It should not have been unexpected that the revolt quickly became more radical, since the problems of the taxpayers were great, nor is it surprising that the powerful in this society refused to acknowledge how deep ran the discontent.

Adrian of Utrecht wrote to the absent monarch in 1521 that the burgeoning strife derived from the inadequacy of municipal leadership: "it is public surmise," he observed, "that one of the main things which caused these revolts was the bad appointment of many unsuitable persons as corregidores."[49] So mono-causal an explanation relieved the regent, his king, and their advisors of blame for their heavy-handed exploitation, and displayed no comprehension of the deep-seated social discontent engendered by the fusion of interests of corregidor and oligarchy. Yet this is also how the 1525 Cortes of Toledo would choose to interpret events: "one of the chief causes for the recent altercations had been the defects of the corregidores and judges . . ."[50] The reason for such curious agreement is not hard to discover. The consensus developed out of the last stage of the revolt, when the once-privileged urban groups became so terrified by the radical consequences of a loss by the king that they rallied to his side. The corregidor provided one convenient, mutually agreed scapegoat who would allow ruling groups to reunify after the revolt with less loss of face all round.

To generalize, if a rebellion is to survive longer than a few days it is necessary that there be more than strong pressure from below. There must also be weakness at the top, such as a split within the ruling group, which will allow elements in opposition an opportunity to exploit the turmoil. As Lenin put it: "For a revolution to break out it is not enough for the 'lower orders to refuse' to live in the old way; it is also necessary that the 'upper classes should be unable' to live in the old way."[51] The urban oligarchy of Castile had gradually allowed itself the luxury of indulging in an intense hostility towards the manifest failings of the monarchy, especially blameworthy for its lackluster representatives at settled urban posts, and for the greedy officials it sent out on special assignment. Resentment was allowed to overshadow gratitude towards the crown for guaranteeing control over virtually hereditary posts. A considerable number of those who mistakenly allowed themselves to be thus alienated from their chief protector were, according to Santa Cruz's chronicle, *caballeros de mediano estado*.[52] The first junta meetings in 1520 were heavily populated by this group. New Christians, who took part in these assemblies in proportion to their number within cities, would also have much to fear if, as a consequence of the weakening of central authority, the prejudiced lower ranks were suddenly to predominate in society.[53]

Although the masses – or, to use a contemptuous phrase of the day, "the men without blood-lines" (*gente sin raíz*) – played a part in disturbances, they at first let others take the lead. This changed rapidly, as a lieutenant of the corregidor at Medina discovered when he noted that the poor were soon making a clear distinction between the *comunidad* of the lower orders and the *comunidad* of ranking citizens.[54] One of the more radical suggestions concerning corregidores, tossed out in the heat of the developing social struggle, was that the official be accompanied in all his juridical duties by two *alcaldes*, one of whom was to be an independent peasant farm proprietor (*labrador*).[55] At Medina, after the great fire, a chief of low extraction exhorted the crowd to kill all traitors. The conflict sharpened when it became possible for a carpenter to head Cuenca's government, or resistance to be directed in Toledo by a brassworker. An alleged plot was uncovered in Soria to murder *regidores*, steal their goods, and burn their homes. The original leadership thus found itself displaced and taxed, with its authority diminished and prestige low.

King Charles intelligently chose to broaden his base of support among the aristocracy by nominating two governors – the constable and admiral of Castile – to act as co-regents, in concert with Cardinal Adrian. As a consequence, the defection of the urban nobility was rapid in 1521, especially after the aristocracy adopted a moderate policy to entice defections to the imperial party.[56] Thirty-three out of

252 leading royalists commended by the regents to receive offices or incomes after the war were *regidores* and *jurados*.[57]

Corregidores were reinstalled by the triumvirate to undertake the internal pacification necessary to restore royal domination. Badajoz received Francisco de Luján peacefully on 6 February 1521. When Valladolid surrendered, *licenciado* de Lugo returned to his post in the train of the conquering army. He was ordered by the regents to begin the sequestering of the goods of rebels in May, and to prohibit all public meetings.[58] That same month, corregidores in Aranda, Avila, Cáceres, Medina, Palencia, Plasencia, Salamanca, Segovia, Toro, and Zamora were told by the government to start recording royal revenues, and to lay plans to collect income due from appropriations made at the two meetings of the Cortes.[59]

During December of the preceding year, in an edict issued from Worms, the king had condemned more than 200 *comuneros*. Corregidores were expected to take charge of carrying out this repression as soon as they arrived at their jurisdictions. Through 1521 they also worked up local lists of those to be proscribed and those to be pardoned. The *licenciado* de Lugo, for example, was ordered in July to inform himself, as secretly as possible, about all in Valladolid who had favored the junta, and to send the details on to a panel of judges set up to punish the guilty. After he had finished this chore, by the end of the summer, he was able to report that the town was at last tranquil.[60] Juan de Ayala, new corregidor at Salamanca, was charged with collecting any correspondence the city had had with other communities through the time of the rising. After assessment for culpability, the documents were to be destroyed, ensuring that the very memory of events would be blotted out – an order later extended by the king to the land as a whole.[61]

Moving from information-gathering to action, corregidores were given maximum powers by the regents to undertake their work of repression. In towns still deemed dangerous, they were assigned personal guards of twenty armed men. Segovia was thought so difficult as to require the service of 100 troops, and when its newly appointed corregidor, the *licenciado* Peralta, arrived at his post on 7 May (five days after the city was liberated), he looked over the continuing disturbances and decided not to assume office. Juan de Acuña, former corregidor of Valladolid, was the next to turn down the hastily proffered job, despite the added inducement of a lifetime position on the municipal council. In a letter to the Royal Council, he stated he refused the offer both because he did not wish to undertake the role of judge, and "for other reasons" he preferred not to put into writing.[62] Less cautious than the nominees to Segovia, the corregidor of Toro, Carlos de Guevara, overawed his jurisdiction by terrorizing citizens after the city was deemed fully pacified. In León, the original corregidor was replaced by the tougher count of Luna, whose brutal repression had such apparently serious consequences that the *regidores* begged the crown to rein him in lest, they alleged, the land become depopulated.[63] For the next few years Avila, Medina, Salamanca, León, Tordesillas, and Segovia suffered a series of investigations, arrests, sequestering of goods, and the destruction of houses that belonged to the condemned.[64]

Even when they were supported by troops, all did not go easily at first for the corregidores, due to the continuing discontent. During February 1521 a crowd in Andújar assailed the home of the corregidor after the city fathers had agitated to name their own man to the spot. Despite the attachment of Cordova to the League of La Rambla, the city was so disturbed during March that the corregidor was assigned a second peace officer, with an additional twenty constables. Diego Osorio issued an order forbidding any meetings in Cordova without his approval or the carrying of arms without his express consent. The corregidor of León, Bernardino de Ledesma, was ordered by the Royal Council to destroy the castles and houses in the possession of the Guzmán family during May. The populace attempted to impede him by force when he started about the demolition of the home of a Guzmán. Hard put to calm the situation, the best he could do was to call upon the constable of Castile for aid.[65] In June the corregidor of Toro, Carlos de Guivera, wrote to inform the crown that, although the city was pacified, there were still occasional disturbances. During the following month the corregidor of Palencia, acting on a tip, uncovered a new conspiracy and was instructed by the Royal Council to punish the guilty severely.[66] After the surrender of Segovia in May, there was consternation in government circles about what to do with the remains of executed leaders of the rebellion. The regents decided to allow the return of Juan Bravo's body to the city early in June, but only on condition that there be a quiet private interment. Instead, an illegal public service was held for the fallen leader which nearly caused a riot. A long cortege of mourners dressed in black hooded robes passed through the poorest sections of town, preceded by a show of the crosses of their confraternities, engendering a sorrow that led to fresh anger against the royalists. The corregidor seized two persons blamed with responsibility for organizing the illegal event and had them hanged.[67]

The tensions in Segovia had been defused by prompt action, but trouble far more difficult to control broke out in Madrid during the summer. In July, some 300 men – mainly agriculturalists – rushed the corregidor's house, and, upon burning it down, moved on to the prison. Among the inmates freed was Juan Negrete, a venerated chief of the *comunidad*. After dispersing the crowd the corregidor, Martín de Acuña, chased some suspects into a church and brought two out to be hanged. A second explosion of resentment took place the following month, triggered by the arrival of ecclesiastical judges to assess the clergy. When some radical clerics who had favored the *comunidad* were arrested, a crowd set out to free them. Some priests escaped, but a few made it only so far as a church, where they claimed sanctuary. This time the corregidor's men broke down the door of the house of worship to get at their catch. In both the July and August incidents, the corregidor and his staff were excommunicated for their actions, but ignored the wrath of pastors. To maintain calm while surrender was being negotiated with Toledo, higher authority did not insist that further action be taken against troublemakers, or that an investigation be launched into alleged plots to return the city to the status of active revolt.[68] Toledo gave up that December, despite the valiant leadership of María Pacheco, after having vainly striven to dictate surrender terms which included the right to a voice in the naming of its corregidores. The archbishop of Bari was entrusted with the administration of the city, until such time as the crown sent whomever it chose for corregidor.[69]

The change of the year brought a relaxation of tensions. During March the corregidor of Valladolid was told by the regents to begin revoking sentences, and in June the crown ordered all cases of persons arrested in León by its brutal corregidor to be transferred to a higher court. On All Saints' Day, the king issued a general pardon which put an end to executions. Thereupon, despite Toledo's incomplete pacification, its corregidor was enjoined by the royal court to reverse all condemnations he had made.[70]

Not unexpectedly, a few corregidores took advantage of emergency conditions to exploit their jurisdictions to the limit, and to claim as much as they could from the crown for services rendered. After the two candidates for the post at Segovia turned it down, as previously mentioned, the title came to rest on the person of Pedro Maldonado, who left his post at Salamanca where he had reduced the city to obedience. As soon as he departed Salamanca he was charged with assorted crimes against the city, in conspiracy with various high clerics.[71] The city fathers of Ronda requested a *residencia* for Alonso de Espinosa, alleging that he favored rebels. Their reiterated demand to be sent a judge hostile to rebellion was a bit of humbug, since the municipality was the only one in its area to join the uprising.[72]

Despite the generosity of the king's pardon he had withheld the restoration of rights and privileges from 293 notorious rebels. Five corregidores made successful supplication to the crown in 1522 for the property and offices of persons exempted from the general pardon.[73] One former corregidor of Valladolid, who gained three such offices then, was still petitioning the crown for favors in 1538, while another long retired corregidor from the same city continued as late as 1541 to apply for royal gifts.[74] Since all municipalities had been left in undisturbed possession of their privileges, despite participation in the rebellion, there was a clear basis for a reconciliation of the country with the crown, once outstanding issues were resolved.

When Charles I disembarked at Santander on 16 July 1522, to the applause of many of his subjects, few corregidores had been at their posts for long. A list (incomplete) drawn up for Charles's perusal at the time shows fifty-four officials in place for seventy localities.[75] Twenty had served less than a year, twenty-one for more than a year, and only eleven for more than two years. In this time of strife, when military men and the titled were far more important than legists, not unexpectedly the list shows only ten licenciates.[76]

Obtaining more satisfactory corregidores than those in place was high on the priorities of parliaments held soon after the king's arrival. *Procuradores* presumed to speak for all subjects in the third estate, but were only drawn from the urban nobility. This bias had been clearly enunciated at least as early as the Cortes of Palencia in 1431, where it was stated that representatives should not be selected from the taxpayers and peasant proprietors so "that the estate and honor of those who send them may be the better safeguarded and that the representatives may be able to agree with each other the more easily when they have to discuss issues at assemblies."[77] The king was not able decisively to select who was chosen from this dominant group to attend the Cortes sessions of 1523 and 1525, but it was unnecessary that he do so, since reconfirmed interests closely bound crown and nobility together to defend privileges against any resumption of assault from the lower orders.[78]

Charles hastened to adopt some of the *Comunero* program as his own, abandoning arbitrary ways in exchange for peaceful cooperation by agreeing to deal fully with all petitions, and although *procuradores* could not get him to settle grievances before voting funds, he did firmly promise that action would be taken to implement each approved petition twenty days after the *servicio* grant was voted. He even opened the first session, in 1523, with an apology, blaming his errors upon youth and inexperience. Petitions regarding the corregidor, put forward by this and the next parliament, were acceded to in their entirety, following along lines of the newly perceived convergence of interests. No official would be allowed to reside at court after appointment, relying entirely upon a lieutenant to do his work in the field. No judge of *residencia* would be permitted to remain at any one location for more than three months, thus ensuring that he would not displace the qualified corregidor. With the proper individuals in place, the king agreed not to send out any more of the special envoys who had plagued cities. The time had also arrived to reduce inflated salaries by reverting to customary remuneration. Most desired of all by cities was their demand, recognized at last by the crown, that no one with judicial responsibilities of any type would be reappointed before a *residencia* was both completed and reviewed. To that end, it was agreed that the Royal Council would oversee judicial work, then send the results to the king in the form of a *consulta*, which report in council would enable him to learn about his servants. Detailed follow-up instructions for the proper behavior of judges and corregidores were soon issued by the Royal Council.[79]

It is not possible to tell, due to the conjoining of interests, which part of all this legislation was favored primarily by the crown and which by the cities. One idea concerning educational qualifications presumably originated with the Royal Council because it marks another significant victory for the legist faction in government. The Cortes decreed the office would only be given to holders of proven ability, who must be as well qualified as other royal servants, which meant that only *letrados* with at least the minimum of ten years' schooling could henceforth be utilized. Such a requirement had rarely been a demand made by cities. On the eve of the revolt, the petition sent by Jerez de la Frontera requesting it be provided with a new official – one who would be a "conscientious person" and a caballero – made no mention that he need be a legist.[80]

The "reform package" fell well within the narrow limits set out by the socially privileged, but it was still necessary to force the pace of royal implementation. Emergency methods were called for to restore confidence in the deeply shaken apparatus of municipal and provincial administration. It was bluntly admitted by the crown that *residencias* had not been revealing whether corregidores had administered their ordinances properly, much less demonstrating how well, or poorly, cities had been governed. The king agreed to send out two honorable caballeros to take testimony for the purpose of castigating the guilty. Charles would have to act promptly because, in the words of the 1525 Cortes, "at no time was it as necessary to show such great diligence and attention as now."[81] Rather than simply wait on the king, the Cortes set up a two-man standing committee (*diputación*) in 1525 to oversee implementation of decrees when parliament was not in session. Its mandate, to make sure that royal promises were kept, was feasible because Charles wished to assure a steady flow of funds.[82]

Panic that there might be after-shocks from the rebellion long held the Cortes, and the city fathers who elected its representatives, in its grip. Murcia, for example, put an abrupt end to its record of bedeviling corregidores by humbly accepting the men sent to govern it. Craven requests were forwarded to the crown begging that the mandate of the royal official be expanded for the good administration of justice and good governance.[83] Affirmation by representatives of municipal councils, assembled in parliament, that corregidores were deemed necessary to urban jurisdictions marks a decisive moment. Completion of the closed system of lifetime appointments which validated the status of oligarchs inevitably called for an equally stable chief, with direct ties to a central power that would guarantee this status. The path trodden is not too divergent from the road taken during the same era by Italian city states, where the fortunes of the patriciate were increasingly tightly tied to despots.[84] The epoch of the medieval corregidor (which I hold extends through the reign of Ferdinand and Isabella) thus came to an end, and the age of the corregidor of the Old Regime commences.[85] The new men would form a permanent corps similarly educated and trained, all prepared to make their careers at postings over a long period, and finally seen by the elite as required for the smooth functioning of municipalities.

Outside Castile

Despite the example of the spectacular growth of the institution in the central Iberian kingdom, Catalonia and Aragon totally escaped the grip of the corregidor. Due to longstanding constraints imposed by the *fueros*, a series of contractual agreements, Ferdinand never tried to install the official in his realms.[86] The idea that kings ever controlled lesser appointments in Aragonese cities has been discredited. Zaragoza, for example, reveals little rupture with the past procedure of self-rule through all the years of the Trastámara monarchy. No new offices were created for designation by the crown, because city government remained a cooperative, collegiate enterprise.[87] In Portugal, however, an official similar to the corregidor was sent out to towns during the reign of João II (1481–95) and Manoel I (1495–1521), in direct imitation of the practice in Castile. The Portuguese nobility acceded to the imposition of the royal representative (*correição*), allowing him to enter estates.[88] Spanish North Africa saw a more tentative imprint of the official upon its sands. Diego de Córdoba, captain-general in Oran in 1507–8 and 1510–22, was entitled corregidor, with the right to nominate officials, pay troops, and administer justice as it suited him.[89] Thereafter the title was abandoned for North Africa, because garrison functions were not rooted in an urban matrix.

Most of all, it was in the New World that the corregidor went on to place his enduring stamp, along with the viceroy, the governor, and the members of the *Audiencia*, as the hallmark of Spanish rule.[90] Similarly to Iberia, the corregidor in the Indies was situated in a large town, where he had municipal responsibilities as well as juridical duties. Here the atmosphere was far more favorable to arbitrary rule than in Castile, for the term of office was securely fixed at five years, and in the majority of instances a corregidor in the Americas could make any ruling he wished regarding judicial matters. Only minimum cooperation was required from the municipal corporation when the corregidor framed an ordinance, which had the full force of law.[91] The distinctiveness of the New World corregidor was that he ranged far beyond his municipal seat to govern vast rural areas, and in distant portions of his domain administered primarily Indian affairs.

All procedures devised in Spain to prevent corruption were copied, including the *residencia*. Instructions to the judge impressively charged him to look into every question and to examine any mandate given any official, from the viceroy down to the meanest *alcalde*, but little so comprehensive could be effected at a vast distance from Madrid.[92] Men who went to the New World to enrich themselves often succeeded in doing so without undue interference. In Peru, a 1672 memorial concerning reforms laments: "The corregidores in that kingdom are like locusts in Castile. Wherever they go they consume everything and lay waste the land."[93] Two-and-a-half centuries passed before the system changed, freeing the Indies from the grip of a medieval legacy.

Conclusions: over the decades

Expansion in the number of jurisdictions receiving corregidores during Isabella's reign was an evolutionary process that grew out of the considerable progress made by her predecessors. Sufficient supervisors were placed in office prior to 1474, for long enough periods, to demonstrate that the prospects of universalizing the office were good if clear-cut policy goals were consistently applied. Isabella was just the person to do this because she had all the vigor and drive one traditionally associates with sovereigns who pick up crowns fallen on the field of battle. She never lacked confidence that her succession was untainted and her right to rule indisputable, despite considerable Castilian and Portuguese support for her niece. The competition for sovereignty was sufficient to force Isabella to surmount challenges which she might not have immediately addressed had she come to the throne uncontested.

Thus, the succession struggle forced the pace of bringing the realm's municipalities under Isabella's sway. Castilian cities were prosperous enough, in an age of freshly vigorous commerce; but this wealth did not translate into political independence, along Italian city state lines, or even into lasting wide-scale military or commercial alliances, as happened among northern German towns. The municipalities of Castile looked instead to balance the territorial aristocracy against the monarchy, thus allowing their own governing bodies to play an often illusory independent hand. When Ferdinand and Isabella neutralized the aristocracy with a potent brew composed of flattery, titles, grants, legitimization of landholdings, patient negotiation, and the resort to military force where absolutely necessary, the cities and towns were left no resort.

The royal formula for pacifying its urban subjects fallen into the trap was composed of five elements: (1) installation of a corregidor with clearly defined powers to supervise the municipal council; (2)

elimination of any residue of open electoral proceedings; (3) confirmation of the privileges of a narrow oligarchy; (4) regulation of the number of council members, along with meticulous balancing of slates representing conflicting leagues of aristocrats; and (5) expropriation of urban fighting forces. Imposing such solutions took up the first decade of Isabella's rule. Municipalities allied with Doña Juana's forces, such as Trujillo, Ciudad Rodrigo, Cáceres, and Castronuño, were repressed by arms, or the threat of force. Corregidores played a military role in these struggles, directing troops and destroying fortifications. Other cities, such as Seville, Cordova, and Toledo, were divided between partisans of both camps, and so took a long time to quieten through a mixture of threats and patient work by a few extraordinary corregidores, handpicked for the work by their queen.

So long as the demands of the War of Succession shackled her, Isabella had to agree to send corregidores only where they were requested, and then only for one year. Assembled representatives from the urban areas of the northern kingdoms of Asturias and of Galicia set restrictions on the corregidores, even though the juntas accepted their direction in principle. Even municipalities initially allied with Isabella – which included Aranda, Alcaraz, Carmona, Jerez de la Frontera, Murcia, and Olmedo – laid obstacles in the path of her domination of their internal affairs. The queen's initial choices for corregidor were totally rejected in Murcia, while opposition to corregidores bubbled along elsewhere. Jerez de la Frontera employed the pretext of the capture of their corregidor by the Moors to overturn his work. Alcaraz several times rose in full rebellion against its overseers.

Once a peace treaty with Portugal was signed, Isabella used the decrees of the Cortes of Toledo to free herself from previous restrictions, so that all jurisdictions open to direct royal influence soon received a representative. In recognition of the continuing problems encountered by its officials as the coverage of the country expanded, the crown began to grope for improved relations with the municipal councils. Ferdinand and Isabella combated corruption by making a start at regularizing a *residencia* exit investigation for all officeholders with juridical responsibilities. The widely held desire of the urban masses, the mendicant friars, and the Old Christian section of the oligarchy to repress the Jews was satisfied, in part, by reviving laws calling for distinguishing markings on clothing and for segregation, making use of corregidores to make sure these decrees were carried out.

Due to royal vacillation over policy, corregidores continued to protect the queen's Jewish subjects from over-enthusiastic private initiatives right up until 1492, at the cost of some mental confusion as to how far these royal officials were obliged to respect the rights of their Jewish charges. The Inquisition, begun to examine the faith of New Christians in the expectation of clearing up questions about wealthy converts who dominated much of urban government, obtained active cooperation from corregidores in Ciudad Real and Toledo in the initial stages of its implementation, but ran into some covert opposition from other corregidores, occasionally themselves from New Christian lines.

The second decade of Isabella's rule proved the golden age for her urban representatives. It appeared at the time that the official had finally become embedded so deeply in the governance of Castile that a glorious future was assured the post. There was a lull in the open rebellions against corregidores which had been going on unabated since the 1450s, while street fighting between aristocratic bands also became a thing of the past. When struggle of this kind flared again in Seville after the Granada War, the *asistente* quickly received augmented powers from the crown sufficient to quell the disturbances, to the applause of city dwellers. Municipal councils sang the praises of their leaders during this time. The reasons for the change in tone are varied. For one thing, the educational level of corregidores improved sharply, as more university graduates entered the ranks. Another cause is that the officials conscientiously supervised the reconstruction of the urban fabric, as under their benevolent guidance walls were repaired, streets cleaned and kept clear of obstructions, and markets regulated. Very high on the list of reasons why the corregidores were so well received during Isabella's second decade is their role in expediting the return of communal lands usurped by aristocrats. Royal encouragement for this policy led to major settlements at Badajoz, Seville, Huete, Avila, and elsewhere – not that corregidores could do any of this on their own, considering the enduring tradition of aristocratic contempt for mere functionaries, but because the crown provided sturdy backing for its men.

Within the narrow limits discovered, corregidores did thus offer certain useful services to their municipalities. Some few corregidores even spoke up for the rights of commoners, in the face of the wrath of oligarchs. Further, a thoroughgoing exit examination which assured probity was applied with some regularity from the late 1480s. These *residencia* investigations reached their peak during this period, although even then they never became automatic upon the expiration of a term. The findings of the investigations reveal surprisingly little corruption, relative to the large number of jurisdictions, for until the later years of the reign communities were generally able to use the inquests to dampen the impulse towards theft and malpractice universally endemic in public service in the age.

There was also a dark side to the willingness of *regidores* to coexist with their royal supervisor, one which grew more somber as the immense financial strain engendered by the Granada War forced the monarchs to loosen their man's grip on urban affairs. Gradually, the minimal protections extended to the lower social levels, by a regime which ritually celebrated its respect for law, began to decay under the impact of the war. To gain the oligarchs' cooperation in raising and collecting taxes, loans, and indulgences, municipal councils were not punished by the crown when they interfered with the corregidor's watchdog functions over treasuries or lands. Corruption began to spread as both property and funds increasingly found their way, unhindered, into private hands.

Many corregidores continued to do an acceptable job for their communities, as others had done throughout the reign, but new obstacles were placed in their way. Pressed by the expenses and necessities of interminable war, the monarchs had leaned ever more heavily upon aristocrats and corporate groups, rewarding them by expanding their privileges. The crown discouraged its officials from initiating new investigations into aristocratic land thefts, and its pressure to halt the construction of new fortifications slackened. Without significant royal protest, great lords reinserted themselves into communal affairs through a resumption of direct payments to municipal council members.

Under royal direction, corregidores cleared away the tangle of unauthorized transit taxes on sheep, and also on mule convoys, so important to supply the material of war. One impact of this shift in tax policy was to keep funds from reaching corregidores, so that they were unable to undertake the repair of roads and bridges, thus dealing a stressful blow to commerce and industry. In addition, although the monarchs disbanded the Council of the Holy Brotherhood in 1498, this action still did not give the corregidores the right to protect their communities from corrupt police or to review decisions handed down by these arbitrary courts. The unattractive picture was made still uglier by a fall-off in the quality of officials in the last decade of the reign. The small pool of acceptable candidates led to their terms being extended to four years or more, at the same time that salaries were reaching high levels. Mistrust and contempt found outlet in anti-corregidor disturbances at Ágreda, Toro, León, Murcia, and elsewhere, which riots the elite declined to repress. Cities like Murcia and Palencia openly renewed complaints that they did not need or want corregidores to oversee their affairs. The last decade of the queen's rule thus saw an unraveling of the informal contract which had held the urban oligarchy to their supervisors.

Vicens Vives suggested that a principal task of modern institutional history should be to define the precise relationships between the theoretic powers of the crown and the actual exercise of these powers.[94] A series of utopian Royal Council decrees, issued in the name of the monarchs, mask the diminished ability of corregidores to fulfill their functions during the latter part of the reign. In 1500, at the very time that corregidores had lost the confidence of much of the urban elite, an elaborate book of ordinances detailing the ideal corregidor was issued, without making it clear who would be able to force the official to fit into the ornate bed the Royal Council had constructed. Despite the need to supervise from sixty to eighty jurisdictions in any one year, no coordinator was ever appointed. The overloaded Royal Council neglected to pay attention to *residencias* when making its virtually automatic renewals, and this at a time when corregidores were finding ways to avoid retaliation for corrupt activities. Another sweeping edict went out in 1500 that no castles were to be built without license – this at exactly the time when corregidores were being restrained from interfering in all vital business pertaining to aristocrats. Corregidores were also pressed, at this moment, by the Royal Council to get poor localities to fix roads and bridges, when the men on the scene realized that exempting heavy users from contributions surely meant that the required funds would never be raised.

After 1504, when the succession wavered, a "fourth period" opened for the corregidores, as aristocrats reasserted control in various locales or successfully harassed royal representatives. Some corregidores took personal advantage of the upheavals to absent themselves from their jurisdictions for long periods, demanding pay all the while, or looked the other way at crime and corruption. Changing rulers paid no attention to complaints, repeated at Cortes after Cortes. By the time the young King Charles left Castile in 1520 to pick up his imperial crown, a thoroughgoing anti-corregidor consensus had coalesced. The oligarchs wanted the office either eliminated or placed under their control because, they alleged, the corregidores no longer promoted good government, and the populace turned hostile because they had not been protected by crown appointees from the assaults of their local overlords.

Speaking through their revolutionary councils, the leaders of the revolt initially revived the demands, once reluctantly accepted by Isabella when she was struggling with a rival, that corregidores be sent only at the request of the communities and they stay for no more than two years, with an automatic judicial examination at the end of the stay. Soon after, a more heartfelt demand rose from revolutionary juntas that cities completely abolish the office. One of the first acts of communities who participated in the *Comuneros* uprising of 1520–1 was therefore to replace their royal corregidores either with locally elected figures, often holding different titles, or with corregidores appointed by the juntas. It was not out of the question for the crown to have resolved the tension by leaving royal corregidores in place with greatly shrunken privileges, or even to eliminate them, for after all the Catholic Sovereigns had earlier completely abandoned the equally useful Holy Brotherhood league, after closing down its royal council. However, Charles and his advisors chose not to take this way out of their difficulties.

As the wave of revolt swelled, pressures from the lower ranks frightened the elite who had begun the struggle, reminding them that they had property and status to lose. At the high tide of egalitarian revolution the urban nobility remembered how to cling to the rock of the monarchy. Cortes proceedings of 1523 and 1525 demonstrate that city fathers came to determine that a royal corregidor was absolutely necessary to them as a bulwark against any resumption of upheaval. The king, too, learned a bitter lesson, and agreed to reform the office, if that was one of the things required to keep the kingdom pacified. What Isabella could not guarantee – civic acceptance of the permanency of corregidores – was achieved by her grandson after the flood of revolution receded.

Limitations and strengths

Corregidores of Isabella's era were less vital to the realms as a whole than they appear to be from a reading of elaborate ordinances, because by far the largest portion of Castile was not under direct royal control. The cities, towns, and villages the queen's men attempted to guide were a small chain of islands in an ocean of aristocratic estates. On their own lands, lords named corregidores or *alcaldes mayor* as they chose, for each seignorial *mayorazgo* was a little kingdom in its own right, visited by outsiders only to question sanctuary, to check on private jailings, or to watch for the augmentation of strongholds. The rich, the powerful, and the privileged thus went their way occasionally hindered, but rarely humbled.

Corregidores raised funds, supplies, and troops for the struggles that placed Isabella on the throne (although few actually performed in combat zones). Much of the assault by corregidores on unauthorized fortresses turns out to have been a part of the War of Succession, or came in the wake of the suppression of localized rebellions, for rarely did they directly challenge great lords or high prelates. Early in the reign the corregidores were also set to work to pacify their jurisdictions through ending street fighting by bands of retainers, notwithstanding the fact that few corregidores could, on their own, bring these struggles to final settlement. Pacts to quiet factions came only after arduous high-level negotiations, sometimes necessitating lengthy visits from the monarchs to the jurisdictions in question. The corregidores were of little account to aristocrats whenever the lords chose to deal over the heads of servants. No matter if the issue were usurpation of land or assaults on residents, the aristocracy took its business directly to the Royal Council or the monarchs.

The clergy, too, stayed clear of control at the local level, for ecclesiastical princes retained full and unrestricted rights over their vassals. Even in royally dominated areas, clerics always had the potential to cause a row or to raise a mob. It took much cajoling to get clerics to release a culprit from sanctuary, to lift an excommunication, or to stop preaching inflammatory sermons; and it was nearly impossible to get churchmen to give up female companionship, despite continued royal interest in the subject. In the main, the clerics relied upon, and were left to, their own judicial and hierarchic systems. Tradition and privilege protected the spiritual estate from significant assault.

When it came to dominating the urban elite, corregidores at first glance appear to be better armed, due to extensive powers mandated by their ordinances. Out in the field, however, these powers could prove parchment bucklers during long-drawn-out combat with well-established municipal councils. *Regidores* in tumultuous jurisdictions outflanked the changing roster of corregidores when they chose to do so, for the royal supervisors might have little experience, or few effective weapons that could be used in cities to control the obstreperous. As far as possible, councilors made sure that a corregidor could not make decisive use of his vote. This negative overall assessment must be balanced by evidence that often corregidores either did not come into conflict with the elite or else could assemble alliances to ensure that the royal will would be obeyed.

For a time, minority religious communities were protected by corregidores from the wrath of their neighbors; but when first Jews, and then Muslims, fell out of royal favor they were segregated by the officials, persecuted, and finally driven from the land. The practical men who predominated in corregidor ranks were a less than perfect instrument, however, when it came to carrying out with precision the schemes of idealistic legists and clerics who walked the halls of state. The confusion deriving from conflicting royal instructions occasionally opened the way for the men on the scene to mitigate the rigor of persecution, although when policy instructions were put clearly, corregidores generally did as they were told.

Those, other than from the separated religious communities, who felt the full brunt of the unimpeded power of corregidores were the burghers, for officials made sure that *ciudadanos* with funds were punished for any slight infraction. Members of the taxpaying estates were constantly harried to undertake the full cost of the physical upkeep of their municipalities, to pay all impositions and tithes requested and, as good Christians, to actively contribute to the crusading effort. In the main, corregidores can be said to have fulfilled royal expectations in the financial exploitation of cities. City fathers thwarted occasional efforts of corregidores to speak for the interests of unrepresented elements of the populace. Residents too poor to pay much in the way of taxes rarely found independent-minded friends in their corregidores, despite a few honorable exceptions. The few royal representatives who took pains to attempt to mediate, as they were mandated to do, between those with status and those with none were made to suffer by the councilors for any excess of compassion.

To suggest that Ferdinand and Isabella had anything like a consistent "urban policy," beyond the points enumerated, would be anachronistic, so conclusions about what the monarchs intended for their municipalities have to be extrapolated from what the crown attempted to impose. The ideal settled area was to be attractive, orderly, and docile, as well as taxable. Stable governments were to meet regularly, in their own buildings, where they would be free of private interference. Streets were to be cleaned, walls, bridges, and outlying roads kept in repair. A controlled economy was desirable, which meant the market-place required regulation, guild activity invigoration, and merchants both protection and close observation. Boundaries were to be respected, and illegally occupied land returned. Petty crime deserved prompt punishment, justice should triumph, and the rich should be kept from preying unduly upon the poor.

These results were often achieved in municipalities under the direct rule of the crown, at least through the mid-point of the queen's reign. The troubles spawned by the Granada War, which only matured into a full-blown crisis for the urban oligarchy during the parade of rulers following Isabella's death, brought corregidores, charged with so many duties, into disrepute. It was left to her grandson, with the help of a municipal elite chastened by a revolt that challenged its status, to undertake a successful reconstruction of what she had so carefully built. Thereafter, the corregidores governed unchallenged in the European realms and spread through the New World, enduring for centuries as exemplars of Spanish rule in the first great empire of modern times.

Table 7. *Castilian corregimientos and some office-holders*

Area	Term	Name	Academic degrees	Offices/other titles (C. = Corregidor of)
Ágreda *see:* Soria				
Aguilar de Campóo, Merindad de				
	1475	Juan Manrique*[1]	Bachiller	Conde de Castañeda; Canciller Mayor
	1487-9	Sancho Díaz de Herrera*[2]	—	—
	1489-90	Rodrigo Guazo*[3]	—	—
	1491-2	Sancho de las Heras*[4]	—	—
	1493-5	Gutierre Guazo*[5]	—	—
Alcalá la Real				
	1488-90	Lope Sánchez del Castillo[6]	Licenciado	C. Alcaraz (1483-4); C. Trujillo (1484-7); C. Carrión-Sahagún (1493-5)
	1490-3	Bartolomé Santa Cruz[7]	Licenciado	—
	1493	Diego Gómez Romani[8]	Licenciado	—
	1493-4	Juan de Portillo[9]	Bachiller	—
	1495-6	Diego Arias de Anaya[10]	—	—
Alcaraz				
	1475	Diego de Madrid[11]	—	(*nomination withdrawn*)
	1477	García del Busto[12]	—	(*nomination withdrawn*)
	1479-81	Juan Pérez de Barradas[13]	—	Trinchante; Comendador de Cieza
	1481-3	Lope Sánchez del Castillo[14]	Licenciado	C. Trujillo (1484-7); C. Alcalá (1488-90); C. Carrión-Sahagún (1493-5)
	1483-4	Antón Martínez de Cascales[15]	Doctor	Continuo Real; Mosén
	1484-6	Fernando de Talavera[16]	Doctor	Mosén
	1486-7	Juan Cabrero[17]	—	Continuo Real; C. Zamora (1485-7)
	1488-9	Juan de la Hoz[18]	—	Alcaide; C. Alcaraz (1492-4)
	1489-90	Pedro Ortiz[19]	—	C. Segovia (1486-8); C. Cuatro Villas (1488-90); C. Madrid (1490); C. Segovia (1492-4); C. Salamanca (1494-6)
	1490-2	Dia Sánchez de Quesada[20]	—	(*see above*)
	1492-3	Pedro Ortiz[21]	—	(*see above*)

1493–6	Juan de Burgos[22]	Bachiller	—
1496–1502	Ortuño de Aguirre[23]	Licenciado	—
1502–4	Gonzalo de Carvajal[24]		—

Alegría *see:* Guipúzcoa
1480	García de Alvarado[25]		

Alfaro *see:* Logroño

Alhama *see:* Loja

Almansa, *see:* Villena, Marquesado de

Almería *see:* Guadix

Almuñécar
1493–5	Juan López Navarro[26]	Licenciado	C. Baza–Vera (1495–6); C. Vélez Málaga (1493–5)
1495–6	Andrés Calderón[27]		C. Granada (1495–6)

Andalucía
1494	—[28]		—

Andújar
1474–8	Alfonso de Aguilar*[29]		Señor de Aguilar; Alcalde Mayor
1478–88	Francisco de Bobadilla[30]		Maestresala; C. Jaén, Marmolejo (1478–88); C. Córdoba (1488–96)
1488–9	Diego de Aguayo[31]		C. Jaén (1488–9)
1489–90	Álvaro de Portugal[32]		—
1496	Licenciado de Herena[33]	Licenciado	

Aranda de Duero–Sepúlveda
1480–1	Pedro del Castillo[34]		Acemilero Mayor
1482–3	Nuño Orejón[35]		Continuo Real
1483–4	Gonzalo Fernández de las Rigas[36]		—
1491–2	Pedro Núñez de Penalever[37]	Bachiller	C. Ávila (1494–5)
1492–4	Francisco González del Fresno[38]	Bachiller	—

Arcos de la Frontera
1490–4	Lope de Porras*[39]		Alcaide

Table 7 (cont.)

Area	Term	Name	Academic degrees	Offices/other titles
Arévalo				
	1485	Pedro de Burgos[*40]	—	—
	1493	Luis Zapata[*41]	—	—
	1494	Juan Paz[*42]	—	—
Asturias de Oviedo, Principado de				
	1475–6	Ladrón de Guevara[43]	—	Guardia Real: Consejero Real; Regidor de Zamora
	1476–8	Pedro de Mazariegos[44]	—	Regidor de Cuenca
	1478–80	Rodrigo de Torres[45]	—	Vasallo del Rey
	1484–6	Luis Mejía[46]	—	Alcaide
	1486–90	Alfonso de Valderrábano[47]	—	C. Carmona (1478–90)
	1490–3	Pedro Dávila[48]	—	Continuo Real
	1493–6	Fernando de Vega[49]	—	—
	1499–1500	Diego Osorio[50]	—	—
	1500–5	Juan Gutiérrez Tello[51]	—	—
Ávila				
	1474–5	Arrual de Chacón[52]	Bachiller	Consejero Real
	1475–7	Juan del Campo[53]	—	Consejero Real
	1477–8	Fernando de Herrera[54]	—	—
	1478–9	Juan Flopeto[55]	—	—
	1479–80	Juan Flores[56]	—	—
	1480–	Pedro Sánchez de Frías[57]	Doctor	Oidor; Consejero Real; C. León (1483–5)
	1485–8	Alfonso Portocarrero[58]	—	—
	1488–93	Álvaro de Santisteban[59]	Licenciado	C. Écija (1492–6)
	1493–4	Antón Rodríguez de Villalobos[60]	Licenciado	C. Aranda–Sepúlveda (1492–4)
	1494–5	Francisco González del Fresno[61]	Bachiller	—
	1495–6	Juan Pérez de la Fuente[62]	Licenciado	—
	1500	Alonso Martínez de Ávila[63]	—	—

Badajoz

Year	Name	Status	Office
1479–80	Pedro de Córdoba[64]	—	Alcaide
1480–1	Francisco Maldonado[65]	—	Continuo Real; C. Cáceres (1476–7); C. Badajoz (1487–9)
1484–5	Álvaro de Villasur[66]	—	
1485–6	Alonso de Carrillo[67]	—	Vasallo del Rey
1486–7	Alfón del Castillo[68]	—	Comendador
1487–9	Francisco Maldonado[69]	—	(see above)
1489	Francisco de Molina[70]	Licenciado	Alcaide
1489–90	Diego López de Trujillo[71]	Licenciado	
1490–1	Alfonso de la Fuente[72]	—	
1491–2	Sancho Sánchez de Montiel[73]	Licenciado	
1492–3	Gonzalo Fernández del Castillo[74]	Bachiller	
1493	Pedro de Cuba[75]	Licenciado	Alcaide de los Alcázares; C. Carmona (1494); C. Toro (1495–6)
1493–5	Alonso Enríquez[76]	—	Continuo Real
1499	Martín Vázquez de Rojas[77]	—	Regidor de Toledo

Baeza–Úbeda

Year	Name	Status	Office
1476–7	Fernando de Covarrubias[78]	—	(Baeza)
1476–7	Rodrigo Manrique[79]	—	(Úbeda) Justicia Mayor
1477–9	Pedro de Rivadeneiya[80]	—	Consejero Real; Mariscal; Alcalde Mayor de Toledo; Caballero de Santiago
1480–3	Juan de Ayala[81]	—	Capitán
1485–8	Diego López de Ayala[82]	—	Capitán; C. Jaén (1491–3)
1488–93	Alonso Enríquez[83]	Licenciado	
1493–4	Diego de Santa Cruz[84]	Bachiller	
1494–5	Lope de Alburquerque[85]	—	Conde de Penamacor
1500	Alfonso Martínez de Angulo[86]	—	Caballero de Santiago; Veinticuatro de Córdoba

Baza–Vera

Year	Name	Status	Office
1492–5	Diego López de Burgos[87]	Licenciado	C. Mojácar, Huéscar (1492–5)
1495–6	Juan López Navarro[88]	—	C. Veléz Málaga (1495–6); C. Almuñécar (1495–6)

Betanzos see: La Coruña

Bierzo, Villafranca del

Year	Name	Status	Office
1494	Miguel Álvarez de Ocaña[89]	—	C. Ponferrada (1494–6)

Table 7 (cont.)

Area	Term	Name	Academic degrees	Offices/other titles
Bilbao see: Vizcaya				
Burgos				
	1475–6	Rodrigo Valderrábano**[90]	—	Maestresala; Regidor de Ávila
	1476	Juan de Gamboa**[91]	—	Alcaide
	1478–90	Andrés de Ribera**[92]	—	C. Ciudad Real (1477–8); C. Salamanca (1483–7); C. Plasencia
	1492–1502	Pedro García de Cotes**[93]	—	(1488); C. Segovia (1488–92)
	1502–4	Gracián de Cotes[94]	—	—
	1504–5	Álvaro Lugo[95]	—	—
Cáceres				
	1475–6	Vasco de Francisco y Vívero[96]	—	Vasallo del Rey; Guardia del Rey
	1476–7	Francisco Maldonado[97]	—	C. Badajoz (1480–1; 1487–9); Diputado General de la Santa Hermandad (1479–); Vasallo del Rey
	1477–8	Ruy González de Puebla[98]	Doctor	C. Segovia (1480–5)
	1478–9	Jerónimo de Valdivieso[99]	—	Trinchante; Continuo Real
	1479–80	Pedro de Velasco[100]	—	C. Trujillo (1479–80)
	1480–5	Sancho de Aguila[101]	—	Alcaide de Trujillo; Capitán
	1488–90	Diego López de Ayala[102]	Bachiller	Capitán; Maestresala; C. Trujillo (1488–90)
	1490–1	Ferrand Sánchez de Tovar[103]	—	—
	1491–2	Diego Ruiz de Montalvo[104]	—	—
	1493–5	Gonzalo Bernaldo Gallego[105]	Licenciado	Oidor de la Audiencia
	1495–6	Fernando de Ribera[106]	—	Continuo Real
	1496–7	Pedro de Paradinas[107]	Licenciado	—
	1497–8	Pedro de Castellanos[108]	—	—
	1500–2	Juan de Villafuerte[109]	—	—
	1503	Sancho Pérez Machuca[110]	—	—
	1504–6	Martín Vázquez de Rojas[111]	—	Regidor de Toledo

Cádiz

1470–92	Rodrigo Ponce de León*[112]		Marqués de Cádiz; Asistente Cádiz (1470–92)
1493–5	Juan de Benavides[113]		Alcaide
1501	Suero de Novoa[114]		Justicia Mayor

Calahorra *see:* Logroño

Canarias, Islas (Gran Canaria)

1478–80	Pedro Fernández de Algaba***[115]		Capitán; Alcaide; Regidor de Jerez
1480–91	Pedro de Vera**[116]		Continuo Real
1492–4	Francisco Maldonado Álvarez*[117]		Capitán General; Continuo Real; Repartidor
1495	Alonso de Fajardo***[118]		
1498–1501	Lope Sánchez de Valenzuela***[119]		
1502–3	Antonio de Torres***[120]	Doctor	
1503–5	Alonso Escudero[121]		

Canarias, Islas (La Palma, Tenerife)

1493–1525	Alonso Fernández de Lugo[122]		Adelantado (1503–25); Gobernador Tenerife (1497–1525)

Carmona

1477–8	Alonso de Deza****[123]		Regidor de Toro
1478–82	Sancho de Ávila****[124]		
1482–4	Alonso Portocarrero****[125]		
1484–90	Pedro Dávila****[126]	Licenciado	Alcaide de los Alcázares; C. Asturias (1490–2)
1491	Pedro de Cuba****[127]		Alcaide de los Alcázares; C. Badajoz (1493); C. Toro (1495–6)
1492–3	Juan de Ulloa****[128]		Alcaide de los Alcázares
1494–9	Pedro Ortiz****[129]		Alcaide de los Alcázares
1499–1504	Bernal Flores del Carpio[130]		
1504–5	Diego Sánchez de Alfaro[131]		

Carrión de los Condes–Sahagún

1475	Alonso Núñez del Castillo[132]	Licenciado	
1480	Diego Carvajal[133]		
1484	Juan de la Hoz[134]		
1485–7	Diego de Ulloa[135]		Receptor
1487–8	Francisco de Anzo[136]		
1488–90	Francisco de Luzón[137]		C. Medina del Campo–Olmedo (1490–2)

Table 7 (cont.)

Area	Term	Name	Academic degrees	Offices/other titles
	1491–2	Juan Ruiz de la Fuente[138]	—	C. Palencia (1490–1)
	1492–3	Juan de Luzón[139]	—	Regidor de Valladolid
	1493–4	Lope Sánchez del Castillo[140]	Licenciado	C. Itero de la Vega, Frómista, Marcilla (1493–4); C. Alcaraz (1481–3); C. Trujillo (1484–7); C. Alcalá (1488–90)
	1494–5	Diego de Sandoval[141]	—	—
	1495–6	Gonzalo Bañuelos[142]	—	Continuo Real; Mosén
Cartagena see: Murcia				
Casarrubios del Monte				
	1494	—[143]		
Castilla				
	1494	—[144]		
Castrogeriz				
	1488	Gonzalo Sánchez[145]	Bachiller	—
	1493	Rodrigo de Torres[146]		—
Chinchilla de Monte Aragón see: Villena				
	1476	Gonzalo de Ávila*[147]		Justicia Mayor; C. Almansa, Sax (1476–80)
	1480–7	Pero Vaca[148]		Maestresala; Fiel Ejecutor Sevilla (1477–); Gobernador Marquesado de Villena (1480–7); C. Huete (1487–93); C. Cuenca (1488–93)
Ciudad Real				
	1475	Juan de Vadillo[149]		—
	1476–7	Juan de Cornaga[150]		—
	1477–8	Pedro García de Cotes[151]		C. Salamanca (1483–7); C. Plasencia (1488); C. Segovia (1488–92); Asistente Burgos (1492–6)
	1478–9	Pedro de Guzmán[152]		Capitán
	1479–80	Alfonso Carrillo[153]		—
	1483–4	Alonso de Cáceres[154]		—

1484–5	Lope de Atuquia*[155]		Comendador; Mosén
1485–7	Juan Pérez de Barradas[156]		Comendador; C. Madrid (1487–9); C. Murcia (1489–92)
1487–90	Diego de Atay[157]		—
1490–1	Francisco Vargas[158]	Licenciado	—
1491–2	Lope Sánchez[159]	Licenciado	—
1492–5	García Alcocer[160]		Continuo Real; C. Marbella–Ronda (1495–6)

Ciudad Rodrigo

1476–80	Diego del Águila****[161]		Consejero Real; Alcaide; Capitán
1480–4	Rodrigo de Peñalosa[162]		C. Molina (1476–7)
1484–5	Pedro Sánchez de Hinestrosa[163]	Licenciado	—
1485–6	Nuño Orejón[164]		—
1486–7	Diego de Mudarra[165]	Licenciado	Regidor de Molina; Alcalde de Casa y Corte; C. Molina (1487–8)
1487–90	Pedro de Mazuelo[166]		Continuo Real; Alcaide de Badajoz
1490–3	Francisco de Vargas[167]	Licenciado	—
1493–4	Diego Bravo[168]		Continuo Real
1499	Francisco Quesado[169]		—
1500	Bernal de Mata[170]		—

Córdoba

1477	Diego de Merlo[171]		Gobernador Jumilla (1475); Asistente Sevilla (1478–82); Guardia Mayor; Contador Mayor; Consejero Real
1477	Diego de Osario[172]		Maestresala
1477–80	Francisco de Valdés[173]		Consejero Real; Alcaide
1483–7	García Fernández Manrique[174]		Alcaide de Málaga
1488–94	Francisco de Bobadilla[175]		Maestresala; Capitán; C. Andújar, Marmolejo (1478–88); C. Jaén (1478–88); Alcaide
1494–5	Juan Fernández de Mora****[176]	Licenciado	Pesquisidor
1495–6	Francisco de Bobadilla[177]		(see above)
1497–8	Alfonso Enríquez[178]		—
1499	Alvaro de San Esteban****[179]	Licenciado	Pesquisidor
1499–1500	Alfonso Enríquez[180]		(see above)
1500	Álvaro de Porras****[181]	Licenciado	Pesquisidor
1500–6	Diego López Dávalos[182]	Licenciado	—

Table 7 (cont.)

Area	Term	Name	Academic degrees	Offices/other titles
La Coruña *see also*: Galicia				
	1477–8	Fernando de Manzuelo[183]	—	Tesorero
	1478–81	Vasco de Vivero[184]	—	Continuo Real; Capitán; Alcaide; C. Betanzos (1478–81)
	1482–5	Juan Díaz de Berlanga[185]	Bachiller	—
	1485–92	Diego López de Haro[186]	—	Justicia Mayor; Gobernador Galicia (1484–95); Corregidor Mayor del Reino (Galicia)
	1493–5	Gonzalo Fernández de las Risas[187]	—	—
	1495–6	Carlos de Cisneros de Camporrenondo[188]	—	C. Betanzos (1495–6)
Cuatro Villas de la Mar (San Vicente de la Barquera, Santander, Laredo, Castro–Urdiales), Merindad de Trasmiera				
	1475–6	Juan de las Casas[189]	—	C. Cuatro Villas (1479–80)
	1476	Hurtado de Luna[190]	—	—
	1476–7	Álvaro de Gaona[191]	—	—
	1479–80	Juan de las Casas[192]	—	(*see above*)
	1480	Juan de Torres[193]	—	—
	1483–7	Diego Álvarez Osorio[194]	—	C. Segovia (1486–8); C. Madrid (1490); C. Alcaraz (1490–2);
	1488–90	Día Sánchez de Quesada[195]	—	C. Segovia (1492–4); C. Salamanca (1494–6)
	1490–3	Fernando de Ribera[196]	—	—
	1493–4	Gonzalo Sánchez de Castro[197]	Bachiller	—
	1494–5	Alonso Maldonado[198]	—	—
	1495	Juan de Deza[199]	—	Regidor de Toro
Cuenca				
	1477–9	Juan de Paz[200]	Bachiller	—
	1480–1	Juan de Osorio[201]	—	Capitán; Alcaide; C. Huete (1475–6, 1478–81)
	1484–5	Rodrigo de Albornoz[202]	—	C. Medina del Campo (1484–5)
	1485–6	Ruy Gómez de Ayala[203]	—	C. Huete (1483–6)
	1488–93	Pero Vaca[204]	—	Maestresala; C. Huete (1487–93); Fiel Ejecutor Sevilla (1477–); Gobernador Marquesado de Villena (1480–7); C. Chinchilla (1480–7)

Year	Name		
1493–5	Francisco Ortiz[205]	Bachiller	—
1500–2	Francisco de Bazán[206]	—	Maestresala
1502–3	Fernando de Rebolledo[207]	—	—
Dueñas			
1492	Adán de Valdés[208]	—	—
Écija			
1476–7	Luis Portocarrero[209]	—	Justicia Mayor; Alcaide
1478–82	Hurtado de Mendoza[210]	Bachiller	—
1482	Diego Rodríguez de San Vicente[211]	—	—
1485–7	Alonso Enríquez[212]	—	Capitán; Alcaide
1487–9	Sancho de Aguilar[213]	—	—
1490–2	Diego de Aguayo[214]	—	—
1492–6	Álvaro de Santisteban[215]	Licenciado	C. Ávila (1488–93)
1499	Sancho Sánchez de Montiel[216]	Licenciado	—
Escalona			
1479	Alonso Fernández de Madrid[217]	—	—
Guadix–Almería			
1490–1	—[218]	—	Adelantado de Cazorla
1493–4	Diego Arias de Anaya[219]	Bachiller	—
1494–5	López de Trujillo[220]	Licenciado	C. Almería (1492–5)
Galicia, Reino de (Betanzos, La Coruña, Mondoñedo, Ponferrada, Vivero)			
1475–6	Enrique Enríquez***[221]	—	Conde de Alba de Liste; Presidente de Galicia (1475–6)
1476–7	Arias del Río***[222]	—	C. Reino de Galicia (1476–7)
1477–80	Pedro de Villandrando***[223]	—	Conde de Ribadeo; Guardia Mayor; Presidente de Galicia (1477–80); C. Mondoñedo, Orense (1476–7)
1480–4	Fernando de Acuña***[224]	—	Justicia Mayor de Galicia (1480–4); Capitán
1484–99	Diego López de Haro***[225]	—	Justicia Mayor de Galicia (1484–99); C. La Coruña (1485–92);
1499–1500	Fernando de la Vega***[226]	—	Corregidor Mayor del Reino (Galicia)
Gibraltar			
1488	Francisco López de Gaja*[227]	—	—

Table 7. (cont.)

Area	Term	Name	Academic degrees	Offices/other titles
Granada (Ciudad)	1492–1500	Andrés Calderón[228]	Licenciado	Alcalde de Casa y Corte; Consejero Real; C. Almuñécar (1495–6); C. Santa Fe (1492–1500)
	1501–2	Diego López de Ávalos[229]	—	
	1503–4	Alonso Enríquez[230]	—	C. Córdoba (1508–11)
Granada, Reino de	1492–1516	Iñigo López de Mendoza***[231]	—	Conde de Tendilla; Marqués de Mondéjar; Capitán General; Alcaide
Guadalajara	1494	—[232]	—	—
Guipúzcoa, Reino de (Alegría, San Sebastián, Vitoria)				
	1477–8	Juan de Sepúlveda[233]	—	—
	1478	Martín Pérez de Alzaga[234]	—	C. Vitoria (1485)
	1484–5	Juan Pascual[235]	—	Consejero Real; Capitán General de la Frontera de Navarra; C. Logroño (1492–4)
	1489–94	Juan de Ribera[236]	—	
	1494–5	Álvaro de Porras[237]	Licenciado	Justicia; C. Trujillo (1491–4)
	1504	Licenciado Vela Nuña[238]	Licenciado	
Hontiveros (Fontiveros)	1494	—[239]	—	—
Huete	1475–6	Juan de Osorio[240]	—	Alcaide; Capitán; C. Cuenca (1480–1)
	1476–7	Juan de Ávila[241]	—	
	1477–8	Diego de Alcocer[242]	—	
	1478	Lope Vázquez[243]	—	
	1478–81	Juan de Osorio[244]	—	(see above)

1483–6	Ruy Gómez de Ayala[245]	—	C. Cuenca (1485–6)
1487–93	Pero Vaca[246]	—	C. Cuenca (1487–93); C. Chinchilla (1480–7); Gobernador Marquesado de Villena (1480–7); Maestresala; Fiel Ejecutor Sevilla (1477–)
1493–5	Sancho de Frías[247]	Licenciado	Alcaide
Jaén			
1475–7	Sancho de la Peña[248]	—	Guarda Real
1478–88	Francisco de Bobadilla[249]	—	Maestresala; C. Andújar (1478–88); C. Córdoba (1488–96)
1488–9	Diego de Aguayo[250]	—	Alcaide; Veinticuatro de Jaén; Juez Ejecutor de la Santa Hermandad (1488–); C. Andújar (1488–9)
1489–91	Francisco Mercado Huete[251]	Licenciado	C. Baeza–Úbeda (1488–95); Capitán
1491–3	Alfonso Enríquez[252]	Licenciado	Pesquisidor (1497)
1494–5	Pedro Díaz de Zumaya[253]		
Jerez de la Frontera			
1472–7	Ponce de León*[254]	—	Marqués de Cádiz
1478–83	Rodrigo Juan de Robles[255]	—	Alcaide; C. Jerez de la Frontera (1488–95)
1484–5	Juan de la Fuente[256]	Licenciado	Alcalde de Casa y Corte; Pesquisidor
1485–7	Pedro de Castro[257]	—	Alcaide
1488–95	Rodrigo Juan de Robles[258]	—	(see above)
1502–4	Gonzalo Gómez de Cervantes[259]	—	Limosnero de Sevilla
Ledesma			
1465–89	Gonzalo Fernández de Mercado*[260]	—	Comendador; Alcalde
León			
1475–7	Álvaro Rodríguez Galdín[261]	Licenciado; Bachiller	—
1478–9	Juan de Soto[262]	—	—
1479–80	Juan de Ulloa[263]	—	—
1480–81	Alfonso Ordóñez de Villaquirán[264]	Doctor	Oidor de la Audiencia; Consejero Real; C. Ávila (1480)
1483–5	Pedro Sánchez de Frías[265]	—	Alcaide
1486–8	Pedro Ortiz[266]	—	—
1488	Díaz de Berlanga[267]	—	—
1489–90	Diego de Carvajal[268]	—	—

Table 7. (cont.)

Area	Term	Name	Academic degrees	Offices/other titles
	1490–3	Juan de Portugal[269]	—	Alguacil
	1493–4	Lope Sánchez del Castillo[270]	Bachiller	—
	1494–6	Pedro Fernández de Aranda[271]	—	—
León, Reino de				
	1494	Diego de Torres[272]		
Logroño–Calahorra–Alfaro				
	1483–4	García de la Cuadra[273]	—	Alcalde
	1484–5	Diego Ruiz de Montalvo[274]	—	Alcaide
	1487–8	Juan Aguado de Hermosilla[275]	—	Alcalde; Alguacil
	1488–91	Juan de Luján[276]	—	—
	1491–2	Vela Núñez[277]	—	—
	1492–4	Juan de Ribera[278]	—	Capitán General de la Frontera de Navarra; C. Guipúzcoa (1489–93)
	1494–6	Francisco Pérez de Vargas[279]	Licenciado	C. Plasencia (1495–6)
Loja–Alhama de Granada				
	1489–90	Juan Serrano[280]	—	—
	1490–1	Álvaro de Luna[281]	—	Alcaide
	1492–4	Alonso Fajardo[282]	—	—
Lorca see: Murcia				
Madrid				
	1475–6	Mendo de Estúñiga [Zúñiga]**[283]	—	Alcalde; Regidor de Medina del Campo
	1477–8	Juan de Bobadilla[284]	—	—
	1478–80	Alonso de Heredia[285]	—	C. Murcia (1484–8); C. Madrid (1495–7)
	1480–3	Rodrigo de Mercado[286]	—	
	1483–4	Juan Martínez de Albelda[287]	Bachiller	Alcaide
	1484–7	García de la Quadra[288]	—	—

1487–9	Juan Pérez de Barradas[289]	—	Comendador de Cieza; C. Ciudad Real (1485–7); C. Murcia (1489–92)
1490	Día Sánchez de Quesada[290]	—	C. Segovia (1486–8); C. Cuatro Villas (1488–90); C. Alcaraz (1490–2); C. Segovia (1492–4); C. Salamanca (1494–6)
1490–2	Tristán de Silva[291]	—	
1492	Juan de Valderrama[292]	—	
1493–4	Cristóbal de Toro[293]	Licenciado	
1494–5	Doctor de Aguilar[294]	Doctor	
1495–7	Rodrigo de Mercado[295]	—	(see above)
1497–9	Juan de Deza[296]	—	Pesquisidor
1499–1502	Alfonso Martínez de Angulo[297]	—	
1502–3	Fernando Rodríguez de Ledesma[298]	—	Pesquisidor
1503	Alonso de Orduña[299]	—	
1503–6	Lorenzo Maldonado[300]	—	
Madrigal de las Altas Torres			
1495	Pascual de Cuellar[301]	—	
Málaga			
1487–92	García Fernández Manrique[302]	Bachiller	Consejero Real; Alcaide
1492–6	Juan Alonso Serrano[303]	Licenciado	Contador
1496–8	Pedro Díaz de Zumaya[304]	—	
1498–9	Alonso Escudero[305]	—	
1499–1504	Juan Gaitán[306]	—	Comendador; C. Vélez Málaga (1499–1504)
Marbella–Ronda			
1487–8	Juan de Villalba[307]	—	(Marbella)
1488–9	Francisco de Villalba[308]	—	(Marbella)
1489–92	Juan de Torres[309]	—	(Marbella); Maestresala; Alcaide
1491–2	Rodrigo de Torres[310]	—	
1493–4	Licenciado Remón[311]	Licenciado	
1495–6	García de Alcocer[312]	—	Continuo Real; C. Ciudad Real (1492–5)
Medellín			
1499	Alonso Téllez[313]	Doctor	—

Table 7. (cont.)

Area	Term	Name	Academic degrees	Offices/other titles
Medina del Campo–Olmedo				
	1475	Diego López de la Encina[314]	—	(Olmedo)
	1475–6	Juan de la Rúa[315]	Licenciado	(Medina)
	1479–80	Juan Rodríguez de Baeza[316]	Bachiller	(Medina)
	1479–80	Juan Ruiz de la Fuente[317]	Licenciado	(Olmedo); Alcalde de Casa y Corte; C. Palencia–Becerril de Campos (1490–1)
	1483–4	Juan López Navarro[318]	Bachiller	—
	1484–5	Rodrigo de Albornoz[319]	—	C. Cuenca (1484–5)
	1485–6	Rodrigo de Céspedes[320]	Bachiller	C. Palencia (1485–6)
	1486–7	Sancho de Arroniz[321]	—	Continuo Real
	1487	Licenciado de Oviedo[322]	Licenciado	—
	1488–90	Ramiro Núñez de Guzmán[323]	—	Regidor de Toledo (1475–)
	1490–2	Francisco de Luzón[324]	—	C. Carrión–Sahagún (1488–90)
	1493–5	Juan Pérez de Barradas[325]	—	Comendador
	1498	Fernando Díaz de Ribaneneira[326]	—	Veinticuatro de Sevilla
Miranda de Ebro				
	1487	Pedro de Orense[327]	—	Regidor de Burgos
Molina				
	1476–7	Rodrigo de Peñalosa[328]	—	C. Ciudad Rodrigo (1480–4)
	1478	Rodrigo de Orejón[329]	—	—
	1485	Alfonso Carrillo de Acuña[330]	—	Alcaide de Lebrija
	1487–8	Diego de Mudarra[331]	Licenciado	Regidor de Molina; Alcalde de Casa y Corte; C. Ciudad Rodrigo (1486–7)
	1488–90	Francisco de Molina[332]	Licenciado	—
	1490–2	Nuño Orejón[333]	—	—
	1492–4	Juan Gómez[334]	Bachiller	—
	1494–6	Alonso Téllez[335]	Bachiller	—

Mondoñedo see also: Galicia

1476–7	Pedro de Villandrando³³⁶	—	Conde de Ribadeo; Guarda Mayor; Gobernador Galicia (1477–80)
1477	Pedro de Tosantos³³⁷	—	—
1489	Sancho Ruiz de Villegas³³⁸	—	Alcaide
1494	Martín de Durango³³⁹	—	—

Murcia–Lorca–Cartagena

1466–75	Alonso López de la Cuadra³⁴⁰	Licenciado	Asistente Murcia (1466–75)
1475–8	Pedro Fajardo**³⁴¹	—	Adelantado Mayor; Consejero Real; Capitán-General; Regidor de Murcia (1469–) (nomination withdrawn)
1478	García de Alcocer³⁴²	Bachiller;	—
1479–81	Lope Sánchez del Castillo³⁴³	Licenciado	—
1481–2	Diego de Carvajal³⁴⁴	—	—
1482–3	Alfonso López³⁴⁵	—	—
1484–7	Rodrigo de Mercado³⁴⁶	—	C. Madrid (1480–3; 1495–7)
1488–9	Juan de Cabrera³⁴⁷	—	Mosén
1489–92	Juan Pérez de Barradas³⁴⁸	—	Trinchante; Comendador; C. Ciudad Real (1485–7); C. Madrid (1487–9)
1493–5	Pedro Gómez de Setúbal³⁴⁹	Licenciado	C. Palencia (1491–3)
1498–9	Fernando de Barrientos³⁵⁰	—	—
1503–4	Diego Roman³⁵¹	Licenciado	—
1504	Juan de Montalvo³⁵²	—	—

Nájera

1487	Alonso de la Peña*³⁵³	—	—

Ocaña

1494	——³⁵⁴	—	—

Olmedo see: Medina del Campo

Los Palacios y Villafranca

1487	Sancho de Bazán**³⁵⁵	—	Justicia Mayor

Palencia

1483–5	Francisco Maldonado³⁵⁶	Bachiller	—

Table 7. (*cont.*)

Area	Term	Name	Academic degrees	Offices/other titles
	1485–6	Rodrigo de Céspedes[357]	—	C. Medina–Olmedo (1485–6)
	1487–8	Alfonso del Águila[358]	—	Alcalde de Segovia
	1488–90	Francisco de Vargas[359]	Bachiller	
	1490–1	Juan Ruiz de la Fuente[360]	Licenciado	Alguacil; C. Carrión–Sahagún (1491–2)
	1491–2	Pedro Gómez de Setúba[361]	Licenciado	C. Murcia–Lorca–Cartagena (1493–5)
	1492–5	Antón Martínez de Aguilera[362]	Bachiller	
Palenzuela				
	1487	Alonso Gómez[363]	Bachiller	—
Palos de la Frontera				
	1477	Alfonso Fernández Rascón[364]	—	Alcalde Mayor
	1492–5	Juan de Cepeda[365]	—	Trinchante
Plasencia				
	1488	Pedro García de Cotes[366]	—	C. Ciudad Real (1477–8); C. Salamanca (1483–7); C. Segovia (1489–92); Asistente Burgos (1492–6); Vasallo del Rey
	1489–90	Antonio de Fonseca[367]	—	Maestresala; Alcaide; Continuo Real
	1490	Bachiller Anaya[368]	Bachiller	
	1490–1	Antonio de Fonseca[369]	—	(*see above*)
	1491–2	Juan Pérez de Segura[370]	Licenciado	
	1493–5	Antonio Cornejo[371]	Doctor	C. Vizcaya (1495–6)
	1495–6	Francisco Pérez de Vargas[372]	Licenciado	C. Logroño (1494–6)
	1496	Francisco de Herrera[373]	Licenciado	—
	1499	Doctor de Neyra[374]	Doctor	—
Ponferrada				
	1489–92	Juan de Torres[375]	—	Alcaide; C. Marbella–Ronda (1489–92); Maestresala
	1494–6	Miguel Álvarez de Ocaña[376]	Bachiller	C. Bierzo (1494)
	1500	Pedro de Vega[377]	—	—
	1503	Juan de Montalvo[378]	—	—

El Puerto de Santa María

1467–78; 1482	Diego de Valera[379]	—	Alcaide-Corregidor; Mosén; C. Palencia (1462); C. Segovia (1478–80)
1490	Pedro de la Peña[380]	—	Alcaide-Corregidor
1504–5	Charles [Carlos] de Valera[381]	—	Alcaide-Corregidor; Capitán

Requena–Utiel

1472–7	Juan Páez de Sotomayor[382]	—	Aposentador Real; (C. Utiel; 1472–7); (Requena, 1476–7)
1478–9	Fernando de Covarrubias[383]	—	—
1479–80	Luis de Velasco[384]	—	Alcaide; Comendador
1484–8	Troilos Carrillo[385]	—	(Requena)
1488–90	Francisco de Molina[386]	—	(Utiel)
1490–4	Francisco de Vaca[387]	Licenciado	—
	Francisco de Bazán[388]	—	Continuo Real; Alcaide

Ronda *see*: Marbella

Sahagún *see*: Carrión de los Condes

Salamanca

1475–6	García Manrique[389]	—	—
1476–7	Vasco Porcallo[390]	—	—
1477–8	García Osorio[391]	—	Capitán
1478–81	Gonzalo de Godoy[392]	—	—
1483–7	Pedro García de Cotes[393]	—	C. Ciudad Real (1477–8); C. Plasencia (1488); C. Segovia (1487–92); Asistente Burgos (1492–6)
1487–9	Pedro López de Ayala[394]	—	Conde de Fuensalida; Alcalde Mayor de Toledo: Aposentador Mayor
1489–91	Pedro de Loaisa[395]	Licenciado	—
1491–4	Honorado Hurtado de Mendoza[396]	—	C. Segovia (1486–8); C. Cuatro Villas (1488–90); C. Madrid (1490); C. Alcaraz (1490–2); C. Segovia (1492–4)
1494–6	Día Sánchez de Quesada[397]	—	
1500–5	Diego Osorio[398]	—	

Sanlúcar de Barrameda

| 1477 | Pedro de Esquivel*[399] | — | Veinticuatro de Sevilla |

Table 7. (cont.)

Area	Term	Name	Academic degrees	Offices/other titles
San Martín de Trevejo				
	1491	Alonso Sánchez Calderón[400]	—	—
Santillana (del Mar), Marquesado de				
	1489–95	Diego Hurtado de la Vega*[401]	—	—
Santo Domingo de la Calzada				
	1491–2	Pedro Pérez de Beamia[402]	Bachiller	—
	1493–4	Sancho de Ayala[403]	—	—
	1494–6	Fernando Gil Mogollón[404]	—	—
	1496–7	Juan de Portillo[405]	—	—
	1498	Licenciado de Tortoles[406]	Licenciado	—
	1502	Francisco Galdin[407]	Licenciado	—
Segovia				
	1475	Juan Velázquez de Cuellar[408]	Licenciado	Oidor de la Audiencia
	1476–8	Andrés López de Castro[409]	Licenciado	Maestresala; Mosén; C. Palencia (1462); C. Puerto de Santa María (1482)
	1478–80	Diego de Valera[410]	—	C. Cáceres (1477–8)
	1480–5	Ruy González de Puebla[411]	Doctor	C. Cuatro Villas (1488–90); C. Madrid (1490); C. Alcaraz (1490–2); C. Segovia (1492–4); C. Salamanca (1494–6)
	1486–8	Día Sánchez de Quesada[412]	—	C. Ciudad Real (1477–8); C. Salamanca (1483–7); C. Plasencia (1488); Asistente Burgos (1492–6)
	1488–92	Pedro Garcia de Cotes[413]	—	(see above)
	1492–4	Día Sánchez de Quesada[414]	—	—
	1494–6	Diego Ruiz de Montalvo[415]	—	—
Sepúlveda see: Aranda				
Sevilla				
	1478–82	Diego de Merlo***[416]	—	Gobernador Jumilla (1475); C. Córdoba (1476–8); Guardia Mayor; Contador Mayor; Consejero Real

Years	Name	Degree	Office
1482–1500	Juan de Silva**[417]	—	Conde de Cifuentes; Consejero Real; Alfares Mayor; Maestresala Presidente Consejo Real; Alcaide Mayor de Toledo (1475–);
1500–10	Íñigo de Velasco**[418]	—	Regidor de Ciudad Rodrigo (1488–)

Soria–Ágreda

Years	Name	Degree	Office
1480–4	Miguel de Chaves[419]	Bachiller	(Ágreda)
1484	Diego Giles[420]	Bachiller	(Soria)
1486–7	Vela Martínez[421]	Licenciado;	(Soria)
1487–96	Ruy Gutiérrez de Escalante[422]	Bachiller	(Ágreda)
1497–8	Pedro Salinas[423]	Licenciado	(Soria)

Toledo

Years	Name	Degree	Office
1475–6	Rodrigo Manrique[424]	—	Conde de Paredes; Maestre de Santiago
1477–90	Gómez Manrique[425]	—	C. Ávila (1465–8)
1491–1506	Pedro de Castilla[426]	—	Gobernador Toledo (1492)

Toro–Tordesillas

Years	Name	Degree	Office
1484–5	Pedro Gómez de Manrique**[427]	—	C. Zamora (1484–5)
1485–8	Diego López de Trujillo[428]	—	Regidor
1488–9	Diego Ruiz de Montalvo[429]	—	—
1491–3	Antón Rodríguez de la Rúa[430]	Licenciado	
1493–5	Diego Fernández de San Millán[431]	Bachiller	Alcalde de la Audiencia
1495–6	Pedro de Cuba[432]	Licenciado	C. Badajoz (1493); Alcaide de los Alcázares; C. Carmona (1491)
1498	Bachiller de Valcarcel[433]	Bachiller	

Trujillo

Years	Name	Degree	Office
1475–6	García Gil de Miranda[434]	—	Consejero Real; Vasallo del Rey
1476	Alonso Enríquez[435]	—	Capitán
1476–7	Juan de Robles[436]	—	Capitán; Alcaide
1477–8	Francisco de Ávila[437]	—	Alcaide
1479–80	Pedro de Velasco[438]	—	C. Cáceres (1479–80)
1480–3	Sancho del Águila[439]	—	Capitán
1483–4	Bachiller Pablo[440]	Bachiller	Alcalde de Trujillo (1483–4)
1484–8	Lope Sánchez del Castillo[441]	Licenciado	C. Alcaraz (1483–4); C. Alcalá (1488–90); Carrión–Sahagún (1493–5)
1488–90	Diego López de Ayala[442]	Bachiller	Maestresala; Capitán; C. Cáceres (1488–90)

Table 7. (cont.)

Area	Term	Name	Academic degrees	Offices/other titles
	1490–1	Diego Arias de Anaya[443]	Bachiller	—
	1491–4	Álvaro de Porras[444]	Licenciado	Justicia; C. Guipúzcoa (1494–5)
	1494–5	Diego Rodríguez de Aylón[445]	Doctor	Consejero Real
Úbeda see: Baeza				
Utiel see: Requena				
Valencia de Alcántara				
	1492	Francisco de Jerez[446]	—	—
Valladolid				
	1475	Alfonso de Deza[447]	—	Consejero Real
	1486–90	Juan de Ayala[448]	—	Fiscal; Alcaide
	1491–1503	Alonso Ramírez de Villaescusa[449]	Doctor	
Vélez Málaga				
	1487–8	Diego Arias de Ayala[450]	Bachiller	C. Abetenis, Abentoniz (1487)
	1488	Francisco Enríquez[451]	—	Capitán
	1491	Pedro Enríquez[452]	—	Adelantado de Andalucía
	1492	Rodrigo Romero[453]	—	C. Almuñécar, Salobreña, Castril de Ferro (1490)
	1493–5	Juan López Navarro[454]	—	C. Almuñécar (1493–5); C. Baza-Vera (1495–6)
	1495–6	Bernaldino Illescas[455]	Bachiller	
	1499–1504	Juan Gaitán[456]	—	Comendador; C. Málaga (1499–1504)
Vera see: Baza				
Villafranca de los Barros				
	1486	Francisco de la Noceda *[457]	—	Comendador
Villalón de Campos				
	1486	Alonso Tinero *[458]	—	—

Villena (Ciudad)

1480–5	Gaspar Fabra***459	—	C. Almansa, Sax, Yecla (1480–5)
1488–93	Lope Sánchez del Castillo***460	—	—

Villena, Marquesado de see also: Chinchilla de Monte Aragon

1475	Diego de Merlo***461	—	—
1476	Gonzalo de Ávila***462	Doctor	Justicia Mayor; Oidor de la Audiencia
1477	Alfonso Navas***463	Doctor	Justicia Mayor
1477	Alfonso Manuel***464	Licenciado	Justicia Mayor; Alcalde de Casa y Corte
1477–9	Fernando de Frías***465		Maestresala; Gobernador Chinchilla (1480–7); C. Cuenca (1488–93); Fiel
1480–7	Pedro Vaca***466		
1488–96	Ruy Gómez de Ayala467	—	Ejecutor de Sevilla (1477–); C. Huete (1487–93); Gobernador Ciudad de Villena (1493–6); Alcalde Mayor, Amo del Príncipe

Vitoria see: Guipúzcoa

Vivero see also: Galicia

1478–94	Fernando Cerón468	—	—

Vizcaya, Contado y Señorío de (Bilbao—Las Encartaciones)

1475–6	Rodrigo Maldonado469	Doctor	Juez de Sevilla (1479); Consejero Real
1476–7	Doctor Villalón470	Doctor	Embajador a Portugal (1474); Francia (1476)
1477–8	Juan de Torres471	Bachiller	—
1478–9	Pedro Alonso de Miranda472	Doctor	—
1479–80	González de Pueblo473	Licenciado	Alcaide de Bilbao (1485); Veedor
1483–8	Lope Rodríguez de Logroño474	Licenciado	Veedor; Alcalde; Juez Mayor
1489–91	Diego Martínez de Astudillo475	Licenciado; Bachiller	Veedor
1491–5	Rodrigo Vela Núñez de Ávila476		
1495–6	Antonio Cornejo477	Doctor	C. Plasencia (1493–5)
1504	Francisco Pérez de Vargas478	—	—

Zamora

1475–6	Juan de Torres479	—	Señor de Retortillo; Alférez de Ciudad Real; Regidor de Ciudad Real
1476–9	Juan de Biedma480	—	Capitán; Regidor de Baeza
1479–80	Alfonso Anguilo481	—	—

Table 7. (cont.)

Area	Term	Name	Academic degrees	Offices/other titles
	1484-5	Pedro Gómez de Manrique[482]	—	C. Toro (1484-5)
	1485-7	Juan de la Hoz[483]	—	C. Alcaraz (1488-9)
	1487-8	Diego de Andrade[484]	—	—
	1490-3	Gutiérrez de Carvajal [Caravaja][485]	—	—
	1493-5	Sancho Maluenda[486]	Licenciado	—
	1498-9	Gonzalo Fernández de Torres[487]	—	—
	1499-1505	Francisco Fernández de Rebollo[488]	—	—

*Seignorial nomination
**Asistente
***Gobernador
****Functioned as corregidor without title

Notes:

1 AGS, *Sello*, 7 Jan. 1475, fol. 315.
2 *Ibid.*, 26 May 1487, fol. 88; 28 Jan. 1489, fol. 295.
3 *Ibid.*, 6 June 1489, fol. 71; 30 Jan. 1490, fol. 173.
4 *Ibid.*, 16 Nov. 1491, fol. 260; 22 May 1493, fol. 255.
5 *Ibid.*, 17 Dec. 1493, fol. 125; 9 July 1495, fol. 305.
6 *Ibid.*, 10 June 1489, fol. 10.
7 *Ibid.*, 28 Jan. 1490, fol. 27; 28 Feb. 1491, fol. 99.
8 *Ibid.*, 4 June 1492, fol. 39; 27 Feb. 1493, fol. 213.
9 *Ibid.*, 7 June 1493, fol. 52.
10 *Ibid.*, 16 Mar. 1495, fol. 64.
11 Area was incorporated into the crown in this year. *Ibid.*, 31 Mar. 1475, fol. 329.
12 *Ibid.*, 9 Sept. 1477, fol. 464.
13 *Ibid.*, 26 Sept. 1479, fol. 39; 26 Sept. 1480, fol. 79.
14 *Ibid.*, 10 Mar. 1484, fol. 36.
15 Pretel Marín, *Integración municipio medieval*, p. 34.

16 *AGS, Sello*, 5 Mar. 1484, fol. 184; 6 Mar. 1485, fol. 85.
17 *Ibid.*, 30 Sept. 1487, fol. 54.
18 *Ibid.*, 22 May 1488, fol. 87; 1 Mar 1489, fol. 16.
19 *Ibid.*, 27 Mar. 1489, fol. 281.
20 *Ibid.*, 17 Sept. 1490, fol. 72; 24 May 1492, fols. 172, 179.
21 *Ibid.*, 29 May 1492, fol. 69; 24 Mar. 1494, fol. 409.
22 *Ibid.*, 28 Mar. 1495, fol. 23.
23 Pretel Marín, *Integración municipio medieval*, p. 35.
24 *Ibid.*
25 *AGS, Sello*, 9 Feb. 1480, fol. 12.
26 *Ibid.*, 30 Jan. 1493, fols. 41, 42.
27 *Ibid.*, 22 Mar. 1495, fol. 63.
28 *AGS, Cámara, Cédulas, Lib.* 1, fols. 13-14r, 15 Mar. 1494.
29 *AGS, Sello*, 3 Dec. 1477, fol. 412; MªC. Quintanilla Raso, *Nobleza y señoríos en el reino de Córdoba: La casa de Aguilar (siglos XIV y XV)* (Cordova, 1979), p. 125.

30 *AGS, Sello,* 20 Mar. 1478, fol. 54; 15 June 1486, fol. 53; Pulgar, *Crónica,* vol. II, p. 237.
31 Pulgar, *Crónica,* vol. II, p. 367.
32 *AGS, Sello,* 21 Jan. 1490, fol. 265.
33 *AM Carmona, AC,* 1496, fol. 219, 2 Sept. 1496.
34 *AGS, Sello,* 26 June 1480, fol. 23.
35 *Ibid.,* 5 Dec. 1483, fol. 82.
36 *Ibid.,* 6 Feb. 1484, fol. 253.
37 *Ibid.,* 14 July 1492, fol. 78.
38 *Ibid.,* 17 Nov. 1492, fol. 154; 7 Feb. 1494, fol. 90.
39 *Ibid.,* 20 Aug. 1490, fol. 297; 5 Dec. 1493, fol. 6.
40 *Ibid.,* 15 Dec. 1485, fol. 159.
41 *Ibid.,* 13 July 1493, fol. 203.
42 *Ibid.,* 20 Sept. 1494, fol. 133.
43 *Ibid.,* 11 Apr. 1475, fol. 402.
44 *Ibid.,* 21 July 1476, fol. 489; 28 June 1478, fol. 155.
45 *Ibid.,* 20 June 1478, fol. 116; 30 May 1480, fol. 117.
46 *Ibid.,* 22 July 1484, fol. 56; 23 Apr. 1486, fol. 54.
47 *Ibid.,* 6 Feb. 1487, fol. 75; 14 Aug. 1490, fol. 360.
48 *Ibid.,* 10 Sept. 1490, fol. 187; 29 Mar. 1493, fol. 209.
49 *Ibid.,* 16 Aug. 1493, fol. 33; 17 Sept. 1495, fol. 14.
50 *RAH,* Salazar A-11, fol. 254, vol. I, p. 154; nd June 1500.
51 *AGS, Sello,* nd Feb. 1505, fol. 450.
52 *Ibid.,* 25 Aug. 1474, fol. 18; José Mayoral Fernández, *El municipio de Ávila* (Avila, 1958), p. 42.
53 *AGS, Sello,* 12 June 1476, fol. 464.
54 *Ibid.,* 23 June 1477, fol. 262.
55 Mayoral Fernández, *Ávila,* p. 55.
56 *AGS, Sello,* 24 Sept. 1480, fol. 199; 22 Sept. 1479, fols. 66, 74, 115.
57 *Ibid.,* 18 Sept. 1480, fol. 130.
58 *Ibid.,* 6 Dec. 1485, fol. 104; 11 June 1488, fol. 221.
59 *Ibid.,* 9 Sept. 1488, fol. 51; 6 Mar. 1494, fol. 179.
60 *Ibid.,* 12 June 1493, fol. 51; 31 Oct. 1494, fol. 333.
61 *Ibid.,* 25 Nov. 1494, fol. 419.
62 *Ibid.,* 28 Apr. 1495, fol. 32.
63 *AGS, Cámara,* 18 Mar. 1500, leg. 2, nf.
64 *AGS, Sello,* 20 Mar. 1480, fol. 71.
65 E. Rodríguez Amaya, "La tierra en Badajoz desde 1250 a 1500," *Revista de Estudios Extremeños,* VII (July-Dec. 1951), p. 451.
66 *AGS, Sello,* 9 Mar. 1484, fol. 123.
67 *AGS, Cámara,* 12 Mar. 1485, leg. 4.
68 *Ibid.,* 9 Sept. 1486, leg. 7.
69 *AGS, Sello,* 8 Sept. 1487, fol. 118; 30 Mar. 1489, fol. 356.
70 *Ibid.,* 5 Apr. 1489, fol. 312.
71 *Ibid.,* 20 Mar. 1489, fol. 357; 17 Mar. 1490, fol. 308.
72 *Ibid.,* nd Feb. 1491, fol. 280.
73 *Ibid.,* 26 Aug. 1491, fol. 73; 20 Mar. 1492, fol. 372.
74 *Ibid.,* 15 Feb. 1492, fol. 255; 13 Aug. 1493, fols. 188, 206.
75 *Ibid.,* 13 Aug. 1493, fol. 206.
76 *Ibid.,* 2 Sept. 1493, fol. 19; 26 Oct. 1494, fol. 405.
77 Rodríguez Amaya, "Badajoz," pp. 456ff.
78 *AGS, Sello,* 28 Feb. 1476, fol. 51.
79 *Ibid.,* 28 Aug. 1477, fol. 338.
80 *Ibid.,* 28 Aug. 1477, fol. 460; nd Aug. 1479, fol. 66.
81 *Ibid.,* 14 Apr. 1480, fol. 167; 25 Aug. 1488, fol. 170.
82 *Ibid.,* 29 Jan. 1485, fol. 56; nd Feb. 1488, fol. 223.
83 *Ibid.,* 5 Feb. 1488, fol. 223; 13 May 1493, fol. 78.
84 *Ibid.,* 4 July 1493, fol. 140.
85 *Ibid.,* 4 Sept. 1494, fol. 90; 6 May 1495, fol. 68.
86 Toral Peñaranda, *Úbeda,* p. 350.
87 *AGS, Sello,* 5 Sept. 1492, fol. 136; 13 Feb. 1495, fol. 334.
88 *Ibid.,* 16 Mar. 1495, fol. 65.
89 *Ibid.,* nd nm 1494, fol. 52.
90 *Ibid.,* 20 Apr. 1475, fol. 416.
91 *Ibid.,* 6 Apr. 1476, fol. 261.
92 *Ibid.,* 13 July 1478, fol. 52; 31 Mar. 1490, fol. 367.
93 *Ibid.,* 3 Apr. 1492, nf; 30 Oct. 1502, fol. 211.
94 *Ibid.,* 9 Nov. 1504, nf.
95 *AGS, Escribanía Mayor de Rentas, Quitaciones de Corte,* leg. 6.
96 *AGS, Sello,* 20 Mar. 1475, fol. 226.

Notes to Table 7 (cont.)

97 Ibid., 29 Oct. 1476, fol. 655.
98 Ibid., 19 Dec. 1477, fol. 512.
99 Ibid., 23 Sept. 1478, fol. 149.
100 Ibid., 30 Sept. 1479, fol. 36.
101 Ibid., 13 Nov. 1480, fol. 46; 30 June 1485, fol. 215.
102 Ibid., 20 Mar. 1489, fol. 17; 9 Mar. 1490, fol. 190.
103 AMC, doc. 196-C, 30 July 1490.
104 AGS, Sello, 23 Dec. 1491, fol. 231.
105 Ibid., 16 Aug. 1493, fol. 275; 14 Mar. 1494, fol. 450.
106 Ibid., 2 Mar. 1495, fol. 61.
107 AMC, doc. 308-O^{12a}, 19 Sept. 1496.
108 Ibid., 327-C, 15 Dec. 1497.
109 Ibid., 339-O^{144}, nd, nm, 1500.
110 AGS, Cámara, 25 Mar. 1503, leg. 8.
111 Ibid., 9 Sept. 1504, leg. 2; AGS, Sello, 5 Apr. 1506, fol. 42.
112 Held the title of asistente from 1470. The area reverted to the crown upon his death in 1493. AGS, PR, leg. 11, docs. 61–3, 66, 27 Jan. 1493; Agustín de Orozco, Historia de la ciudad de Cádiz (Cádiz, 1845), p. 149.
113 AGS, Sello, 30 Sept. 1493, fol. 45; 17 July 1495, fol. 103.
114 José Sánchez Herrero, Cádiz: La ciudad Medieval y Cristiana (1260–1525) (Cordova, 1981), p. 177.
115 AGS, Sello, 25 Nov. 1478, fol. 58.
116 Ibid., 4 Nov. 1480, fols. 11, 174; 22 Sept. 1483, fol. 135; 21 July 1489, fol. 349; 5 Nov. 1490, fol. 7.
117 Ibid., 21 May 1491, fol. 110; 28 Apr. 1492, fol. 156; 4 July 1494, fol. 134.
118 Ibid., 30 Jan 1495, fol. 122; 12 May 1496, fol. 29.
119 AGS, Diversos, leg. 9, no. 20, 12 Sept. 1501; S. Zavala, "Las conquistas de Canarias y América: estudio comparativo," Estudios indianos (Mexico, 1948), p. 53.
120 José de Viera y Clavijo, Noticias de la Historia General . . . Santa Cruz de Tenerife (4 vols), Santa Cruz de Tenerife, 1952), vol. IV, p. 483.
121 Ibid., vol. IV, p. 484.
122 AGS, Sello, 20 Dec. 1493, fol. 52; L. de la Rosa Olivera and E. Serra

Ráfols, El Adelantado D. Alonso de Lugo y su residencia por Lope de Sosa (La Laguna, 1949), pp. 147f.
123 AGS, Sello, 23 Aug. 1477, fol. 449.
124 Manuel González Jiménez, El concejo de Carmona a fines de la edad media (1464–1523) (Seville, 1973). p. 135.
125 Ibid., p. 136.
126 AGS, Sello, 8 Aug. 1478, fol. 79; 18 Jan. 1490, fol. 28.
127 Ibid., nd Jan. 1491, fol. 50.
128 Ibid., 17 May 1491, fol. 116; 26 Apr. 1494, fol. 505.
129 Ibid., 27 Mar. 1494, fol. 48; 17 Sept. 1495, fol. 13.
130 Ibid., 15 May 1499, fol. 12; 8 Sept. 1503, fol. 22.
131 Ibid., 12 Apr. 1504, fol. 321; 12 Sept. 1505, fol. 87.
132 Ibid., 2 Apr. 1475, fol. 383.
133 Ibid., 19 Oct. 1480, fol. 146.
134 Ibid., 28 Sept. 1484, fol. 153.
135 Ibid., 9 Sept. 1485, fol. 234; 16 Mar. 1487, fol. 27.
136 Ibid., 6 June 1488, fol. 44.
137 Ibid., 4 May 1488, fol. 185; 3 Feb. 1490, fols. 86, 87; nd Feb. 1491, fol. 287.
138 Ibid., 25 Sept. 1490, fol. 231.
139 Ibid., 26 Nov. 1492, fol. 190.
140 Ibid., 27 June 1493, fol. 247.
141 Ibid., 28 Mar. 1495, fol. 379.
142 Ibid., 15 May 1495, fol. 276.
143 AGS, Cámara, Cédulas, lib. 1, fols. 13–14r, 15 Mar. 1494.
144 Ibid.
145 AGS, Sello, 18 Nov. 1488, fol. 196.
146 Ibid., 25 Oct. 1493, fol. 239.
147 Ibid., 25 Nov. 1476, fol. 725.
148 Ibid., 22 Feb. 1480, fol. 1475; 12 Jan. 1485, fol. 65; 10 Oct. 87, fol. 200.
149 Luis Delgado Merchán, Historia documentada de Ciudad Real (Ciudad Real, 1907), p. 185.
150 AGS, Sello, 3 Apr. 1476, fol. 209.

151 *Ibid.*, 9 Feb. 1477, fol. 57.
152 *Ibid.*, 25 Jan. 1478, fol. 77.
153 *Ibid.*, 10 Sept. 1479, fol. 40.
154 *Records of the Trials at the Spanish Inquisition in Ciudad Real*, ed. Haim Beinart (4 vols., Jerusalem, 1974), vol. I, pp. 198ff.
155 *AGS, Sello*, 7 Sept. 1484, fol. 41.
156 *Ibid.*, 24 Sept. 1485, fol. 165; 11 Apr. 1487, fol. 147.
157 *Ibid.*, 5 July 1487, nf; 5 Feb. 1490, fol. 261.
158 *Ibid.*, 13 Dec. 1490, fol. 90.
159 *Ibid.*, 9 Mar. 1491, fol. 453; 13 Mar. 1492, fol. 145.
160 *Ibid.*, 3 Sept. 1493, fol. 20; 4 Jan. 1495, fol. 245.
161 *AGS, Cámara*, 9 Mar. 1476, *leg.* 12; *AGS, Sello*, 12 Nov. 1476, fol. 698; 9 June 1478, fol. 98.
162 *AGS, Cámara*, 9 July 1480, fols. 6, 7; 22 May 1483, fol. 17; 12 Oct. 1484, fol. 121.
163 *Ibid.*, 7 Feb. 1484, fol. 199.
164 *Ibid.*, 13 June 1484, fol. 206.
165 *Ibid.*, 10 May 1486, fol. 76.
166 *Ibid.*, 27 Mar. 1488, fol. 76; 15 Oct. 1490, fol. 296.
167 *Ibid.*, 20 Mar. 1491, fol. 199; 25 Sept. 1493, fol. 38.
168 *Ibid.*, 20 July 1494, fol. 53.
169 *Ibid.*, nd Sept. 1499, nf
170 D. de Nogales Delicado y Rendón, *Historia de la muy noble y leal ciudad de Ciudad Rodrigo* (Ciudad Rodrigo, 1880), p. 219.
171 *AGS, Sello*, 24 Sept. 1477, fol. 558.
172 *Ibid.*, 22 June 1477, fol. 12; 3 Sept. 1477, fol. 42; 7 Nov. 1477, fol. 283.
173 *Ibid.*, 7 Nov. 1477, fol. 283; 29 Jan. 1480, fol. 46.
174 *Ibid.*, 4 Nov. 1483, fol. 275; 30 June 1486, fol. 124.
175 *Ibid.*, 3 July 1488, fol. 304; 10 Feb. 1494, fol. 22.
176 *Ibid.*, 10 Feb. 1494, fol. 22.
177 Edwards, *Christian Córdoba*, p. 195.
178 *Ibid.*
179 *Ibid.*
180 *Ibid.*
181 *Ibid.*

182 *Ibid.*; *AGS, Sello*, 12 Aug. 1506, nf.
183 *AGS, Sello*, 4 Mar. 1478, fol. 77.
184 *Ibid.*, 20 July 1478, fol. 1; 16 Dec. 1480, fol. 21.
185 *Ibid.*, 9 May 1484, fol. 56; 23 July 1485, fol. 103.
186 *Ibid.*, 12 Feb. 1485, fol. 24; nd Sept. 1492, fol. 295.
187 *Ibid.*, nd July 1494, fol. 214.
188 *Ibid.*, nd Nov. 1495, fol. 194.
189 *Ibid.*, 20 Feb. 1475, fol. 190.
190 *Ibid.*, 23 Jan. 1476, fol. 21.
191 *Ibid.*, 25 Nov. 1476, fol. 723; 12 Dec. 1480, fol. 234.
192 *Ibid.*, 12 Dec. 1479, fol. 234.
193 *Ibid.*, 12 Dec. 1480, fol. 233.
194 *Ibid.*, 12 July 1483, fol. 83; 22 Mar. 1487, fol. 110.
195 *Ibid.*, 15 Nov. 1488, fol. 129; 23 Jan. 1490, fol. 169.
196 *Ibid.*, 22 Mar. 1490, fol. 26; 13 May 1493, fol. 203.
197 *Ibid.*, 19 Oct. 1493, fol. 48.
198 *Ibid.*, nd July 1494, fol. 353.
199 *Ibid.*, 30 Jan. 1495, fol. 19.
200 *Ibid.*, 5 Mar. 1480, fol. 162.
201 *Ibid.*, 15 June 1480, fol. 29.
202 *Ibid.*, 24 May 1484, fol. 29.
203 *Ibid.*, 7 Jan. 1485, fol. 125.
204 *Ibid.*, 8 Jan. 1488, fol. 241; 19 Mar. 1493, fol. 224.
205 *Ibid.*, 12 June 1493, fol. 53; 6 Aug. 1495, fol. 151.
206 *AGS, Cámara*, nd, May 1501, *leg.* 7, nf.
207 *Ibid.*, 30 Aug. 1502, *leg.* 7, fol. 59; *AGS, Diversos, leg.* 10, fol. 31, 23 Aug. 1503.
208 *AGS, Sello*, 23 June 1492, fol. 166.
209 *Ibid.*, 1 Aug. 1476, fol. 559; 24 Feb. 1477, fol. 326.
210 *Ibid.*, 12 Apr. 1478, fol. 39.
211 *AM Carmona, AC*, 1482, fol. 60; nd, nm 1482, fol. 30.
212 *AGS, Sello*, 14 Mar. 1486, fol. 178.
213 *Ibid.*, 28 Jan. 1480, fol. 328.
214 *Ibid.*, 29 Apr. 1490, fol. 271; 4 Mar. 1492, fol. 444.
215 *Ibid.*, 26 Sept. 1492, fol. 45; 9 Feb. 1495, fol. 12.

Notes to Table 7 (cont.)

216 AMS, *Diversos*, sec. 16ª, no. 768.
217 AGS, *Sello*, 12 July 1479, fol. 52.
218 *Ibid.*, 14 Dec. 1490, fol. 65.
219 *Ibid.*, 19 Mar. 1493, fol. 147; 7 May 1494, fol. 451.
220 *Ibid.*, 21 June 1492, fol. 25, 10 Jan. 1495, fol. 33 (Almería); 10 Jan. 1495, fol. 33 (Guadix).
221 *Ibid.*, 8 Nov. 1475, fol. 723.
222 A. López Ferreiro, *Galicia en el último tercio del siglo XV* (Vigo, 1968), p. 74.
223 AGS, *Sello*, 30 Nov. 1476, fol. 222; 24 Jan. 1478, fol. 116; 9 June 1478, fol. 55.
224 *Ibid.*, 2 Feb. 1480, fol. 207; 3 July 1480, fol. 15.
225 *Ibid.*, 12 Mar. 1484, fols, 170, 199; 12 Mar. 1492, fol. 198.
226 AGS, *Escribanía Mayor de Rentas, Nóminas de Corte*, leg. 1.
227 Manuel Acien Almansa, *Ronda y su serranía en tiempo de los Reyes Católicos* (3 vols., Málaga, 1979), vol. I p. 62. Doc. no. 9.
228 AGS, *Sello*, 1 June 1492, fol. 340; BNM, ms 226/137, 3 Jan. 1500.
229 A. Cotarelo y Valledor, *Fray Diego de Deza, ensayo biográfico* (Madrid, 1902), p. 149.
230 AM Málaga, *Provisiones*, vol. IV, fols. 151–3; 162v–163; 12 Sept. 1503, 2 May 1504.
231 His co-administrator was Hernando de Zafra. Erika Spivakovsky, *Son of the Alhambra: Don Diego Hurtado de Mendoza, 1504–1575* (Austin, Texas, 1970), pp. 3ff.
232 AGS, *Cámara, Cédulas, lib.* 1, fols. 13–14ª, 15 Mar. 1494.
233 AGS, *Sello*, 14 Mar. 1477, fol. 441.
234 *Ibid.*, 28 July 1478, fol. 38.
235 *Ibid.*, 14 Oct. 1484, fol. 86; 21 July 1485, fol. 76.
236 *Ibid.*, 9 Feb. 1490, fol. 108; 26 Oct. 1493, fol. 47.
237 *Ibid.*, 9 Sept. 1494, fol. 148; 6 Nov. 1495, fol. 155.
238 *Ibid.*, 23 Sept. 1504, nf
239 AGS, *Cámara, Cédulas, lib.* 1, fols. 13–14ª, 15 Mar. 1494.
240 AGS, *Sello*, 10 Sept. 1476, fol. 32.
241 *Ibid.*, 20 Dec. 1476, fol. 818.

242 *Ibid.*, 24 Oct. 1477, fol. 163.
243 *Ibid.*, 5 Feb. 1478, fol. 65.
244 *Ibid.*, 5 Feb. 1478, fol. 65; 12 Dec. 1480, fol. 20.
245 *Ibid.*, 26 Apr. 1484, fol. 28.
246 *Ibid.*, 14 June 1487, fols. 26, 30.
247 *Ibid.*, 28 July 1494, fol. 55; 13 Dec. 1495, fol. 29.
248 *Ibid.*, 15 Feb. 1475, fol. 27; 22 Dec. 1477, fol. 543.
249 *Ibid.*, 2 June 1488, fol. 77.
250 *Ibid.*, 20 July 1488, fol. 157.
251 *Ibid.*, 15 Dec. 1489, fol. 87.
252 *Ibid.*, 30 Mar. 1491, fol. 393.
253 *Ibid.*, 20 May 1494, fol. 467.
254 Cádiz returned to the crown under an accord of 13 Sept. 1477. AGS, PR, leg. 11, fol. 40.
255 He was imprisoned in Granada during 1483. AGS, *Sello*, 20 Oct. 1477, fol. 125; 15 Feb. 1484, fol. 203.
256 Pulgar, *Crónica*, vol. II, ch. 3, p. 189.
257 AGS, *Sello*, 5 Dec. 1485, fol. 43; nd Mar. 1487, fol. 58.
258 *Ibid.*, 10 Jan. 1488, fol. 320; 10 July 1495, fol. 441.
259 AMS, *Tumbo*, book IV, fol. 154, 28 Feb. 1502; AM Málaga, *Provisiones*, book IV, fols. 104v–116, 15 Jan. 1504.
260 AGS, *Sello*, nd Aug. 1487, fol. 174; 23 Feb. 1489, fol. 62; M. Villar y Macías, *Historia de Salamanca* ... (4 vols., Salamanca, 1887), vol. II, p. 47.
261 *Ibid.*, 16 Oct. 1475, fol. 657; 8 Oct. 1476, fol. 654.
262 *Ibid.*, 11 Sept. 1479, fol. 134.
263 *Ibid.*, 3 Mar. 1480, fol. 51.
264 *Ibid.*, 31 Jan. 1480, fol. 7; 10 Dec. 1480, fol. 19.
265 *Ibid.*, 24 Dec. 1483, fol. 186; 7 Feb. 1485, fol. 247.
266 *Ibid.*, 21 Aug. 1486, fol. 81; 13 June 1488, fol. 173.
267 A twenty-day appointment. *Ibid.*, 18 Aug. 1488, fol. 102.
268 *Ibid.*, 24 Mar. 1489, fol. 18; 31 Mar. 1490, fol. 272.
269 *Ibid.*, 4 Nov. 1490, fol. 169; 26 Nov. 1493, fol. 68.
270 *Ibid.*, 28 Mar. 1494, fol. 367.
271 *Ibid.*, 7 Apr. 1494, fol. 405; 10 Nov. 1495, fol. 46.

272 AGS, Cámara, Cédulas, lib. I, fols. 13–14ʳ, 15 Mar. 1494.
273 AGS, Sello, 15 Nov. 1483, fol. 233.
274 Ibid., 10 Mar. 1484, fol. 189.
275 Ibid., 28 Jan. 1488, fol. 100.
276 Ibid., 6 Feb. 1488, fol. 152; 19 Apr. 1491, fol. 206.
277 Ibid., nd Apr. 1491, fol. 304.
278 Ibid., 16 Apr. 1492, fol. 204.
279 Ibid., 12 May 1494. fol. 268; 27 June 1494, fol. 39.
280 Ibid., nd Feb. 1490, fol. 279.
281 Ibid., 4 Apr. 1490, fol. 158; 18 July 1491, fol. 77.
282 Ibid., 22 May 1492, fol. 293; 10 Sept. 1494, fol. 11.
283 AM Madrid, Cédulas, M-340, fol. 65v, 13 Sept. 1476; AGS, Sello, 9 July 1476, fol. 534.
284 AM Madrid, Acuerdos, 1477, 25 Apr. 1477.
285 Ibid., 1479, 29 Sept. 1479.
286 AGS, Sello, 23 Nov. 1480, fol. 34; 12 Dec. 1483, fol. 200.
287 AM Madrid, Acuerdos, 1483, 7 Dec. 1483.
288 AGS, Sello, 14 Mar. 1484, fol. 233; AM Madrid, Horadado, M-338, fols. 233–234v, 28 Jan. 1487.
289 AGS, Sello, 11 Apr. 1487, fol. 147; 14 May 1489, fol. 287.
290 Ibid., 11 May 1490, fol. 71.
291 Ibid., 5 Jan. 1491, fol. 250.
292 Ibid., 6 Dec. 1492, fol. 45.
293 Ibid., 22 Feb. 1493, fol. 22; 26 Sept. 1494, fol. 328.
294 AM Madrid, Horadado, M-338, fol. 105v, 8 Sept. 1494.
295 AGS, Sello, 28 Feb. 1494, fol. 79.
296 AM Madrid, Horadado, M-338, fol. 219ʳ, 11 Apr. 1497.
297 AM Madrid, AC, V-1498, fol. 172ʳ, 19 Oct. 1498; AM Madrid, Cédulas, M-340, fol. 205, 2 Oct. 1501.
298 AM Madrid, AC, V-1502, fol. 124ʳ, 11 Mar. 1502.
299 Ibid., V-1503, fol. 166, 27 Oct. 1503.
300 AM Madrid, Cédulas, M-340, fols. 70ʳ–74ʳ, 15 Nov. 1503–5 Aug. 1506.
301 AGS, Sello, 26 June 1495, fol. 23.
302 Ibid., 14 Oct. 1487, fol. 188; 4 June 1492, fol. 100.
303 Ibid., 15 May 1492, fol. 62; 21 Oct. 1495, fol. 261.

304 AM Málaga, Provisiones, vol. I, fols. 75–9, 82v–87, 10 June 1496, 12 Aug. 1498.
305 Ibid., vol. I, fols. 102v–107v, 12 Aug. 1498, 15 Jan. 1499.
306 Ibid., vol. I, fols. 102v–107v, 15 Jan. 1499: vol. IV, fols. 165–165v, 26 Nov. 1504.
307 AGS, Sello, 28 Aug. 1488, fol. 123.
308 Given office upon death of his father. Ibid.
309 Ibid., 3 June 1489, fol. 100; 6 Mar. 1492, fol. 361.
310 Ibid., nd Mar. 1491, fol. 88. His jurisdiction included Gaucín.
311 Ibid., 29 Mar. 1493, fol. 48; 17 Apr. 1494, fol. 449; 30 July 1495, fol. 443.
312 Ibid., 17 Sept. 1495, fol. 66.
313 AGS, Cédulas, 5 Dec. 1499, leg. 3.
314 AGS, Sello, 9 Jan. 1475, fol. 52.
315 Ibid., 23 Dec. 1475, fol. 790.
316 Ibid., 26 May 1480, fol. 249.
317 Ibid., 28 Feb. 1480, fol. 14.
318 Listed as teniente, not corregidor. Ibid., 3 Feb. 1484, fol. 234.
319 Ibid., 23 June 1484, fol. 20; 23 Dec. 1484, fol. 42.
320 Ibid., 30 Sept. 1485, fol. 137.
321 Ibid., 6 May 1486, fol. 200; 26 Apr. 1487, fol. 155.
322 Ibid., 14 Nov. 1487, nf.
323 Ibid., 9 Dec. 1488, fol. 42; 12 Feb. 1490, fols. 84–5.
324 Ibid., 30 July 1490, fols. 115, 336; 18 Nov. 1492, fol. 37.
325 Ibid., 26 Jan. 1493, fol. 57; 5 May 1495, fol. 392.
326 AMS Diversos, sec. 16ª, no. 749.
327 AGS, Sello, 8 Aug. 1487, fol. 52.
328 Ibid., 17 Nov. 1476, fol. 721.
329 Ibid., 30 May 1478, fol. 34.
330 Ibid., 4 July 1485, fol. 82.
331 Ibid., 6 Feb. 1488, fol. 37.
332 Ibid., 26 Nov. 1488, fol. 35.
333 Ibid., 7 Apr. 1490, fol. 280; 9 Mar. 1491, fol. 105.
334 Ibid., 14 Oct. 1493, fol. 45; 3 Sept. 1493, fol. 21.
335 Ibid., 7 Mar. 1494, fol. 504; nd Feb. 1495, fol. 78.
336 Ibid., 30 Nov. 1476, fol. 222; 24 Jan. 1478, fol. 116; 9 June 1478, fol. 55.

Notes to Table 7 (cont.)

337 Ibid., 22 Feb. 1477, fol. 36.

338 Ibid., 15 Dec. 1489, fol. 157.

339 Ibid., 17 Apr. 1494, fol. 475.

340 Ibid., 18 May 1475, nf. Named to govern municipalities and kingdom of Murcia by "King" Don Alfonso in 1464. Privilege to "guard and govern" reconfirmed by Isabella in 1475.

341 AM Murcia, 1453-75, fols. 234ff.

342 Appointment withdrawn. AM Murcia, CR, 1478-88, fol. 9, 12 Sept. 1478.

343 AGS, Sello, 11 Jan. 1478, fol. 135; AM Murcia, CR, 1478-88, fols. 44r-45, 18 June 1479.

344 AM Murcia, CR, 1478-88, 19 Oct. 1481, fol. 66.

345 Ibid., fols. 71-2, 26 Jan. 1482.

346 AGS, Sello, 29 Mar. 1484, fol. 165; nd Sept. 1487, fol. 102.

347 Ibid., 15 Dec. 1488, fol. 54; 29 July 1489, fol. 153.

348 Ibid., 22 June 1490, fol. 16; nd Mar. 1492, fol. 302.

349 Ibid., 23 Aug. 1493, fol. 99; 11 Mar. 1494, fol. 306.

350 Rafael Serra Ruiz, "Notas Sobre el Juicio de Residencia en la época de los Reyes Católicos," Anuario de estudios medievales 5 (1968), 538-46.

351 Owens, Oligarquía murciana, p. 142.

352 Ibid., p. 144.

353 AGS, Sello, 1 Feb. 1487, fol. 84.

354 AGS, Cámara, Cédulas, lib. 1, fols. 13-14r, 15 Mar. 1494.

355 AGS, Sello, 15 May 1487, fol. 91.

356 Ibid., 8 Sept. 1484, fol. 161.

357 Ibid., 10 May 1486, fol. 57.

358 Ibid., 17 Nov. 1488, fol. 128.

359 Ibid., 4 Dec. 1488, fol. 150; 26 Mar. 1490, fol. 235.

360 Ibid., 9 Aug. 1490, fols. 48, 59; 10 Oct. 1491, fol. 142.

361 Ibid., 8 Mar. 1492, fol. 366; 11 Jan. 1493, fol. 253.

362 Ibid., nd Sept. 1492, fol. 46; 27 Nov. 1495, fol. 52.

363 Ibid., 20 Sept. 1487, fol. 160.

364 Ibid., 28 Nov. 1491, fol. 380.

365 Ibid., 31 July 1492, fol. 63; 14 May 1495, fol. 48.

366 Ibid., 2 Dec. 1488, fol. 197.

367 Ibid., 4 Feb. 1489, fol. 275; 12 Feb. 1491, fol. 126.

368 AGS, Cédulas, 7 Apr. 1490, leg. 4.

369 Ibid., 12 Sept. 1490, leg. 22; AGS, Sello, 8 Feb. 1491, fol. 32.

370 Ibid., AGS, Sello, 4 May 1492, fol. 261.

371 Ibid., 26 Jan. 1493, fol. 54; 14 Feb. 1495, fol. 205.

372 Ibid., 2 Mar. 1495, fol. 60.

373 AGS, Cédulas, 9 Sept. 1496, leg. 12.

374 Ibid., nd Apr. 1499, leg. 3.

375 AGS, Sello, 18 Feb. 1489, fol. 214; 16 Dec. 1491, fol. 160.

376 Ibid., nd Apr. 1494, fol. 54; 27 June 1496, nf.

377 Ibid., 12 June 1500, nf.

378 AGS, Cédulas, 19 June 1503, leg. 48.

379 Ibid., 13 Aug. 1478, nf; H. Sancho Mayi, Historia del Puerto de Santa María (Cádiz, 1943), p. 548.

380 AGS, Sello, 19 Mar. 1490, fol. 533.

381 Lucas de Torre, "Diego de Valera," pp. 374f.

382 Named asistente Requina and corregidor Utiel. AGS, Sello, 6 Apr. 1486, fol. 186.

383 Named asistente Requina and corregidor Utiel. Ibid., 4 Feb. 1478, fols. 63-4.

384 Named asistente Requina and corregidor Utiel. Ibid., 13 Sept. 1479, fol. 237; Torres Fontes, "Marquesado de Villena," p. 107.

385 Named corregidor to Requina. His lieutenant, Francisco de Molina, named corregidor to Utiel. AGS, Sello, 15 Apr. 1485, fol. 201; 20 Mar. 1486, fol. 43.

386 Ibid., 20 Mar. 1486, fol. 168; 12 Apr. 1488, fol. 43.

387 Ibid., 28 Oct. 1490, fol. 148.

388 Ibid., 29 Oct. 1490, fol. 39; 18 Mar. 1494, fol. 363.

389 Ibid., 8 Mar. 1475, fol. 255.

390 Ibid., nd, nm, 1476, fol. 36.

391 Uncle of the marquis of Astorga. Ibid., 27 June 1477, fol. 218.

392 Ibid., 9 July 1478, fol. 60; 8 Dec. 1480, fol. 18.

393 Ibid., 26 Apr. 1484, fol. 27; 28 Jan. 1487, fol. 18.

[394] Died in office. Position granted to son Pedro de Loaisa in 1489. *Ibid.*, 7 Aug. 1487, fol. 331; 20 Apr. 1489, fol. 8; Benito Ruano, *Toledo*, p. 129.
[395] *AGS, Sello*, 29 Jan. 1491, fol. 162.
[396] *Ibid.*, 16 Sept. 1491, fol. 280; 15 Oct. 1494, fol. 459.
[397] *Ibid.*, 3 Oct. 1494, fol. 46; 3 Oct. 1495, fol. 212.
[398] *AGS, Cédulas*, 4 Dec. 1501, leg. 12 *AGS, Sello*, 11 Aug. 1505, nf.
[399] *AGS, Sello*, 15 Sept. 1477, fol. 511.
[400] *Ibid.*, 14 July 1491, fol. 157.
[401] *Ibid.*, 14 Jan. 1489, fol. 99; 19 Mar. 1495, fol. 320.
[402] *Ibid.*, 26 Jan. 1492, fol. 73.
[403] *Ibid.*, 16 Dec. 1493, fol. 97.
[404] *Ibid.*, 20 May 1494, fol. 36; 6 May 1495, fol. 43.
[405] *Ibid.*, 12 Nov. 1497, fol. 42.
[406] *Ibid.*, 13 May 1498, nf.
[407] *Ibid.*, 4 May 1502, nf.
[408] *Ibid.*, 15 Oct. 1475, fol. 11.
[409] *Ibid.*, 8 Apr. 1477, fol. 100.
[410] *Ibid.*, 26 Aug. 1478, fol. 104.
[411] *Ibid.*, 4 Nov. 1480, fol. 18; 26 Jan. 1485, fol. 100.
[412] *Ibid.*, 8 Mar. 1486, fol. 66; 14 Jan. 1488, fol. 263.
[413] *Ibid.*, 24 Mar. 1488, fol. 74; 1 Mar. 1492, fol. 293.
[414] *Ibid.*, 16 Mar. 1492, fol. 27; 15 Feb. 1493, fol. 6.
[415] *Ibid.*, 4 Oct. 1495, fol. 300; 12 Jan. 1506, nf.
[416] *AMS Tumbo*, 2 Aug. 1478, transcr. *AMS Tumbo*, ed. Carande, vol. I, p. 288.
[417] *AMS Tumbo*, ed. Carande, vol. II, p. 168, 22 Sept. 1482; *AGS, Diversos*, leg. 43, fol. 51, nd, nm, 1506.
[418] *AMS, Tumbo*, bk. V, p. 395, 25 Sept. 1500; *RAH*, no. 346, appendix B, 2 June 1510.
[419] *AGS, Sello*, 20 Mar. 1480, fol. 299; 20 Feb. 1484, fol. 80.
[420] *Ibid.*, 19 Mar. 1484, fol. 95.
[421] *Ibid.*, 18 May 1487, fol. 39.
[422] *Ibid.*, 13 Aug. 1487, fol. 204; 6 Apr. 1495, fol. 30.

[423] *Ibid.*, 26 Oct. 1497, nf; 15 May 1498, fol. 34.
[424] Francisco de Pisa, *Descripción de la imperial ciudad de Toledo* (Toledo, 1617), vol. IV, ch. XXXVII.
[425] *AGS, Sello*, 20 Feb. 1477, fol. 298.
[426] *Ibid.*, 11 Feb. 1491, fol. 23; 12 Dec. 1506, nf.
[427] *AGS, Sello*, 26 Apr. 1484, fol. 37; 18 Jan. 1485, fol. 25.
[428] *Ibid.*, 20 Dec. 1485, fol. 116; 25 Mar. 1487, fol. 68.
[429] *Ibid.*, 6 Mar. 1489, fol. 157.
[430] *Ibid.*, 10 Oct. 1491, fol. 116; 23 Apr. 1493, fol. 83.
[431] *Ibid.*, 10 Oct. 1493, fol. 48; 18 Nov. 1494, fol. 198.
[432] *Ibid.*, 16 May 1495, fol. 159.
[433] *Ibid.*, 6 Feb. 1498, nf.
[434] *Ibid.*, 9 Nov. 1475, fol. 729; 9 Mar. 1476, fol. 155.
[435] *AGS, Cédulas*, 8 Apr. 1476, leg. 88.
[436] *AGS, Sello*, 20 Feb. 1477, fol. 277.
[437] *Ibid.*, 28 Oct. 1477, fol. 202.
[438] *Ibid.*, 23 Sept. 1479, fol. 65.
[439] *AGS, Cédulas*, nd July 1480, leg. 11; *AGS, Sello*, 12 Sept. 1483, fol. 18.
[440] *AGS, Sello*, 9 Dec. 1483, fol. 87; 12 Feb. 1484, fol. 84.
[441] *Ibid.*, 10 Mar. 1484, fol. 34; 26 Feb. 1487, fol. 65.
[442] *Ibid.*, 19 May 1488, fol. 29; nd Mar. 1499, fols. 190, 392.
[443] *Ibid.*, 8 July 1490, fol. 333.
[444] *Ibid.*, 18 Jan. 1492, fol. 84; 29 Nov. 1493, fol. 76.
[445] *Ibid.*, 13 Oct. 1494, fol. 49; 22 Aug. 1495, fol. 41.
[446] *Ibid.*, 5 June 1492, fols. 315–16.
[447] *Ibid.*, 24 Apr. 1475, fol. 426.
[448] *Ibid.*, 19 May 1486, fol. 181; nd Mar. 1490, fol. 392.
[449] *Ibid.*, 28 June 1491, fol. 41; *AMV, AC*, 1503, fol. 136v, 9 Oct. 1503.
[450] *AGS, Sello*, 10 Oct. 1487, fol. 246.
[451] *Ibid.*, 28 July 1488, fol. 221.
[452] *Ibid.*, 2 Apr. 1491, fol. 62.
[453] *Ibid.*, nd, nm, 1492, fol. 166.
[454] *Ibid.*, 17 Jan. 1493, fol. 65.
[455] *Ibid.*, 10 May 1495, fol. 167.

Notes to Table 7 (cont.)

456 AM *Málaga, Provisiones*, vol. 1, fols. 102–107v, 15 Jan. 1499; fols. 165–165v, 26 Nov. 1504.

457 AGS, *Sello*, 18 Oct. 1486, nf.

458 *Ibid.*, 22 May 1486, fol. 170.

459 *Ibid.*, 11 Apr. 1485, fol. 148.

460 *Ibid.*, nd July 1488, fol. 26; 3 June 1491, fol. 192; 5 Dec. 1493, fol. 4. The city was reintegrated into the *Marquesado* during 1493.

461 *Ibid.*, 8 Nov. 1475, fol. 726; 22 Feb. 1477, fol. 36.

462 *Ibid.*, 22 Nov. 1476, fol. 725.

463 *Ibid.*, 10 Apr. 1477, fol. 99.

464 *Ibid.*, 24 Oct. 1477, fol. 12.

465 *Ibid.*, 7 Nov. 1477, fol. 287; Sept. 1479 to Requena–Utiel.

466 *Ibid.*, 22 Feb. 1480, fol. 75; 12 Jan. 1485, fol. 65; 10 Oct. 1487, fol. 200. Territory returned to the crown in 1488 from Don Diego López Pacheco. *Ibid.*, 14 Jan. 1488, nf; 13 Sept. 1488, fol. 42; nd June 1493, fol. 16.

468 *Ibid.*, 27 June 1478, fol. 71; 18 Nov. 1494, fol. 112.

469 *Ibid.*, 7 Feb. 1475, fol. 153.

470 T. López Mata, *La ciudad y el castillo de Burgos* (Burgos, 1949), p. 93.

471 AGS, *Sello*, 4 Nov. 1477, nf.

472 *Ibid.*, 23 Sept. 1478, fol. 133.

473 *Ibid.*, 31 Jan. 1480 nf.

474 *Ibid.*, 15 Oct. 1483, fol. 216; 29 Oct. 1488, fol. 16.

475 *Ibid.*, 7 Mar. 1489, fol. 161; 21 Feb. 1491, fol. 310.

476 *Ibid.*, 10 Dec. 1491, fol. 38; nd Mar. 1494, fol. 377.

477 *Ibid.*, 6 Apr. 1495, fol. 33.

478 *Ibid.*, 8 July 1504, nf.

479 *Ibid.*, 10 Mar. 1474, fol. 269.

480 *Ibid.*, 10 Feb. 1476, fol. 49.

481 *Ibid.*, 26 Apr. 1480, fol. 56.

482 *Ibid.*, 26 Apr. 1484, fol. 37; 18 Jan. 1485, fol. 25.

483 *Ibid.*, 5 Nov. 1485, fol. 125; 29 May 1487, fol. 50.

484 *Ibid.*, 24 Apr. 1487, fol. 44; 22 Dec. 1488, fol. 194.

485 *Ibid.*, 17 Mar. 1490, fol. 64; 20 Sept. 1493, fols. 55, 71.

486 *Ibid.*, 7 Mar. 1494, fol. 383; 27 June 1496, nf.

487 *Archivo Municipal de Zamora, Documentos varios, S. XV; Documentos Reales – Reyes Católicos, leg.* 19, fol. 31, 5 Oct. 1498.

488 Fernández Duro, *Memorias históricas de la ciudad de Zamora, su provincia y obispado* (Madrid, 1882–3), vol. IV, p. 621.

Notes

Abbreviations

A. Archives

AGS	*Archivo General de Simancas*
Cámara	*Cámara de Castilla*
Cédulas	*Libros de Cédulas*
Contaduría	*Contaduría Mayor de Cuentas, 1ª época*
Diversos	*Diversos de Castilla*
Estado	*Estado, Castilla*
PR	*Patronato Real*
Sello	*Registro General del Sello*
AHN	*Archivo Histórico Nacional* (Madrid)
Diversos	*Sección de Diversos*
AMB	*Archivo Municipal de Burgos*
AC	*Actas Capitulares*
AMC	*Archivo Municipal de Cáceres*
AC	*Actas Capitulares*
AM Carmona	*Archivo Municipal de Carmona*
AC	*Actas Capitulares*
PR	*Provisiones Reales*
AM Madrid	*Archivo Municipal de Madrid*
AC	*Actas Capitulares*
Acuerdos	*Libro de Acuerdos*
Cédulas	*Libro de Cédulas y Provisiones*
Horadado	*Libro de Horadado*
AM Málaga	*Archivo Municipal de Málaga*
AC	*Actas Capitulares*
Originales	*Colección de Originales*
Provisiones	*Libro de Provisiones*
AM Murcia	*Archivo Municipal de Murcia*
AC	*Actas Capitulares*
CR	*Cartas Reales*
AMS	*Archivo Municipal de Sevilla*
AC	*Actas Capitulares*
Tumbo	*El Tumbo de los Reyes Católicos*
AMV	*Archivo Municipal de Valladolid*
AC	*Actas Capitulares*
BNM	*Biblioteca Nacional* (Madrid)
RAH	*Real Academia de la Historia, Biblioteca de* (Madrid)
Salazar	*Colección de Don Luis de Salazar y Castro*

B. *Documents*

fol./fols.	folio/folios
leg.	*legajo* (bundle)
lib.	*libro* (book)
mrs	*maravedís*
nd	no day
nf	no folio number
nm	no month
no.	number
pet.	*petición* (petition)
r	*reverso* (reverse of page)
v	*vuelta* (unnumbered back of numbered page)
1^a	first

C. *Series*

AHDE	*Anuario de Historia del Derecho Español*
BAE	*Biblioteca de Autores Españoles*
B(R)AH	*Boletín de la (Real) Academia de la Historia*
CDI	*Colección de documentos inéditos para la historia de España*
HAHR	*Hispanic American Historical Review*
RABM	*Revista de Archivos, Bibliotecas, y Museos*

1. The omnicompetent servant

1. *Max Weber: Essays in Sociology*, tr., ed., and with intro. by H. H. Gerth and C. W. Mills (New York, 1946), ch. 7, "Bureaucracy."
2. "Los Reyes Católicos confían el gobierno a una clase social selecta, con la suficiente preparación moral y profesional para desempeñar adecuadamente sus funciones. Este intento de crear una *élite* gobernante es una de las más felices iniciativas de los monarcas, y para ello, teniendo en cuenta la necesidad absoluta de eliminar la levantisca y anárquica nobleza, se acude a los letrados, que se reclutaban entre los hidalgos y los burgueses" (Fernando de Albi, *El corregidor en el municipio español bajo la monarquía absoluta. Ensayo histórico-crítico* (Madrid, 1936), p. 56).
3. William D. Phillips, Jr., *Enrique IV and the Crisis of Fifteenth-Century Castile, 1425–1480* (Cambridge, Mass., 1978), pp. 49ff.
4. See Table 7, pp. 196ff.
5. "la cristalización definitiva de una figura institucional que por su propia naturaleza exigía flexibilidad para adaptarse a las circunstancias cambiantes y dispares en que se desenvolvía" (Benjamín González Alonso, *El corregidor castellano (1348–1808)* (Madrid, 1970), p. 81).
6. See Jaime Vicens Vives, *Historia crítica de la vida y reinado de Fernando II de Aragón* (Zaragoza, 1962); Tarsicio de Azcona, *Isabel la Católica: Estudio crítico de su vida y su reinado* (Madrid, 1964).
7. Jaime Vicens Vives, *Approaches to the History of Spain*, tr. and ed. J. C. Ullman (Berkeley and Los Angeles, 1967) p. xvii.
8. Stephen Haliczer, *The Comuneros of Castile: The Forging of a Revolution, 1475–1521* (Madison, Wis., 1981), p. 32.
9. Felipe Fernández-Armesto, *Ferdinand and Isabella* (London, 1975), p. 85.
10. "... sin ser ella creadora de la institución, pudo Isabel modernizarla y manejarla

como medio tremendamente eficaz para hacer llegar a los municipios la mano, a veces pasada y a veces bienhechora, del poder real" (Azcona, *Isabel*, p. 344).

11. Henry Kamen, *Spain 1469–1714: A Society of Conflict* (London and New York, 1983), p. 26.

12. J. H. Elliott, *Imperial Spain 1469–1716* (London, 1963; 2nd edn., 1975), pp. 96f.

13. Clauses 57–107, 1480 Cortes of Toledo, *Cortes de los antiguos reinos de León y Castilla*, ed. Manuel Colmeiro y Penido (5 vols., Madrid, 1861–1903), vol. IV, pp. 136–83. *Archivo Municipal de Toledo*, 1482, fols. 19r–31r, transcr. Emilio Sáez Sánchez, "El Libro del Juramento de ayuntamiento de Toledo," *AHDE*, vol. XVI (1945), pp. 530–624 (referred to hereafter as *Capítulos de corregidores, 1482*). A 1493 version, issued to Cordova, virtually identical with the regulations of 1500, found in the *AMS, Carpeta 5ª*, no. 32, fols. 1–6v, 18 July 1493 (referred to hereafter as *Capítulos de corregidores, 1493*). "Capítulos de corregidores, 1500," transcr. in González Alonso, *Corregidor castellano*, pp. 299–317 (referred to hereafter as *Capítulos de Corregidores, 1500*). See facsimile reprint and study by A. M. Orejón, *Los Capítulos de Corregidores de 1500* (Madrid, 1963).

14. D. Agustín Bermúdez Aznar, *El corregidor en Castilla durante la Baja Edad Media (1348–1474)* (Murcia, 1974), pp. 209ff. See also Luis García de Valdeavellano, "Las 'Partidas' y los orígenes medievales del Juicio de Residencia," *B(R)AH* 153 (1963), pp. 205–46.

15. Perez Zagorin, *Rebels and Rulers, 1500–1660* (2 vols., London and New York, 1982), vol. I, *Society, States and Early Modern Revolution. Agrarian and Urban Rebellions*, p. 254.

2. Establishing authority

1. Text in *Cancionero de Gómez Manrique*, intro. Antonio Paz y Melía, *Colección de escritores castellanos*, ed. R. Foulché-Delbosc (2 vols., Madrid, 1885), vol. I, p. 26; Clemente Palencia Flores, "El poeta Gómez Manrique, corregidor de Toledo," *Boletín de la Real Academia de Bellas Artes y Ciencias Históricas de Toledo* 22 (1943–4), p. 42 (reprinted 1944).

2. José Mª Font Rius, "Las instituciones administrativas y judiciales de las ciudades en la España Medieval," *Anales de la Universidad de Valencia* 26 (1952–3), p. 103.

3. J. M. García Marín, *El oficio público en Castilla durante la Baja Edad Media* (Seville, 1974), pp. 157ff. See also Rogelio Pérez Bustamante, *El gobierno y la administración de los reinos de la corona de Castilla, 1230–1474* (2 vols., Madrid, 1976).

4. M. A. Ladero Quesada, *España en 1492* (Madrid, 1978), p. 59.

5. See H. Lapeyre, *Une famille de marchands: Les Ruiz* (Paris, 1955), and R. S. Smith, *The Spanish Guild Merchant: A History of the Consulado, 1250–1700* (Durham, NC, 1940).

6. Rafael Gibert y Sánchez de la Vega, *El Concejo de Madrid: Su organización en los siglos XII a XV* (Madrid, 1949), pp. 154ff.

7. García Marín, *Oficio público en Castilla*, pp. 169ff.

8. J. H. Edwards, *Christian Córdoba: The City and its Region in the late Middle Ages* (Cambridge, 1982), p. 39.

9. In Murcia it was the custom to provide 5,000 mrs to allow *jurados* to go to court to make their complaint: see J. B. Owens, *Rebelión, monarquía y oligarquía murciana en la época de Carlos V* (Murcia, 1980), p. 36.

10. *AGS Sello*, 25 May 1466, fol. 96.

11. Edwards, *Christian Córdoba*, p. 38.

12. Ladero Quesada, *España en 1492*, p. 33. Urban population figures presented throughout my text without citation are drawn from his summary, unless

specifically noted otherwise. See also 1541 and 1591 census figures in Pierre Chaunu, *La España de Carlos V*, tr. E. Riambau Saurí (2 vols., Barcelona, 1976), vol. I, pp. 68f.

13. J. A. García de Cortázar, *La época medieval*, vol. II, *Historia de España Alfaguara*, dir. Miguel Artola (Madrid, 1976), p. 390.

14. Jane Jacobs, *The Economy of Cities* (New York, 1969), p. 262.

15. Bermúdez Aznar, *Corregidor en Castilla*, pp. 55f.

16. María del Carmen Carlé, *Del concejo medieval castellano-leonés* (Buenos Aires, 1968), pp. 132ff.

17. Pet. 47, Cortes of Alcalá de Henares, *Cortes*, vol. I, p. 608; Bermúdez Aznar, *Corregidor en Castilla*, p. 49.

18. Albi, *Corregidor en monarquía absoluta*, p. 150.

19. Bermúdez Aznar, *Corregidor en Castilla*, pp. 28, 97ff.

20. Julio Valdeón Baruque, *Enrique II de Castilla: La guerra civil y la consolidación del régimen (1366–1371)* (Valladolid, 1966), pp. 78ff., 322ff.

21. Emilio Mitre Fernández, *La extensión del régimen de corregidores en el reinado de Enrique III de Castilla* (Valladolid, 1969), pp. 20f.

22. Pedro López de Ayala, *Crónica de Don Enrique III . . . Crónicas de los Reyes de Castilla*, *BAE*, vol. LXVIII (Madrid, 1779–80), p. 247.

23. Pet. 5, 1419 Cortes of Madrid, *Cortes*, vol. III, pp. 14f.; see also José Manuel Pérez-Prendes, *Cortes de Castilla* (Barcelona, 1974).

24. Palencia Flores, "Gómez Manrique," p. 20.

25. Antonio Álvarez de Morales, *Las hermandades, expresión del movimiento comunitario en España* (Valladolid, 1974), p. 122.

26. Juan Torres Fontes, *Don Pedro Fajardo, adelantado mayor del reino de Murcia* (Madrid, 1953), pp. 196ff.

27. Francisco Layna Serrano, *Historia de Guadalajara y sus Mendozas en los siglos XV y XVI* (4 vols., Madrid, 1942), vol. II, p. 131.

28. Lorenzo Galíndez de Carvajal, "Crónica de Enrique IV" in *Estudio sobre la "Crónica de Enrique IV" del Dr Galíndez de Carvajal*, ed. Juan Torres Fontes (Murcia, 1946), ch. 7, p. 84.

29. Letter dated 1462, in *Epístolas de Mosén Diego de Valera . . .*, *BAE* vol. 116 (Madrid, 1828), p. 18.

30. Diego de Valera, *Memorial de diversas hazañas. Crónica de Enrique IV*, ed. Juan de Mata Carriazo (Madrid, 1941), ch. 20, p. 73.

31. Alonso de Palencia, *Crónica de Enrique IV*, ed. A. Paz y Meliá (Madrid, 1904), vol. I, bk. VI, ch. 8, p. 380.

32. López Mata, *La ciudad y el castillo de Burgos* (Burgos, 1949), p. 76.

33. P. L. Serrano y Serrano, *Los Reyes Católicos y la ciudad de Burgos, desde 1451 a 1492* (Madrid, 1943), pp. 71f.

34. Bermúdez Aznar, *Corregidor en Castilla*, p. 206.

35. *AM Murcia, CR*, 1453–78, fol. 119, 18 March 1461, transcr. D. A. Bermúdez Aznar, "El asistente real en los concejos castellanos bajomedievales," *Actas II Symposium de Historia de la Administración* (Madrid, 1971), doc. 6, pp. 246ff.

36. *AM Murcia, CR*, 1453–78, 12 September 1462, fol. 144, *transcr.* Bermúdez Aznar, *Corregidor en Castilla*, doc. 8, p. 249.

37. *AM Murcia, AC*, 1464, nf, 22 September 1464, transcr. Bermúdez Aznar, "Asistente real," doc. 9, p. 206.

38. *AM Madrid*, sec. 2, *leg.* 397, no. 78, transcr. Bermúdez Aznar, "Asistente real," doc. 3, pp. 239f.

39. José Amador de los Ríos, *Historia social, política y religiosa de los judíos de España*

y Portugal (3 vols., Madrid, 1875, reprinted 1960), vol. II, pp. 662f.

40. See L. W. Newton, "The development of the Castilian peerage" (unpublished PhD dissertation, Tulane University, 1972) for a study of a branch of the Álvarez de Toledo family.

41. Angus MacKay, *Money, Prices and Politics in 15th Century Castile* (London, 1981), pp. 99f.

42. Mohammed III (1595–1603) had nineteen brothers strangled, according to a dispatch of Marco Venier, *Calendar of State Papers . . . Venice . . .* (38 vols.), vol. 9, transcr. in *Pursuit of Power. Venetian Ambassadors' Reports on Turkey, France and Spain in the Age of Philip II, 1560–1600*, ed. J. C. Davis (New York, 1970), p. 169.

43. Alonso de Palencia is the original source for most of these stories.

44. The group consisted of Pacheco's uncle, Alfonso Carillo de Acuña (archbishop of Toledo), and his brother Pedro Girón (master of Calatrava). Their clan was joined by Fadrique Enríquez (admiral of Castile) and a son, Enrique (count of Alba de Liste). Further support came from the counts of Plasencia (Álvaro de Estúñiga), Benavente (Rodrigo Alonso Pimentel), Alba de Tormes (García Álvarez de Toledo), Haro (Pedro Fernández de Velazco, constable of Castile), Paredes de Nava (Rodrigo Manrique), and others. See Palencia, *Crónica*, vol. I, bk. VII, ch. 10, pp. 171ff. and Galíndez de Carvajal, *Crónica*, ch. 65, pp. 238ff.

45. Palencia, *Crónica*, vol. I, bk. VII, ch. 8, pp. 167f.; Diego Enríquez del Castillo, *Crónica del Rey D. Enrique el cuarto . . . Colección de Crónicas de Castilla . . .* (Madrid, 1887), ch. 74, pp. 128ff.

46. The title was changed to corregidor the following year. Torres Fontes, *Pedro Fajardo*, pp. 103f.

47. *AGS, Diversos, leg.* 40, no. 49.

48. See Baltasar Cuartero y Hurta, *El pacto de los Toros de Guisando y la venta del mismo nombre* (Madrid, 1952). Charges of forgery are set out by Orestes Ferrara, *Un pleito sucesorio: Enrique IV, Isabel de Castilla y La Beltraneja* (Madrid, 1945), pp. 251ff.; Phillips, *Enrique IV*, p. 109.

49. Copies of pact in *BNM, Mss.* 13109, fols. 199–207; 18736, no. 1; 13110, fols. 26–32*v*; version in *AM Murcia, CR,* 1453–1478, fols. 211–219*v*, 21 March 1471, transcr. Juan Torres Fontes, "La contratación de Guisando," *Anuario de estudios medievales* 2 (1965), pp. 418ff., doc. 3.

50. *AGS, Diversos, leg.* 40, no. 48, transcr. M. I. del Val Valdivieso, *Isabel la Católica, princesa (1468–1474)* (Valladolid, 1974), doc. 30, pp. 475ff.

51. Clause 7, 24 January 1472, Archivo Municipal de Sepúlveda, no. 51, transcr. *Los fueros de Sepúlveda*, ed. Emilio Saez *et al.* (Segovia, 1953), doc. 44, pp. 278–82; M. I. del Val Valdivieso, "Resistencia al dominio señorial durante los últimos años del reinado de Enrique IV," *Hispania* 34 (1974), pp. 67ff.

52. Estanislao Labayru y Goicoechea, *Historia general del Señorío de Vizcaya* (Bilbao, 1968), vol. III, doc. 15, pp. 649f.

53. Val Valdivieso, "Resistencia señorial," p. 76.

54. Diego de Valera, *Memorial de diversas hazañas. Crónica de Enrique IV*, ed. and with study by Juan de Mata Carriazo (Madrid, 1941), ch. 53, p. 167.

55. Val Valdivieso, "Resistencia señorial," p. 91.

56. The most important of these municipalities were Ágreda, Aranda de Duero, Avila, Burgos (excluding the castle), Murcia, Salamanca, Segovia, Sepúlveda, Toledo, Tordesillas, and Trujillo.

57. Phillips, *Enrique IV*, p. 119; Luis Suárez Fernández, *La España de los Reyes Católicos*,

1475–1516. Historia de España, dir. Ramón Menéndez Pidal (Madrid, 1969), vol. 17, pt. I, p. 99.

58. These areas were Cáceres, Alcalá de Guerra, and Vizcaya. Torres Fontes, *Itinerario de Enrique IV de Castilla* (Murcia, 1955), pp. 227, 235, 247. See also Diego de Colmenares, *Historia de la insigne ciudad de Segovia* (Segovia, 1763; reprinted 1969), pp. 88f.

59. See table in Bermúdez Aznar, *Corregidor en Castilla*, pp. 69–88.

60. Bermúdez Aznar, "Asistente real," p. 227.

61. Seville (1459–70); Toledo (1458, 1460, 1462, 1464–7, 1471–3); Murcia (1460–4, 1466); Madrid (1464–6, 1471–2); Burgos (1465); Guadalajara (1460). *Memorias de D. Enrique IV de Castilla*, vol. 2, *Colección diplomática*, ed. Real Academia de Historia (Madrid, 1835–1913), doc. 31.

62. Pet. 2, 1462 Cortes of Toledo; pet. 2, 1465 Cortes of Salamanca, *Cortes*, vol. III, pp. 705, 750f.

63. See Table 7, pp. 196ff.

64. See Table 7. Murcia and Guadalajara were sent corregidores instead of the *asistentes* assigned by Enrique IV.

65. *AGS, Sello*, 10 September 1494, fol. 49.

66. *Ibid.*, 31 March 1477, fol. 449 (Guipúzcoa); 28 January 1477, fol. 233; 20 February 1477, fol. 318 (Toledo).

67. Benjamín González Alonso, *Gobernación y gobernadores: Notas sobre la administración de Castilla en el período de formación del estado moderno* (Madrid, 1974), p. 36.

68. Miguel Lucas de Iranzo was granted merely the titles of *alcalde mayor* for Baeza (1454) and *alcalde* for Jaén and Alcalá la Real (1458). *Relación de los hechos del muy magnífico e más virtuoso señor el señor Don Miguel Lucas, muy digno condestable de Castilla. (Crónica del siglo XV). Colección de Crónicas Españolas*, ed. Juan de Mata Carriazo (Madrid, 1940), pt. xxxix, ch. 1, p. 4.

69. González Alonso, *Gobernación*, pp. 39ff., 48, 52, 59.

70. See Table 7.

71. *AGS, Sello*, nd March 1484, fol. 199; 30 June 1487, fol. 15.

72. See Table 7.

73. Felipe Fernández-Armesto, *The Canary Islands After the Conquest. The Making of a Colonial Society in the Early Sixteenth Century* (Oxford, 1982), p. 115.

74. *Ibid.*, pp. 140f.; Eduardo Aznar Vallejo, *La integración de las Islas Canarias en la Corona de Castilla (1478–1526). Aspectos administrativos, sociales y económicos* (Seville, 1983), pp. 74ff.

75. Letter of 6 June 1511, *Colección de documentos inéditos relativas al descubrimiento . . . ultramar*, 2nd ser. (Madrid, 1885, reprinted 1967), vol. I, doc. 1, pp. 1ff.

76. González Alonso, *Gobernación*, pp. 96ff.

77. Clauses cited, 1480 Cortes of Toledo, *Cortes*, vol. IV, pp. 137f.

78. *Capítulos de corregidores, 1482*, p. 530.

79. *AMS, Carpeta, 5ᵃ*, no. 32, fols. 1–6v, 18 July 1493.

80. *Capítulos de corregidores, 1500*, p. 299.

81. The order became "*corregidor, asistente, gobernador, alcalde mayor* . . ."; *AHN, Consejo de Castilla. Sala de Casa y Corte*, bk. 1474, doc. 32, 12 December 1669.

82. Suárez Fernández, *Historia de España*, vol. 17, pt. I, pp. 86f.; letter to Murcia in *AM Murcia, CR*, 1453–74, fol. 221r, 16 December 1474, transcr. Torres Fontes, *Pedro Fajardo*, doc, 23, pp. 237f.

83. See preface to Melveena McKendrick, *Women and Society in the Spanish Drama of the Golden Age. A study of the Mujer Varonil* (Cambridge, Mass., 1974).

84. Instituto Diego Colmenares, *Acta de proclamación* (Segovia, 1952); Fernando del Pulgar, *Crónica de los Reyes Católicos*, ed. with a study, Juan de Mata Carriazo (2

vols., Madrid, 1943), vol. I, ch. 21, p. 65 gives an alternative version which places Ferdinand first.

3. The naked sword (1474–85)

1. *Cuatro Décadas de Alonso de Palencia*. Translation and study by José López de Toro (Madrid, 1970), *Década III*, bk. I, ch. 2, p. 317; Palencia, *Crónica*, vol. II, bk, x, ch. 10, pp. 154f.
2. Analysis of the controversy is provided by Marvin Lunenfeld, "Isabella I of Castile and the company of women in power," *Historical Reflections/Réflexions Historiques* (Waterloo, Ont.), IV (1978) pp. 207–29.
3. See R. García y García, *Virtudes de la Reina Católica* (Madrid, 1951) or Rodríguez Valencia, *Isabel la Católica en la opinión de españoles y extranjeros* (Valladolid, 1970).
4. See J. B. Sitges, *Enrique IV y la Excelente Señora: Llamada vulgarmente Doña Juana la Beltraneja* (Madrid, 1913); Gregorio Marañón, *Ensayo biológico sobre Enrique IV de Castilla y su tiempo* (Madrid, 1934, reprinted 1964); Orestes Ferrara, *Un pleito sucesorio: Enrique IV, Isabel de Castilla y La Beltraneja* (Madrid, 1945).
5. A full list of supporters is given in J. Fernández Domínguez Valencia, *La guerra civil a la muerte de Enrique IV: Zamora–Toro–Castronuño* (Zamora, 1929), pp. 10f. The argument put forth by Suárez Fernández for an ideological component to the aristocratic leagues is refuted by Phillips, who finds only pragmatic causes: see Luis Suárez Fernández, *Nobleza y monarquía: puntos de vista sobre la historia castellana del siglo XV* (Valladolid, 1959), pp. 102ff., 132ff., 161ff.; Phillips, *Enrique IV*, pp. 121ff.
6. *Documentos referentes a las relaciones con Portugal durante el reinado de los Reyes Católicos*, ed. Antonio de La Torre y del Cerro and Luis Suárez Fernández (3 vols., Valladolid, 1959–63), vol. I, pp. 254–84.
7. Suárez Fernández, *Historia de España*, vol. 17, pt. II, p. 169.
8. *Crónica incompleta de los Reyes Católicos (1469–1476): según un manuscrito anónimo de su época*, ed. Julio Puyol y Alonso (Madrid, 1934), ch. 19, pp. 158ff.
9. J. Torres Fontes, "La conquista del marquesado de Villena en el reinado de los Reyes Católicos," *Hispania* 13 (1953), pp. 79ff.
10. See Table 7, pp. 196ff.
11. *AGS, Sello*, 28 February 1476, fol. 51; 11 June 76, fol. 405.
12. See Table 7.
13. Suárez Fernández, *Historia de España*, vol. 17, pt. I, p. 339.
14. *AGS, Diversos, leg.* 11, fol. 18.
15. M. A. Ladero Quesada, *La Ciudad Medieval, 1248–1492*, dir. Francisco Morales Padrón, (5 vols., Seville, 1976), vol. II, *Historia de Sevilla*, p. 216.
16. J. H. Edwards, "Oligarchy and merchant capitalism in Lower Andalucía under the Catholic kings: the case of Córdoba and Jerez de La Frontera," *Historia Instituciones Documentos* 4 (1977), pp. 22f.
17. *AGS, Sello*, 28 August 1478, fol. 77 (Baeza–Úbeda); 30 October 1478, fol. 29 (Jaén).
18. Edwards, "Oligarchy and merchant capitalism," pp. 22f.
19. Palencia, *Crónica* vol. IV, bk. xxix, ch. 6, pp. 401ff.; Edwards, *Christian Córdoba*, pp. 30f., 151f.; M. A.; Ladero Quesada, *Andalucía en el siglo XV. Estudios de historia política* (Madrid, 1973), p. 47.
20. M. C. Quintanilla Raso, *Nobleza y señoríos en el reino de Córdoba: La casa de Aguilar (siglos XIV y XV)* (Cordova, 1979), pp. 131ff.
21. Ladero Quesada, *Ciudad Medieval*, p. 118.

22. Suárez Fernández, *Historia de España*, vol. 17, pt. II, pp. 275ff.

23. *El Tumbo de los Reyes Católicos del concejo de Sevilla*, eds. Ramón Carande and Juan de Mata Carriazo (5 vols., Seville, 1929–68; 1971–), vol. I, p. 288, 2 August 1478.

24. Joaquín Guichot y Parody, *Historia del Excmo. Ayuntamiento . . . Sevilla* (8 vols., Seville, 1896–1903), vol. I, pp. 173ff.

25. Ladero Quesada, *Ciudad Medieval*, p. 72.

26. AMS, *Archivo de Privilegios "Ordenanzas de Sevilla,"* 1492 (1531 edn.) fols. 1ff.

27. AMS, *Tumbo*, ed. Carande, vol. I, p. 288, 2 August 1478.

28. *Ibid.*

29. AMS, *Tumbo*, ed. Carande, vol II, p. 5, 28 August 1479.

30. *Ibid.*, vol. II, p. 58, 15 June 1480.

31. *Ibid.*, vol. II, p. 63, 28 June 1480; vol. II, p. 62, 31 (*sic*) June 1480.

32. Diego Ortiz de Zúñiga, *Anales eclesiásticos y seculares de la . . . ciudad de Sevilla* (5 vols. Madrid, 1677), vol. III, pp. 99ff.

33. Pulgar, *Crónica*, vol. II, ch. 1, p. 237; ch. 6, pp. 291f.

34. Ortiz de Zúñiga, *Anales de Sevilla*, vol. III, p. 129.

35. See Table 7, pp. 196ff.

36. Bermúdez Aznar, "Asistente real," pp. 168, 243; Ortiz de Zúñiga, *Anales de Sevilla*, vol. III, p. 112.

37. Antonio Herrera García, "El testamento de asistente de Sevilla Diego de Merlo (1482)," *En la España Medieval. Estudios dedicados al profesor D. Julio González González* (Madrid, 1981), pp. 162–8.

38. AMS, *Tumbo*, ed. Carande, vol. II, p. 157, 20 June 1482; vol. II, pp. 158ff., 6 September 1482.

39. *Ibid.*, vol. II, p. 163, 5 September 1482; vol. II, p. 166, 19 October 1482.

40. Francisco Tomás Valiente, "La venta de oficios de regidores y la formación de oligarquías urbanas en Castilla (siglos XVII y XVIII)," *Historia Instituciones Documentos* (1975), p. 529.

41. Ladero Quesada, *Andalucía*, pp. 77ff.

42. AGS, *Sello*, 20 March 1475, fol. 313.

43. A. C. Floriano y Cumbreño, *La villa de Cáceres y la Reina Católica* (Cáceres, 1917), pp. 25f.; M. A. Ortí Belmonte, "Cáceres baja le Reina Católica y su camarero Sancho Paredes Golfín," *Revista de Estudios Extremeños*, Badajoz 1–4 (1954), pp. 193ff.

44. AMC, 129–0[45], 9 July 1477, *Ordenanzas de los cargos concejiles*.

45. AMC, 136 C, 30 August 1479.

46. AGS, *Sello*, 30 August 1479, fol. 14.

47. Pulgar, *Crónica*, vol. II, ch. 69, p. 323.

48. Treaty of concord, transcr. Luis Delgado Merchán, *Historia documentada de Ciudad Real* (Ciudad Real, 1907), pp. 424–7.

49. *Ibid.*

50. Eloy Benito Ruano, *Toledo en el siglo XV: Vida política* (Madrid, 1961), p. 129.

51. Francisco de Pisa, *Descripción de la imperial ciudad de Toledo* (Toledo, 1617), bk. I, ch. 117, p. 32.

52. AGS, *Sello*, 20 February 1477, fol. 289, transcr. Benito Ruano, *Toledo*, pp. 293f.

53. AGS, *Sello*, 30 March 1477, fol. 422, transcr. Benito Ruano, *Toledo*, pp. 296f.

54. *Ibid.*, pp. 124f.

55. Pulgar, *Crónica*, vol. I, ch. 97, pp. 340ff.

56. Benito Ruano, *Toledo*, p. 126; This personal force, reduced to twenty-five men, remained in existence until 1520. AGS, *PR*, 27 February 1520, nf.

57. Concord of 12 December 1506, transcr. Benito Ruano, *Toledo*, doc. 97, pp. 305ff.

58. Palencia Flores, "Gómez Manrique," pp. 23ff., 44.
59. Benito Ruano, *Toledo*, pp. 124f.; Palencia Flores, "Gómez Manrique," pp. 36f.
60. P. L. Murugarren, *Evolución de la industria textil castellana en los siglos XIII–XVI* (Salamanca, 1974), p. 88.
61. *AGS, Sello*, 20 August 1477, fol. 378.
62. Inventory in *Archivo General de la Casa Ducal de Medinaceli*, leg. 266, no. 33, 22 July 1487, transcr. Antonio Paz y Melía, *Serie de más importantes documentos . . . Medinaceli. Primera Serie: Histórica* (Madrid, 1915, reprinted 1918), vol. III, p. 42.
63. Avila, Burgos, Medina, Olmedo, Palencia, Salamanca, Segovia, and Zamora. Pulgar, *Crónica*, vol. I, ch. 70, pp. 230ff.; Fernández Domínguez Valencia, *Guerra civil*, p. 85.
64. The thirty-two signatures on the pledge of 9 April 1476 to uphold Isabella's right of succession include representatives from jurisdictions in dispute. *AGS, PR, leg.* 7, fol. 60; see Pulgar, *Crónica*, vol. I, ch. 95, pp. 425f. for list of municipalities habitually in attendance.
65. *AGS, Sello*, 3 February 1475, fol. 205.
66. *Archivo Municipal de Alcaraz*, no. 66, 15 April 1475, transcr. Aurelio Pretel Marín, *Una ciudad castellana en los siglos XIV y XV (Alcaraz, 1300–1475)* (Albecete, 1978), p. 295.
67. Pet. 28, 1476 Cortes of Madrigal, *Cortes*, vol. IV, p. 97.
68. See Table 7, pp. 196ff. Aguilar de Campóo, Andújar, Principado de Asturias de Oviedo, Avila, Burgos, Cáceres, Carrión de los Condes–Sahagún, Ciudad Real, Cordova, Cuatro Villas de la Mar, a governor in Galicia, Huete, Jaén, León, Madrid, Medina del Campo, Olmedo, Sahagún, Salamanca, Segovia, Toledo, Trujillo, Valladolid, Vizcaya (including Bilbao and Las Encartaciones), and Zamora.
69. See Table 7. Baeza–Úbeda, Chinchilla de Monte Aragón, a governor in Ciudad Rodrigo, Écija, Molina, Olmeda, Soria, Requena–Utiel, an *asistente* in Toledo, and a governor in the Marquesado de Villena.
70. See Table 7. Carmona, a corregidor for La Coruña, Cuenca, Guipúzcoa, and Jerez de la Frontera.
71. See Table 7. Alcaraz, Badajoz, Murcia, and an *asistente* in Seville.
72. Pulgar, *Crónica*, vol. I, ch. 115, p. 423.
73. Clauses 57–107, 1480 Cortes of Toledo, *Cortes*, vol. IV, pp. 136–83.
74. *AGS, Cámara*, vol. I (1485).
75. Chinchón, set up by Enrique IV in 1486, was dropped. Álvarez Laviada, *Chinchón histórico y diplomático . . .* (Madrid, 1931), pp. 127, 143, 210.
76. Avila, Burgos, Cordova, Cuenca, Guadalajara, Jaén, León, Madrid, Murcia, Salamanca, Segovia, Seville, Soria, Toledo, Toro, Valladolid, and Zamora.
77. Two municipalities separated out of Galicia for *corregimientos* in the 1480s were Ponferrada and Mondoñedo. See Table 7.
78. Aznar Vallego, *Islas Canarias*, p. 75.
79. David E. Vassberg, *Land and Society in Golden Age Castile* (Cambridge, 1984), pp. 91, 103f.
80. M. Cuartas Rivero, *Asturiensia medievalia*. Oviedo, 1975, pp. 295ff.
81. González Alonso, *Gobernación*, p. 128.
82. See Table 7.
83. *AGS, Sello*, 7 October 1480, fol. 22.
84. They included Túy, Lugo, Orense, and Mondoñedo.
85. Pulgar, *Crónica*, vol. I, ch. 117, pp. 420ff.
86. Fajardo was appointed in 1464 by "King" Don Alfonso, and reappointed by

Isabella in 1475. There was also a corregidor for the town from 1466 until 1475, until he was superseded by Fajardo. Torres Fontes, *Pedro Fajardo*, pp. 101ff., 245ff.

87. *Ibid.*, pp. 164f., 182.

88. *Ibid.*, p. 183.

89. Owens, *Oligarquía murciana*, p. 137.

90. *AGS, Sello* 20 October 1483, fols. 140, 158; 22 October 1483, fol. 246; 23 October 1483, fol 217.

91. *Ibid.*, 15 September 1480, fol. 146; 19 October 1480, fol. 128.

92. *Ibid.*, 22 March 1483, fol. 17; 27 March 1489, fol. 378; 12 May 1489, fol. 235.

93. *AM Carmona, AC*, 1478, 28 May 1478.

94. *Ibid.*, 1480, fols. 1, 39, 3 and 24 November 1480; 1481, fols. 31–31v, 7 March 1481; 1484, fols. 63, 67, 1 and 8 August 1484.

95. AGS, *Sello*, 16 April 1478, fol. 41; 22 November 1478, fol. 94; 13 September 1480, fol. 27.

96. Benito de Cárdenas, *Memoria y verdadera relacion* . . . transcr. José Moreno de Guerra, *Bandos en Jerez. Los del puesto de abajo*. . . (2 vols., Madrid, 1929–32), vol. I, pp. 87–143; Hipólito Sancho de Sopranis, *Historia social de Jerez de la Frontera* . . . (2 vols., Jerez, 1964–5), vol. I, *1255–1492*, pp. 156ff.

97. AGS, *Sello*, 13 September 1483, fol. 27.

98. *AMC, AC*, 276–0¹²², 4 September 1493.

99. *AMV, Libro de Acuerdos*, 1497/1501, fol. 17v, transcr. A. M. Guilarte, *El régimen señorial en el siglo XVI* (Madrid, 1962), 397f.

100. 1482–8 Pedro de Rojas; –1483 *Bachiller* Pablo; 1483–5 Juan Pérez de Treviño (*licenciado*); 1485–8 Fernán Yáñes de Lobón (*licenciado*); 1490–2 Juan de Valderrama (*bachiller*); 1492– Rodrigo Romero; 1492– Luis de la Casas; 1493– Lorenzo Comeño; 1496– Juan de Ayala; 1498–9 Mateo de la Cuadra (*bachiller*); 1498–1503 Luis Portocarrero (*señor de Palma*).

    AMS, Tumbo, ed. Carande, vol. II, pp. 218, 363, 259, 385; vol. III, p. 64, 28 April 1483 (internal letter 5 July 1482), 30 August 1483, 26 August 1484, 20 October 1484, 20 November 1485; *AMS, Tumbo*, bks. V, fol. 163, VI, fol. 214v, 22 July 1498, 29 July 1503; *AMS*, Sección 16a – *Diversos*, fols. 748, 760; *AGS, Sello*, nd November 1488, fol. 275, 12 February 1491, fol. 82, 10 May 1492, fol. 564, 26 October 1493, fol. 244.

101. Alonso Morgado, *Historia de Sevilla* . . . (Seville, 1587), pp. 188f.; Francisco Morales Padrón, *La ciudad del Quinientos* (Seville, 1977), p. 214.

102. See Table 7.

103. Owens, *Oligarquía murciana*, p. 32.

104. Pet. 96, 1480 Cortes of Toledo, *Cortes*, vol. IV, p. 178. Corregidor control of subordinates was not always clear-cut. The selection of *fieles* was hedged with restrictions in Burgos. There the corregidor had to send an *alcalde* to meet with the council for the purpose of selecting eight men to fill positions. Neither the corregidor nor his *alcalde* were to interfere when the *regidores* voted. J. G. Sáinz de Baranda, *La ciudad de Burgos y su concejo en la Edad Media* (2 vols., Burgos, 1967), vol. II, p. 94.

105. *AGS, Sello*, 12 December 1480, fol. 233.

106. Owens, *Oligarquía murciana*, p. 31.

107. R. S. Chamberlain, "The 'corregidor' in Castile in the sixteenth century and the 'residencia' as applied to the 'corregidor'," *HAHR* 23 (1943), pp. 226f.

108. A. C. Floriano y Cumbreño, *Documentación histórica del Archivo Municipal de Cáceres* (Cáceres, 1934), pp. 119–43, 159, 166–72, 304.

109. *AGS, Sello*, 20 March 1486, fols. 167, 168.

110. *AMS, Tumbo*, ed. Carande, vol. I, p. 288, 2 August 1478.
111. *Ibid.*, vol. II, p. 25, 3 April 1483.
112. García Marín, *Oficio público en Castilla*, pp. 54–64, 239–42.
113. Pet. 5, 1419 Cortes of Madrid, *Cortes*, vol. III, pp. 14–15.
114. Pet. 17, 1476 Cortes of Madrigal, *Cortes*, vol. IV, pp. 76–7.
115. Gibert, *Concejo de Madrid*, p. 175.
116. The commission set up to introduce the 1480 Cortes of Toledo reforms in Madrid included the corregidor. Gibert, *Concejo de Madrid*, p. 190.
117. *AGS, Sello*, 23 November 1480; *AM Madrid, Horadado*, M–338, 1480, fol. 17r–v, 24 November 1480. Prescribed ceremonial forms are recapitulated in Juan de Havia Bolaños, *Curia philipica* . . . (2 vols., Valladolid, 1615, reprinted Madrid, 1753), vol. I, p. 1, para. 2.
118. This provoked the queen's ire in 1488 and 1489. *Documentos del Archivo General de la Villa de Madrid*, ed. Timoteo Domingo Palacio (4 vols., Madrid, 1889), vol. III, pp. 303–7, 312–15, 319–22.
119. Meetings held by municipal bodies seem not to change much over the centuries. I witnessed virtually identical complaints raised at Toronto's City Council in 1977, during a half-year with the office of the Metropolitan Chairman of Toronto, and again in 1980 at the City Council of New York, while I was serving for a year as consultant to the City Council President.
120. Data for the above paragraphs was drawn from the *AM Madrid, Acuerdos*, vol. I, 1481, fols. 1–195v, 5 January – 31 December 1481.
121. This lasted until 1488, when a majority of *regidores* imposed their will that henceforth they would do without participation by the commoners, except for a consultative role in fiscal matters. Gibert, *Concejo de Madrid*, pp. 315f.
122. *AM Madrid, Acuerdos*, vol. I, 1481, fols. 3, 189, 195v.
123. *Ibid.*, vol. II, 1483, fol. 185r–v, 14 May 1483.
124. *Ibid.*, vol. II, 1483, fol. 169r, 18 March 1483, fols 118r–119v, 1 December 1483.
125. See Marvin Lunenfeld, *The Council of the Santa Hermandad: A Study of the Pacification Forces of Ferdinand and Isabella* (Coral Gables, Florida, 1970); Celestino López Martínez, *La Santa Hermandad de los Reyes Católicos* (Seville, 1921); Antonio Álvarez de Morales, *Las hermandades, expresión del movimiento comunitario en España* (Valladolid, 1974).
126. In 1465, for example, key appointments in the *hermandad general* between Aranda, Arévalo, Avila, Burgos, and Valladolid went to corregidores from the three most important jurisdictions. Luis Suárez Fernández, "Evolución histórica de las hermandades castellanas," *Cuadernos de Historia de España* (Buenos Aires) 16 (1951), p. 11; Julio Puyol y Alonso, *Las hermandades de Castilla y León. Estudio histórico seguido de las Ordenanzas de Castronuño* (Madrid, 1913), p. 51.
127. J. A. García de Cortázar and Ruiz de Aguirre, *Vizcaya en el siglo XV. Aspectos económicos y sociales* (Bilbao, 1966), pp. 187f.
128. *AGS, Sello*, 30 August 1479, fol. 12 (Cáceres); nd February 1488, fol. 177 (Jaén).
129. *Ibid.*, 25 March 1477, fol. 445.
130. *AHN, Diversos, leg.* 83, doc. 22, 1484 (transcription).
131. *AGS, Sello*, 20 August 1479, fol. 76 (Trujillo); 9 September 1488, fol. 102, 15 November 1488, fol. 143 (Avila); 1 August 1488, fol. 99 (Badajoz); 16 October 1491, fol. 94 (Cordova); *AM Carmona, PR*, 1500–16, 30 January 1504.
132. *AGS, Sello*, 23 September 1487, fol. 12 (Vizcaya); 21 October 1486, fol. 69 (Trujillo); 3 July 1478, fol. 88 (Medina).
133. *Ibid.*, 29 November 1483, fol. 262.
134. Aurelio Pretel Marín, *Alcaraz, un enclave castellano en la frontera del siglo XIII* (Albacete, 1974), pp. 49f.; see also Pretel Marín, *La integración de un municipio*

medieval en el estado autoritario de los Reyes Católicos (*La ciudad de Alcaraz, 1455–1525*) (Albacete 1979); and *Fondos Medievales del Archivo Municipal de Alcaraz* (Alcaraz, 1976).

135. Pretel Marín, *Integración Alcaraz*, p. 43.
136. *Ibid.*, p. 10; *AM* Alcaraz, no. 66, 15 April 1475, transcr. Pretel Marín, *Ciudad castellana*, doc. 47, p. 295.
137. Torres Fontes, "Marquesado de Villena," p. 69; Pretel Marín, *Ciudad castellana*, p. 14.
138. *AGS, Sello*, 9 September 1477, nf, transcr. Pretel Marín, *Ciudad castellana*, doc. 40, pp. 308f.
139. Pretel Marín, *Ciudad castellana*, pp. 174f.
140. *AGS, Sello*, 11 July 1478, fol. 116, transcr. Pretel Marín, *Ciudad castellana*, doc. 62, pp. 310f.
141. *AGS, Sello*, 26 September 1479, fol. 39.
142. Pretel Marín, *Ciudad castellana*, pp. 174f.
143. Pardons granted upon payment of fines are found in *AGS, Sello*, 8 December 1485, fols. 90, 93, 100, 140. The last of these documents is transcribed in Pretel Marın, *Ciudad castellana*, doc. 56, pp. 318f.
144. Pretel Marín, *Integración Alcaraz*, pp. 46f.
145. *Ibid.*, pp. 20f.

4. Faithful servants (1485–94)

1. *Epistolario de Pedro Mártir de Anglería*, ed. and tr. José López de Toro (4 vols., Madrid, 1953–7), letter 79, vol. 1, pp. 131f.
2. *AM Madrid, Acuerdos*, 1485, fol. 112r, 25 February 1485; fol. 116, 26 April 1485; *AM Madrid, Cédulas*, M–339, fols. 46r–47v, 2 June 1485.
3. Haliczer, *Comuneros*, pp. 81f.
4. *AGS, Sello*, 4 June 1492, fol. 356.
5. A misleading but often quoted document used by Tarsicio de Azcona and González Alonso lists 56 jurisdictions. It neglects *corregimientos* in the kingdom of Granada, the Basque area, the Cantabrian coast, and the Canaries, as well as missing various jurisdictions on the Meseta, in Galicia, in Andalusia, and in the Murcia area. *AGS, Cámara, Cédulas, lib.* 1, fols. 13–14r, 15 March 1494; see Table 7, pp. 196ff.
6. *AGS, Diversos, leg.* 9, fol. 36, undated, 1–6.
7. Julio Caro Baroja, *Linajes y bandos en Vascongada* (Madrid, 1957), pp. 22f.
8. Transcr. A. Marichalar y Manrique, *Historia de los fueros de Navarra, Vizcaya, Guipúzcoa y Alava* (Madrid, 1868), appendix III, pp. 586–604.
9. *AGS, Sello*, 20 December 1488, fol. 112; 17 March 1490, fol. 308.
10. Enrique Toral Peñaranda, *Úbeda (1442–1510)* (Madrid and Jaén, 1975), pp. 345f.
11. Marie-Claude Gerbet, *La noblesse dans le royaume de Castille: Etude sur ses structures sociales en Estrémadure (1454–1516)* (Paris, 1979), p. 452.
12. *AGS, Sello*, 23 June 1492, fol. 23.
13. Ladero Quesada, *Ciudad Medieval*, p. 44.
14. *AGS, Sello*, 26 April 1484, fol. 11.
15. *AGS, Diversos*, 30 November 1493, *leg.* 10, no. 36.
16. Pet. 106, 1480 Cortes of Toledo, *Cortes*, vol. IV, pp. 182f.
17. P. L. Serrano y Serrano, *Los Reyes Católicos y la ciudad de Burgos, desde 1451 a 1492* (Madrid, 1943), p. 208.
18. *AGS, Sello*, 28 March 1495, fol. 546 (Baeza); 22 February 1495, fol. 30 (Asturias).

19. *Capítulos de corregidores, 1482*, clause 18, p. 564.
20. *AGS, Sello*, 30 April, 1495, fol. 90.
21. Saínz de Baranda, *Burgos*, vol. ii, p. 121.
22. B. H. Firoozye, "Warfare in fifteenth-century Castile" (unpublished PhD dissertation, University of California at Los Angeles, 1974), p. 103; L. Sprague de Camp, *The Ancient Engineers* (New York, 1936), p. 176.
23. *AGS, Sello*, 25 February 1492, fol. 246 (Málaga); 1 January 1488, fol. 44 (Molina); 4 April 1486, fol. 20 (Palencia); 30 June 1490, fol. 58 (Murcia).
24. *AMC*, 238 C, December 1491; 258 O¹¹², 8 March 1492.
25. *AGS, Sello*, 13 February 1494, fol. 346 (Ciudad Real); 8 May 1494, fol. 293 (Logroño – for subject village); 12 March 1494, fol. 187 (S. Domingo de la Calzada); 8 March 1486, fol. 66 (Segovia – for subject village).
26. *AGS, Sello*, 22 February 1495, fol. 30 (Asturias); 17 February 1494, fol. 322 (Valladolid – for subject village).
27. *Capítulos de corregidores, 1500*, clause 33, p. 306.
28. The grandiose bridge which replaced it was built during the reign of Philip II.
29. *AGS, Sello*, 28 March 1495, fol. 145.
30. *AM Madrid, Acuerdos*, 1485, fol. 18r, 23 November 1485; *AM Madrid, Horadado*, M–338, 1489, fol. 311–311v, 8 September 1489, transcr. Domingo Palacio, *Madrid*, vol. iii, p. 431.
31. *Capítulos de corregidores, 1500*, clause 17, p. 303.
32. *AM Madrid, Cédulas*, M–340, fol. 66r, 20 February 1491; fol. 82r, 4 April 1494.
33. *AGS, Sello*, 25 October 1494, fol. 52; 30 October 1494, fol. 14.
34. *Ibid.*, 4 May 1496, fol. 5.
35. R. W. Bulliett, *The Camel and the Wheel* (Cambridge, Mass., 1975), pp. 224ff.
36. No citation, Leopoldo Torres Balbás, "La Edad Media," *Resumen histórico del urbanismo en España*, ed. García Bellidea *et al.* (Madrid, 1968), p. 96.
37. *AGS, Sello*, 14 April 1488, fol. 88 (Segovia); 19 January 1490, fol. 189 (Vizcaya).
38. *AGS, Sello*, nd February 1492, fol. 246.
39. T. F. Glick, *Islamic and Christian Spain in the Early Middle Ages* (Princeton, NJ, 1979), pp. 121ff.
40. *AMV, AC*, no. 2, *hoja* 137, 12 July 1494.
41. *AGS, Sello*, 26 January 1493, fol. 73.
42. *Ibid.*, 26 March 1489, fol. 233; 18 March 1491, fol. 448.
43. *Ibid.*, 4 March 1492, fol. 444.
44. *Ibid.*, 14 January 1495, fol. 117.
45. *Ibid.*, 19 August 1493, fol. 192.
46. Jaime Vicens Vives and Jorge Nadal, *Manual de historia ecónomica de España* (Barcelona, 3rd edn, 1959), pp. 280f.
47. See Angus MacKay, "Popular movements and pogroms in fifteenth-century Castile," *Past and Present* 55 (1972), pp. 33ff.
48. *AGS, Sello*, 25 February 1493, fol. 144.
49. *AMS, Tumbo*, ed. Carande, vol. i, p. 329, 24 August 1487; p. 330, 30 September 1478; p. 336, 2 November 1487; *AGS, Sello*, 17 May 1495, fol. 310.
50. *Capítulos de corregidores, 1500*, clause 17, p. 303.
51. *AGS, Sello*, 5 May 1490, fol. 263.
52. *Libro de las bulas y pragmáticas de los Reyes Católicos*, Juan Ramírez (2 vols., Alcalá, 1503, facsimile reprint Madrid, 1973), vol. i, p. 50, 3 August 1488; i, p. 68, 20 December 1491; i, p. 143, 3 August 1498; i, p. 175, 6 June 1500; i, p. 180, 30 July 1500; i, p. 251, 11 February 1503.
53. *AGS, Sello*, 23 March 1489, fol. 154.
54. *Ibid.*, 15 June 1487, fol. 10 (Alcaraz); 10 March 1489, fol. 246 (Alfaro).

55. *Ibid.*, 26 November 1493, fol. 123 (Cuatro Villas); 21 February 1495, fol. 419 (Baeza).

56. Antonio Palomeque Torres, "Derechos de arancel de la justicia civil y criminal en los lugares de los propios y montes de la ciudad de Toledo anteriores al año de 1500," *AHDE* 24 (1954), p. 87n.

57. Elliott, *Imperial Spain*, pp. 34, 113.

58. Pet. 82, 1480 Cortes of Toledo, *Cortes*, vol. IV, pp. 155f.

59. *AGS, Sello*, 15 October 1483, fol. 216 (Vizcaya); 24 August 1490, fol. 188(Avila); 14 February 1491, fol. 22 (Avila); 17 January 1493, fol. 68 (Málaga).

60. During 1480 the crown pressed the corregidor of Huete to get Lope Vázquez de Acuña to return Villajudíos. At Vitoria, in 1483, the corregidor was told to investigate land manipulations in Burgos by Íñigo de Guevara. *AGS, Sello*, 17 May 1480, fol. 72; 30 December 1483, fol. 118.

61. Jean-Pierre Molénat, "Tolède et ses finages au temps des Rois Catholiques: Contribution à l'histoire sociale et économique de la cité avant la révolte des comunidades," *Mélanges de la Casa de Velázquez* 8 (1972), pp. 335ff.

62. *Ibid.*, p. 345.

63. *AM Madrid, Horadado*, M–338, 1481, fols. 116r–v, 18 September 1481, fols. 117r–v, 5 June 1482.

64. Pulgar, *Crónica*, vol. II, ch. 167, pp. 141ff.

65. *AMS, Tumbo*, ed. Carande, vol. III, p. 261, 22 October 1488.

66. *AMS, Sec. 1ª, carpeta* 63, no. 44, fols. 77–103, 26 May 1491; *carpeta* 65, no. 50, fols. 210–18, 222–31, 233–8, 341–7, 5 November 1494.

67. *AGS, Sello*, 5 June 1493, fol. 96; 12 June 1496, fol. 99.

68. E. Rodríguez Amaya, "La tierra de Badajoz desde 1230 a 1500," *Revista de estudios Extremeños* (Badajoz) 7 (1951), pp. 446ff.

69. M. A. Ladero Quesada, *La hacienda real en Castilla en el siglo XV* (La Laguna, 1973), p. 44.

70. M. A. Ladero Quesada, *La hacienda real castellana entre 1480 y 1492* (Valladolid, 1967), p. 35.

71. Lunenfeld, "Isabella I," p. 225, and "The royal image: symbol and paradigm in portraits of early modern female sovereigns and regents," *Gazette des Beaux-Arts* (April, 1981), p. 158.

72. Vicens Vives, *Historia ecónomica*, ch. 23; Jerónimo López de Ayala Álvarez de Toledo del Hierro, *Contribuciones e impuestos en León y Castilla durante la Edad Media* (Madrid, 1896), pp. 8off.

73. Pets. 60, 98, 1480 Cortes of Toledo, *Cortes*, vol. IV, pp. 138, 179.

74. *Capítulos de corregidores, 1484*, clauses 12, 13, p. 562.

75. Salvador de Moxó, "Los Cuadernos de Alcabalas: Orígenes de la legislación tributaria castellana," *AHDE* 39 (1969), p. 327, and *La Alcabala: Sobre sus orígenes, concepto y naturaleza* (Madrid, 1963), p. 47.

76. *AGS, Diversos, leg.* 4, fol. 114 (1484), 4–80 (1491) "Leyes del Cuaderno sobre las Escribanías de Rentas."

77. *Capítulos de corregidores, 1500*, clauses 13, 14, p. 303.

78. *Ibid.*, clause 24, pp. 304f.

79. Ladero Quesada, *Hacienda, 1480 y 1492*, p. 36.

80. Ladero Quesada, *Hacienda en siglo XV*, p. 30.

81. *AM Madrid, Cédulas*, M–339, fols. 83v–84v, 18 October 1489; *AMS, Tumbo*, ed. Carande, vol. I, p. 324, 30 September 1484.

82. Lunenfeld, *Council Santa Hermandad*, table pp. 68f.

83. *AGS, Sello*, 3 March 1480, fol. 351; *AMS, Tumbo*, ed. Carande, vol. VI, p. 145, 27 August 1492; *AMS, Tumbo*, bk. IV, fol. 418, 16 May 1495; bk v. fol. 174, 10

October 1498; *AGS, Sello*, 23 December 1484, fol. 81 (Galicia); 14 July 1488, fol. 234 (Vizcaya); 10 September 1488, fol. 36, 19 December 1488, fol. 60 (Ciudad Real); 23 August 1493, fol. 99 (Murcia).

84. *AGS, Sello*, 31 March 1493, fol. 163; 30 April 1493, fol. 81.
85. Lunenfeld, *Council Santa Hermandad*, pp. 40, 57f.
86. *Ibid.*, p. 69.
87. *AMS, Tumbo*, ed. Carande, vol. III, p. 269, 3 January 1489.
88. *AGS, Sello*, 17 September 1487, fol. 94; *AM Madrid, Horadado*, 1493, fols. 159*r*–160*r*, 15 April 1493.
89. Juan de Mata Carriazo y Arroquia, "Historia de la Guerra de Granada," in "La España de los Reyes Católicos (1474–1516)," *Historia de España*, dir. Ramón Menéndez Pidal (Madrid, 1969), vol. 17, pt. I, pp. 751ff.
90. Vicens Vives, *Historia económica*, p. 727.
91. M. A. Ladero Quesada, *Milicia y economía en la Guerra de Granada* (Valladolid, 1964), table 7, p. 130.
92. José Goñi Gaztambide, *Historia de la bula de Cruzada en España* (Vitoria, 1958), ch. 13.
93. *Capítulos de corregidores, 1500*, clause 51, p. 311.
94. *AGS, Sello*, 2 February 1488, fol. 204; nd February 1490, fol. 279.
95. *Ibid.*, 21 May 1491, fols. 28, 29.
96. Azcona, *Isabel*, pp. 532ff.
97. *Ibid.*, pp. 361f.
98. *AGS, Sello*, 10 July 1493, fol. 276 (Burgos); 13 September 1494, fol. 142 (Valladolid); Ladero Quesada, *Hacienda siglo XV*, p. 45.
99. Mateo Alemán, *Vida del pícaro Guzmán de Alfarache* (1599), ed. Guili y Gayal (Madrid, 1958), ch. 8, p. 171.
100. Lunenfeld, *Council Santa Hermandad*, table p. 78.
101. *BNM, Sección de Manuscritos*, ms. R22905, "Leyes Nuevas de la Hermandad."
102. *AGS, Sello*, 4 February 1485, fol. 203; 10 September 1488, fol. 36; 20 November 1488, fol. 261; 29 November 1494, fol. 83.
103. *Ibid.*, 20 June 1489, fol. 151.
104. Albi, *Corregidor en monarquía absoluta*, p. 157.
105. *Capítulos de corregidores, 1500*, clause 30, pp. 305f.
106. Albi, *Corregidor en monarquía absoluta*, pp. 158ff.
107. Some 25 out of 114 letters are specifically addressed to the corregidor. Eighteen letters cover the cost of war; 14 deal with lawsuits; 11 concern officials of the municipal council; and 10 treat taxes. These totals are drawn from over 2,000 items in Manuel González Jiménez, *Catálogo de documentación medieval del Archivo Municipal de Carmona* (Seville, 1975).
108. *AMC* 199 C – 29 August 1489; 268 C – 7 September 1492.
109. *Ibid.*, 248 C – 30 January 1492; 266 O[116] – 16 April 1492.
110. *Ibid.*, 270 C – 15 September 1492.
111. *AGS, Sello*, 13 February 1493, fol. 94; 20 March 1493, fols. 278–9; 8 April 1493, fol. 213; 10 July 1493, fol. 191; 15 May 1494, fol. 399; 26 April 1494, fol. 505.
112. *Ibid.*, 2 May 1489, fol. 181 (Cordova); 5 May 1491, fol. 117 (Cordova); 1 December 1491, fol. 2 (Cáceres); 13 March 1492, fol. 45 (Cordova); 6 August 1492, fol. 134 (Miranda de Ebro); 14 August 1492, fol. 75 (Ágreda); 14 October 1492, fol. 49 (Murcia).
113. *Ibid.*, 20 November 1485, fol. 31.
114. *Ibid.*, 13 August 1483, fol. 153; 30 October 1483, fol. 93; 13 December 1486, fol. 62; 29 November 1488, fol. 214.

115. *Ibid.*, 9 April 1488, fols. 26, 28; 10 April 1488, fol. 32; 15 January 1490, fol. 98; 18 February 1490, fol. 321.
116. *Ibid.*, 11 May 1490, fol. 313.
117. *AM Madrid, Cédulas*, M–340, 17 December 1490; *AGS, Sello*, nd April 1492, fols. 81, 107; 30 May 1492, fol. 581; 16 July 1492, fol. 129.
118. *AGS, Sello*, 4 January 1493, fol. 47; 19 October 1493, fol. 70; 12 April 1494, fol. 564.
119. *Ibid.*, 4 June 1492, fol. 39; 18 July 1492, fol. 82; 30 August 1493, fol. 103.
120. *Ibid.*, 13 August 1493, fols. 188, 206; 24 August 1493, fol. 44; 16 September 1493, fol. 194; 22 May 1494, fol. 86; nd May 1494, fol. 76; 12 April 1494, fol. 486.
121. S. E. Morison, *Admiral of the Ocean Sea* (2 vols., Boston, 1942), vol. I, p. 358.

5. Careers open to talent: judicature, remuneration, *residencia*

1. Bartolomé de Góngora, *El corregidor sagaz. Avisos, y documentos morales* . . . (Madrid, 1620, reprinted 1960), ch. 9, p. 125.
2. Gustavo Villapalos Salas, *Los recursos contra las actas de gobierno en la Baja Edad Media. Su evolución histórica en el reino castellano (1252–1504)* (Madrid, 1976), pp. 23f., 262–71.
3. David Torres Sanz, *La administración central castellana en la Baja Edad Media* (Valladolid, 1982), pp. 181–211; Angus MacKay, *Spain in the Middle Ages: From Frontier to Empire, 1000–1500* (London, 1977), pp. 143f.
4. *RAH, Colección diplomática*, doc. 109.
5. Salustiano de Dios, *El Consejo Real de Castilla (1385–1522)* (Madrid, 1982), ch. 4. See M. J. Gounon-Loubens, *Essais sur l'administration de la Castille au XVIe siécle* (Paris, 1860), p. 166, and Mariano Alcocer y Martínez, "Consejo Real de Castilla," *Revista Histórica* (Valladolid) 1925, pp. 33–44.
6. Pets. 1–31, 1480 Cortes of Toledo, *Cortes*, vol. IV, pp. 111ff.
7. *Ibid.*, pets. 1, 3, 9, 11–15, 21, 32; Dios, *Consejo Real*, p. 160.
8. *AM Carmona, PR*, 1476–89, 18 February 1486.
9. *AGS, PR*, 5126, 22 May 1496.
10. *AMC*, 307 O¹²⁷ – 3 August 1496.
11. Helen Nader, *The Mendoza Family in the Spanish Renaissance: 1350 to 1550* (New Brunswick, NJ, 1979), ch. 1.
12. *Ibid.*, see also: J. Cepeda Adán, *En torno al concepto del estado en tiempos de los Reyes Católicos* (Madrid, 1956).
13. Directed to Diego Ruíz de Montalvo. *AGS, Sello*, 4 January 1495, fol. 272 to 22 December 1495, fol. 18.
14. Letters from *AMS, Tumbo*, ed. Carande.
15. *Ibid.*, vol. II, p. 205, 3 April 1483.
16. Letters from *AGS, Sello*, 1487–8.
17. Gonzalo Fernández de Oviedo, *Las Quincuagenas de la nobleza de España* (3 vols., Madrid, 1880 edn.), vol. III, p. 11.
18. Dios, *Consejo Real*, pp. 384–7; Azcona, *Isabel*, p. 328.
19. M. de la S. Martín Postigo, *La cancillería castellana de los Reyes Católicos* (Valladolid, 1959), p. 123.
20. Pets. 23–6, 1480 Cortes of Toledo, *Cortes*, vol. IV, pp. 117ff.
21. Dios, *Consejo Real*, p. 384; Gounon-Loubens, *Administration de la Castille*, p. 193.
22. Gounon-Loubens, *Administration de la Castille*, pp. 208ff.
23. R. L. Kagan, *Lawsuits and Litigants in Castile, 1500–1700* (Chapel Hill, NC, 1981), pp. 79f.
24. *AGS, Sello*, 11 January 1488, fol. 110; 14 April 1488, fol. 27; 6 August 1493, fol. 47; 27 November 1493, fol. 56.

25. *Ibid.*, 7 September 1485, fol. 68; nd January 1499, fol. 96.
26. Gounon-Loubens, *Administration de la Castille*, pp. 208ff.
27. Kagan, *Lawsuits and Litigants*, p. 10.
28. *AGS, Sello*, 21 August 1495, fol. 247; 10 September 1495, fol. 252.
29. *Ibid.*, 26 January 1495, fol. 136; 5 April 1495, fol. 12.
30. Kagan, *Lawsuits and Litigants*, p. 21.
31. *Ibid.*, p. 237.
32. *AGS, Sello*, 17 July 1484, fol. 80.
33. Vassberg, *Land and Society*, pp. 64, 83, 137.
34. *AGS, Sello*, 30 June 1488, fol. 58; 20 April 1490, fol. 61.
35. *Ibid.*, 25 July 1495, fol. 62; *AM Madrid, Acuerdos*, 1482, fol. 198r.
36. *Bulas y pragmáticas*, vol. I, p. 103, fols. 37v–38v, 18 November 1494 (Valladolid); p. 198, fols. 41v–44v, 29 April 1501 (Salamanca).
37. *AGS, Sello*, 30 August 1487, fol. 49.
38. The term is not used in the 1480 Cortes decrees. It makes its first appearance in *Capítulos de corregidores, 1500*, clause 47, p. 310.
39. *Ibid.*, pp. 305ff., clauses 29, 47, 50.
40. *AGS, Sello*, 3 October 1494, fols. 53, 255.
41. *Ibid.*, 8 July 1490, fol. 333.
42. *Ibid.*, 10 July 1495, fol. 307.
43. *Ibid.*, 30 April 1487, fol. 63.
44. *Ibid.*, 13 February 1488, fol. 153.
45. *Ibid.*, 1 June 1492, fol. 340.
46. *Ibid.*, 12 January 1493, fol. 256; 31 January 1493, fol. 234.
47. *Ibid.*, 9 July 1495, fol. 305; 10 July 1495, fol. 306.
48. *Ibid.*, 12 August 1489, fol. 153.
49. *Ibid.*, 19 October 1480, fol. 225.
50. *Ibid.*, 6 March 1484, fol. 39; 2 July 1484, fol. 63; 6 September 1484, fol. 71.
51. Haim Beinart, *Trujillo: A Jewish Community in Extremadura on the Eve of the Expulsion from Spain* (Jerusalem, 1980), p. 95.
52. *AGS, Sello*, 14 December 1487, fol. 112; 15 January 1488, fols. 42, 178; nd December 1488, fol. 96.
53. M. F. Landreda, *Estudios históricos sobre los códigos de Castilla* (La Coruña, 1896), pp. 165f.
54. *AGS, Sello*, 20 April 1475, fol. 418; 29 August 1477, fol. 374.
55. See Table 2, p. 84.
56. *AGS, Sello*, 20 October 1494, fol. 212 (*merindad de Trasmeira*).
57. *Ibid.*, 19 June 1493, fol. 101; 14 March 1493, fol. 169.
58. *AGS, Sello*, 14 January 1489, fol. 203; 7 June 1493, fol. 89.
59. *Ibid.*, 23 November 1492, fol. 178 (Sahagún); 29 October 1494, fol. 377 (Avila).
60. *Ibid.*, 27 April 1493, fol. 48 (Baeza); 9 October 1493, fol. 92 (Toro); nd July 1494, fol. 214 (La Coruña); royal decree dated 1501, *Inventario del Archivo de Excmo. Ayuntamiento de Ciudad Real* (Ciudad Real, 1952), p. 47.
61. Francisco Chacón Jiménez, "Una contribución al estudio de las economías municipales en Castilla: La coyuntura económica concejil murciana en el período 1496–1515," *Miscelánea Medieval Murciana* III (1977), pp. 238ff.; *AM Madrid, Acuerdos*, 1482, fol. 198r.
62. *AGS, Sello*, 22 November 1480, fol. 66; 13 December 1480, fol. 128; 4 November 1494, fol. 39.
63. 1436 Cortes of Toledo, *Cortes*, vol. III, p. 272.
64. *AGS, Sello*, 9 January 1478, fol. 89; 11 September 1479, fol. 134; 13 June 1480, fol. 304; 2 September 1485, fol. 251; 20 September 1485, fol. 235; 12 December 1488, fol. 115; 14 January 1493, fol. 266; 30 July 1493, fol. 250; 1 August 1493,

fol. 242; 12 September 1493, fol. 198; 7 May 1494, fol. 451; 27 November 1494, fol. 355; nd October 1494, fol. 151; 18 November 1494, fol. 323; 4 March 1495, fol. 507; 30 April 1495, fol. 175.

65. *Ibid.*, and March 1487, fol. 58; 29 October 1487, fol. 190; 20 March 1489, fol. 145.

66. *Ibid.*, 8 March 1492, fol. 289; 23 November 1492, fol. 128; 26 November 1492, fol. 190; 28 November 1492, fol. 117; 14 January 1493, fol. 266; 30 July 1493, fol. 250; 12 September 1493, fol. 273.

67. *AMS, Tumbo*, ed. Carande, vol. II, p. 163, 5 September 1482; p. 166, 19 October 1482.

68. *Ibid.*, vol. III, p. 220, 4 July 1488; p. 221, 4 June 1488.

69. Bermúdez Aznar, *Corregidor en Castilla*, tables pp. 153, 155; MacKay, *Money in Castile*, pp. 101ff.; see also Octavio Gil Farrés, *Historia de la moneda española* (Madrid, 1959).

70. *AGS, Sello*, 26 January 1493, fol. 57 (Medina); 19 December 1477, fols. 511f. (Cáceres); Chacón Jiménez, *Concejil murciana*, pp. 241ff.

71. *AMS, Tumbo*, ed. Carande, vol. II, p. 169, 10 September 1482; vol. III, p. 65, 25 November 1485.

72. *AGS, Sello*, 20 March 1480, fol. 375 (Badajoz); 8 October 1495, fol. 265 (León); 30 July 1478, fol. 56 (Toledo); 3 February 1485, fol. 9 (Medina del Campo).

73. *AGS, Contaduría, leg.* 104.

74. *AM Málaga, Provisiones*, vol. IV, fols. 58–60, 12 September 1503; 78–9, 17 November 1502; 2 May 1503, 162v–163, 5 July 1504.

75. *AGS, Sello*, 28 August 1488, fol. 123; 20 February 1489, fol. 14; *AM Málaga, Provisiones*, vol. IV, fol. 157, 26 January 1504.

76. Lorenzo Guardiola y Sáez, *El corregidor perfecto . . .* (Madrid, 1789), p. 63.

77. Benjamín González Alonso, "El juicio de residencia en Castilla. I: Origen y evolución hasta 1480," *AHDE* 48 (1978), p. 194; Luis García de Valdeavellano, "Las 'Partidas' y los orígenes medievales del juicio de residencia," *B(R)AH* 153 (1963), pp. 212f. See also his *Curso de historia de las instituciones españolas de los orígenes al final de la Edad Media* (Madrid, 1968).

78. Title XXXII, law 44, cited García de Valdeavellano, "Orígenes medievales residencia," p. 212; González Alonso, "Juicio de residencia," pp. 210ff., 221ff.

79. Their petition marks the first time *rresidençia* (original spelling) appears with its normative meaning. Pet. 6, 1419 Cortes of Madrid, *Cortes*, vol. III, p. 15.

80. Pet. 18, 1435 Cortes of Madrid; pet. 15, 1436 Cortes of Toledo; pet. 19, 1438 Cortes of Madrigal; pet. 2, 1462 Cortes of Toledo, *Cortes*, vol. III, pp. 206f., 272f., 327f. 704f.

81. Pet. 58, 1480 Cortes of Toledo, *Cortes*, vol. IV, pp. 136f.

82. Pet. 59, ibid., vol. IV, p. 137.

83. This position is adopted by González Alonso, *Corregidor castellano*, p. 98, and Haliczer, *Comuneros*, pp. 31f.

84. Pulgar, *Crónica*, vol. II, chs. 196, 256, pp. 251, 436.

85. Gonzaléz Alonso, *Gobernación*, p. 89.

86. *AGS, Sello*, 30 March 1491, fol. 64.

87. L. de la Rosa Olivera and E. Serra Rafols, *El Adelantado Don Alonso de Lugo y su residencia por Lope de Sosa* (La Laguna, 1949), p. xlii; Antonio Ruméu de Armas, *Alonso de Lugo en la corte de los Reyes Católicos (1496–1497)* (Madrid, 1952), appendix 2, pp. 190f.

88. Fernández-Armesto, *Canary Islands*, pp. 146f.; Aznar Vallejo, *Islas canarias*, pp. 74f.

89. This interpretation was suggested by a reading of chapter 2 of M. R. Weisser, *Crime and Punishment in Early Modern Europe* (Atlantic Highlands, NJ, 1979).

90. The twenty-two paragraph document is transcribed in Rafael Serra Ruiz, "Notas sobre el juicio de residencia en la época de los Reyes Católicos," *Anuario de Estudios Medievales* (Barcelona) 5 (1968), pp. 531–46.

91. Clauses dropped in 1500 had merely emphasized that the judge must not be a native of the jurisdiction under review; that any appearance of collusion with residents must be avoided; and that the church was not to impede justice. The one insignificant addition made in 1500 was that local scribes were made responsible for publicity to alert the community that an investigation was about to begin. Serra Ruiz, "Juicio de residencia," pp. 531ff.

92. Jerónimo Castillo de Bovadilla, *Política para corregidores y señores de Vasallos en Tiempo de paz, y de guerra* (1597; 2 vol. facsimile of 1640 Valladolid edn., Madrid, 1978), vol. ii, bk. 5, ch. 1, no. 260.

93. Serra Ruiz, "Juicio de residencia," pp. 538ff.

94. *Ibid.*

95. *Novísima Recopilación de las leyes de España* (6 vols., Madrid, 1805–7 edn.), bk. vii, tit. xii, law 3.

96. García Marín, *Oficio público en Castilla*, p. 295.

97. *AMS, Tumbo*, ed. Carande, vol. iii, p. 451, 23 September 1491; p. 462, 29 October 1491.

98. *AGS, Sello*, 20 February 1493, fols. 51, 62; 22 May 1493, fol. 141 (Salamanca); 9 March 1490, fol. 190; 8 July 1490, fol. 312; 14 July 1490, fol. 254 (Cáceres).

99. *Ibid.*, 23 June 1488, fol. 228.

100. *Ibid.*, 16 March 1494, fol. 386; 7 May 1494, fol. 224; 7 October 1494, fol. 239.

101. *Ibid.*, 30 July 1495, fol. 443.

102. A *residencia* report in Burgos on Alonso Pérez de Arteaga runs to more than 100 fat folios. The corregidor emerged untainted, but his lieutenant was judged guilty of varied infractions. *Archivo General de Simancas, Consejo Real, leg.* 46, no. 5, i–ii, 4 July 1561. This file was called to my attention by Paul Hiltpold.

103. Decree of 1493, reprinted in *Novísima Recopilación*, bk. iii, tit. ix, law 2.

104. García Marín, *Oficio público en Castilla*, pp. 183f.

105. Twenty-two had the bachelor's degree and eleven the doctorate. See Table 4, pp. 95ff.

106. See Table 4, pp. 95ff.

107. The Cortes of 1512 requested reappointment not be made until at least two years had passed. Pet. 3, 1512 Cortes of Burgos, *Cortes*, vol. iv, pp. 240f.

108. During the reign of Charles V, judges sometimes stayed on, without warrant, for as long as the corregidores whose terms they had investigated. Philip II regularized the practice by automatically appointing each judge as the new official. Chamberlain, "Corregidor in Castile," pp. 249f.

109. *AGS, Sello*, 18 February 1490, fol. 321; 16 March 1490, fol. 193.

110. *Ibid.*, 20 April 1493, fols. 68, 69; 20 September 1493, fols. 55, 71, 145; 13 August 1493, fol. 50; 20 September 1493, fol. 237; nd September 1493, fol. 185; 22 March 1494, fol. 481; nd November 1494, fol. 529; 8 December 1494, fol. 100.

111. *Ibid.*, 26 March 1493, fol. 106 (Cuenca); 29 August 1495, fol. 250 (Carmona).

112. *AM Málaga, Provisiones*, vol. iv, fols. 100v–101v, 26 February 1504.

113. Bermúdez Aznar, *Corregidores en Castilla*, pp. 157f.

114. *Capítulos de corregidores, 1482*, clause 7, p. 560.

115. Copy in *AMC*, 117 – O⁷⁴, 26 May 1488.

116. *AGS, Sello*, 9 April 1488, fols. 26, 28 (Jerez de la Frontera); 6 June 1488, fol. 44 (Carrión); 17 July 1488, fol. 72 (Murcia); 9 February 1490, fol. 224 (Carmona); 3 September 1490, fol. 52 (Alcaraz); 2 October 1490, fol. 194 (Carrión); 23 March 1491, fol. 355 (Badajoz); *AMC*, 275 O¹²¹, 25 September 1493.

117. *AGS, Sello*, 9 April 1488, fols. 26, 86 (Jerez de la Frontera); 8 May 1488, fol. 200 (Madrid); 6 June 1488, fol. 44, 25 March 1491, fol. 355 (Carrión); 10 December

1490, fol. 290 (Frengal); 30 January 1491, fol. 23 (Palencia); 13 December 1494, fol. 92 (Azcoitia).

118. *Ibid.*, 26 January 1492, fol. 73; 1 February 1492, fol. 276; 24 March 1492, fol. 336 (S. Domingo de la Calzada).

119. *Ibid.*, 4 November 1488, fol. 263 (Segovia); 23 March 1491, fol. 355 (Badajoz).

120. *AMC*, 275 – O^{121}, 25 September 1493.

121. *AM Madrid, Cédulas*, M–340, fol. 208r, 4 February 1503.

122. *AGS, Sello*, 5 June 1478, fol. 80; 27 January 1490, fol. 125.

123. *AMC*, 370 – O^{168}, 28 June 1503.

124. *AM Málaga, Provisiones*, vol. VII, fols. 113–14, 177–177v, 15 September 1514.

125. *AGS, Sello*, 22 February 1493, fol. 228.

126. Albi, *Corregidor en monarquía absoluta*, pp. 117f.

127. Pet. 65, 1480 Cortes of Toledo, *Cortes*, vol. IV, pp. 140f.

128. *Bulas y pragmáticas*, 1–55, fols. 119v–20v, 30 May 1489; 1–58, fols. 119r–v, 31 July 1489.

129. *AGS, Sello*, 24 March 1491, fol. 372; 19 July 1493, fol. 170; Alonso de Santa Cruz, *Crónica de los Reyes Católicos*, ed. and with study by Juan de Mata Carriazo (Seville, 1951), ch. 18, p. 25.

130. In 1520 the revolutionary junta demanded that all fines go to the royal treasury: letter of 20 May 1520, tr., Prudencio de Sandoval, *Historia de la vida y hechos del Emperador Carlos V* (5 vols., *BAE* Madrid, 1955–6 edn.), vol. 1, p. 309.

131. *AGS, Sello*, 23 May 1476, fol. 283.

132. See Table 7, pp. 196ff.

133. Honorato Hurtado de Mendoza, corregidor of Salamanca, rejected him as his judge of *residencia*. *AGS, Sello*, 15 October 1494, fol. 459.

134. *Ibid.*, 1 September 1487, fol. 62; 22 January 1489, fol. 391; 23 January 1490, fol. 169; 3 September 1490, fol. 52; nd, nm 1492, fol. 196; 23 April 1493, fol. 113; 24 May 1493, fols. 172, 179; 27 November 1493, fol. 44; 4 December 1493, fol. 110; 7 April 1494, fol. 401; 20 May 1494, fol. 361; 15 October 1494, fol. 459.

135. *Ibid.*, 22 September 1479, fols. 66, 74, 115; 4 November 1479, fol. 114; 18 September 1480, fol. 130; 11 March 1493, fol. 317; 18 July 1493, fol. 224; 17 August 1493, fol. 144; 6 March 1494, fol. 179; 22 April 1494, fol. 579; 15 May 1494, fol. 20.

136. *Ibid.*, 3 February 1490, fols. 86, 87; 12 July 1490, fol. 185; 2 October 1490, fols. 194; 29 April 1491, fols. 160, 300; 26 November 1492, fol. 190; 1 April 1493, fol. 76; 12 September 1493, fol. 273; 30 October 1494, fols. 191, 256.

137. *Ibid.*, 10 March 1484, fol. 36; 23 October 1484, fols. 142, 143.

138. Pretel Marín, *Integración Alcaraz*, p. 44.

139. *AGS, Sello*, 17 March 1493, fol. 169; 3 June 1493, fol. 199; 13 September 1493, fol. 120; 24 March 1494, fol. 409; nd March 1494, fol. 291.

140. Pretel Marín, *Fondos Medievales*, no. 154, p. 27.

141. *Ibid.*, no. 177, 3 August 1500, p. 30.

142. *Capítulos de corregidores, 1500*, clause 4, p. 300.

143. *AGS, Sello*, 1 April 1493, fol. 76; *AGS, Diversos, lib.* 10, fol. 31.

144. The right of appointment was not subject to restraint by higher authority until the end of the sixteenth-century. Pet. 70, 1576 Cortes of Madrid, *Actas de las Cortes de Castilla: 1563–1627* (39 vols., Madrid, 1862–1925), vol. V, p. 78.

145. *AM Madrid, Cédulas*, M–340, fols. 85r–86r, 31 July 1489.

146. *AGS, Sello*, 9 February 1491, fol. 87.

147. *Ibid.*, 2 October 1494, fol. 545; 31 October 1494, fol. 333; nd February 1495, fol. 268.

148. Drawn from *AGS, Sello*.

149. Peace officers: *ibid.*, 23 December 1485, fol. 58 (Medina del Campo); 8 July 1490, fol. 333 (Trujillo); 31 December 1491, fol. 33 (Écija); cell-keepers: *ibid.*, nd September 1492, fol. 97 (Gran Canaria); 26 March 1493, fol. 106; 27 March 1493, fol. 220 (Cuenca), where the charge was that too many people were being locked up.

150. *Ibid.*, 15 April 1493, fol. 27; 5 September 1493, fol. 156 (Jerez de la Frontera); 8 September 1493, fol. 133 (Asturias).

151. *Ibid.*, 14 July 1492, fol. 64; 16 July 1492, fol. 104; nd December 1492, fol. 86; 20 January 1493, fol. 159; 24 April 1493, fol. 150; 14 October 1493, fol. 127.

152. *Ibid.*, 7 October 1494, fol. 239 (Burgos).

153. *Ibid.*, 13 August 1490, fol. 241 (Medina del Campo); 18 February 1493, fol. 129 (Segovia); 27 November 1494, fol. 355 (Gaudix); 27 June 1495, fol. 80 (Alcaraz).

154. *Ibid.*, 24 April 1494, fol. 73.

155. *Ibid.*, 7 February 1488, fol. 116 (Huete); 18 January 1493, fol. 123 (Écija).

156. *AMC*, 324 – O[139], 30 June 1497.

157. Weisser, *Crime and Punishment*, p. 63.

158. P. S. Lewis, *Later Medieval France: the Polity* (New York and London, 1968), p. 239; J. H. Shennan, *Government and Society in France 1461–1661* (London, 1969).

159. Donald Queller, *The Venetian Patriciate: Reality versus Myth* (Urbana, Illinois, 1986), pp. 189–211.

6. Lords and prelates: a matter of privilege

1. Andrés Bernáldez, *Memorias del reinado de los Reyes Católicos*, ed. with study by Manuel Gómez-Moreno and Juan de Mata Carriazo (Madrid, 1962), vol. I, ch. 202, p. 485.

2. Valentín Vázquez de Parda, *Historia social y económica de España y América*, dir. Jaime Vicens Vives (5 vols., Barcelona, 1959), vol. II, pp. 438f.; see also J. R. L. Highfield, "The Catholic kings and the titled nobility of Castile," *Europe in the Late Middle Ages*, ed. J. R. Hale *et al.* (London, 1965), pp. 358–85.

3. Suárez Fernández, *Historia de España*, vol. 15, p. 96.

4. Edwards, "Oligarchy and merchant capitalism," pp. 11ff.

5. See Bartolomé Clavero, *Mayorazgo, propiedad feudal en Castilla, 1369–1836* (Madrid, 1974).

6. *AGS, Sello*, 21 April 1480, fol. 77; nd December 1491, fol. 50.

7. Mitre Fernández, *Régimen de corregidores*, pp. 44ff.

8. Salvador de Moxó, *Los antiguos señoríos de Toledo* (Madrid, 1973), p. 248.

9. *AGS, Sello*, 30 June 1490, fol. 173.

10. *AGS, PR, leg.* 11, fols. 61–3, 27 January 1493.

11. *Ordenanzas reales de Castilla*, law 25, tit. III, compiled by Alfonso Díaz de Montalvo, cited J. M. Antequera, *Historia de la legislación española* ... (Madrid, 1890), pp. 417ff.

12. Guilarte, *Régimen señorial*, p. 78.

13. Castillo de Bovadilla, *Política para corregidores*, vol. I, bk. 2, ch. 19.

14. Guilarte, *Régimen señorial*, p. 117.

15. Corregidores guaranteed the right of peasants to receive protection if they fled to the "free air" of the towns. Directives to Madrid, also intended for aristocrats, affirmed that when peasants declared their intention to stay they were to be safeguarded. Issued 15 January 1480, with reissue 18 November 1492; transcr. Domingo Palacio, *Madrid*, vol. III, pp. 257ff.

16. No *Junta General* actually met that year. *AGS, Sello*, 6 April 1475, fol. 371; clauses

xiv, xxv transcr. Juan Uría Ríu, *Estudios sobre la Baja Edad Media Asturiana* (Girón, 1979), pp. 142–52.

17. Pets. 60, 66, 1480 Cortes of Toledo, *Cortes*, vol. iv. pp. 137ff.; *Capítulos de corregidores, 1500*, p. 305.

18. *AGS, Sello*, 26 April 1484, fol. 37 (Zamora); 13 September 1492, fol. 142 (Segovia); 19 May 1488, fol. 29, 5 April 1489, fol. 41 (Trujillo); 28 February 1492, fol. 245 (Avila).

19. *Ibid.*, 12 January 1478, fol. 121 (Galicia); 5 February 1478, fol. 53 (Huete); 2 March 1478, fol. 36, 20 March 1478, fol. 54 (Andújar); nd January 1478, fol. 221 (Úbeda).

20. *Ibid.*, 20 July 1479, fol. 131 (Countess Teresa de Torres); 9 February 1480, fol. 12 (Leonor de Zúñiga).

21. *Ibid.*, 12 July 1484, fol. 139.

22. *Ibid.*, 7 January 1485, fol. 125; 19 September 1488, fol. 134.

23. *Ibid.*, 5 July 1487, fol. 94 (Ciudad Rodrigo); 26 February 1487, fols. 65, 135 (Trujillo); 25 May 1489, fols 144, 145 (León).

24. *Ibid.*, 18 January 1493, fol. 162.

25. *Ibid.*, nd September 1492, fol. 93; 25 October 1493, fol. 239; 26 October 1493, fol. 238.

26. Edward Cooper, *Castillos señoriales de Castilla de los siglos XV y XVI* (2 vols., Madrid, 1980–1), vol. I, pp. 72f., 77f.

27. 9 June 1500 in *Novísima Recopilación*, bk. 7, tit. I, law vi; Cooper, *Castillos señoriales*, vol. ii, docs. 40, 78, 102, 145, 158–9, 169, 171, 174, 209, 217.

28. Cooper, *Castillos señoriales*, vol. i, pp. 72f., 77f.

29. *AGS, Sello*, 17 July 1490, fol. 244; 3 September 1490, fol. 56.

30. *AGS, Cámara*, 30 August 1502, *leg.* 7, fols. 55f.

31. Bartolomé Bennassar, *Valladolid au siècle d'or* . . . (Paris, 1967), pp. 404ff.

32. Modesto Sarasola, *Vizcaya y los Reyes Católicos (1455–78)* (Madrid, 1950), p. 200.

33. Manuel Balbás Fernández, "La institucionalización de los bandos en la sociedad bilbaína y vizcaína al comienzo de la Edad Moderna," *La sociedad Vasca rural y urbana en el marco de la crisis de los siglos XIV y XV*, ed. José Valdeón Baruque (Bilbao, 1973), pp. 13–23.

34. Torres Fontes, "Marquesado de Villena," p. 79.

35. See Table 7, pp. 196ff.

36. Torres Fontes, "Marquesado de Villena," pp. 133f.

37. Pulgar, *Crónica*, vol. i, ch. 99, p. 352.

38. *AGS, Sello*, 13 June 1478, fol. 56; 11 May 1478, fol. 39.

39. See Table 7.

40. González Alonso, *Gobernación*, p. 83.

41. M. Enrique de Vedia y Gossens, *Historia y descripción de la ciudad de La Coruña* (La Coruña, 1845, reprinted 1972), p. 31.

42. Antonio López Ferreiro, *Historia de la Santa A. M. Iglesia de Santiago de Compostela* (Santiago, 1904), vol. ii, p. 109.

43. *AGS, Sello*, 4 May 1486, fols. 90–2, 207; 6 June 1486, fol. 59.

44. The count resumed his rebellion soon after Isabella died. A. López Ferreiro, *Galicia en el último tercio del siglo XV* (Vigo, 1896, reprinted 1968), pp. 109ff.

45. *AGS, Sello*, 22 December 1486, fol. 64, transcr. González Alonso, *Gobernación*, doc. 8, pp. 185ff.

46. *AGS, Sello*, 9 January 1487, fol. 19. transcr. González Alonso, *Gobernación*, doc. 9, pp. 189ff.

47. *AGS, Sello*, 8 June 1490, fol. 96; 5 December 1491, fol. 50.

48. *Ibid.*, 2 August 1492, fol. 20.

49. *Ibid.*, 7 August 1489, fol. 227.

50. *Ibid.*, 27 March 1488, fol. 109; 14 July 1488, fol. 147; 4 June 1489, fol. 140.

51. *Ibid.*, 24 December 1483, fol. 186.

52. *Ibid.*, 29 April 1487, fol. 158; 23 August 1487, fol. 35; 25 August 1487, fols. 355–6, 358–9.

53. *Ibid.*, 1 January 1488, fol. 119; 4 March 1488, fol. 78; 30 March 1488, fols. 142, 170.

54. The corregidor in Asturias struggled with the count in 1487 over who should possess the alcázar of Oviedo, and there were complaints the following year about attacks by the count's men on residents of Huerga. *Ibid.*, 6 February 1487, fol. 75; 30 March 1488, fol. 170.

55. *Ibid.*, 24 January 1491, fol. 146.

56. *Ibid.*, 4 August 1489, fols. 175, 176.

57. *AGS, Cédulas*, 1, fols. 1, 287; 3, fols. 29–33; Emma Solano Ruiz, *La Orden de Calatrava en el siglo XV. Los señoríos castellanos de la Orden al fin de la Edad Media* (Seville, 1978), pp. 109–23; L. P. Wright, "The military orders in sixteenth- and seventeenth-century Spanish society," *Past and Present* 43 (1969), pp. 34–70; D. W. Lomax, *Las órdenes militares en la Península Ibérica durante la Edad Media* (Salamanca, 1976).

58. C. R. Phillips, *Ciudad Real, 1500–1750* (Cambridge, Mass., 1979), p. 9.

59. *AMC*, 203 O[88] – 29 March 1490; 206 C – 19 July 1490; 207 C – 20 July 1490; 208 C – 20 July 1490; 209 C – 20 July 1490; 210 C – 22 July 1490; 211 C – 23 July 1490; 212 C – 23 July 1490; 213 C – 24 July 1490; 214 O[91] – 24 July 1490; 215 O[92] – 1 August 1490; 216 O[93] – 13 August 1490; 218 O[95] – nd October 1490.

60. *Ibid.*, 225 O[98] – 8 March 1491; 226 C – 10 March 1491; 227 O[99] – 11 March 1491; 231 C – 27 June 1491; 232 C – 8 September 1491; 233 C – 8 September 1491; 234 C – 14 November 1491; 235 C – 24 November 1491; 236 C – 24 November 1491; 301 C – 2 December 1495; 303 O[124] – 4 February 1496; 306 O[126] – 19 June 1496; 307 O[127] – 3 August 1496.

61. Francisco Rades de Andrada, *Crónica de las tres Órdenes y Cauallerías de Santiago, Calatraua y Alcántara* (Toledo, 1572).

62. Lope de Vega (Félix Lope de Vega Carpio), *Fuenteovejuna*. tr. Roy Campbell, *The Classic Theater* vol. III, ed. Eric Bentley, p. 230.

63. E. Cabrera *et al.*, "La sublevación de Fuenteovejuna contemplada en su V centenario," *Actas del I Congreso de Historia de Andalucía: Andalucía Medieval* (Cordova, 1982), vol. II, pp. 113–21.

64. Quintanilla Raso, *Casa de Aguilar*, p. 129.

65. Raul García Aguilera and M. Hernández Osorno, *Revuelta y litigios de los villanos de la encomienda de Fuente Ovejuna (1476)* (Madrid, 1975), doc. 3, 163–94.

66. *Ibid.*, pp. 197ff.

67. *AGS, Sello*, 28 March 1495, fol. 181.

68. C. E. Aníbal, "The historical elements in Lope de Vega's *Fuenteovejuna*," *PMLA*, XLIX, 3 (1934), pp. 657–718; R. Ramírez de Arellano, "Rebelión de Fuenteovejuna contra el comendador mayor de Calatrava, Fernán Gómez de Guzmán," *B(R)HA* 34 (1901), pp. 446ff.

69. Tarsicio de Azcona, *La elección y reforma del episcopado español en tiempo de los Reyes Católicos* (Madrid, 1960), pp. 236ff. José García Oro, "Conventualismo y observancia. La reforma de las órdenes religiosas en los siglos XV y XVI," *Historia de la Iglesia en España*, dir. Ricardo García-Villoslada (Madrid, 1980), vol. III, pt. 1, pp. 211–349.

70. *AGS, Diversos*, 652, *leg.* 4, no. 27, 10 August 1503.
71. *AGS, Sello*, 7 October 1485, fol. 31; 9 December 1485, fol. 45; 24 March 1495, fol. 285; 24 November 1495, fol. 115.
72. *AM Málaga, Originales*, 1, fol. 160, 28 July 1494.
73. *Capítulos de corregidores, 1482*, clause 25, pp. 566f.; *Capítulos de corregidores, 1500*, clause 47, p. 310; Azcona, *Isabel*, pp. 473ff.
74. *AGS, Sello*, 2 February 1488, fol. 66; *AGS, Cédulas*, 8 fols. 36v–37, 20 November 1488.
75. *AGS, Sello*, 18 July 1492, fol. 105; 4 December 1493, fol. 48.
76. *Ibid.*, 7 April 1494, fol. 401; 20 May 1494, fol. 362; 28 May 1494, fol. 361.
77. José García Oro, *Cisneros y la reforma del clero español en tiempo de los Reyes Católicos* (Madrid, 1971), p. 279.
78. *AGS, Sello*, 24 January 1495, fol. 293.
79. García Oro, *Cisneros*, pp. 281f., 293.
80. *Ibid.*, pp. 295ff.
81. F. B. de San Román, "Cisneros y el cabildo primado al finalizer el año 1503," *Boletín de la Real Academia de Bellas Artes y Ciencias Históricas de Toledo* 2 (1919), pp. 95ff.
82. Pulgar, *Crónica*, vol. II, ch. 95, pp. 248ff.
83. *AGS, Sello*, 18 August 1487, fol. 354.
84. *Ibid.*, 14 January 1485, fol. 96; 27 January 1485, fol. 80; 12 February 1485, fol. 18.
85. *AGS, Cámara*, nd October 1504, *leg.* 4.
86. Elliott, *Imperial Spain*, p. 99.
87. *AGS, Sello*, 12 December 1493, fol. 185 (Asturias).
88. *Ibid.*, 30 July 1485, fol. 52.
89. *Ibid.*, 29 March 1494, fol. 367.
90. *Ibid.*, 3 March 1492, fol. 203.
91. *Ibid.*, 27 March 1488, fol. 76; 8 December 1488, fol. 98.
92. *Ibid.*, 6 December 1485, fol. 104 (Avila); 14 January 1489, fol. 171 (Salamanca); 16 November 1487, fol. 27 (Toro); 23 November 1493, fol. 140 (Valladolid); 14 January 1495, fol. 132 (Burgos).
93. *Ibid.*, 14 August 1479, fol. 49; 30 June 1489, fol. 271.
94. *Ibid.*, 29 May 1487, fol. 50; *AM Málaga, Originales*, vol. II, fol. 119, 24 December 1500.
95. Azcona, *Reforma del episcopado*, p. 59.
96. First spelled out in *Capítulos de corregidores, 1482*, clause 19, pp. 564f.
97. Pulgar, *Crónica*, vol. II, ch. 181, pp. 203ff.
98. Azcona, *Reforma del episcopado*, pp. 60f.
99. *AGS, PR*, 5137, 2 fols., 16 August 1499.
100 *AGS, Sello*, 20 March 1492, fol. 354.

7. The end of *convivencia*: Jews, Christians, and Muslims

1. Tr. G. A. Bergenroth, *Calendar of Letters, Dispatches and State Papers . . . Spain . . . Henry VIII, 1485–1509* (London, 1862), vol. I, p. xn.
2. Francisco Guicciardini, *Ricordi politici e civili*, tr. Mario Domandi, *Maxims and Reflections. (Ricordi)* (Philadelphia, 1972), p. 77.
3. *AGS, Sello*, 28 February 1480, fol. 92; 10 June 1486, fol. 47.
4. *Ibid.*, 19 January 1480, fol. 49.
5. *Ibid.*, 4 November 1488, fol. 200, transcr. *Documentos acerca de la Expulsión de los judíos*, ed. Luis Suárez Fernández (Valladolid, 1964), no. 118, pp. 310f.

6. *AGS, Sello*, 28 May 1488, fol. 8.

7. *Ibid.*, 3 June 1489, fol. 94, transcr. Suárez Fernández, *Expulsión*, no. 130, pp. 326f.

8. *AGS, Sello*, 12 August 1490, transcr. Yitzhak Baer, *Die Jüden in christlichen Spanien* (2 vols., Berlin, 1936), no. 371, vol. II, pp. 397f.

9. See Justiniano Rodríguez Fernández, *La juderías de la provincia de León* (León, 1976).

10. Beinart, *Trujillo*, p. 103.

11. *AGS, Sello*, 15 April 1485, fol. 300, transcr. Suárez Fernández, *Expulsión*, no. 86, pp. 258f.

12. *AGS, Sello*, 24 April 1487, fol. 44.

13. *Ibid.*, 21 May 1491, fols. 28–9, transcr. Suárez Fernández, *Expulsión*, nos. 159–60, pp. 363ff.

14. The change to persecution is credited to religious commitment by J. N. Hillgarth, *The Spanish Kingdoms: 1250–1516* (2 vols., Cambridge, 1976–8), vol. II, pp. 463, 482f., 605f. and Antonio Domínguez Ortiz, *Los judeoconversos en España y América* (Madrid, 1971), pp. 38f. Economic motivations receive emphasis in Vicens Vives, *Historia económica*, p. 270.

15. *AGS, Sello*, 8 February 1478, fol. 52.

16. *Archivo Municipal de Ávila*, 1–34, 30 October 1478, transcr. Pilar León Tello, "La judería de Ávila durante el reinado de los Reyes Católicos," *Sefarad* 23 (1963), pp. 50ff., doc. VIII..

17. *AGS, Sello*, 26 August 1478, fol. 30 transcr. Suárez Fernández, *Expulsión*, no. 29, pp. 140f.

18. Pet. 76, 1480 Cortes of Toledo, *Cortes*, vol. IV, pp. 149ff; Roger Collins, *Early Medieval Spain: Unity in Diversity* (New York, 1983), pp. 129–45.

19. *AGS, Sello*, 20 May 1480, fol. 80; nd March 1486, fol. 89.

20. *AM Ávila*, 155, 7 February 1483, transcr. León Tello, "Judería de Ávila," doc. 20, pp. 73f.

21. *AGS, Sello*, nd March 1486, fol. 64.

22. *Ibid.*, nd March 1486, fol. 89; 22 May 1491, fol. 108.

23. R. D. Laing, *Self and Others* (New York, 1969), pp. 125ff.

24. *AGS, Sello*, 17 November 1489, fol. 71.

25. *Ibid.*, 30 September 1489, fol. 157, transcr. Suárez Fenández, *Expulsión*, no. 33, pp 330f.

26. *AM Madrid, Horadado*, M–338, 1482, fols. 112r–v, 26 July 1482.

27. Hipólito Sancho de Sopranis, "Contribución a la historia de la judería de Jerez de la Frontera," *Sefarad*, 11 (1951), pp. 364ff.

28. Benito de Cárdenas, *Memoria*, in Moreno de Guerra, *Bandos en Jerez*, vol. I, p. 102; see also Henry Kamen, *Inquisition and Society in Spain in the Sixteenth and Seventeenth Centuries* (London, 1985), pp. 13f., 41.

29. *AGS, Sello*, 23 December 1490, fol. 57; 19 January 1491, fol. 167; 22 March 1491, fol. 206, transcr. Suárez Fernández, *Expulsión*, nos. 145–6, 152, pp. 348ff., 355f.

30. *AGS, Sello*, 22 May 1491, fol. 108; 8 June 1491, fol. 47, transcr. Suárez Fernández, *Expulsión*, nos. 161, 163, pp. 367f., 370f.

31. *AGS, Sello*, 25 March 1475, fol. 321, transcr. Baer, *Die Jüden*, no. 325, vol. II, pp. 336f.

32. *AGS, Sello*, 18 September 1479, fol. 57, transcr. Suárez Fernández, *Expulsión*, no. 37, pp. 158ff.

33. *AGS, Sello*, 31 August 1485, nf; 7 September 1485, nf, transcr. Baer, *Die Jüden*, no. 352, vol. II, pp. 376ff.

34. *AGS, Sello*, 6 September 1487, fol. 25; 7 September 1487; fol. 191.

35. *Ibid.*, 7 March 1491, fol. 113 (Cáceres); 15 March 1491, fol. 141 (Murcia).
36. *Ibid.*, 1 July 1490, fol. 89.
37. *AGS, Sello,* 22 December 1491, fols. 271, 276, transcr. Suárez Fernández, *Expulsión,* nos. 171–2, pp. 383ff.
38. Suárez Fernández, *Historia de España,* vol. 17, pt. II, p. 247; Yitzhak Baer, *A History of the Jews in Christian Spain* (2 vols., Philadelphia, 1961–6), vol. II, pp. 330f.
39. *AGS, Sello,* 1 March 1486, fol. 41, transcr. Suárez Fernández, *Expulsión,* no. 96, pp. 276ff.
40. *AGS, Sello,* 4 December 1488, fol. 119; 19 December 1488, fol. 159; 30 January 1489, fol 284, transcr. Suárez Fernández, *Expulsión,* nos. 120–1, 123, pp. 312ff., 317ff.
41. Baer, *Jews in Spain,* vol. II, p. 420.
42. *Ibid.*, vol. II, pp. 398ff.; see also F. Fita, "La verdad sobre el martirio del Santo Niño de La Guardia . . .," *B(R)HA* 11 (1877), pp. 7–134.
43. Edict of expulsion in *AGS, PR, leg.* 28, fol. 6, transcr. Baer, *Die Jüden,* no. 378, vol. II, pp. 404ff.
44. Bernáldez, *Memorias,* ch. 110, pp. 251ff.
45. *AGS, Sello,* 18 June 1492, fol. 99, transcr. Suárez Fernández, *Expulsión,* no. 200, pp. 434f.
46. S. E. Morison, *Christopher Columbus, Mariner* (New York, 1955, reprinted 1960), pp. 32f.
47. The juridical basis of action was a law of the 1476 Cortes of Madrigal. The corregidor of Carrión, at the command of the Royal Council, seized Jewish goods in 1476 in response to complaints from nearby villagers. Similarly in Ágreda during 1478, the corregidor canceled "usurious" debts. A Jew in Atienza was charged with usury by a corregidor in 1491. Pet. 36, 1476 Cortes of Madrigal, *Cortes,* vol. IV, pp. 102ff.; *AGS, Sello,* 3 December 1476, fol. 792; 19 January 1487, fol. 48; 23 July 1491, fol. 15.
48. *AGS, Sello,* 5 July 1492, fol. 171 (Castrogeriz); 6 July 1492, fol. 100 (Salamanca).
49. *AGS, Sello,* 5 May 1492, fol. 307, transcr. Suárez Fernández, *Expulsión,* no. 181, p. 401; *AGS, Sello,* 17 August 1492, fol. 225.
50. *AGS, Sello,* 26 November 1492, fol. 132, transcr. Suárez Fernández, *Expulsión,* no. 232, pp. 489ff.
51. *AGS, Sello,* 13 November 1492, fol. 77.
52. *Ibid.*, 26 June 1492, fol. 289, transcr. Suárez Fernández, *Expulsión,* no. 206, pp. 442ff.
53. *AGS, Sello,* 6 February 1494, fol. 167.
54. Hillgarth, *Spanish Kingdoms,* vol. II, p. 449.
55. *AGS, Sello,* 4 February 1492, fol. 84 (Valencia de Alcántara).
56. *AGS, Diversos,* 29 May 1492, *leg.* 8, no. 100.
57. *AGS, Sello,* 2 February 1493, fol. 5 (Badajoz); 21 May 1493, fol. 102 (Madrid).
58. *Ibid.*, 21 May 1492, fol. 173.
59. *Ibid.*, 20 December 1494, fol. 8.
60. *Ibid.*, 19 January 1495, fol. 263; 18 September 1495, fol. 4.
61. *Ibid.*, 28 January 1495, fol. 398 (Burgos); 9 February 1495, fol. 221 (Trujillo); 18 March 1495, fol. 336 (Badajoz); 3 April 1495, fol. 161 (Burgos); nd May 1495, fol. 112 (Segovia).
62. *Ibid.*, 30 April 1494, fol. 364.
63. *AGS, Sello,* 3 February 1493, fol. 134, transcr. Suárez Fernández, *Expulsión,* no. 243, pp. 505f.
64. Suárez Fernández, *Historia de España,* vol. 17, pt. II, pp. 264f.
65. *AGS, Sello,* 25 June 1493, fol. 135, transcr. Suárez Fernández, *Expulsión,* no. 252, pp. 517f.

66. *AGS, Sello*, 2 December 1492, fol. 73 (Atienza); 25 February 1493, fol. 36 (Avila).
67. Suárez Fernández, *Historia de España*, vol. 17, pt. II, pp. 261f.
68. *Archivo Municipal de Ávila*, 1/131, 132, transcr. León Tello, Judería de Ávila," doc. 39, pp. 109f.
69. *Capítulos de corregidores, 1482*, clause 39, p. 573; *Capítulos de corregidores, 1500*, clause 42, p. 308.
70. Francisco Márquez Villanueva, "The Converso problem: an assessment," *Collected Studies in Honor of Américo Castro's Eightieth Year*, ed. M. P. Hornick (Oxford, 1965), p. 515.
71. Haim Beinart, *Conversos on Trial. The Inquisition in Ciudad Real* (Jerusalem, 1981), p. 83; Luis Delgado Merchán, *Historia documentada de Ciudad Real* (2 vols., Ciudad Real, 1907), vol. I, pp. 424f.
72. *AHN, Inquisición Toledo, leg.* 1481, no. 267, fols. 1r–16r (new numbers: 148, no. 6), transcr. with commentary in *Records of the Trials of the Spanish Inquisition in Ciudad Real*, ed. Haim Beinart (4 vols., Jerusalem, 1974–7), vol. I, pp. 198–211.
73. *Cancionero castellano del siglo XV*, ed. R. Foulché–Delbosc (2 vols., Madrid, 1912–15), vol. II, pp. 100f.
74. Beinart, *Conversos*, pp. 150f.; Benito Ruano, *Toledo*, pp. 244ff., 248f.
75. Henry Kamen, *The Spanish Inquisition* (New York, 1966), pp. 163f.
76. Baer, *Jews in Spain*, vol. II, p. 339.
77. Text in Benito Ruano, *Toledo*, p. 137.
78. Kamen, *Spanish Inquisition*, p. 45.
79. Márquez Villanueva, "Converso," p. 515; Benito Ruano, *Toledo*, p. 137.
80. Baer, *Jews in Spain*, vol. II, p. 339; Amador de los Ríos, *Historia de los judíos*, vol. III, pp. 692ff.
81. Beinart, *Ciudad Real*, p. 186n.
82. A. Cotarelo y Valledor, *Fray Diego de Deza. Ensayo biográfico* (Madrid, 1902), p. 149; Nader, *Mendoza*, p. 159.
83. Santa Cruz, *Crónica de los Reyes Católicos*, vol. I, ch. 60, p. 248.
84. *AGS, Sello*, 6 June 1485, fol. 221; 20 March 1492, fol. 350; 11 March 1495, fol. 536.
85. Fermín Caballero, *Conquenses ilustres*, vol. III, *Dr Alonso Díaz de Montalvo* (Madrid, 1873), pp. 38f., 55, 509.
86. Márquez Villanueva, "Converso," p. 507n; Haliczer, *Comuneros*, p. 69.
87. See Table 7, pp. 196ff.; Márquez Villanueva, "Converso," p. 508.
88. Biographical material from preliminary study by Juan de Mata Carriazo (ed.), Diego de Valera, *Memorial de diversas hazañas* (Madrid, 1941), pp. xiv–xxvi, and Lucas de Torre, "Mosén Diego de Valera. Su vida y sus obras," *B(R)HA* 64 (1914), pp. 9–168, 249–76, 365–412.
89. Lucas de Torre, "Diego de Valera," pp. 374f.
90. Márquez Villanueva, "Converso," pp. 539f.
91. The figure is for 1500: M. A. Ladero Quesada, *Los Mudéjares de Castilla en tiempos de Isabel I* (Valladolid, 1969), p. 20.
92. *Ibid.*; for the small Burgos and Avila populations, see Leopoldo Torres Balbás, *Algunos aspectos del mudejarismo urbano medieval . . .* (Madrid, 1954), pp. 25–46.
93. *AGS, Sello*, 25 March 1475, fol. 321; 18 September 1479, fol. 57; 23 April 1486, fol. 111, transcr. Suárez Fernández, *Expulsión*, nos. 4, 37, 98, pp. 85f., 158f., 280f.
94. Juan Torres Fontes, "El alcalde mayor de las aljamas de moros," *AHDE* 32 (1962), pp. 156f.
95. *Ibid.*, pp. 157ff.
96. Pet. 25, 1476 Cortes of Madrigal, *Cortes*, vol. IV, pp. 94f.
97. *AGS, Sello*, 16 June 1489, fol. 176.
98. *Ibid.*, 10 January 1493, fol. 252; 12 January 1493, fol. 259.

99. Pet. 76, 1476 Cortes of Madrigal, *Cortes*, vol. IV, pp. 194ff.

100. *AGS, Sello*, 29 January 1480, fol. 46, 3 May 1480, fol. 87 (Cordova); 4 November 1480 (Segovia); see Edwards, *Christian Córdoba*, pp. 178f.

101. *AGS, Sello*, 9 September 1489, fol. 31.

102. *Ibid.*, 2 July 1489, fol. 300.

103. Carriazo, *Historia de España*, vol. 17, pt. 1, p. 585.

104. D. W. Lomax, *The Reconquest of Spain* (London and New York, 1978), p. 169.

105. Pulgar, *Crónica*, vol. II, ch. 135, pp. 29ff., ch. 146, pp. 61ff.; Carriazo, *Historia de España*, vol. 17, pt. 1, pp. 489ff.

106. J. F. Powers, "Townsmen and soldiers: the interaction of urban and military organization in the militias of medieval Castile," *Speculum* XLVI, 4 (October 1971), pp. 649ff.; P. J. Stewart, Jr., "Army of the Catholic Kings: Spanish military organization and administration in the reign of Ferdinand and Isabella, 1474–1516" (unpublished PhD dissertation, University of Illinois, 1961), pp. 187f.

107. Chamberlain, "Corregidor in Castile," pp. 239f.

108. Owens, *Oligarquía murciana*, p. 44.

109. See Table 7, pp. 196ff.

110. This differs from González Alonso, who maintains that corregidores could not be captains at the same time as they held the municipal title. See his *Corregidor castellano*, p. 109.

111. *AM Carmona, AC*, 1483, fols. 17–18, 16 May 1483.

112. Pulgar, *Crónica*, vol. II, ch. 157, p. 109.

113. Carriazo, *Historia de España*, vol. 17, pt. 1, pp. 567ff.

114. Pulgar, *Crónica*, vol. II, ch. 198, pp 258ff.

115. Carriazo, *Historia de España*, vol. 17, pt. 1, pp. 721ff.

116. Pulgar, *Crónica*, vol. II, pp. 61, 77, 109, 193, 237, 290, 336.

117. *Ibid.*, vol. II, ch. 176, pp. 188ff.

118. *AM Málaga, Originales*, vol. I, fol. 25, 30 September 1489.

119. Francisco Bejarano Robles, "Constitución del concejo y del primer cabildo de Málaga," *Jábega* 22 (1978), pp. 3ff.

120. Carriazo, *Historia de España*, vol. 17, pt. 1, pp. 721ff.

121. *AMS, Tumbo*, ed. Carande, vol. III, p. 152, 22 March 1487; p. 167, 28 May 1487; p. 252, 12 November 1488; p. 277, 14 March 1489; p. 381, 12 July 1490; p. 394, 7 August 1490; p. 412, 31 January 1491; p. 471, 1 December 1491; p. 475, 13 December 1491.

122. *AGS, Sello*, 4 October 1488, fol. 39 (Diego López de Haro, Galicia); 24 February 1486, fol. 13 (Alfonso de Valderrábano, Asturias); Laderdo Quesada, *Milicia de Granada*, table, p. 110.

123. *AGS, Sello*, 6 July 1486, fol. 59; 22 September 1488, fol. 122 (Vizcaya).

124. Letter to corregidor of Galicia, 7 April 1487, transcr. Antonio Vallecillo, *Legislación militar de España* . . . (13 vols., Madrid, 1853–6), vol. IV, p. 147.

125. Pulgar, *Crónica*, vol. II, ch. 254, pp. 432ff.; Carriazo, *Historia de España*, vol. 17, pt. 1, pp. 783ff.

126. Carriazo, *Historia de España*, vol. 17, pt. 1, chs. 27–40.

127. Nader, *Mendoza*, p. 155.

128. *Ibid.*, pp. 156, 159.

129. Biographical details from Ángel González Palencia and Eugenio Mele, *Vida y obras de Don Hurtado de Mendoza* (3 vols., Madrid, 1943), vol. I, pp. 4ff.; and José Cepeda Adán, "El gran Tendilla medieval y renacentista," *Cuadernos de Historia* 1 (1967), pp. 159–68.

130. González Palencia, *Mendoza*, vol. I, p. 10.

131. *Correspondencia del conde Tendilla*, ed. Emilio Meneses García (2 vols., *Archivo Documental Español*, Madrid, 1973), vol. II, pp. 541–2.

132. See Table 7.
133. *Correspondencia Tendilla*, vol. I, p. 57.
134. Last testament, transcr. appendix, doc 2, Meneses García, *Tendilla*, vol. I, p. 57.
135. *Ibid.*, vol. I, p. 60.
136. Quoted in Nader, *Mendoza*, p. 234.
137. *CDI*, vol. VIII, pp. 411–82.
138. *Correspondencia Tendilla*, vol. II, pp. 271–4.
139. Suárez Fernández, *Historia de España*, vol. 17, pt, II, pp. 291ff.
140. Transcr. González Palencia, *Mendoza*, vol. I, pp. 11–12.
141. *Correspondencia Tendilla*, vol. I, p. 64.
142. *AM Málaga*, *Provisiones*, vol. II, fols. 9–9*v*, 29 January 1501; fol. 23*v*, 26 February 1501.
143. Suárez Fernández, *Historia de España*, vol. 17, pt. I, p. 300.
144. *AGS*, *Sello*, 4 June 1492, fol. 100; *AM Málaga*, *Provisiones*, vol. II, fol. 110, 26 July 1501; vol. IV, fol. 354–354*v*, 24 May 1502.
145. Nader, *Mendoza*, p. 160.
146. *Ibid.*, p. 159.

8. Difficult governance (1495–1504)

1. Castillo de Bovadilla, *Política para corregidores*, vol. II, epilogue.
2. See Table 7, pp. 196ff.
3. *AMS*, *Tumbo*, bk. IV, fols. 283–4.
4. *AM Málaga*, *Originales*, vol. I, fol. 175, 28 July 1494.
5. Stewart, "Army of the Catholic Kings", pp. 193f.
6. *Bulas y pragmáticas*, pp. 84*v*–86*v*; version in *AMS*, *Tumbo*, bk. 5, fols. 152–4.
7. Pet. 54, 1525 Cortes of Valladolid, *Cortes*, vol. IV, pp. 435f.; Álvarez de Morales, *Hermandades*, p. 172.
8. David Ringrose, "The government and the carters in Spain: 1476–1700," *Economic History Review*, 2nd ser., 22 (1969), pp. 46ff.; Gonzalo Menéndez Pidal, *Los caminos en la historia de España* (Madrid, 1951, reprinted 1962), pp. 71f.
9. Julius Klein, *The Mesta: A study in Spanish Economic History, 1273–1836* (Cambridge, Mass., 1920), p. 104.
10. *Novísima Recopilación*, bk. 7, tit. 28, laws 1–4, tit. 35, law 2.
11. Ringrose, "Carters," p. 50; see also map in Menéndez Pidal, *Los caminos*, p. 70.
12. Jean-Pierre Molénat, "Chemins et ponts du Nord de la Castille au temps des Rois Catholiques," *Mélanges de la Casa de Velázquez* 7 (1971), pp. 134f.
13. *Ibid.*, pp. 123ff.
14. *AGS*, *Sello*, 26 November 1491, fol. 164; 8 March 1492, fol. 366.
15. Molénat, "Chemins et ponts," docs. 1–2, pp. 157f.
16. C. J. Bishko, "Sesenta años Después: La *Mesta* de Julius Klein a la luz de la investigación subsiguiente," *Historia Instituciones Documentos* 8 (1982), pp. 33f.
17. Felipe Ruiz Martín, "Pastos y ganaderos en Castilla: La Mesta (1450–1600)," *Atti della prima settimana di studio (18–24 aprile 1969): La lana come materia prima: i fenomeni della sua produzione e circolazione nei secoli XIII–XVII*, ed. Marco Spallanzani (Florence, 1974), p. 275.
18. Vicens Vives, *Historia económica*, pp. 232ff.
19. C. J. Bishko, "The Castilian as plainsman: the medieval ranching frontier in La Mancha and Extremadura," *The New World Looks at its History*, eds. A. R. Lewis and T. F. McGann (Austin, Texas, 1963), p. 63.
20. Bishko, "Castilian as plainsman," p. 49; and his "El castellano, hombre de llanura. La explotación ganadera en el área fronteriza de La Mancha y

Extremadura durante la Edad Media," *Homenajo a Jaime Vicens Vives*, ed. J. Maluquer de Montes (2 vols., Barcelona, 1965), vol. I, p. 203.

21. *AMC*, 204 O[83] – 2 April 1490.
22. *AGS, Sello*, 10 May 1486, fol. 56.
23. Klein, *Mesta*, p. 218.
24. *Ibid.*, p. 44.
25. C. J. Bishko, "The Andalusian municipal mestas in the 14th–16th centuries: Administrative and social aspects," *Actas I Congreso de Historia de Andalucía: Andalucía Medieval* (Cordova, 1982), vol. I, pp. 349f.
26. *Ibid.*, vol. I, pp. 368ff.
27. Edwards, *Christian Córdoba*, pp. 117, 120.
28. *AGS, Sello*, 19 October 1494, fol. 63.
29. Klein, *Mesta*, p. 324.
30. See table in M. T. Oliveros de Castro and Julio Jordana de Pozas, *La agricultura de los reinos españoles en tiempo de los Reyes Católicos* (Madrid, 1968), pp. 225f.
31. Vicens Vives, *Approaches*, p. 94.
32. Ruiz Martín, "Pastos y ganaderos," pp. 273ff.
33. M. A. Ladero Quesada and Manuel González Jiménez, *Diezmo eclesiástico y producción de cereales en el reino de Sevilla (1408–1503)* (Seville, 1979), pp. 79, 85, 117 (graph); M. A. Ladero Quesada, "Los cereales en Andalucía durante el siglo XV," *Revista de la Universidad de Madrid* 18 (1969), pp. 223ff.
34. Fernand Braudel, *Capitalism and Material Life (1400–1800)*, tr. Miriam Kochan (New York, 1974), p. 89.
35. *AGS, Sello*, 15 June 1487, fol. 10; 21 February 1495, fol. 419.
36. Bernáldez, *Memorias*, ch. 209, pp. 516f.
37. *Bulas y pragmáticas*, fol. 314, 23 December 1502.
38. Eduardo Ibarra y Rodríguez, *El problema cerealista en España durante el reinado de los Reyes Católicos (1475–1516). Anales de Economía* (Madrid, 1944), pp. 119ff.
39. *AGS, Diversos*, 639, *leg.* 42, no. 33, 5–6 April 1503.
40. *AM Málaga, Originales*, vol. II, fol. 364, 3 April 1503; fol. 67, 23 April 1503; fol. 339, 22 June 1503.
41. Haliczer, *Comuneros*, ch. 4.
42. Edwards, "Oligarchy and merchant capitalism," pp. 22f.
43. *AMC*, 318 C – 29 April 1494, 320 O[135] – 5 June 1497; 321 O[136] – 7 June 1497.
44. *AGS, Sello*, 12 November 1497, fol. 42.
45. *AGS, Cámara*, 18 March 1500, *leg.* 2; 19 December 1501, *leg.* 7, nf; 23 July 1502, *leg.* 7, fol. 59; 25 July 1502, *leg.* 7, fol. 3.
46. See G. Sáinz de Zúñiga Ajo, *Historia de las Universidades Hispánicas . . .* (7 vols., Madrid and Avila, 1957–67), vol. II, *El siglo de oro universitario.*
47. R. L. Kagan, *Students and Society in Early Modern Spain* (Baltimore, 1974), p. 129.
48. Bermúdez Aznar, *Corregidor en Castilla*, pp. 69–88, 135.
49. See Table 7, pp. 196ff.
50. Pet. 2, 1462 Cortes of Toledo, *Cortes*, vol. III, pp. 704f.
51. Guilarte, *Régimen señorial*, p. 80n.
52. Phillips, *Enrique IV*, pp. 49f.
53. Kagan, *Students and Society*, p. 132.
54. Incorporated into the (*Nueva*) *Recopilación de todas las leyes de estos reinos* (2 vols., Alcalá de Henares, 1566, reprinted 1569), vol. I, bk. II, tit. IX, law II.
55. *Ibid.*
56. See Table 7.
57. Pet. 59, 1480 Cortes of Toledo, *Cortes*, vol. IV, p. 137.
58. See Table 7.
59. Primarily from the *AGS, Sello* and *PR*.

60. Toral Peñaranda, *Úbeda*, pp. 168f.

61. *Ibid.*, pp. 121ff., 175.

62. *AGS, Sello*, 4 September 1494, fol. 90; 6 May 1495, fol. 68.

63. Toral Peñaranda, *Úbeda*, pp. 247f., 350.

64. Marie-Claude Gerbet, "Les guerres et l'accès à noblesse en Espagne de 1465 à 1592," *Mélanges de la Casa de Velázquez* 8 (1972), pp. 321ff., tables i and ii.

65. Manuel González Jimenez, *El Concejo de Carmona a fines de la Edad Media (1464–1523* (Seville, 1976), pp. 293ff.

66. See Table 7.

67. The enumeration of caballeros throughout the tables excludes aristocrats.

68. See Table 7.

69. Guipúzcoa (1489–94); Huete (1487–93); Jerez de la Frontera (1488–95); Murcia (1489–92); Ponferrada (1489–92); Segovia (1488–92); Soria (1487–96). See Table 7.

70. Asturias (1500–5); Burgos (1492–1502); Carmona (1494–9 and 1499–1503); Écija (1492–6); Granada (1492–1500); Málaga (1499–1504); Requena–Utiel (1490–4); Salamanca (1500–5); Soria (1487–96); Toledo (1491–1506); Valladolid (1491–1503); Vélez Málaga (1499–1504); Vivero (1478–94); Vizcaya (1491–5); Zamora (1499–1505). See Table 7.

71. *AGS, Sello*, 16 March 1494, fol. 386; 7 May 1494, fol. 224; 7 October 1494, fol. 239.

72. *Ibid.*, 4 November 1495, fol. 56; *AGS, Diversos, leg.* 42, no. 28, 25 January 1499.

73. *AM Carmona, AC*, 1501, fol. 243, 30 November 1501; 1503, fol. 63v, 18 April 1503; 1504, fol. 41, 9 January 1504; *AM Carmona, PR*, 1500–1516, 16 December 1503, nf.

74. *AGS, Cámara*, 11 May 1501, *leg.* 7, fol. 44; nd May 1501, *leg.* 7.

75. Pretel Marín, *Fondos Medievales*, p. 31, and *Integración Alcaraz*, p. 16.

76. The corregidor of Alcaraz ordered the city to pay expenses involved in a trip by a *regidor* to the court to secure the royal official's appointment. *AGS, Sello*, 29 May 1492, fol. 69; 4 June 1492, fol. 356.

77. Ladero Quesada, *Hacienda, 1480 y 1492*, pp. 35, 74, 85, 90, 93.

78. J. M. Carretero Zamora, "Andalucía en las cortes de los Reyes Católicos," *Actas II Coloquios Historia de Andalucía: Andalucía Moderna* (Cordova, 1980), vol. ii, pp. 43ff. Wladimir Piskorski, *Las Cortes de Castilla en el período de tránsito de la Edad Media a la Moderna, 1188–1520*, tr. C. Sánchez-Albornoz (Barcelona, 1930), pp. 53f.

79. *AMS, Tumbo*, bk. v, fols. 137v, 144, 16 March 1498, 2 April 1498; Carretero Zamora, "Andalucía," p. 45 and (doc. transcr. from *AGS, PR, leg.* 69, fol. 27, 5 April 1498), p. 53.

80. José Martínez Caadós, "Las Cortes de Castilla en el siglo XVI," *Revista de la Universidad de Madrid* 4ª época, 6 (1957), p. 583.

81. Letter convoking session transcr. Manuel Dánvila y Collado, *Historia crítica y documentada de las comunidades de Castilla* (6 vols., *Memorial Histórico Español*, Madrid, 1897–1900), vol. i, doc. 7, p. 18.

82. Martínez Caadós, "Cortes," pp. 583ff.

83. E. H. Kantorowicz, *The King's Two Bodies: A Study in Medieval Political Theology* (Princeton, NJ, 1957), p. 159.

84. J. B. Owens, "'Feudal' monarch and 'just' monarch: an interpretation of fifteenth-century Castilian politics" (paper delivered at 5th Annual Convention of the Society for Spanish and Portuguese Historical Studies, San Diego, 22 March 1974).

85. *AGS, Sello*, 25 September 1494, fol. 149; 11 October 1494, fol. 544; 14 April 1495, fol. 97.

86. *Ibid.*, 16 May 1495, fol. 159.

87. *Ibid.*, 10 November 1495, fol. 46.
88. Owens, *Oligarquía murciana*, pp. 77, 136.
89. Haliczer, *Comuneros*, p. 108.
90. J. H. Elliott, "Revolution and continuity in early modern Europe," *Past and Present* 42 (1969), pp. 52f.

9. The queen in heaven: troubled aftermath

1. Baldassare Castiglione, *The Book of the Courtier*, tr. C. S. Singleton (New York, 1959), bk. III, p. 238.
2. *CDI*, vol. 81, pp. 25ff. Sarmiento's complaint may have been drawn up to curry favor with Philip I, according to Hillgarth, *Spanish Kingdoms*, vol. II, p. 592.
3. Antonio de La Torre y del Cerro, *Testamentaria de Isabel la Católica* (Barcelona, 1974), transcriptions pp. 61–91, 93–101.
4. Toral Peñaranda, *Úbeda*, pp. 387ff.
5. Alonso de Santa Cruz, *Crónica del Emperador Carlos V* (5 vols., Madrid, 1920–5 edn.), vol. I, p. 218.
6. Owens, *Oligarquía murciana*, pp. 145ff.
7. *AGS, Cámara*, 26–7 November 1506, *leg.* 20, nf.
8. Bartolomé Yun Casalilla, *Crisis de subsistencias y conflictividad social en Córdoba a principios del siglos XVI. Una ciudad andaluza en los comienzos de la modernidad* (Cordova, 1980), pp. 71ff.
9. *Ibid.*, pp. 167f.; Edwards, *Christian Córdoba*, p. 157.
10. Edwards, *Christian Córdoba*, p. 158.
11. Owens, *Oligarquía murciana*, p. 140.
12. Pretel Marín, *Integración Alcaraz*, p. 27.
13. *AGS, Cámara*, 12 August 1506, *leg.* 7, fol. 73.
14. Haliczer, *Comuneros*, p. 107.
15. *AGS, Estado, leg.* 4, fol. 24 transcr. Jerónimo López de Ayala, *El cardenal Cisneros. Gobernador del reino. Estudio histórico y documentos* (2 vols., Madrid, 1928), doc. 358, vol. II, pp. 603–9.
16. It again became customary from 1520. Martínez Caadós, "Cortes," p. 590.
17. Responses to pet. 23, 1506 Cortes of Salamanca–Valladolid, *Cortes*, vol. IV, p. 230 and to pet. 13, 1512 Cortes of Valladolid, *Cortes*, vol. IV, 241.
18. Pets. 13–14, 1512 Cortes of Valladolid; pet. 10, 1515 Cortes of Burgos; pets. 28–9, 34, 1518 Cortes of Valladolid, *Cortes*, vol. IV, pp. 240f., 253, 269f.
19. *AGS, Diversos, leg.* 9, fol. 36, 1–6. The document is dated 1512 by Tarsicio de Azcona and 1515 by González Alonso. A 1516 date is accepted by M. A. Ladero Quesada and by Emilio Mitre Fernández. I believe the list was prepared at the later date, not for Cisneros but for Charles who, arriving shortly afterwards in the kingdom to receive its homage, would require it to be spelled out, for example, that Francisco de Bazán had been at Requena "for many years." The listing appears to have been hastily drawn, since it contains an admission that in several instances figures are lacking for emoluments, and seven locations show no salary.
20. A list of 80 individuals available to fill posts shows that *letrados* constitute 42 per cent (34) of the total, with 58 per cent (46) from the higher nobility, generally caballeros. *AGS, Diversos, leg.* 9, fol. 5v–6.
21. See J. A. Maravall, *Las Comunidades de Castilla: Una primera revolución moderna* (3rd edn., Madrid, 1963); J. I. Gutiérrez Nieto, *Las Comunidades como movimiento antiseñorial: La formación del bando realista en la guerra castellana de 1520–1521* (Barcelona, 1973); Joseph Pérez, *La révolution des "Comunidades" de Castille (1520–21)* (Bordeaux, 1970); H. L. Seaver, *The Great Revolt in Castile: a Study of the Comunero Movement of 1520–21* (London, 1928).

22. Zagorin, *Rebels and Rulers*, vol. I. p. 261.
23. Phillips, *Ciudad Real*, p. 15.
24. Zagorin, *Rebels and Rulers*, vol. I, p. 261.
25. *AGS, Estado, leg.* 3, fol. 154, transcr. López de Ayala, *Cisneros*, doc. 340, vol. I, pp. 568–9.
26. Ramón Alba, *Acerca de algunas particularidades de las Comunidades de Castilla* . . . (Madrid, 1975), p. 111.
27. Letter to corregidor of Salamanca. *AGS, Cámara, leg.* 35, fol. 239, transcr. Dánvila, *Comunidades*, vol. II, p. 92.
28. Dánvila, *Comunidades*, vol. I, pp. 99, 287ff., 305, 322.
29. *Ibid.*, vol. I, p. 283.
30. *Ibid.*, vol. I, pp. 98, 283; Pérez, *Comunidades*, pp. 51f.
31. Sandoval, *Carlos V*, vol. I, p. 215; Seaver, *Great Revolt*, pp. 85ff.
32. Santa Cruz, *Crónica Carlos V*, vol. I, p. 235.
33. *Ibid.*, vol. I, pp. 236ff.
34. Dánvila, *Comunidades*, vol. I, pp. 361ff., 366ff.
35. Dánvila, *Comunidades*, vol. VI, pp. 246–7, 306–9.
36. *AGS, PR, Comunidades de Castilla, leg.* I, fol. 185, transcr. Dánvila, *Comunidades*, vol. I, pp. 434–7.
37. *AGS, Estado, leg.* 12, fol. 14, transcr. Dánvila, *Comunidades*, vol. II, pp. 214–15, 455.
38. Dánvila, *Comunidades*, vol. I, pp. 525ff., vol. III, p. 154.
39. Pérez, *Comunidades*, p. 518.
40. Maravall, *Comunidades*, ch. 5.
41. J. L. Bermejo Cabrero, "La gobernación del reino de las Comunidades de Castilla," *Hispania* 124 (1973), pp. 259ff.; Sandoval, *Carlos V*, pp. 211ff.
42. See R. García Cárcel, *Las Germanías de Valencia* (Barcelona, 1975), and *La revolta de les Germanies* (Valencia, 1981); L. Bonilla, *Las revoluciones españolas en el siglo XVI* (Madrid, 1973), chs. 8–9; Eulàlia Durán, *Les Germanies als Països Catalans* (Barcelona, 1982).
43. Tarsicio de Azcona, *San Sebastián y la provincia de Guipúzcoa durante la guerra de las Comunidades (1520–1521): Estudio y documentos* (San Sebastián, 1974), pp. 22ff.
44. *AGS, Diversos*, 6–111, fols. 20–24v, 30 November 1520, 2 March 1521, transcr. Azcona, *San Sebastián*, docs. 4, 10, pp. 75ff., 84ff.
45. *AGS, Diversos*, 6–110, fols. 16r–19v, 24 December 1525, transcr. Azcona, San Sebastián, doc. 11, pp. 95ff.
46. Dánvila, *Comunidades*, vol. II, p. 125.
47. *AGS, PR, leg.* 5–5v, f. 13 (20 October 1520), transcr. Sandoval, *Carlos V*, vol. I, pp. 113ff.; Santa Cruz, *Crónica Carlos V*, vol. I, pp. 311f.
48. Dánvila, *Comunidades*, vol. II, pp. 262ff.
49. *Ibid.*, vol. III, p. 39.
50. Pet. 7, 1525 Cortes of Toledo, *Cortes*, vol. IV, p. 407.
51. Cited by Theda Skocpol, *States and Social Revolutions* (Cambridge, 1981), p. 47.
52. i.e. Pedro Pimentel and Juan de Padilla: Santa Cruz, *Crónica Carlos V*, vol. I, pp. 335, 421.
53. Maravall, *Comunidades*, pp. 181ff.
54. Gutiérrez Nieto, *Comunidades*, p. 337n.
55. Probably issued by the junta at Avila: *CDI*, vol. I, pp. 272ff.
56. Gutiérrez Nieto, *Comunidades*, pp. 337ff.
57. *AGS, PR, Comunidades de Castilla, leg.* 5, fol. 320, transcr. Dánvila, *Comunidades*, vol. V, pp. 292–301.
58. Dánvila, *Comunidades*. vol. III, pp. 371, 784; vol. IV, p. 51.

59. Dánvila, *Comunidades*, vol. IV, p. 177.
60. *AGS, PR, Comunidades de Castilla, leg.* 5, fol. 236, transcr. Dánvila, *Comunidades*, vol. IV, pp. 301–2, 399–400.
61. *AGS, Cédulas, lib.* 52, fol. 156, transcr. Dánvila, *Comunidades*, vol. IV, p. 105; Alba *Comunidades*, p. 107.
62. Dánvila, *Comunidades*, vol. IV, pp. 76–8; Pérez, *Comunidades*, p. 571.
63. Dánvila, *Comunidades*, vol. VI, p. 154; Pérez, *Comunidades*, p. 579.
64. Dánvila, *Comunidades*, vol. V, pp. 72, 193, 233, 257, 502.
65. Eloy Díaz-Jiménez y Molleda, *Historia de los Comuneros de León y su influencia en el movimiento general de Castilla* (2nd edn., León, 1978), p. 134; Dánvila, *Comunidades*, vol. III, pp. 542f.
66. Dánvila, *Comunidades*, vol. III, pp. 163; vol. IV, p. 317; L. Redonet, "Comentarios sobre las Comunidades y Germanías," *B(R)AH* 145 (1959), p. 65.
67. Alba, *Comunidades*, p. 127.
68. Dánvila, *Comunidades*, vol. IV, pp. 424f.; Alba, *Comunidades*, pp. 76f.
69. Alba, *Comunidades*, p. 44.
70. Dánvila, *Comunidades*, vol. V, pp. 402, 450, 503.
71. *AGS, Cámara, leg.* 143, nf, transcr. Dánvila, *Comunidades*, vol. IV, pp. 99–102
72. *AGS, PR, Comunidades de Castilla, leg.* 4, fols. 191f., transcr. Dánvila, *Comunidades*, vol. IV, p. 254.
73. García Álvarez Ortiz (Seville), Diego Osorio (Cordova), and three from Valladolid: Juan de Acuña, the *licenciado* de Lugo, and Martín de Acuña. *AGS, PR, Comunidades de Castilla, leg.* 5, fol. 320 transcr. Dánvila, *Comunidades*, vol. V, pp. 299–301.
74. Dánvila, *Comunidades*, vol. V, p. 653.
75. *AGS, Estado, leg.* 27, fols. 313–18, transcr. Dánvila, *Comunidades*, vol. V, pp. 186–7.
76. *Ibid.*
77. Pet. 9, 1431 Cortes of Palencia, *Cortes*, vol. III, p. 101.
78. Francisco Tomás Valiente, "La Diputación de las Cortes de Castilla," *AHDE* 32 (1962) p. 368.
79. Pet. 92, 1523 Cortes of Valladolid; Pets. 28, 38, 40, 55–6, 63, 73, 1525 Cortes of Toledo, *Cortes*, vol. IV, pp. 383f., 397, 418f., 422f., 436.
80. *AGS, PR, Comunidades de Castilla, leg.* 4, fol. 193, transcr. Dánvila, *Comunidades*, vol. I, p. 205.
81. Pet. 7, 1525 Cortes of Toledo, *Cortes*, vol. IV, p. 407.
82. Tomás Valiente, *Diputación*, pp. 368f.
83. Owens, *Oligarquía murciana*, pp. 211f.
84. Lauro Martines, *Power and Imagination: City-States in Renaissance Italy* (New York, 1980), pp. 139ff.
85. The domination gained by corregidores when Valencia's *fueros* were breached in 1707 is studied in V. L. Simó Santonia, *Valencia en la época de los corregidores* (Valencia, 1975), p. 420.
86. Jaime Vicens Vives, *Ferran II i la ciutat de Barcelona, 1479–1516* (3 vols., Barcelona, 1939), vol. III, docs. 182, 188, 195.
87. M. I. Falcón Pérez, *Organización municipal de Zaragoza en el siglo XV* (Zaragoza, 1978), p. 33.
88. A. H. de Oliveira Marques, *History of Portugal* (2 vols., New York, 2nd edn., 1976), vol. II, p. 180; see also Henrique de Gama Barios, *História de administração pública em Portugal nos séculos XII a XV* (2nd edn., Lisbon, 1954), ch. 11.
89. "Mémoire du corregidor d'Oran sur la manière dont cette ville est administrée," *Documents sur l'occupation espagnole en Afrique (1506–1574)*, ed. F. Elie de la Primaudae (Algiers, 1875), pp. 312f.

90. See Guillermo Lohmann Villena, *El corregidor de Indios en el Perú bajo los Austrias* (Madrid, 1957), and Carlos Castañeda, "The corregidor in Spanish colonial administration," *HAHR* 9 (1929), pp. 446–70.

91. Alonso de Villadiego Vascuña y Montoya, *Instrucción politica y práctica judicial conforme al estilo de los concejos* (Madrid, 1766), pp. 148ff., 190ff.

92. G. Céspedes del Castillo, "La visita como institución indiana," *Anuario de Estudios Americanos* 3 (1946), p. 987; see also J. M. Ots Capdequí, *El juicio de residencia en la historia del derecho indiano* (Mexico, 1964).

93. Juan de Aponte Figueroa, *Memorial . . . CDI* 51 (1867), pp. 324ff.

94. Jaime Vicens Vives, "Estructura administrativa estatal en los siglos XVI y XVII," *Coyuntura económica y reformismo burgués* (Barcelona, 1968), p. 107.

Select bibliography

I (a) Archival sources and guides

The *Archivo General de Simancas*, Castile's principal repository, supplied the major documentation for this study. An introduction to the vast collection has been prepared by Ángel de la Plaza Bores, *Guía del Archivo General de Simancas* (Valladolid, 1962). A voluminous correspondence directed at corregidores by the sovereigns and the Royal Council of Castile is found in the sections *Registro General del Sello* and *Patronato Real*. These letters contain summaries of investigations, appeals to lower court judgements, instructions, and admonishments. The well-preserved *Sello* papers are being catalogued in a series of volumes first issued at Valladolid in 1950. Beginning with volume 6 (for 1489) the entries are more detailed, with each volume devoted to a single year. A less useful catalogue for the *Patronato Real* was prepared by A. Prieto Cantero, *Patronato Real: 834–1851* (Valladolid, 1946–9). Edicts promulgated by the monarchs are preserved in the section *Cámara de Castilla. Libros de Cédulas*. Supplemental bundles of correspondence are located in *Diversos de Castilla*. Account books and fragments of bills are found in the section *Contaduría Mayor de Cuentas, 1ª época*.

The *Archivo Histórico Nacional* (Madrid) provided a few documents from the sixteenth-century in the sections *Colección de Reales Cédulas*, *Sección de Consejos Suprimidos*, and *Sección de Diversos*. Some codes and compilations are found at the *Biblioteca Nacional* (Madrid) in the *Sección de Manuscritos*.

The state of preservation of documents in municipal archives varies. A valuable guide has been prepared by Vicenta Cortés Alonso, *Manual de Archivos Municipales* (Madrid, 1982). A thorough – but unannotated – listing of printed sources for Andalusia's archives is provided by Martinez del C. Hernández, *Indice Histórico Andaluz: Época Moderna* (Cordova, 1981). A major source of information concerning relations between the crown and Seville's *asistentes* is the five massive volumes of royal correspondence from the *Tumbo de los Reyes Católicos*. Documentation for the years 1474–92 has been transcribed by Ramón Carande. For the remaining years, see the index of subject headings by Claudio Sanz Arizmendi, "Indice del 'Tumbo de los Reyes Católicos'," *Revue Hispanique* 62 (1924), pp. 1–272.

A brief overview of Seville's municipal holdings is provided by José Velázquez y Sánchez, *El archivo municipal de Sevilla* (Seville, 1864). The *Actas Capitulares* are badly deteriorated. A catalogue for the years 1474 onward is in the process of preparation. A number of letters from the *Reyes Católicos* to the city and its subject villages are filed under *Diversos*. See the *Catálogo de la Sección*

1b: Diversos, I, 1280–1515 (Seville 1977). The *Archivo de Privilegios* contains the 1492 *Ordenanzas de Sevilla*.

Proceedings of council meetings and collections of royal correspondence are found at Cáceres. A. C. Floriano y Cumbreño provides a guide in *Documentación histórica del Archivo Municipal de Cáceres* (Cáceres, 1934). For Málaga in this period there is an analytic assessment in *Documentos del reinado de los Reyes Católicos. Catálogo de los documentos existentes en el Archivo Municipal de Málaga* (Málaga, 1961), edited by Francisco Bejarano.

Madrid's *concejo* proceedings are well-preserved in that town's *Archivo General de la Villa de Madrid*. This material is collected in the books of the *Libro de Acuerdos del Concejo Madrileño* and the *Libro de Horadado*. Royal correspondence is found in the volumes of the *Libro de Cédulas y Provisiones*. Some of these sources have been indexed or abstracted by Agustín Carlo Millares. For Alcaraz, brief summaries of documents contained in its archives were published by Aurelio Pretel Marín, *Fondos Medievales del Archivo Municipal de Alcaraz* (Alcaraz, 1976). There are a number of significant records at Carmona. A guide is provided by the *Ordenanzas del Concejo de Carmona: Fuentes para la historia del antiguo reino de Sevilla*, ed. M. González Jiménez (Seville, 1972).

The judicial records of early medieval *residencias* have apparently been destroyed. Judges presumably discarded court registers and other documents upon completion of their work. Many summaries of *residencia* proceedings for the reign of Isabella I are found scattered through the documents in the *Archivo General de Simancas*, section *Registro General del Sello de Corte*, along with an occasional full proceeding. Owing to changed procedures in later reigns, some judicial records for the mid-sixteenth century are found in the same archive under *Consejo Real*, along with bills for the expenses of judges in *Escribanía Mayor de Rentas: Residencias*. Reports for the seventeenth-century are located in the *Archivo Histórico Nacional* (Madrid) in the section *Consejos Suprimidos*. New World *residencia* records are to be found in the *Archivo General de Indias* (Seville), in the section *Escribanía de Cámara*.

Law codes governing the activities of the corregidores have almost all found their way into print. The relevant laws of the Cortes proceedings of 1476 and 1480 are found in volume IV of *Cortes de los antiguos reinos de León y Castilla*, ed. Manuel Colmeiro y Penido (5 vols., Madrid, 1861–1903). A royal code of conduct for corregidores from Toledo dated 1482 has been transcribed by Emilio Sáez Sánchez, "El Libro del Juramento de ayuntamiento de Toledo," *Anuario de Historia del Derecho Español*, vol. XVI (Madrid, 1945), pp. 530–624. An unpublished 1493 version is found in the *Archivo Municipal de Sevilla, Carpeta* 5ª, no. 32, fols. 1–6v. The "definitive" 1500 decree governing the officials has been transcribed by Benjamín González Alonso, *El corregidor Castellano (1348–1808)* (Madrid, 1970), and in a facsimile reprint with study by A. Muro Orejón, *Los Capítulos de corregidores de 1500* (Madrid, 1963).

Royal decrees are found in *Libro de las bulas y pragmáticas de los Reyes Católicos*, ed. Juan Ramírez, Alcalá, 1503 (facsimile reprint, Madrid, 1973). Compilations of laws following the corregidores into the sixteenth-century are found in *Los códigos españoles concordados y anotados* (12 vols., Madrid, 1872–84); the

Novísima Recopilación de las leyes de España (6 vols., Madrid, 1805–7); and the (*Nueva*) *Recopilación de todas las leyes de estos reinos* (2 vols., Alcalá de Henares, 1566; reprinted 1569).

I (b) Printed sources

Alemán, Mateo, *Vida del pícaro Guzmán de Alfarache* (1599), ed. Guili y Gayal (Madrid, 1958).

Baer, Yitzhak, *Die Jüden in christlichen Spanien* (2 vols., Berlin, 1936).

Beinart, Haim, *Records of the Trials of the Spanish Inquisition in Ciudad Real* (4 vols., Jerusalem, 1974–7).

Bernáldez, Andrés, *Memorias del reinado de los Reyes Católicos*, ed. and with a study by Manuel Gómez-Moreno and Juan de Mata Carriazo (Madrid, 1962).

Cancionero castellano del siglo XV, ed. R. Foulché-Delbosc (2 vols., Madrid, 1912–15).

Cancionero de Gómez Manrique, intro. Antonio Paz y Melía, *Colección de escritores castellanos*, ed. R. Foulché-Delbosc (2 vols., Madrid, 1885).

Cárdenas, Benito de, *Memoria y verdadera relación* . . . transcr. José Moreno Guerra, *Bandos en Jerez. Los del puesto de abajo* . . . (2 vols., Madrid, 1929–32), vol. I, pp. 87–143.

Carretero Zamora, J. M., "Andalucía en las cortes de los Reyes Católicos," *Actas II coloquios Historia de Andalucía, Andalucía Moderna* (Cordova, 1980), vol. II, pp. 43–53.

Castillo de Bovadilla, J., *Política para corregidores y señores de Vasallos en tiempo de paz, y de Guerra* (1597) (2 vols., Madrid, 1978; facsimile reprint of 1640 edition).

Celso, Hugo de, *Reportorio de las leyes de todos los reynos de Castilla* . . . (1547).

Colmeiro y Penido, Manuel, *Cortes de los antiguos reinos de León y Castilla* (5 vols., Madrid, 1861–1903).

Correspondencia del conde de Tendilla, ed. Emilio Meneses García (2 vols., *Archivo Documental Español*, Madrid, 1973).

Crónica incompleta de los Reyes Católicos (1469–1476): según un manuscrito anónimo de su época, ed. Julio Puyol y Alonso (Madrid, 1934).

Dánvila y Collado, Manuel, ed., *Historia crítica y documentada de las comunidades de Castilla* (6 vols., *Memorial Histórico Español*, Madrid, 1897–1900).

Delgado Merchán, Luis, *Historia documentada de Ciudad Real* (Ciudad Real, 1907).

Documentos referentes a las relaciones con Portugal durante el reinado de los Reyes Católicos, ed. Antonio de la Torre y del Cerro and Luis Suárez Fernández (3 vols., Valladolid, 1959–63).

Domingo Palacio, Timoteo, *Documentos del Archivo General de la Villa de Madrid* (4 vols., Madrid, 1889).

Élie de la Primaudae, F., ed., *Documents sur l'occupation espagnole en Afrique (1506–1574)* (Algiers, 1875).

Enríquez del Castillo, Diego, *Crónica del Rey D. Enrique el cuarto* . . . *Colección de Crónicas de Castilla* . . . (Madrid, 1887).

Fernández de Oviedo, Gonzalo, *Las Quincuagenas de la nobleza de España* (3 vols., Madrid, 1880 edn.).

Galíndez de Carvajal, Lorenzo, *Crónica de Enrique IV*. In *Estudio sobre la "Crónica de Enrique IV" del Dr. Galíndez de Carvajal*, ed. Juan Torres Fontes (Murcia, 1946).

González Palencia, Ángel and Eugenio Mele, *Vida y obras de Don Hurtado de Mendoza* (3 vols., Madrid, 1943).

Herrera García, Antonio, "El testamento de asistente de Sevilla Diego de Merlo (1482)," *En la España Medieval. Estudios dedicados al profesor D. Julio González González* (Madrid, 1981), pp. 155–68.

Hevia Bolaños, Juan de, *Curia philipica* . . . (2 vols., Valladolid, 1615; reprinted Madrid, 1753).

La Torre y del Cerro, Antonio de, *Testamentaria de Isabel la Católica* (Barcelona, 1974).

Leyes de Toro (Valladolid, 1505), tr. and intro. M. Soledad Arribás, with foreword by Ramón Falcón Rodríguez (facsimile edn., Madrid, 1976).

Lope de Vega [Félix Lope de Vega Carpio], *Fuenteovejuna*, tr. Roy Campbell, *The Classic Theater*, vol. III, ed. Eric Bentley (New York, 1959).

López de Ayala, Jerónimo, *El cardenal Cisneros. Gobernador del reino, Estudio histórico y documentos* (2 vols., Madrid, 1928).

López de Ayala, Pedro, *Crónica de Don Enrique III, Crónicas de los Reyes de Castilla*, *BAE*, vol. LXVIII (Madrid, 1779–80; reprinted 1953) pp. 161–271.

Martire d'Anghera, Pietro, *Epistolario de Pedro Mártir de Anglería*, ed. and tr. José López de Toro (4 vols., Madrid, 1953–7).

Memorias de Don Enrique IV de Castilla, vol. II, *Colección diplomática* (*RAH*, Madrid, 1835–1913).

Millares Carlo, Agustín, ed., *Contribuciones documentales a la historia de Madrid* (Madrid, 1971).

Indice y extractos del "Libro Horadado" del concejo madrileño (siglos XV–XVI) (Madrid, 1927).

Libros de Acuerdos del concejo de Madrid (Madrid, 1932).

Palencia, Alonso de, *Crónica de Enrique IV*, tr. and ed. A. Paz y Meliá (4 vols., *BAE*, Madrid, 1904–9).

Cuatro Décadas de Alonso de Palencia, tr. and with a study by José López de Toro (Madrid, 1970).

Pulgar, Fernando del, *Crónica de los Reyes Católicos*, ed. and with a study by Juan de Mata Carriazo (2 vols., Madrid, 1943)

Rades de Andrada, Francisco, *Crónica de las tres Ordenes y Cauallerías de Santiago, Calatraua y Alcántara* (Toledo, 1572).

Santa Cruz, Alonso de, *Crónica de los Reyes Católicos*, ed. and with a study by Juan de Mata Carriazo (Seville, 1951).

Crónica del emperador Carlos V (5 vols., Madrid, 1920–5).

Suárez Fernández, Luis, ed., *Documentos acerca de la Expulsión de los judíos* (Valladolid, 1964).

El Tumbo de los Reyes Católicos del concejo de Sevilla, eds. Ramón Carande and Juan de Mata Carriazo (5 vols., Seville, 1929–68; 1971–).

Valera, Diego de, *Epístolas de Mosén Diego de Valera enviadas en diversos tiempos a diversas personas* (*BAE*, vol. 116, Madrid, 1878).
Memorial de diversas hazañas, ed. and with a study by Juan de Mata Carriazo (Madrid, 1941).
Vallecillo, Antonio, *Legislación militar de España, antigua y moderna, recogida, ordenada y recopilada* (13 vols., Madrid, 1853–6).

II Secondary bibliography

Acien Almansa, Manuel, *Ronda y su serranía en tiempo de los Reyes Católicos* (3 vols., Málaga, 1979).
Ajo, G. Sainz de Zúñiga, *Historia de las Universidades Hispánicas. Orígenes y desarrollo desde su aparición hasta nuestros días* (7 vols., Madrid and Avila, 1957–67), vol. II, *El siglo de oro universitario.*
Alba, Ramón, *Acerca de algunas particularidades de las Comunidades de Castilla tal vez relacionadas con el supuesto acaecer terreno del Milenio Igualitario* (Madrid, 1975).
Albi, Fernando de, *El corregidor en el municipio español bajo la monarquía absoluta. Ensayo histórico-crítico* (Madrid, 1943).
Alcocer y Martínez, Mariano, "Consejo Real de Castilla," *Revista Histórica* Valladolid (1925), pp. 33–44.
Alijo Hidalgo, Francisco, "Estudio demográfico y urbanístico de la ciudad de Antequera (1492–1518)," *Jábega* 23 (1979), pp. 11–16.
Alonso Romero, María Paz, *El proceso penal en Castilla, siglo[s] XIII–XVIII* (Salamanca, 1982).
Álvarez de Morales, Antonio, *Las hermandades, expresión del movimiento comunitario en España* (Valladolid, 1974).
Amador de los Ríos, José, *Historia social, política y religiosa de los judíos de España y Portugal* (3 vols., Madrid, 1875; reprinted 1960).
Azcona, Tarsicio de, *La elección y reforma del episcopado español en tiempo de los Reyes Católicos* (Madrid, 1960).
Isabel la Católica. Estudio crítico de su vida y su reinado (Madrid, 1964).
San Sebastián y la provincia de Guipúzcoa durante la guerra de las Comunidades (1520–1521): Estudio y documentos (San Sebastián, 1974).
Aznar Vallejo, Eduardo, *La integración de las islas canarias en la Corona de Castilla (1478–1526). Aspectos administrativos, sociales y económicos* (Seville, 1983).
Baer, Yitzhak, *A History of the Jews in Christian Spain* (2 vols., Philadelphia, 1961–6).
Barbadillo Delgado, Pedro, *Historia antigua y medieval de Sanlúcar de Barrameda* (Cadiz, 1945).
Basas Fernández, Manuel, "La institucionalización de los bandos en la sociedad bilbaína y vizcaína al comienzo de la Edad Moderna," *La sociedad Vasca rural y urbana en el marco de la crisis de los siglos XIV y XV*, ed. José Valdeón Baruque (Bilbao, 1973), pp. 38–92.

Beinart, Haim, *Conversos on Trial. The Inquisition in Ciudad Real* (Jerusalem, 1981).

Trujillo: A Jewish Community in Extremadura on the Eve of the Expulsion from Spain (Jerusalem, 1980).

Bejarano Robles, Francisco, "Constitución del concejo y del primer cabildo de Málaga," *Jábega* 22 (1978), pp. 3–7.

Beneyto Pérez, Juan, *Historia de la administración española e hispanoamericana* (Madrid, 1986).

Benito Ruano, Eloy, *Toledo en el siglo XV: Vida política* (Madrid, 1961).

Los orígenes del problema converso (Barcelona, 1976).

Bennassar, Bartolomé, *Valladolid au siècle d'or* . . . (Paris, 1967).

Bermejo Cabrero, J. L., "La gobernación del reino de las Comunidades de Castilla," *Hispania* 124 (1973), pp. 249–64.

Bermúdez Aznar, D. Agustín, "El asistente real en los concejos castellanos bajomedievales," *Actas II Symposium de Historia de la Administración* (Madrid, 1971), pp. 225–51.

El corregidor en Castilla durante la Baja Edad Media (1348–1474) (Murcia, 1974).

Bernardo Ares, José Manuel de, "El municipio cordobés en el Antiguo Régimen. Fuentes y métodos para su estudio," *Estudios de historia de España: Homenaje a Manuel Tuñón de Lara*, ed. Santiago Castillo *et al.* (2 vols., Santander, 1981), vol. I.

"Los juicios de residencia como fuente para la historia urbana," *Actas II Coloquios de Historia de Andalucía: Andalucía Moderna* (Cordova, 1980), vol. II, pp. 1–24.

Bishko, C. Julian, "The Andalusian municipal mestas in the 14th–16th centuries: administrative and social aspects," *Actas I Congreso de Historia de Andalucía: Andalucía Medieval* (Cordova, 1982), vol. I, pp. 347–74.

"El castellano, hombre de llanura. La explotación ganadera en el área fronteriza de La Mancha y Extremadura durante la Edad Media," *Homenaje a Jaime Vicens Vives*, ed. J. Maluquer de Montes (2 vols., Barcelona, 1965), vol. I, pp. 201–18.

"The Castilian as plainsman: The medieval ranching frontier in La Mancha and Extremadura," *The New World Looks at its History*, ed. A. R. Lewis and T. F. McGann (Austin, Texas, 1963), pp. 47–69.

"Sesenta años despúes: La *Mesta* de Julius Klein a la luz de la investigación subsiguiente," *Historia Instituciones Documentos* 8 (1982), pp. 1–49.

Braudel, Fernand, *Capitalism and Material Life (1400–1800)* (New York, 1974). Translation by Miriam Kochan of *Civilisation Matérielle et Capitalisme* (Paris, 1967).

Bulliett, R. W., *The Camel and the Wheel* (Cambridge, Mass., 1975).

Caballero, Fermín, *Conquenses ilustres*, vol. III, *Dr. Alonso Díaz de Montalvo* (Madrid, 1873).

Cabrera, E. *et al.*, "La sublevación de Fuenteovejuna contemplada en su v centenario," *Actas I Congreso de Historia de Andalucía: Andalucía Medieval* (Cordova, 1982), vol. II, pp. 113–21.

Carande, Ramón, "La económica y expansión de España bajo el reinado de los Reyes Católicos," *B(R)AH* 86 (1952), pp. 213–55.

Carlé, María del Carmen, *Del concejo medieval castellano-leonés* (Buenos Aires, 1968).

Caro Baroja, Julio, *Linajes y bandos en Vascongada* (Madrid, 1957).

Carriazo y Arroquia, Juan de Mata, "Historia de la Guerra de Granada," in "La España de los Reyes Católicos (1474–1516)," *Historia de España*, dir. Ramón Menéndez Pidal (Madrid, 1969), vol. 17: I, pt. III.

Castañeda, Carlos, "The corregidor in Spanish colonial administration," *HAHR* 9 (1929), pp. 446–70.

Cepeda Adán, José, "El gran Tendilla medieval y renacentista," *Cuadernos de Historia* I (1967), pp. 159–68.

Cerda, Joaquin, "Hombres buenos, jurados y regidores en los municipios castellanos de la Baja Edad Media," *Actas I Symposium de Historia de la Administración* (Madrid, 1970), pp. 161–206.

Chacón Jiménez, Francisco, "Una contribución al estudio de las economías municipales en Castilla: La coyuntura económica concejil murciana en el período 1496–1514," *Miscelánea Medieval Murciana* (Murcia), vol. 3 (1977).

Chamberlain, R. S., "The 'corregidor' in Castile in the sixteenth century and the 'residencia' as applied to the 'corregidor'," *HAHR* 23 (1943), pp. 222–57.

Chaunu, Pierre, *La España de Carlos V* (2 vols., Barcelona, 1976). Translation by E. Riambau Sauri of *L'Espagne de Charles Quint* (Paris, 1973).

Clavero, Bartolomé, *Mayorazgo, propiedad feudal en Castilla, 1369–1836* (Madrid, 1974).

Clemencín, Diego de, *Elogio de la Reina Católica Doña Isabel*... (Madrid, 1820). *Ilustraciones sobre varios asuntos del reinado de Isabel la Católica* (Madrid, 1821).

Collantes de Terán Sánchez, A., *Sevilla en la Baja Edad Media: la ciudad y sus hombres* (Seville, 1977).

Colmenares, Diego de, *Historia de la insigne ciudad de Segovia*... (Segovia, 1637; reprinted 1969).

Cooper, Edward, *Castillos señoriales de Castilla de los siglos xv y xvi* (2 vols., Madrid, 1980–1).

Cotarelo y Valledor, A., *Fray Diego de Deza. Ensayo biográfico* (Madrid, 1902).

Díaz-Jiménez y Molleda, Eloy, *Historia de los Comuneros de León y su influencia en el movimiento general de Castilla* (2nd edn., León, 1978).

Dios, Salustiano de, *El Consejo Real de Castilla (1385–1522)* (Madrid, 1982).

Dominguez Ortiz, Antonio, "Historical research on Spanish Conversos in the last 15 years," *Collected Studies in Honour of Américo Castro's Eightieth Year*, ed. M. P. Hornick (Oxford, 1965), pp. 63–82.

Los judeoconversos en España y América (Madrid, 1971).

"Salario y atribuciones de los asistentes de Sevilla," *Archivo Hispalense* VII, 20 (1946), pp. 209–13.

Edwards, J. H. *Christian Córdoba. The City and its Region in the Late Middle Ages* (Cambridge, 1982).

"Oligarchy and merchant capitalism in lower Andalucía under the

Catholic Kings: the case of Córdoba and Jerez de la Frontera," *Historia Instituciones Documentos* (Seville) 4 (1977), pp. 11–33.

Elliott, J. H. *Imperial Spain 1469–1716* (London, 1963; 2nd edn., 1975).

"Revolution and continuity in early modern Europe," *Past and Present* 42 (February, 1969), pp. 35–56.

Enrique de Vedia y Gossens, M., *Historia y descripción de la ciudad de La Coruña* (La Coruña, 1845; reprinted 1972).

Falcón Pérez, María Isabel, *Organización municipal de Zaragoza en el siglo xv* (Zaragoza, 1978).

Fernández-Armesto, Felipe, *The Canary Islands after the Conquest. The Making of a Colonial Society in the Early Sixteenth Century* (Oxford, 1982).

Ferdinand and Isabella (London, 1975).

Fernández Domínguez Valencia, J., *La guerra civil a la muerte de Enrique IV, Zamora–Toro–Castronuño* (Zamora, 1929).

Ferrara, Orestes, *Un pleito sucesorio: Enrique IV, Isabel de Castilla y La Beltraneja* (Madrid, 1945).

Firoozye, B. H. "Warfare in fifteenth-century Castile" (unpublished PhD dissertation, University of California at Los Angeles, 1974).

Fita, F., "La verdad sobre el martirio del Santo Niño de La Guardia . . .," *B(R)AH* 11 (1877), pp. 7–134.

Floriano y Cumbreño, A. C., *La villa de Cáceres y la Reina Católica* (Cáceres, 1917).

Font Rius, José M, "Las instituciones administrativas y judiciales de las ciudades en la España Medieval," *Anales de la Universidad de Valencia* xxvi (1952–3), pp. 19–158.

García Aguilera, Raul and M. Hernández Osorno, *Revuelta y litigios de los villanos de la encomienda de Fuente Ovejuna (1476)* (Madrid, 1975).

García de Cortázar, José Ángel, *La época medieval*, vol. ii, *Historia de España alfaguara*, dir. Miguel Artola (Madrid, 1976).

Vizcaya en el siglo XV. Aspectos económicos y sociales (Bilbao, 1966), with Ruiz de Aguirre.

García de Valdeavellano, Luis, *Curso de historia de las instituciones españolas de los orígenes al final de la Edad Media* (Madrid, 1968).

"Las 'Partidas' y los orígenes medievales del juicio de residencia," *B(R)AH* 153 (1963), pp. 205–46.

García Marín, José María, *El oficio público en Castilla durante la Baja Edad Media* (Seville, 1974).

García Oro, José, *Cisneros y la reforma del clero español en tiempo de los Reyes Católicos* (Madrid, 1971).

García Sáinz de Baranda, Julián, *La ciudad de Burgos y su concejo en la Edad Media* (2 vols., Burgos, 1967).

Gerbet, Marie-Claude, "Les guerres et l'accès à noblesse en Espagne de 1465 à 1592," *Mélanges de la Casa de Velázquez* 8 (1972), pp. 295–326.

La noblesse dans le royaume de Castille: Etude sur ses structures sociales en Estrémadure (1454–1516) (Paris, 1979).

Gibert y Sánchez de la Vega, Rafael, *El Concejo de Madrid: Su organización en los siglos xii a xv* (Madrid, 1949).

Glick, Thomas F., *Islamic and Christian Spain in the Early Middle Ages* (Princeton, NJ, 1979).

Goñi Gaztambide, José, *Historia de la bula de la Cruzada en España* (Vitoria, 1958).

González Alonso, Benjamín, *El corregidor castellano (1348–1808)* (Madrid, 1970).

Gobernación y gobernadores: Notas sobre la administración de Castilla en el período de formación del estado moderno (Madrid, 1974).

"El juicio de residencia en Castilla. 1: Origen y evolucion hasta 1480," *AHDE* 48 (1978), pp. 193–247.

González Jiménez, Manuel, "El concejo de Alanis en el siglo xv," *Archivo Hispalense* 171–3 (1973), pp. 135–41.

El concejo de Carmona a fines de la Edad Media (1464–1523) (Seville, 1976).

González Varges, A., *El ceremonia del cabildo municipal sevillano* (Seville, 1967).

Gounon-Loubens, M. J. *Essais sur l'administration de la Castille au xvi͏ᵉ siècle* (Paris, 1860).

Guichot y Parody, Joaquín, *Historia del Excmo. Ayuntamiento . . . Sevilla* (8 vols., Seville, 1896–1903).

Guilarte, A. M., *El régimen señorial en el siglo xvi* (Madrid, 1962).

Gutiérrez Nieto, J. I., *Las Comunidades como movimiento antiseñorial: La formación del bando realista en la guerra castellana de 1520–1521* (Barcelona, 1973).

Haliczer, Stephen, *The Comuneros of Castile: The Forging of a Revolution, 1475–1521* (Madison, Wis., 1981).

Highfield, J. R. L., "The Catholic kings and the titled nobility of Castile," *Europe in the Late Middle Ages*, ed. John R. Hale *et al.* (London, 1965), pp. 358–85.

Hillgarth, J. N., *The Spanish Kingdoms: 1250–1516* (2 vols., Oxford, 1978), vol. II, *1410–1516 Castilian Hegemony.*

Ibarra y Rodríguez, Eduardo, *El problema cerealista en España durante el reinado de los Reyes Católicos (1475–1516)*, *Anales de Economía* (Madrid, 1944).

Irurita Lusarreta, María Ángeles, *El municipio de Pamplona en la Edad Media* (Pamplona, 1959).

Kagan, R. L., *Lawsuits and Litigants in Castile, 1500–1700* (Chapel Hill, NC, 1981).

Students and Society in Early Modern Spain (Baltimore, 1974).

Kamen, Henry, *Inquisition and Society in Spain in the Sixteenth and Seventeenth Centuries* (London, 1985).

Spain 1469–1714: A Society of Conflict (London and New York, 1983).

The Spanish Inquisition (New York, 1966).

Kantorowicz, E. H., *The King's Two Bodies: A Study in Medieval Political Theology* (Princeton, NJ, 1957).

Klein, Julius, *The Mesta: A Study in Spanish Economic History, 1273–1836* (Cambridge, Mass., 1920).

Labayru y Goicoechea, Estanislao, *Historia general del Señorío de Vizcaya* (Bilbao, 1968).

Ladero Quesada, M. A., *Andalucía en el siglo xv. Estudios de historia política* (Madrid, 1973).

"Los cereales en Andalucía durante el siglo xv," *Revista de la Universidad de Madrid*, xviii (1969), pp. 223–40.

La Ciudad Medieval 1248–1492, vol. ii in *Historia de Sevilla*, dir. Francisco Morales Padrón (5 vols., Seville, 1976).

España en 1492 (Madrid, 1978).

Granada: Historia de un país islámico (1232–1571) (Madrid, 1969).

La hacienda real castellana entre 1480 y 1494 (Valladolid, 1967).

La hacienda real de Castilla en el siglo xv (La Laguna, 1973).

Milicia y economía en la Guerra de Granada (Valladolid, 1964).

Los Mudéjares de Castilla en tiempos de Isabel I (Valladolid, 1969).

El siglo xv en Castilla: Fuentes de renta y política fiscal (Barcelona, 1982).

Ladero Quesada, M. A. and González Jiménez, Manuel, *Diezmo eclesiástico y producción de cereales en el reino de Sevilla (1408–1503)* (Seville, 1979).

Ladreda, Manuel F., *Estudios históricos sobre los códigos de Castilla* (La Coruña, 1896).

Laing, R. D., *Self and Others* (New York, 1969).

Laviada, Alvarez, *Chinchón histórico y diplomático hasta finalizar el siglo xv* (Madrid, 1931).

Layna Serrano, Francisco, *Historia de Guadalajara y sus Mendozas en los siglos xv y xvi* (4 vols., Madrid, 1942).

León Tello, Pilar, "La judería de Ávila durante el reinado de los Reyes Católicos," *Sefarad* 23 (1963), pp. 36–153.

Judíos de Toledo (2 vols., Madrid, 1979).

Lomax, Derek W., *Las órdenes militares en la Península Ibérica durante la Edad Media* (Salamanca, 1976).

The Reconquest of Spain (London and New York, 1978).

López de Ayala Álvarez de Toledo del Hierro, Jerónimo, *Contribuciones e impuestos en León y Castilla durante la Edad Media* (Madrid, 1896).

López Ferreiro, Antonio, *Galicia en el último tercio del siglo xv* (Vigo, 1896; reprinted 1968).

Historia de la Santa A. M. Iglesia de Santiago de Compostela (Santiago, 1904).

López Martínez, Celestino, *La Santa Hermandad de los Reyes Católicos* (Seville, 1921).

López, Mata, T., *La ciudad y el castillo de Burgos* (Burgos, 1949).

Lunenfeld, Marvin, *The Council of the Santa Hermandad. A Study of the Pacification Forces of Ferdinand and Isabella* (Coral Gables, Fla., 1970).

"Governing the cities of Isabella the Catholic: the *corregidores*, governors and assistants of Castile," *Journal of Urban History* 9, 1 (1982), pp. 31–55.

"Isabella of Castile and the company of women in power," *Historical Reflections/Réflexions Historiques* (Waterloo, Ont.) iv, 2 (1978), pp. 207–29.

"The royal image: symbol and paradigm in portraits of early modern female sovereigns and regents," *Gazette des Beaux-Arts* (April, 1981), pp. 157–62.

MacKay, Angus, *Money, Prices and Politics in Fifteenth Century Castile* (London, 1981).

Spain in the Middle Ages: From Frontier to Empire, 1000–1500 (New York, 1977).

Marañón, Gregorio, *Ensayo biológico sobre Enrique IV de Castilla y su tiempo* (Madrid, 1934; reprinted 1964).

Maravall, J. A., *Las Comunidades de Castilla: Una primera revolución moderna* (3rd edn., Madrid, 1963).

Márquez Villanueva, Francisco, "The Converso problem: an assessment," *Collected Studies in Honour of Américo Castro's Eightieth Year*, ed. M. P. Hornick (Oxford, 1965), pp. 316–33.

Martín Postigo, M. de la S., *La cancillería castellana de los Reyes Católicos* (Valladolid, 1959).

Martínez Caadós, José, "Las Cortes de Castilla en el siglo XVI," *Revista de la Universidad de Madrid*, 4th época, 6 (1957), pp. 583–605.

Mayoral Fernández, José, *El municipio de Ávila* (Avila, 1958).

Menéndez Pidal, Gonzalo, *Los caminos en la historia de España* (Madrid, 1951; reprinted 1962).

Mitre Fernández, Emilio, *La extensión del régimen de corregidores en el reinado de Enrique III de Castilla* (Valladolid, 1969).

Molénat, Jean-Pierre, "Chemins et ponts du nord de la Castille au temps des Rois Catholiques," *Mélanges de la Casa de Velazquez* (Paris) 7 (1971), pp. 115–62.

"Tolède et ses finages au temps des Rois Catholiques: Contribution à l'histoire sociale et économique de la cité avant la révolte des comunidades," *Mélanges de la Casa de Velázquez* 8 (1972), pp. 327–77.

Morales Padrón, Francisco, *La ciudad del Quinientos*, vol. III, *Historia de Sevilla* (Seville, 1977).

Morison, S. E., *Admiral of the Ocean Sea* (2 vols., Boston, 1942).

Christopher Columbus, Mariner (New York, 1955; reprinted 1960).

Moxó, Salvador de, *La Alcabala: Sobre sus orígenes, concepto y naturaleza* (Madrid, 1963).

"Los Cuadernos de Alcabalas: Orígenes de la legislación tributaria castellana," *AHDE* no. 1, 39 (1969), pp. 317–450.

Murugarren, P. L., *Evolución de la industria textil castellana en los siglos XIII–XVI* (Salamanca, 1974).

Nader, Helen, *The Mendoza Family in the Spanish Renaissance: 1350 to 1550* (New Brunswick, NJ, 1979).

Newton, L. W., "The development of the Castilian peerage" (unpublished PhD dissertation, Tulane University, 1972).

Oliveira Marques, A. H. de, *History of Portugal* (2 vols., New York, 1976 edn.).

Oliveros de Castro, M. T. and Julio Jordana de Pozas, *La agricultura de los reinos españoles en tiempo de los Reyes Católicos* (Madrid, 1968).

Ortí Belmonte, Miguel Ángel, "Cáceres baja la Reina Católica y su camarero · Sancho Paredes Golfin, *Revista de Estudios Extremeños* (Badajoz), 1–4 (1954), pp. 193–328.

Ortiz de Zúñiga, Diego, *Anales eclesiásticos y seculares de la . . . ciudad de Sevilla* (5 vols., Madrid, 1677), vol. III.

Owens, John B., *Rebelión, monarquía y oligarquía murciana en la época de Carlos V* (Murcia, 1980).

Palencia Flores, Clemente, "El poeta Gómez Manrique, corregidor de Toledo," *Boletín de la Real Academia de Bellas Artes y Ciencias Históricas de Toledo* (Toledo) 22–3 (1943–4; reprinted 1944), pp. 35–50.

Pérez, Joseph, *La révolution des "Comunidades" de Castille (1520–21)* (Bordeaux, 1970).

Pérez Bustamante, Rogelio, *El gobierno y la administración de los reinos de la corona de Castilla, 1230–1474* (2 vols., Madrid, 1976).

Pérez-Prendes, José Manuel, *Cortes de Castilla* (Barcelona, 1974).

Pescador del Hoyo, María del Carmen, "Los orígenes de la Santa Hermandad," *Cuadernos de la Historia de España* 55–6 (1972), pp. 400–43.

Phillips, Carla Rahn, *Ciudad Real, 1500–1750* (Cambridge, Mass., 1979).

Phillips, William D., Jr., *Enrique IV and the Crisis of Fifteenth Century Castile, 1425–1480* (Speculum Anniversary Monographs, Cambridge, Mass., 1978).

Pisa, Francisco de, *Descripción de la imperial ciudad de Toledo* (Toledo, 1617).

Powers, J. F., "Townsmen and soldiers: the interaction of urban and military organization in the militias of medieval Castile," *Speculum* XLVI (October 1971), pp. 641–55.

Pretel Marín, Aurelio, *Alcaraz, un enclave castellano en la frontera del siglo* XIII (Albacete, 1974).

Una ciudad castellana en los siglos XIV–XV *(Alcaraz, 1300–1475)* (Albacete, 1978).

La integración de un municipio medieval en el estado autoritario de los Reyes Católicos (La ciudad de Alcaraz, 1475–1525) (Albacete, 1975).

Puyol y Alonso, Julio, *Las hermandades de Castilla y León. Estudio histórico seguido de las Ordenanzas de Castronuño* (Madrid, 1913).

Quintanilla Raso, M. C., *Nobleza y señoríos en el reino de Córdoba: La casa de Aguilar (siglos* XIV y XV) (Cordova, 1979).

Ringrose, David, "The government and the carters in Spain: 1476–1700," *Economic History Review*, 2nd ser., no. 1, 22 (April, 1969), pp. 45–57.

Ríos, J. Amador de los, *Historia social, política y religiosa de los judíos de España y Portugal* (Madrid, 1960).

Rodríguez Amaya, E., "La tierra de Badajoz desde 1230 a 1500," *Revista de Estudios Extremeños* (Badajoz) 7 (1951), pp. 395–497.

Rosa Olivera, L. de la, and E. Serra Rafols, *El Adelantado Don Alonso de Lugo y su residencia por Lope de Sosa* (La Laguna, 1949).

Ruiz Martín, Felipe, "Pastos y ganaderos en Castilla: La Mesta (1450–1600)," *Atti della 'prima settimana di studio' (18–24 aprile 1969): La lana come materia prima: i fenomeni della sua produzione e circolazione nei secoli* XIII–XVII, ed. Marco Spallanzani (Florence, 1974), pp. 271–85.

Ruméu de Armas, Antonio, *Alonso de Lugo en la corte de los Reyes Católicos (1496–1497)* (Madrid, 1952).

Sáinz de Baranda, J. G., *La ciudad de Burgos y su concejo en la Edad Media* (2 vols., Burgos, 1967).

Sancho de Sopranis, Hipólito, "Contribución a la historia de la judería de Jerez de la Frontera," *Sefarad* 11 (1951), pp. 349–70.

Historia social de Jerez de la Frontera . . . (2 vols., Jerez, 1964–5).

"La judería del Puerto de Santa María de 1483 a 1492," *Sefarad* 13 (1953), pp. 309–24.

Sandoval, Prudencio de, *Historia de la vida y hechos del Emperador Carlos V* (*BAE*, vols. 80–2, Madrid, 1955–6 edn.).

Sarasola, Modesto, *Vizcaya y los Reyes Católicos (1455–78)* (Madrid, 1950).

Seaver, H. L., *The Great Revolt in Castile: A Study of the Comunero Movement of 1520–21* (London, 1928).

Serra Ruiz, Rafael, "Notas sobre el juicio de residencia en la época de los Reyes Católicos," *Anuario de Estudios Medievales* (Barcelona) 5 (1968), pp. 531–46.

Serrano y Serrano, P. L., *Los Reyes Católicos y la ciudad de Burgos, desde 1451 a 1492* (Madrid, 1943).

Simó Santonia, V. L., *Valencia en la época de los corregidores* (Valencia, 1975).

Sitges, J. B., *Enrique IV y la Excelente Señora: Llamada vulgarmente Doña Juana la Beltraneja, 1425–1530* (Madrid, 1913).

Solano Ruiz, Emma, *La Orden de Calatrava en el siglo XV: Los señoríos castellanos de la Orden al fin de la Edad Media* (Seville, 1978).

Stewart, P. J., Jr., "The army of the Catholic kings: Spanish military organization and administration in the reign of Ferdinand and Isabella, 1474–1516" (unpublished PhD dissertation, University of Illinois, 1961).

Suárez Fernández, Luis, *La España de los Reyes Católicos, 1475–1516, Historia de España*, vol. 17, parts I and II, dir. Ramón Menéndez Pidal (Madrid, 1969).

"Evolución histórica de las hermandades castellanas," *Cuadernos de Historia de España* (Buenos Aires) 16 (1951) (pamphlet).

Nobleza y monarquía: Puntos de vista sobre la historia castellana del siglo XV (Valladolid, 1959).

Tomás Valiente, Francisco, "La Diputación de las Cortes de Castilla," *AHDE* 32 (1962), pp. 347–469.

Toral Peñaranda, Enrique, *Úbeda (1442–1510)* (Madrid and Jaén, 1975).

Torre, Lucas de, "Mosén Diego de Valera: Su vida y sus obras," *B(R)AH* LXIV (April, 1914), pp. 9–168, 249–76, 365–412.

Torres Balbás, Leopoldo, *Algunos aspectos del mudejarismo urbano medieval* . . . (Madrid, 1954).

"La Edad Media," *Resumen histórico del urbanismo en España*, ed. García Bellidea *et al.* (Madrid, 1968), pp. 67–149.

Torres Fontes, Juan, "El alcalde mayor de las aljamas de moros," *AHDE* 32 (1962), pp. 131–82.

"La conquista del marquesado de Villena en el reinado de los Católicos," *Hispania* 13 (1953), pp. 37–151.

"La contratación de Guisando," *Anuario de estudios medievales* 2 (1965), pp. 214–428.

Don Pedro Fajardo, adelantado mayor del Reino de Murcia (Madrid, 1953).

Itinerario de Enrique IV de Castilla (Murcia, 1955).

Torres Sanz, David, *La administración central castellana en la Baja Edad Media* (Valladolid, 1982).

Uría Ría, Juan, *Estudios sobre la Baja Edad Media Asturiana* (Girón, 1979).

Val Valdivieso, María Isabel del, *Isabel la Católica, princesa (1468–1474)* (Valladolid, 1974).

"Resistencia al dominio señorial durante los últimos años del reinado de Enrique IV," *Hispania* 34 (1974), 53–104.

Valdeón Baruque, Julio, *Los conflictos sociales en el reino de Castilla en los siglos XIV y XV* (Madrid, 1950).

Enrique II de Castilla: La guerra civil y la consolidación del régimen (1366–1371) (Valladolid, 1966).

Vassberg, D. E., *Land and Society in Golden Age Castile* (Cambridge, 1984).

Vedia y Goossens, Enrique de, *Historia y descripción de la ciudad de La Coruña* (La Coruña, 1845; reprinted 1942).

Vicens Vives, Jaime, *Approaches to the History of Spain*, tr. and ed. J. C. Ullman (Berkeley and Los Angeles, 1967). Translation of *Aproximación de la historia de España* (2nd edn., Barcelona, 1960).

"Estructura administrativa estatal en los siglos XVI y XVII," *Coyuntura económica y reformisto burgués* (Barcelona, 1968).

Vicens Vives, Jaime with Jorge Nadal, *Manual de historia económica de España* (Barcelona, 1959). Translated by Frances M. López-Morillas as *An Economic History of Spain* (Princeton, NJ, 1966).

Vigón, Jorge, *El ejército de los Reyes Católicos . . .* (Madrid, 1953; reprinted 1968).

Villapalos Salas, Gustavo, *Los recursos contra los actos de gobierno en la Baja Edad Media. Su evolución histórica en el reino castellano (1252–1504)* (Madrid, 1976).

Weisser, M. R., *Crime and Punishment in Early Modern Europe* (Atlantic Highlands, NJ, 1979).

Yun Casalilla, Bartolomé, *Crisis de subsistencias y conflictividad social en Córdoba a principios del siglo XVI. Una ciudad andaluza en los comienzos de la modernidad* (Cordova, 1980).

Zagorin, Perez, *Rebels and Rulers, 1500–1600* (2 vols.), vol. 1, *Society, States and Early Modern Revolutions. Agrarian and Urban Rebellions* (London and New York, 1982).

Index

276